Moral Development, Moral Education, and Kohlberg

Moral Development, Moral Education, and Kohlberg
Basic Issues in Philosophy, Psychology, Religion, and Education

Edited by
BRENDA MUNSEY

Religious Education Press
Birmingham Alabama

Library of Congress Cataloging in Publication Data

Main entry under title:

Moral development, moral education, and Kohlberg.

  Includes bibliographies and index.
  1. Moral development.   2. Moral education.
3. Kohlberg, Lawrence, 1927-   I. Munsey, Brenda.
II. Title.
BF723.M54M684   370.11'4   80-50
ISBN 0-81935-020-9

Religious Education Press, Inc.
1531 Wellington Road
Birmingham, Alabama 35209
10 9 8 7 6 5 4 3 2

*Religious Education Press publishes books and educational materials exclusively in religious
education and in areas closely related to religious education. It is committed to enhancing
and professionalizing religious education through the publication of significant scholarly
and popular works.*

PUBLISHER TO THE PROFESSION

TO MY PARENTS, JOSEPH AND POLLY MUNSEY

Contents

Part I

INTRODUCTION

Chapter 1

Multidisciplinary Interest in Moral Development and Moral Education

BRENDA MUNSEY

There has been an upsurge of interest in moral development and moral education in recent years, on the part of the broader society as well as within the scholarly community. This book of essays addresses some major issues in the current multidisciplinary inquiry into moral development and education.

The construction of a coherent theory of moral education is an inherently multidisciplinary endeavor, requiring the participation of scholars with divergent questions and methods of approaching that topic. This collection presents some concerns of scholars from those fields which have (probably) maintained the most active interest in moral education, i.e., philosophy, psychology, religion, and education. Our goal is a collective analysis, the scope of which is broad enough to provide a realistic perspective on the multiplicity of philosophical, empirical, and practical questions involved in recent scholarly debate about moral education.

Our point of departure in this endeavor has been Lawrence Kohlberg's important account of the development of moral judgment. Because of the reach of his theoretical conclusions, Kohlberg has been a catalyst for interdisciplinary exchanges about morality and moral development. Kohlberg's desire to develop the educational implications of his psychological findings led him to enlarge the scope of his theorizing and to deal explicitly with some ques-

1

tions falling properly in other areas of theory. His efforts in this regard greatly enhanced the cross-disciplinary interest in his findings. However, Kohlberg's willingness to address the interdisciplinary significance of his research is only partially explained by his interest in its educational applications. The other bases for his efforts are his specific assumptions about the relationship between empirical and philosophical studies of morality.

Of the many contemporary social scientists to have studied these phenomena, Kohlberg is one of the few to have shown a real appreciation for the fact that a scientific study of morality cannot be ethically neutral. Necessarily, any actual psychological paradigm for studying moral judgment would embody certain moral epistemological assumptions. Yet psychologists consistently have failed to defend these aspects of their theories, probably because their (implicit) epistemological hypotheses were rarely acknowledged in their own statements of the theories. Given that the complete statement of any psychological theory of morality would include specific normative ethical positions, it follows that at least part of the task of validating such theories falls in the realm of moral philosophy Being theoretically sophisticated, Kohlberg appreciates this metapsychological fact. Hence his interest in developing and defending his ethical presuppositions within the philosophical community is, in reality, but an extension of his interest in defining and defending an adequate psychological account of moral judgment.

Kohlberg's assumptions about the dependence of a psychological study of moral phenomena on a prior epistemological inquiry are relatively uncontroversial (at least among philosophers). As noted above, the way a psychologist conceptualizes and interprets such phenomena presupposes specific philosophical positions on morality. However, Kohlberg also claims that the validity of moral philosophical positions is to some degree dependent on the results of moral psychological research. He asserts that "since the psychological study of concepts presupposes an epistemological position, must not the results of psychological inquiry lead to both partial validation and partial correction of its initial epistemology?"[1] While this naturalistic metaethical stance would be totally unacceptable to moral philosophers who treat the validation of normative ethical theories as a purely a priori matter, many philosophers now seem open to the relevance of moral psychological findings for moral philosophy. Some, especially those favoring a pragmatic paradigm for philosophical inquiry, agree with Kohlberg's claim that psychological findings are relevant to the validation of ethical theories. But whatever their specific views concerning the relationship between their respective investigations, it is evident that a growing number of philosophers and psychologists are eager for interdisciplinary exchanges about moral phenomena.

As noted earlier, concern about moral education is an important practical motive for interdisciplinary inquiry. The task of formulating sound educational proposals presents distinctive groups of scholars with issues falling outside their respective boundaries with other disciplines. Psychologists seeking to apply their findings about the process of cognitive development to the task of shaping that development are confronted with issues which can be resolved only by an ethical inquiry. Likewise, moral philosophers interested in the educational applications of their positions are faced with integrating those positions with a sound psychological account of moral development. In a similar way, an interest in moral education on the part of philosophers, psychologists, theologians, curriculum-instruction scholars, and others would inevitably lead to joint demands for greater interdisciplinary communication about moral development.

This volume serves as a forum for interdisciplinary analysis of Kohlberg's developmental theory and his proposals for moral education. Given the dual nature of scholarly interest in these topics, two levels of concern are expressed in this collection. The essays deal both with theoretical matters related to Kohlberg's proposals and research and with practical matters related to curricular-instructional applications. There is a somewhat heavier emphasis on theoretical matters in the sections focusing on issues within disciplines contributing to moral education theory, i.e., Part III, "Basic Issues in the Psychology of Moral Development," Part IV, "Basic Issues in Moral Philosophy," and to a lesser degree in Part V, "Basic

Issues in Religion and Religious Education." In contrast, Part VI, "Basic Issues in Moral Education," lays a somewhat heavier emphasis on practical questions related to Kohlberg's theory as a framework for moral education.

Part II consists of Kohlberg's essay, "Stages of Moral Development as a Basis for Moral Education." The only essay not written specifically for this volume, it provides a relatively comprehensive statement of Kohlberg's classic positions on moral development: philosophical, psychological, and educational. Kohlberg wrote this essay for an interdisciplinary symposium on moral education held in Toronto at the Ontario Institute for Studies in Education (June, 1968). This selection is useful reading for readers wanting a solid exposition of Kohlberg's findings and positions. Having breadth, and a fair amount of depth, it provides an excellent entry into the wide range of issues addressed in the rest of the book. The multiple positions Kohlberg outlines in this 1968 essay constitute the classic theory of moralization we have come to associate with his name.

Some of Kohlberg's positions have been modified since the Toronto symposium, partly as a result of his own ongoing research and involvement in educational programs, and partly in response to the wealth of related studies and critiques continuing to surface within the scholarly community. This collection has been designed to project something of the dynamic character of both Kohlberg's positions and the scholarly debate in which they figure. Kohlberg's Postscript (Part VII) is especially important in this regard because it provides a timely updating of some of the findings and positions stated in "Stages of Moral Development as a Basis for Moral Education" (Part II). In Chapter 16, "Educating for a Just Society: An Updated and Revised Statement," Kohlberg explains the theoretical and empirical basis of post-1968 modifications in his proposals for education. In 1968, Kohlberg had claimed that his research on moral development, both cross-cultural and in experimental programs of moral discussion in American schools, supported adopting a stage 6 vision of the task of moral education. However, research conducted between 1968 and 1976 did not confirm Kohlberg's theoretical hypothesis about a sixth and highest stage.

Kohlberg's longitudinal subjects, still adolescents in 1968, had come to adulthood by 1976 and yet none had attained stage 6. Also, by 1976, serious questions had been raised about the ethical theory embodied in Kohlberg's stage 6; questions still at issue in an ongoing scholarly debate in moral philosophy. Such developments led Kohlberg to reassess his educational positions and, in 1976, he proposed a retrenchment from stage 6 to a stage 5 conception of the goals of moral education. In contrast to the negative findings regarding stage 6, longitudinal research had shown stage 5 to be "a natural stage of development found in Israel and Turkey as well as in the United States." In chapter 16, Kohlberg explains why he now advocates a still further retrenchment: from a stage 5 to a stage 4 conception of the proximate ends of civic education. Kohlberg's new stage 4 educational model requires direct experience with participatory democracy. Because of this requirement, Kohlberg cautions against confusing his new stage 4 approach with what he describes as the "old fashioned indoctrinative civic education for stage 4."

Parts III, IV, V, and VI, respectively, focus on different aspects of the scholarly debate over moral development and moral education: issues in psychology, issues in philosophy, issues in religion and religious education, and issues in education. As the editor, my goal has been that the three essays in each of these sections offer three different perspectives on the issues, resulting in a somewhat balanced overall treatment for each division. My goal is a balanced, rather than exhaustive, examination, and, given the book's scope, no effort has been made to assure that all important points of view would be represented in each section.

The selections in Part III, "Basic Issues in the Psychology of Moral Development," deal with Kohlberg's cognitive-developmental account from the point of view of both metapsychological issues (Munsey, chapter 5), and issues within developmental psychology (Rest, chapter 3, and Fowler, chapter 4). James Rest's "Developmental Psychology and Value Education" reviews the available research in developmental psychology bearing on major aspects of Kohlberg's theory. Following an explication of the major psychological assumptions of Kohlberg's approach to moral education, Rest assesses the

evidence regarding the identification of structures of moral judgment, evidence that moral judgment follows a developmental sequence, evidence that moral judgment is largely determined by cognitive processes, evidence relating moral judgment with values and
behavior, and, finally, evidence bearing on the effectiveness of moral
educational interventions. Based on this review, Rest concludes that,
while some aspects of Kohlberg's theory are not well supported by
available data, in general, the evidence is highly supportive of his
cognitive-developmental approach.

In chapter 4 James Fowler is concerned with the relationship,
logical as well as empirical, between Kohlberg's stages of moral
reasoning and Fowler's own stages of faith development. The specific issue being addressed is the question of whether moral development is prior to faith development, or vice versa. Kohlberg's
empirical hypothesis is that "development to a given moral stage
precedes development of the parallel faith stage"; and his Kantian
epistemological assumption is that faith is grounded on moral reasons. Fowler defends the opposite philosophical position, i.e., that
faith stages are broader constructs which comprehend and contextualize stages of moral judgment. Furthermore, regarding
Kohlberg's empirical hypothesis, Fowler points to empirical studies
which tend to support his own thesis that faith development is
psychologically prior to moral development.

In the final chapter in Part III, "Cognitive-Developmental
Theory of Moral Development: Metaethical Issues," I raise questions about the metaphilosophical criteria assumed by Kohlberg's
analysis of cognitive moral stages. I argue that developmental psychology's study of moral judgment would be better served if its
paradigm incorporated pragmatic, rather than formalistic, epistemological criteria in interpreting the greater adequacy of
emergent cognitive structures.

The essays in Part IV, "Basic Issues in Moral Philosophy," were
written by three philosophers holding radically different views
about the proper philosophical basis of moral education. Dwight
Boyd (chapter 6) is an ethical rule theorist (as is Lawrence
Kohlberg), while Bernard Rosen (chapter 8) is an ethical act

theorist. In contrast to these, John Wilson (chapter 7) advocates basing the design of moral education programs on an analysis of ordinary moral discourse. These are important differences, touching metaethical questions which may not be obvious to readers lacking a good grasp of technical philosophy. However, what will be obvious to all readers are the distinctive concerns and normative perspectives embodied in each author's practical proposals. These differences are especially evident in the Wilson and Rosen chapters. In each of these two chapters the author devotes relatively little attention to a critical analysis of Kohlberg's approach and is primarily concerned with explaining a rival paradigm for moral education.

John Wilson has consistently raised grave doubts about the whole methodology and procedures of developmental psychology. In chapter 7, he questions the vagueness of the phrase "moral development" and the whole concept of "stages," whether based on logical or psychological criteria. Finally, he rejects the "simple-mindedness of psychological techniques which fail to take into account what the respondent *means* by such words as 'ought,' 'right,' etc." Wilson's basic charge is that psychological studies such as Kohlberg's are based on an inadequate philosophical analysis of morality and thus cannot produce sound empirical results. Having rejected the empirical basis of Kohlbergian developmental approaches to moral education, Wilson contends that there is no compelling reason why moral understanding and reasoning cannot be taught directly to children of all ages.

Bernard Rosen's essay, "Moral Dilemmas and Their Treatment," advocates an approach to moral education developed from ethical act theory starting points. Since Kohlberg is an ethical rule theorist, he and Rosen differ on such basic matters as the nature of moral principles and their significance in moral judgment. In this chapter Rosen is primarily concerned with contrasting his own act theory treatment of moral dilemmas with Kohlberg's rule theory orientation, and arguing for the act theory analysis.

Unlike Rosen and Wilson, Dwight Boyd's basic philosophical orientation falls within the same ethical rule theory tradition as Kohlberg's. John Rawls is also in this tradition, and in chapter 6,

"The Rawls Connection," Boyd examines Kohlberg's ethical theory
in terms of its much discussed connection to John Rawls's theory of
justice.[2] Such a topic is especially appropriate for Boyd, who first
aroused Kohlberg's interest in Rawls's theory as an example of the
stage 6 form of moral judgment. In this chapter Boyd argues that
Kohlberg's substantive conception of justice is strikingly similar to
that of Rawls—and that this similarity can best be understood in
terms of how both theorists use the notion "respect for persons."

Part V addresses questions regarding the significance of
Kohlberg's theory of moral development for religion (chapter 9) and
for religious education (chapters 10 and 11). As Ernest Wallwork
points out in chapter 9, "No recent scientific theory of morality has
sparked as much interest on the part of religious ethicists and
educators as Kohlberg's work." Wallwork briefly examines the reasons for this interest and then undertakes the primary task of chapter 9—a philosophical critique of Kohlberg's views on the relationship between religion and morality. Kohlberg's controversial claim
about the logical independence of morality from religion is analyzed
in terms of several distinctive interpretations assigned to the opposite thesis (i.e., that morality depends on religion). Wallwork also
considers James Fowler's dispute with Kohlberg over these issues
(see chapter 4). Siding with Kohlberg, Wallwork argues that
morality is indeed logically independent of religion. Finally, he
asserts that while morality is not logically dependent on religion,
nevertheless religion exerts important "positive influences" on
moral judgment.

Some of the themes raised in the Wallwork analysis (and in the
earlier Fowler chapter) occur again in the remaining two chapters in
Part V, which deal with Kohlberg's theory and religious education.
Barry Chazan examines the significance of Kohlberg's theory from
the point of view of Jewish education (chapter 10) and James Michael
Lee considers Kohlberg's significance for Christian religious education (chapter 11). The specific question Chazan addresses in chapter
10 is whether Kohlberg's theories of moral development and moral
education are compatible with or contradictory to "Jewish education." Chazan's analysis focuses on two of the multiple meanings of

"Jewish education," i.e., "classical Jewish education" and "contemporary nonorthodox Jewish education." In both instances, Chazan argues that Kohlberg is either contradictory to or irrelevant to Jewish education.

In chapter 11 James Michael Lee examines the significance of Kohlberg's psychological research for two major views regarding the relevance of such studies for the design and enactment of Christian religious education. According to the traditional *theological approach,* the validation of Christian religious education comes almost entirely from sources outside the learner, namely from God, the Bible, and church pronouncements. Given that theology is the field which investigates these phenomena, it is said to be the proper basis for Christian religious education. In contrast to the theological approach, the starting point of the *social-science approach* to Christian religious education is social-scientific data about the learning process and how to facilitate learning. This approach is said to be congenial to the view that God is immanent in the process of human development. In chapter 10, Lee argues that, although Kohlberg's conclusions pose serious challenges to many of the basic tenets of the theological approach, they offer promising data for the social-science approach. Lee, himself an advocate of the social-science approach, concludes that studies such as Kohlberg's provide useful empirical data on the way God actually works within the "progressive flow of human development."

Part VI is concerned with issues specifically related to Kohlberg's approach to moral education. The first two chapters in this section deal with the Kohlbergian approach in terms of practical, instructional, and curricular considerations. In contrast, chapter 14 proposes a radical alternative to Kohlberg's theory of moral education. Chapter 12, Linda Rosenzweig's "Kohlberg in the Classroom: Moral Education Models," provides a timely analysis and assessment of actual Kohlbergian programs. Rosenzweig sketches the history of the cognitive developmental approach and reviews the range of current Kohlbergian intervention efforts. She contends that such efforts reflect four basic models: occasional classroom discussions of moral dilemmas; special courses focusing on moral issues through

academic and experiential components; infusion of ethical considerations and supplementary materials into existing formal curricular
materials; and establishment of participatory democratic governance
structures. Rosenzweig, herself involved in the Carnegie-Mellon
Civic Education Program (which incorporates a cognitive developmental perspective), details and assesses this project as a case study
of an intervention based on a Kohlbergian perspective.

In chapter 13, "A Look at the Kohlberg Curriculum Framework
for Moral Education," James Macdonald, a curriculum theorist,
analyzes Kohlberg's approach from the standpoint of curriculum
theory. Utilizing established criteria, he attempts to determine
whether the Kohlberg framework is indeed a complete curriculum.
Concluding that it is, Macdonald then examines the soundness of
this framework in light of its philosophical, psychological, and
social assumptions. Finally, he compares it to its current major
competitors and argues that the Kohlberg model has major advantages over these.

The concluding selection in Part VI, by Israela Ettenberg Aron,
offers a radical critique of Kohlberg's framework for moral education. Aron challenges Kohlberg's educational theory on the basis of
its formalistic ethical premises and argues for an alternative approach to moral education, an approach which is rooted in John
Dewey's ethical theory. In point of metatheoretical presuppositions,
Aron's theoretical recommendations for moral education are in the
same tradition as my recommendations for moral psychology (chapter 5) and Rosen's moral philosophical proposals (chapter 8). Aron,
Rosen, and I challenge the ethical formalism of some aspect of
Kohlberg's multifaceted theory and argue for an alternative approach based on ethical pragmatism—myself in psychology, Rosen
in normative ethics, and Aron in education.

Part VII, "Postscript: Updating Kohlberg's Positions and Response to the Issues," provides a revised statement on moral education by Lawrence Kohlberg (chapter 14, described above) and a
Kohlbergian response to criticisms put forth in the present volume
(chapter 15). In "Kohlbergian Forms and Deweyan Acts: A Response,"
Bill Puka responds from a Kohlbergian perspective to issues raised

in the book's critical essays. Puka, a philosopher and close associate of Kohlberg at the Center for Moral Development and Moral Education (Harvard University) has a solid grasp of both Kohlberg's positions and the types of objections which have heretofore been raised against those positions. Given that some of the objections raised in this collection have been addressed elsewhere, Puka, in conferring with Kohlberg, chose to concentrate on the more novel criticisms. Thus Puka's response focuses on the essays by Munsey (chapter 5), Rosen (chapter 8), and Aron (chapter 14). As noted above, these chapters critique Kohlbergian positions in psychology, philosophy, and education from the standpoint of similar philosophical perspectives; Deweyan ethics in the Aron chapter and ethical act theory in the Munsey and Rosen chapters.

In concluding this introduction, I would like first to comment on the way citations have been handled throughout the volume. To preserve the distinctive flavor of each contribution I have chosen not to regularize the references and have left intact the manner in which the various contributors made their scholarly citations. Second, I would like to express my thanks to those whose encouragement and support of this project helped assure its completion: to the contributors for their intelligent, conscientious treatments of their topics; to Lawrence Kohlberg for his receptiveness to this endeavor and helpful counsel; and to my publisher for encouraging me to initiate this project and for his continuing support and guidance.

NOTES

1. Lawrence Kohlberg, "From Is to Ought: How to Commit the Naturalistic Fallacy and Get Away with It in the Study of Moral Development," in *Cognitive Development and Epistemology,* p. 151, edited by Theodore Mischel (New York: Academic Press, 1971).

2. John Rawls, *A Theory of Justice* (Cambridge, Mass.: Belknap Press, 1971).

Part II

KOHLBERG ON MORAL DEVELOPMENT
AND MORAL EDUCATION

Chapter 2

Stages of Moral Development as a Basis for Moral Education

LAWRENCE KOHLBERG

INTRODUCTION

Conferences on morality and moral education tend toward the equal-time view, one anthropologist, one psychologist, one theologian, one social commentator. The present conference is organized with the recognition that there are only two disciplines that have

This paper is reprinted with permission of the University of Toronto Press, which holds international rights, exclusive of U.S. rights. Paulist Press holds the U.S. rights on the volume in which this essay ("Stages of Moral Development as a Basis for Moral Education") originally appeared: *Moral Education: Interdisciplinary Approaches,* edited by C. M. Beck, B. S. Crittenden, and E. V. Sullivan (Toronto: University of Toronto Press, 1971, pp. 23-92). The editor would like to thank the University of Toronto Press and Paulist Press for permission to reprint this article.

The research reported in this paper was supported by NICHD GRANT H.D. 02469-01. Philosophic positions of the paper are in part drawn from the writer's conference paper "From Is to Ought" in T. Mischel (ed.) *Cognitive Development and Epistemology* New York: Academic Press 1971. Psychological findings are amplified in Kohlberg and Turiel (eds.) *Moralization Research, the Cognitive-Developmental Approach* New York: Holt, Rinehart and Winston 1971. An amplification of the practical implications of our approach for teachers is presented in Kohlberg and Turiel "Developmental Methods in Moral Education" in G. Lesser (ed.) *Psychological Approaches to Teaching* Chicago: Scott, Foresman 1971. The writer wishes to acknowledge the helpful editorial comments of Clive Beck and Edmund Sullivan.

any basic scholarly generalizations to make about moral education; these are developmental social psychology and moral philosophy. Many other scholarly fields have an interest in moral education, but insofar as this interest leads to scholarly generalizations discussed on their intellectual merits, they are generalizations about either developmental social psychology or the nature of ideal morality. Let me cite two examples. A Catholic theologian and educator may have a great deal of interest in, and working knowledge of, the aims and processes of Catholic moral education. This knowledge will be of use to non-Catholic educators, however, only insofar as the Catholic educator has formulated a conception of morality that is defensible by reference to moral philosophy, rather than Catholic theology, and insofar as he has studied the development of such morality in terms of the general methods and concepts of developmental social psychology. Similarly, an anthropologist's study of socialization in a tribe in New Guinea may provide a fresh perspective on moral education, but it will do so only by generating social psychological generalizations about development in terms of philosophically defensible goals of moral education.

But not only is it the case that there are just two basic "disciplines" or ways of thinking central to moral education. It seems to me that anything worthwhile any of us can say about moral education requires our being simultaneously a social psychologist and a philosopher. An approach to moral education based on putting together some consensus of current psychology and current philosophy is the typical camel, the committee-constructed animal, whose only virtue is that it does not drink. In other places (e.g., Kohlberg 1969—see the references at the end of this chapter), I have argued that the social psychology of moral development has spent the last two generations in the wilderness because it thought it could carry on its studies without attention to the issues of moral philosophy. I suspect that Edel, Scriven, and Baier might say something similar about moral philosophy's neglect of psychology. Certainly there have been no classical or exciting treatments of moral education in the last two generations to compare with the work of Dewey (1909) and Durkheim (1925), in which a moral philosophy and a social psychology form a single unified whole.

While somewhat embarrassed at my own presumption, I have, in this and other papers, joined the list of aspirants to the grand tradition and claimed to have defined an approach to moral education which unites philosophic and psychological considerations and meets, as any "approach" must, the requirements (a) of being based on the psychological and sociological facts of moral development, (b) of involving educational methods of stimulating moral change, which have demonstrated long-range efficacy, (c) of being based on a philosophically defensible concept of morality, and (d) of being in accord with a constitutional system guaranteeing freedom of belief.

The chief focus of this paper (as distinct from my previous papers in the area) is the attempt to set forth explicitly the philosophic basis for my definition of moral maturity. However, I would like to propose to this conference that my conception of moral maturity be criticized and discussed with regard to its adequacy as a starting point for planned moral education in the public schools, not just in terms of its congruity with particular disciplinary perspectives. In order to lead the discussion in this direction, I have begun by considering two approaches to moral education alternative to mine, the ethically relative "hidden curriculum" approach dominant in the United States, and the "bag of virtues" approach which is favored when the implicit moral education of a "hidden curriculum" is traded for explicit moral education. In criticizing these approaches, I have tried to bring out a set of standards for moral education which can then be used to test my own approach. For purposes of discussion, I have made the strongest possible claim, namely, that I can define a culturally and historically universal pattern of mature moral thought and action that meets philosophic criteria of rationality or optimality about as well as such criteria can be met. It is not necessary to accept such a strong claim in order to accept my general approach to moral education, but to the extent to which the claim can be accepted, it certainly provides a more adequate basis for the approach.

THE HIDDEN CURRICULUM

Most teachers are not fully aware that they must deal with issues of moral education, that they have no clear views on the subject, and that they have never had any training or education in it. Nevertheless, they are constantly acting as moral educators, because they are continually telling children what to do, continually making evaluations of their behavior, continually monitoring their social relations in the classroom, and doing all of this as part of a larger social institution called the school, which is defined by a still larger institution called society. For example, my second-grade son one day told me that he did not want to be one of the bad boys in school, and when asked "who are the bad boys?" he replied "the ones who don't put their books back where they belong." His teacher would probably be surprised to know that her trivial classroom-management concerns defined for children what she and her school thought were basic moral values, and that as a result she was unconsciously miseducating them morally.

In recent years, these moralizing activities of the teacher have been called the "hidden curriculum," and some writers (Jackson 1968, Dreeben 1968) have argued that the unconscious shaping of teachers' activities by the demands of classroom management and of the school as a social system performs hidden services in adapting children to society.

Jackson (1968) summarizes three central characteristics of school life: the crowds, the praise, and the power. Learning to live in the classroom means, first, learning to live and to be treated as a member of a crowd of same-age, same-status others. Second, it means learning to live in a world in which there is impersonal authority, in which a relative stranger gives orders and wields power. Dreeben (1968) emphasizes similar characteristics, especially learning to live with authority. Both Jackson and Dreeben stress the fact that the hidden curriculum provides a way-station between the personal relations of the family and the impersonal achievement and authority-oriented roles of adult occupational and sociopolitical life. The perspectives of Jackson and Dreeben derive from a long and a great tradition of educational sociology founded by Emile Durkheim in France at the end of the nineteenth century. According to Durkheim (1925),

There is ... a great distance between the moral state in which the child finds himself as he leaves the family and the one toward which he must strive. Intermediaries are necessary. The school environment is the most desirable. It is a more extensive association than the family or the little societies of friends. It results neither from blood relationships nor from free choice, but from a fortuitous and inevitable meeting among subjects brought together on the basis of similar age and social conditions. In that respect it resembles political society. On the other hand, it is limited enough so that personal relations can crystallize. . . . It is precisely groups of young persons, more or less like those constituting the social system of the school, which have enabled the formation of societies larger than the family. . . . [Even in simple societies without schools] the elders would assemble the young after they had reached a given age, to initiate them collectively into . . . the intellectual and moral patrimony of the group (1925, pp. 230–2).

These views of the hidden curriculum depend upon the value-perspective of functional sociology, the perspective that the invisible hand of societal survival guides the shaping of human institutions and gives them a value or wisdom not apparent at first glance. Durkheim understood that functional sociology (which he founded) was not value-free but essentially represented a moral point of view. He articulately and explicitly argued that the sociologist's definition of the invisible hand of the social system was also the definition of the rational or scientific morality. Durkheim goes further than saying that acceptance of authority is one of the key elements of the child's moral development. He argues that the crowds, the praise, and the power which look so wasteful from the point of view of intellectual development are the necessary conditions for the moral development of the child. According to Durkheim,

Although . . . familial education is an excellent first preparation for the moral life, its usefulness is quite restricted—above all, with respect to the spirit of discipline. That which is essential to the spirit of discipline, that is to say, respect for the rule, can scarcely develop in the familial setting. The family . . . is a very small group of persons . . . their relationships are not subject to any general impersonal, immutable regulation; they always have and normally should have an air of freedom. . . . But meanwhile the child must learn respect for the rule; he must learn to do his duty because it is his duty . . .even though the task may not seem an easy one. Such an apprenticeship . . . must devolve upon the school. . . . Too often, it is true, people conceive of school discipline so as to preclude endowing it with such an important moral function. Some see in it a simple way of guaranteeing superficial peace and order in the class. Under such conditions, one can quite reasonably come to view these imperative requirements as barbarous—as a tyranny of complicated rules. . . . In reality, however, the nature and function of discipline is something altogether different. It is not a simple device for securing superficial peace in the classroom. . . . It is the morality of the classroom (as a small society) (1925, pp. 146–8).

I shall not go into Durkheim's system of moral education in detail in this paper except to say it is the most philosophically and scientifically comprehensive, clear, and workable approach to moral education extant. Its workability has been demonstrated, not in France, but in Soviet Russia where it has been elaborated from the point of view of Marxist rather than Durkheimian sociology. Like Durkheim, the Russians hold that altruistic concern or sacrifice, like the sense of duty, is always basically directed toward the group rather than toward another individual or toward an abstract principle. Durkheim reasons that altruism is always sacrificing the self for something greater than the self, and another self can never be greater than the self except as it stands for the group or for society. Accordingly a central part of moral education is the sense of belonging to, and sacrificing for, a group.

One of the logical but to us rather horrifying innovations in the hidden curriculum that Durkheim and the Russians suggest on this basis is the use of collective responsibility, collective punishment and reward. Here is how a Russian moral education manual (quoted by Bronfenbrenner 1968) tells us these and other aspects of moral education are to be handled in a third-grade classroom:

Class 3-B is just an ordinary class; it's not especially well disciplined.

The teacher has led this class now for three years, and she has earned affection, respect, and acceptance as an authority from her pupils. Her word is law for them.

The bell has rung, but the teacher has not yet arrived. She has delayed deliberately in order to check how the class will conduct itself.

In the class all is quiet. After the noisy class break, it isn't so easy to mobilize yourself and to quell the restlessness within you! Two monitors at the desk silently observe the class. On their faces is reflected the full importance and seriousness of the job they are performing. But there is no need for them to make any reprimands: the youngsters with pleasure and pride maintain scrupulous discipline; they are proud of the fact that their class conducts itself in a manner that merits the confidence of the teacher. And when the teacher enters and quietly says "be seated," all understand that she deliberately refrains from praising them for the quiet and order, since in their class it could not be otherwise.

During the lesson, the teacher gives an exceptional amount of attention to collective competition between "links." (The links are the smallest unit of the Communist youth organization at this age level.) Throughout the entire lesson the youngsters are constantly hearing which link has best prepared its lesson, which link has done the best at numbers, which is the most disciplined, which has turned in the best work.

The best link not only gets a verbal positive evaluation but receives the right to leave the classroom first during the break and to have its notebooks checked before the others. As a result the links receive the benefit of collective education, common responsibility, and mutual aid.

"What are you fooling around for? You're holding up the whole link," whispers Kolya to his neighbor during the preparation period for the lesson. And during the break he teaches her how better to organize her books and pads in her knapsack.

"Count more carefully," says Olya to her girl friend. "See, on account of you our link got behind today. You come to me and we'll count together at home."

I do not need to say any more to indicate that Durkheim and the Russians know how to make the hidden curriculum work. Furthermore, it is clear that Durkheim has simply taken to its logical conclusion a justification of the hidden curriculum which many teachers vaguely assume, the justification that the discipline of group life directly promotes moral character. We see, however, that when this line of thinking is carried to its logical conclusion, it leads to a definition of moral education as the promotion of collective national discipline which most of us feel is consistent neither with rational ethics nor with the American constitutional tradition. What I am arguing is that the trouble with Durkheim's approach to the hidden curriculum is not that he starts from a conception of moral development, but rather that he starts from an erroneous conception of moral development.

Oddly enough, permissive rejection of Durkheim's worship of

collective authority can open the way for educational practices which, just as much as Durkheim's, are based upon a culturally relative notion of the moral. A.S. Neill says: "We set out to make a school in which we should allow children freedom to be themselves. To do this we had to renounce all discipline, all direction, all moral training. We have been called brave but it did not require courage, just a complete belief in the child as a good, not an evil, being. A child is innately wise and realistic. If left to himself without adult suggestion of any kind he will develop as far as he is capable of developing. I believe that it is moral instruction that makes the child bad, not good" (1960, p. 4).

A philosopher could while away a pleasant afternoon trying to find out just what ethical framework Neill is using when he says children are good but morality is bad. It is more instructive, however, to recognize that even at Summerhill moral problems arise, and to see how Neill handles them. Some years ago, Neill says,

we had two pupils arrive at the same time, a boy of seventeen and a girl of sixteen. They fell in love with each other and were always together. I met them late one night and stopped them. "I don't know what you two are doing," I said, "and morally I don't care for it isn't a moral question at all. But economically, I do care. If you, Kate, have a kid, my school will be ruined. You have just come to Summerhill. To you it means freedom to do what you like. Naturally, you have no special feeling for the school. If you had been here from the age of seven, I'd never have had to mention the matter. You would have such a strong attachment to the school that you would think of the consequences to Summerhill" (1960, p. 57).

What the quotation makes clear, of course, is that the hidden moral curriculum of Summerhill is the "explicit" curriculum of Durkheim and the Russians. Unquestioned loyalty to the school, to the collectivity, seems to be the ultimate end of moral education at Summerhill. The radically child-centered approach, which denies morality, has a "hidden curriculum" which is the same "hidden curriculum" as that of the teacher who preached that moral virtue was putting your books away. For both the radical libertarian and the Philistine bureaucrat a point comes where the wish of the child conflicts with the convenience and welfare of the school (or its managers) and, for both, the latter is the ultimate good. If exposed to reflection, and made explicit as moral education, this implicit teaching of conformity to the school becomes Durkheim's use of loyalty to the school and its rules as a symbol of, and preparation for, loyalty to the national society.

The term "hidden curriculum," then, refers to the fact that teachers and schools are engaged in moral education without explicitly and philosophically discussing or formulating its goals and methods. On the face of it, engaging in moral education without thinking about its goals and methods seems as dubious as it would be in intellectual education. There is, however, a school of functional sociology which claims that unreflective moral education reflects the unconscious wisdom of society and its needs for "socializing" the child for his own welfare as well as that of society. When such "socialization" or rule enforcement is viewed as implying explicit positive educational goals, it generates a philosophy of moral education in which loyalty to the school and its rules is consciously cultivated as a matter of breeding loyalty to society and its rules.

RELATIVITY AND UNIVERSALS IN MORAL DEVELOPMENT

Although Durkheim's philosophical and psychological development of the hidden curriculum of everyday public-school practice seems repellent, we shall argue that it is the only logically consistent rationale for deliberate moral education under the central common assumption of most social scientists, the assumption of the cultural and historical relativity of moral values. Before we can consider other approaches to moral education, then, we must consider the issue of value-relativity.

Most contemporary psychologists and sociologists who write about moral values in child development and education start with the assumption that there are no universal, nonarbitrary moral principles and that each individual acquires his own values from the external culture. The following definition of moral values clearly reflects such a relativistic view: "moral values are evaluations of actions generally believed by the members of a given society to be either 'right' or 'wrong,'" (Berkowitz 1964, p. 44). While there are major theoretical differences among sociological role-theorists, psychoanalytic theorists, and learning theorists, and among different learning theorists themselves, they all do have a common characteristic: they view moral development and other forms of socialization as "the whole process by which an individual, born with behavioral potentialities of enormously wide range, is led to develop actual behavior which is confined within a much narrower range—the range of what is customary and acceptable for him according to the standards of his group" (Child 1954 p. 655). Thus, development is defined as the direct internalization of external cultural norms. The growing child is trained to behave in such a way that he conforms to societal rules and values.

The first educational position derived from the assumption of relativity is Durkheim's advocacy of moralization by collective discipline. According to this position, although all values are relative, the child must be taught to accept the dominant values of his society for his own adaptation and for the survival of his society, and the school plays a necessary role in this process.

A second position derived (in America) from the assumption of the relativity of values is that the public schools cannot teach the moral values of American society to children without infringing the rights of minority groups, and hence that value education should be conducted by having publicly supported schools which teach one or another system of values, leaving parents free to send their children to a Catholic parochial school, a school teaching black nationalistic values, etc.

A third position (the Neill position) derived from the assumption is that moral values should not be taught or enforced in schools at all, since they are arbitrary and irrational.

In practice, most working educators who believe in ethical relativity shuttle from one of these three positions to the other depending upon the situation with which they are confronted. They have no assurance about the nature of any universal ethical principles to be transmitted to children, but they cannot be completely ethically neutral either. The customary result is to focus moral instruction on the trivial and immediate, rather than on the universal and important, because this approach gives rise to fewer headaches about philosophic or ethical justification.

An example of this shuttling between positions based on relativity comes from my observation of an enlightened and effective young fourth-grade teacher. The teacher was at the back of the room working with a project group, while the rest of the class were engaged with their workbooks. In the front row, a boy said something to his neighbor who retaliated by quietly spitting in his face. The first boy equally quietly slugged the other without leaving his seat, by which time the teacher noted the disturbance. She said calmly, "Stop that and get back to your workbooks." The boy who had done the slugging said, "Teacher, I hit him because he spit in my face." The teacher replied, "That wasn't polite, it was rude, now get back to work, you're supposed to be doing your workbooks." As they went back to work, the boy who had done the spitting said to his opponent with a grin, "I will grant you that, it was rude."

A later discussion with this teacher about her general views on moral education explained why she handled the situation as she did. In her master's thesis she had reviewed writings and research on "middle-class values in education and their application to the disadvantaged child." She said that her paper had made her realize that she was transmitting middle-class values. Nevertheless, she said, politeness was just very important to her and she was bent on transmitting it to her students. The point is that she had absorbed from educational sociology the conflictful concept that "all values are relative" and had resolved the conflict by the decision to support the "middle-class" value of "politeness," which was emotionally central to her. The result was that she attempted to avoid moralizing, but, when she finally did moralize, she perceived the moral issue in terms of the superficial "middle-class" value of "politeness" rather than the deeper and more universal value of human dignity. The boys themselves recognized that some deeper value than politeness was involved, as the smiling "I'll grant you that, it was rude" indicated. I do not presume to advise the teacher as to what she should have said in this situation. My point is that the teacher must resolve the issues involved in moral relativity more systematically if she is to carry out her moral-educational activities in a positive fashion.

When confronted with uncertainty about the relativity of ethical principles, the customary resort of the teacher is to retreat to a committee or group. Uneasy about her own arbitrary authority, she passes this authority over to the group, a good strategy for non-moral policy decisions within the democratic process, but not a strategy for arriving at valid ethical principles.

The teacher just mentioned had gathered together suggestions of the class in the form of a moral code put up on a poster at the back of the class. The code had the following commandments: (1) Be a good citizen; (2) Be generous by helping our friends; (3) Mind your own business; (4) Work quietly; (5) No fighting; (6) Play nicely and fairly; (7) Be neat and clean; (8) Be prepared; (9)Raise your hand; (10) Be polite. Even if some of us feel that the original Ten Commandments could stand restatement, I doubt if these ten would be considered an improvement.

Now, we shall claim that this teacher's problems arise because of faulty thinking about ethical relativity which she shares with all the writers we have so far quoted or discussed. In this section I will present evidence that the factual assumptions made by theories of ethical relativity are not correct; that there are in fact universal human ethical values and principles.

In this section I will also present evidence which leads us to question a second common assumption closely linked to the assumption of ethical relativity. This is the assumption, accepted by all the writers quoted, that morality and moral learning are fundamentally emotional, irrational processes. Durkheim (1925) and Dreeben (1968) assume that learning to accept rules and authority is a concrete nonrational process based on repetition, emotion, and sometimes sanctions. The child is assumed to be controlled by primitive and selfish drives which he is reluctant to give up, and the steady experience of authority and discipline is necessary for his learning to live with rules. This conception of moral learning contrasts with that of Dewey (1925) and Piaget (1932), who hold that the child learns to accept authority genuinely when he learns to understand and accept the reasons and principles behind the rules, or more generally that "ethical principles" are the end point of sequential "natural" development in social functioning and thinking (Kohlberg 1969, Kohlberg and Turiel 1971). This is a very different point of view from that taken by most teachers who either, like Durkheim, assume that "ethical principles" are the accepted rules of their own nation and culture, which should be taught to children by the teacher's deliberate instruction, example, and discipline, or else, like Neill, assume that "ethical principles" are relative and arbitrary. It will be our contention that ethical principles are distinguishable from arbitrary conventional rules and beliefs and that the stimulation of their development is a matter quite different from the inculcation of arbitrary cultural beliefs.

Before presenting our evidence, it is important to note that the value-relativity issue is not solely one of fact. As usually held by adults, value relativism is both a doctrine that "everyone has his own values," that all men do not adhere to some set of universal standards, and a doctrine that "everyone ought to have his own values," that there are no universal standards to which all men ought to adhere. Thus, the value-relativity position often rests on logical confusion between matters of fact, what "is," and matters of value, what "ought to be."

To illustrate, I shall quote a typical response of one of my graduate students to the following moral dilemma:

In Europe, a woman was near death from a very bad disease, a special kind of cancer. There was one drug that the doctors thought might save her. It was a form of radium that a druggist was charging ten times what the drug cost him to make. He paid $200 for the radium and charged $2,000 for a small dose of the drug. The sick woman's husband, Heinz, went to everyone he knew to borrow the money, but he could only get together about $1,000, which is half of what it cost. He told the druggist that his wife was dying, and asked him to sell it cheaper or let him pay later. But the druggist said, "No, I discovered the drug and I'm going to make money from it." So Heinz got desperate and broke into the man's store to steal the drug for his wife.

Should the husband have done that? Why?

Part of her reply was as follows: "I think he should steal it because if there is any such thing as a universal human value, it is the value of life, and that would justify stealing it." I then asked her, "Is there any such thing as a universal human value?" and she answered, "No, all values are relative to your culture."

I quote the response because it illustrates a typical confusion of the relativist. She starts out by claiming that one ought to act in terms of the universal value of human life, implying that human life is a universal value in the sense that it is logical and desirable for all men to respect all human life, and that one can demonstrate to other men that it is logical and desirable to act in this way. If she were clear in her thinking she would see that the *fact* that all men do not always act in terms of this value does not contradict the claim that all men *ought* always to act in accordance with it. Because she has this confusion, she ends up denying the possibility of making a judgment of should or ought going beyond the self.

Very typically, the doctrine of relativity is used as an argument for tolerance. When the relativist says, "Everyone has his own bag," he means, "Everyone ought to be allowed and encouraged to have his own bag," which is a postulation of liberty as something which ought to be a universal human value. Frequently, however, the desire to postulate the principle of tolerance as an ideal leads to a postulation of the factual claim that there is cultural relativity, a complete logical confusion.

If the relativist could clearly separate the question "Are there universal moral values?" from the question "Ought there to be universal human values?" he could get an affirmative answer to both questions. Let us take the "is" question first.

For twelve years, I have been studying the development of moral judgment and character primarily by following the same group of seventy-five boys at three-year intervals from early adolescence (at the beginning the boys were ten to sixteen years of age) through young manhood (they are now twenty-two to twenty-eight years of age). This study has been supplemented by a series of studies of development in other cultures, and by a set of experimental studies, some designed to change the child's stage of moral thought, some to find the relation of an individual's moral thought to moral action.

The first assumption behind our approach has been that the key to understanding a man's moral conduct or "character" is to understand his moral philosophy, that is, the assumption that we all, even and especially young children, are moral philosophers. By this I mean, in the first place, that the child has a morality of his own. Adults are so busy trying to instill in children their own morality, that they seldom listen to children's moralizing. If the child repeats a few of the adult's clichés and behaves himself, most parents think he has now adopted or "internalized" parental standards. A great deal of anthropology and psychology makes this assumption, which can be made only if we fail to talk to children. As soon as we do, we find that they have lots of standards which do not come in any obvious way from parents, peers, or teachers.

A consideration of somewhat more advanced moral philosophies leads us to stages defined in Appendix 1. We have defined these stages by means of the analysis of responses to hypothetical moral dilemmas, deliberately "philosophical," some found in medieval works of casuistry. (A more complete treatment of the dilemmas and sample responses to them can be found in Kohlberg and Turiel 1971). When I first decided to explore development in other cultures by this method, I did so with fear and trembling induced by predictions by some of my anthropologist friends that I would have to throw away my culture-bound moral concepts and stories and start from scratch learning the values of that culture. In fact, something quite different happened. My first try was a study of two villages—one Atayal (Malaysian aboriginal), one Taiwanese. My guide was a young Chinese ethnographer who had written an account of the moral and religious patterns of the village. When he started to translate for me the children's responses, he'd start to laugh at something at which I had laughed when I first heard it from American children. Cultural differences there are, but they are not what made him laugh. To illustrate, let me quote for you a dilemma, similar to the Heinz dilemma on stealing (see above), adapted for the villages investigated:

A man and wife had just migrated from the high mountains. They started to farm but there was no rain and no crops grew. No one had enough food. The wife got sick from having little food and could only sleep. Finally she was close to dying from having no food. The husband could not get any work and the wife could not move to another town. There was only one grocery store in the village, and the storekeeper charged a very high price for the food because there was no other store and people had no place else to go to buy food. The husband asked the storekeeper for some food for his wife, and said he would pay for it later. The storekeeper said, "No, I won't give you food unless you pay first." The husband went to all the people in the village to ask for food but no one had food to spare. So he got desperate and broke into the store to steal food for his wife.

Should the husband have done that? Why?

The stage-2 children in the Taiwanese village would reply to the above story as follows: "He should steal the food for his wife because if she dies he'll have to pay for her funeral and that costs a lot." In the Atayal village, funerals weren't such a big thing and the stage-2 boys would say, "He should steal the food because he needs his wife to cook for him." In other words, we have to consult our ethnographer to know what content a stage-2 child will include in his instrumental exchange calculations, but what made our anthropologist laugh was the difference in form between the child's thought and his own, a difference definable independently of the particular culture.

It is this emphasis on the distinctive form (as opposed to the content) of the child's moral thought which allows us to call all men moral philosophers.

The actual definition of our stages is detailed and is based on a treatment of 28 basic aspects of morality (moral concepts or values) to be found in any culture (Appendix 2). Appendix 3 presents one of these 28 concepts, the concept of the value of life. Appendix 3 defines and gives examples of the way this value is defined at each of the six stages of development.

The progression, or set of stages, just described implies something more than age trends. In the first place, stages imply invariant sequence. Each individual child must go step by step through each of the kinds of moral judgment outlined. It is, of course, possible for a child to move at varying speeds and to stop (become "fixated") at any level of development, but if he continues to move upward, he must move in accord with these steps. The longitudinal study of American boys at ages 10, 13, 16, 19, and 23 suggests that this is the case. An example of such stepwise movement is provided in Appendix 3. Tommy is stage 1 at age 10, stage 2 at age 13, and stage 3 at age 16. Jim is stage 4 at age 10, stage 5 at 20, and stage 6 at 24. (See Kohlberg 1963; 1969, and Kohlberg and Turiel 1971 for a more detailed discussion of empirical findings.)

Second, stages define "structured wholes": total ways of thinking, not attitudes towards particular situations. Another of the 28 different aspects contributing to stage definitions concerns the motives of moral action. As can be seen in Appendix 4, which illustrates prepared arguments for and against stealing the drug in the first dilemma described, a stage is a way of thinking, which may be used to support either side of an action choice; that is, it illustrates the distinction between moral form and moral content (action choice). Our correlational studies indicate a general factor of moral level which cross-cuts aspect. An individual at stage 6 on a "cognitive" aspect (universalized value of life) is also likely to be at stage 6 on an "affective" aspect (motive for difficult moral action in terms of internal self-condemnations). An individual at stage 6 on a situation of stealing a drug for a wife is likely to be at stage 6 on a story involving civil disobedience (helping slaves escape before the Civil War). It should be noted that any individual is usually not entirely at one stage. Typically, as children develop they are partly in their major stage (about 50 percent of their ideas), partly in the stage into which they are moving, and partly in the stage they have just left behind. Seldom, however, do they use stages at developmental stages removed from one another.

Third, a stage concept implies universality of sequence under varying cultural conditions. It implies that moral development is not merely a matter of learning the verbal values or rules of the child's culture but reflects something more universal in development, something that would occur in any culture. In general, the stages in moral judgment just described appear to be culturally universal.

Figures 1 and 2 indicate the cultural universality of the sequence of stages that we have found. Figure 1 presents the age trends for middle-class urban boys in the United States, Taiwan, and Mexico.

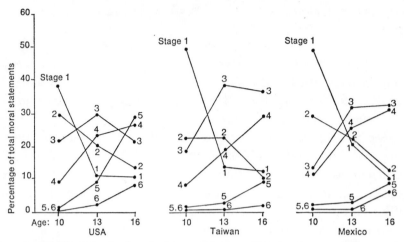

FIGURE 1 Middle-class urban boys in the U.S., Taiwan, and Mexico. At age 10 the stages are used according to difficulty. At age 13, stage 3 is most used by all three groups. At age 16, U.S. boys have reversed the order of age 10 stages (with the exception of 6) In Taiwan and Mexico, conventional (3-4) stages prevail at age 16, with stage 5 also little used. (From L. Kohlberg and R. Kramer: Continuities and discontinuities in childhood and adult moral development *Human Development* 1969 *12* 93-120 (S. Karger, Basel/New York).)

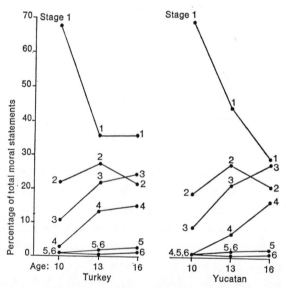

FIGURE 2 Two isolated villages, one in Turkey, the other in Yucatan, show similar patterns in moral thinking. There is no reversal of order, and preconventional (1-2) does not gain a clear ascendancy over conventional stages at age 16. (From L. Kohlberg and R. Kramer: Continuities and discontinuities in childhood and adult moral development *Human Development* 1969 *12* 93-120 (S. Karger, Basel/New York).)

At age 10 in each country the greater number of moral statements are scored at the lower stages. In the United States by age 16, the order is reversed, so that the greater proportion use higher stages, with the exception of stage 6 which is rarely used. The results in Mexico and Taiwan are the same, except that development is a little slower. The most conspicuous feature is that stage-5 thinking is much more salient in the United States than in Mexico or Taiwan at age 16. Nevertheless, it is present in the other countries, so we know that it is not purely an American democratic construct. The second figure indicates results from two isolated villages, one in Yucatan, one in Turkey. The similarity of pattern in the two villages is striking. While conventional moral thought (stages 3 and 4) increases steadily from age 10 to age 16, at 16 it still has not achieved a clear ascendancy over premoral thought (stages 1 and 2). Stages 5 and 6 are totally absent in this group. Trends for lower-class urban groups are intermediate in rate of development between those for the middle class and the village boys.

The first and most obvious implication of these findings is that many social scientific notions of "the cultural relativity of morals" are false. As Brandt's careful analysis indicates (1959), "cultural relativity in morals" has been based upon striking cultural differences in customs, but has not taken account of the meaning of such customs with regard to differences in principles or forms of moral judgment. A comparison of American college students' quaint springtime rite of sitting-in in the sixties with their quaint rites of panty-raiding in the fifties would not tell us anything about moral changes unless we looked at the way in which the students thought about the values involved in what they were doing. Our own studies are the first effort to examine this question, and suggest that the same basic ways of moral valuing are found in every culture and develop in the same order.

A second, related, fallacy is the notion that basic moral principles are dependent upon a particular religion, or any religion at all. We have found no important differences in development of moral thinking between Catholics, Protestants, Jews, Buddhists, Moslems, and atheists. Children's moral values in the religious area seem to go through the same stages as their general moral values, so that a stage-2 child is likely to say, "Be good to God and he'll be good to you." Both cultural values and religion are important factors in selectively elaborating certain themes in the moral life but they are not unique causes of the development of basic moral values. Our data do not indicate that all values are universal, but rather that basic moral values are universal. For example, a Taiwanese boy recommends stealing the drug "because if she dies, he'll have to pay for her funeral and that costs a lot." No American boy ever says that. But American boys will (like the Atayal) recommend stealing the drug because otherwise "there'll be no one to cook your food." In other words, big funerals are a value in Taiwan and not in the United States. Both the value of life and a stage of instrumental-pragmatic thinking about this value are culturally universal, however.

If basic moral values are universal, the relativists' next defense is to say that the ordering or hierarchy of these values is idiosyncratic and relative. For instance, one might agree that everyone would value both life and property rights in the Heinz dilemma, but argue that which is valued most would depend upon a culturally relative hierarchy of values. In fact, however, basic hierarchies of moral values are primarily reflections of developmental stages in moral thought. Anyone who understands the values of life and property will recognize that life is morally more valuable than property. Even at stage 2 boys know that the druggist in the story would rather save his own life than his own property so that the druggist's property is less valuable than the woman's life. Appendix 3, defining the six steps or stages in the development of conceptions of the value of life, suggests these are steps not only in conceptions of life's value, but also in the differentiation of life from other values and in the hierarchical dominance of life over such values as that of property.

Another example concerning hierarchies of value is the current American problem of law and order versus justice which I have discussed in more detail elsewhere (Kohlberg and Turiel 1971). A person at stage 4 thinks law and order is justice, or as one respondent said, "If we have law and order, what do we need justice for?"

Governor Reagan of California thinks civil disobedience is automatically unjust. By contrast, people at stages 5 and 6 know that the
purpose of law and order is the maintenance of justice. As stated in
the old-fashioned terms of the founding fathers, governments are
formed to protect the equal rights of citizens. Development in
conceptions of justice leads to a hierarchical relation between "law
and order" and "justice."

   In summary, the doctrine of ethical relativity assumes that different cultures or groups hold different basic fundamental moral
values or hierarchies of values, and that these different values or
value hierarchies cannot themselves be judged as more or less
adequate or more or less moral. When extended to individual differences within cultures, the doctrine holds that individuals, too,
have different values because of differences in basic needs, and that
these values also are determined by extramoral considerations and so
cannot be judged as more or less adequate morally. There are two
portions to the doctrine, one about matters of fact, one normative.
The normative portion denies that one can *judge* or evaluate cultural
or individual differences in moral judgment as better or worse. The
empirical portion claims that the explanation of cultural differences
in moral values is to be sought apart from a general concept of
morality as such. Concretely, there have been moderate and extreme
doctrines of relativity in both empirical and normative aspects. The
moderate doctrine is represented by Durkheim, who holds that the
concept of morality is scientifically meaningful and that an individual's attitude to the norms of his group is more or less moral,
depending upon the extent to which he displays respect for, and
attachment to these norms. One can characterize at least certain
delinquents and psychopaths as being not moral. One cannot, however, characterize the differences in norms from one society or group
to another as being more or less moral, since the essence of morality
is respect for norms, and differences in the content of these norms
are irrelevant to the fact that they involve the moral form (respect).
As a doctrine about the empirical nature of morality, Durkheim's
doctrine assumes that theories explaining differences in norms from
culture to culture are not theories about why some individuals (or

groups) are more or less moral (feel more or less respect) than others. As a normative doctrine, it holds that children within a culture may be judged as more or less moral, and that the less moral child should be made more moral, but that cultural differences as such cannot be morally evaluated and that moral education should be one thing in one culture, another in another.

The strong form of the doctrine of ethical relativity would deny the usefulness of defining individual differences in moral terms at all. It holds that labelling individual differences as more or less moral is simply judging them from the arbitrary standards of some individual or group or making a judgment of praise or blame which has no scientific value or meaning. When the teacher labelled "putting books away" as "good behavior" or as moral, she did not add anything to the scientific understanding of the behavior by introducing moral terminology. The extreme relativist would say the same with regard to more sophisticated efforts by psychologists to describe "moral character" (as we discuss in our final section). To label children who put their books away as more moral than those who do not, not only adds nothing to the scientific understanding of the behavior but is not based on a moral norm of any rational validity. The extreme relativist would say the same for all discussions of individual and cultural differences in terms of morality.

In contrast to both schools of relativism, we have first pointed out that there are universal moral concepts, values, or principles. As a matter of fact, there is less variation between individuals and cultures than usually has been maintained: (a) almost all individuals in all cultures use the same 28 basic moral categories, concepts, or principles; (b) all individuals in all cultures go through the same order or sequences of gross stages of development, although varying in rate and terminal point of development.

Second, we have pointed out that the marked differences which exist between individuals and cultures are differences in stage or developmental status. There are marked individual and cultural differences in the definition, use, and hierarchical ordering of these universal value-concepts, but the major source of this variation both within and between cultures is developmental. Insofar as they are developmental, they are not morally neutral or arbitrary. This means empirically that the theory which explains cultural and individual differences in values is also the same general theory of why children become capable of moral judgment and action at all. It means normatively that there is a sense in which we can characterize moral differences between groups and individuals as being more or less adequate morally.

The basic educational conclusions we shall draw from this position are that the only philosophically justifiable statement of aims of moral education, the only one which surmounts the problem of relativity, is a statement in terms of the stimulation of moral development conceived of as the encouragement of a capacity for principled moral judgment and of the disposition to act in accordance with this capacity. To support this conclusion we shall need to clarify our philosophical conception of the nature of moral principles and of the relation of moral principles to moral action. Before doing this, however, we need to go back over the research findings just presented in terms of their implications for a psychological theory of moralization. We need to do this because we believe that the only psychological theory consistent with our findings is so different from that entertained by most philosophers, educators, and psychologists, that communication is impossible without some clarification of this theory.

THE COGNITIVE-DEVELOPMENTAL THEORY OF MORALIZATION

Almost all psychology textbooks which discuss moral development treat it as the product of internalization of the norms and values of parents and of the culture through processes of identification, reward, or punishment. Our findings concerning stages obviously lead us to reject the theories of internalization which are the unquestioned "truths" of textbook social science, but also require a positive alternative explanation. Often, notions of stages are assimilated to a conception of natural biological growth and unfolding. In the area of morality, such maturational theories lead to a conception of "giving the child freedom to grow in his own way" such as was represented by our quotations from A. S. Neill. Such a maturational theory, however, is far from our own view of the implications of moral stages. Instead, we have elaborated a "cognitive-developmental" theory of moralization which attempts to explain universals and natural trends in development without assuming that these trends are the innate unfolding of the nervous sytem, and which specifies the kind of environmental conditions necessary to facilitate moral development (Kohlberg 1969; Kohlberg in preparation).

I have used the term "cognitive-developmental" to refer to a set of assumptions common to the moral theories of Dewey (1909), G. H. Mead (1934), J. M. Baldwin (1906), Piaget (1932), and myself. All have postulated stages of moral development representing cognitive-structural transformations in the conception of self and society. All have assumed that these stages represent successive modes of "taking the role of others" in social situations, and hence that the social-environmental determinants of development are its opportunities for role-taking. More generally, all have assumed an active child who structures his perceived environment, and hence they have assumed that moral stages and their development represent the interaction of the child's structuring tendencies and the structural features of the environment.

There are two assumptions of our theory which we shall stress here, because they are central for educators and philosophers concerned with morality. One is our second assumption, the assumption that moral development has a cognitive core. This assumption is central to any intellective approach to moral education and contrasts sharply with irrational-emotive theories of moral development such as those of Durkheim and Freud. The other assumption is of the interactional origins of morality. This assumption is central to an intellective approach to moral education as not a process of transmission of fixed moral truth but rather a stimulation of the child's restructuring of his experience.

There are two issues which require clarification in labelling our theory as "cognitive." First, the label does not imply that we consider moral judgment to be cognitive in the sense held by philosophers holding "descriptivistic" metaethical views, that is, that moral judgments describe states of the world in somewhat the same way as scientific judgments describe states of the world. (In this camp are utilitarians who believe that moral judgments describe the welfare or happiness consequence of action, intuitionists who believe moral judgments reflect immediately apprehended moral qualities of action, and Durkheimian sociological ethicists.) As I elaborate in later sections, my metaethical position is "prescriptivistic" and "constructionistic" rather than "descriptivistic" or "emotive." Put differently, moral judgments and norms are to be understood ultimately as universal constructions of human actors which regulate their social interaction rather than as passive reflections of either external states of other humans or of internal emotions.

It should be noted, however, that although "descriptivism" and "objectivism" are inadequate metaethical views, they are the views of most of humanity. Below the principled stage of morality, it is simply assumed that judgments of right and wrong correspond to a right and wrong external to the judger, that "almost everyone knows right from wrong," and that "right and wrong" are the rules of society or of God. This is most patently true at stage 1. When stage-1 ten-year-old children are asked, "Is there a right answer to these questions (moral dilemmas)?" they are likely to respond, "You must have the right answers in the back of your book." While children at the conventional stage discriminate between moral problems and arithmetic problems, they still believe moral judgments reflect an objective "right and wrong" external to the judger. In light of the fact that moral judgments are usually believed to be cognitions by their makers, it is psychologically correct to analyze moral judgment in terms of general principles and theories of cognitive development.

The second issue raised by the label "cognitive" is that of the role of affect in moral judgment. Discussions of cognition and affect usually are based on the assumption that cognitions and affects are different mental states, leading to the question, "Which is quantitatively more influential in moral judgment, states of cognition or states of affect?" In contrast, the cognitive-developmental view holds that "cognition" and "affect" are different aspects of, or perspectives on, the same mental events, that all mental events have both cognitive and affective aspects, and that the development of mental dispositions reflects structural changes recognizable in both cognitive and affective perspectives. It is evident that moral judgments often involve strong emotional components. It is also evident that the presence of strong emotion in no way reduces the cognitive component of moral judgment, although it may imply a somewhat different functioning of the cognitive component than is implied in more neutral areas. An astronomer's calculation that a comet will hit the earth will be accompanied by strong emotion but this does not make his calculation less cognitive than a calculation of a comet's orbit which had no earthly consequences. And just as the quantitative strength of the emotional component is irrelevant to the theoretical importance of cognitive structure for understanding the development of scientific judgment, so too the quantitative role of affect is relatively irrelevant for understanding the structure and development of moral judgment. The dilemmas we present to our children are hypothetical and involve relatively mild emotional arousal. Several studies have compared stages of moral judgment in real dilemmas and our hypothetical ones and indicate a quite high correlation between moral stage in the real and hypothetical dilemmas. The example of the astronomer's calculation can be misleading, however, in that moral judgments differ from scientific judgments in the way in which they involve affective aspects of mental functioning. Moral judgments are largely about sentiments and intuitions of persons and to a large extent they express and are justified by reference to the judger's sentiments. The development of sentiment, as it enters into moral judgment, is, however, a development of structures with a heavy cognitive component. We presented in Appendix 4 six stages in the development of sentiments of fear, shame, and guilt as they enter into moral judgment. The emergence of self-condemnation, for example, as a distinctive sentiment in moral judgment, is the final step in a series of differentiations which, like all differentiations in development, are cognitive in nature. The sequential differentiations are defined in the parentheses of Appendix 4 (e.g., disapproval from punishment, moral condemnation from disapproval, self-condemnation from moral condemnation by others). The series of differentiations involved in the emergence of guilt is related to the series of differentiations (presented in Appendix 3) involved in the development of human life, on the face of it not an "affective" concept. Both spring from the central differentiations involved in the stages as a whole. The fact that this is true is shown by the fact that there is a good correlation between a child's stage on the life concept and on the guilt concept. This consistency enters into "real life" measures of guilt as well. Ruma and Mosher (1966) obtained a correlation of 0.56 between real-life measures of guilt by delinquents over confessed offenses and stage of moral judgment, a correlation as high as that between one measure of guilt and another. In general, then, the quality (as opposed to the quantity) of affects involved in moral judgment is determined by its cognitive-structural development, a development which is part and parcel with the general development of the child's conceptions of a moral order. Two adolescents, thinking of stealing, may have the same feeling of anxiety in the pit of their stomachs. One adolescent (stage 2) interprets the feeling as "being chicken," "being afraid of the police," and ignores it. The other (stage 4) interprets the feeling as "the warning of my conscience" and decides accordingly. The difference in reaction is one in cognitive-structural aspects of moral judgment, not in emotional "dynamics" as such.

The exact psychological meaning for moral judgment of the contentions just made has been clarified by several empirical findings. Maturity of moral judgment is correlated with cognitive maturity but is clearly distinguishable from it. Among children of a given age, the correlations between IQ and moral maturity are 0.35 to 0.50 in various samples, accounting for about one-fourth of the variation in moral judgment. In large part, older children are more mature in moral judgment because they are in general more cognitively mature. This is true to an extent greater than is suggested by the correlations with tests of IQ. IQ tests are poor tests of maturity of reasoning processes in moral judgment, processes more adequately measured by Piaget's tests of reasoning. Piaget's tests predict maturity of moral judgment independently of the relation of both moral judgment and Piaget reasoning to IQ. Furthermore, the empirical relations between general cognitive maturity and maturity of moral judgment are both greater and less than is suggested by these correlations. The correlations are not one-to-one but of the order that a certain level of cognitive maturity is a necessary but not sufficient condition for a given level of moral judgment. In other words, all morally advanced children are bright but not all bright children are morally advanced (or, all intellectually dull children are morally retarded but not all bright children are morally advanced). Moral maturity requires cognitive maturity but it also requires further features of development.

To summarize, our view implies that cognitive-structural features are the core of moral development, but moral judgment is not simply the application of intelligence in the sense of logical-technological thought to moral situations and problems. Our theory implies the untestable hypothesis that a child deprived of all moral-social stimulation until adolescence might perhaps develop "principled" or formal–operational logical thought in adolescence, but would still have to go through all the stages of morality before developing moral principles. If this were not so, it would be difficult to explain invariant sequence within the moral domain. Our notion of the cognitive-structural as broader than the usual conceptions of "knowing" and of "rationality" becomes evident when we consider the sense in which higher stages are more adequate than lower stages. Both psychological and philosophical analyses suggest that the more mature stage of moral thought is the more structurally adequate. This greater adequacy of more mature moral judgments rests on structural criteria more general than those of truth-value or efficiency. These general criteria are the *formal* criteria developmental theory holds as defining all mature structures, the criteria of increased differentiation and integration. These formal criteria (differentiation and integration) of development fit the formal criteria which philosophers of the formalist school have held to characterize genuine or adequate moral judgments.

From Kant to Hare, formalists have stressed the distinctively *universal* and *prescriptive* nature of adequate moral judgments. The increasingly prescriptive nature of more mature moral judgments is reflected in the series of differentiations we have described, which is a series of increased differentiations of "is" from "ought" (or of morality as internal principles from external events and expectations). As I elaborate later, this series of differentiations of the morally autonomous or categorical "ought" from the morally heteronomous "is" also represents a differentiation of the sphere of value judgments.

Corresponding to the criterion of integration is the moral criterion of universality, which is closely linked to the criterion of consistency, as formalists since Kant have stressed. The claim of principled morality is that it defines the right for anyone in any situation. In contrast, conventional morality defines good behavior for a Democrat but not for a Republican, for an American but not for a Vietnamese, for a father but not for a son.

The way in which these criteria are embodied in our stages is indicated by Appendix 3, the moral worth of human life. The series approaches prescriptivity because the moral imperative to value life becomes increasingly independent of the factual properties of the life in question. First the person's furniture becomes irrelevant to his value, next whether he has a loving family, and so on. (It is correspondingly a series of differentiations of moral considerations from other value-considerations.) In parallel fashion it is movement toward increased universality of the moral value of human life. At stage 1 only important persons' lives are valued, at stage 3 only family members, at stage 6 all life has equal moral value.

These combined criteria, differentiation and integration, are considered by developmental theory to entail a better equilibrium of the structure in question. A more differentiated and integrated moral structure handles more moral problems, conflicts, or points of view in a more stable or self-consistent way. Because conventional morality is not fully universal and prescriptive, it leads to continual self-contradictions, to definitions of right which are different for Republicans and Democrats, for Americans and Vietnamese, for fathers and sons. In contrast, principled morality is directed to resolving these conflicts in a stable, self-consistent fashion.

In this way a psychological explanation of why the child moves from stage to stage converges with a philosophical explanation of why one stage is "better" than another. A series of studies (Turiel 1966, Rest, Turiel, and Kohlberg 1969, Rest 1968) indicates that children and adolescents comprehend all stages up to their own, but not more than one above their own. The material in Appendix 4 was taken from one of these studies (Rest 1968). Adolescents were asked to restate each of the statements in their own words and to rank the statements in order of how good they were (Rest 1968). Statements at stages two or more above the subject's own were restated in terms of lower-stage thinking. Stages below the subject's own were disapproved or ranked low. Statements more than one stage above the subject's own are typically liked, but usually assimilated to the subject's own stage or the one above. Subjects prefer the stage one above their own to their own stage or to all the lower stages because, in developmental jargon, it represents a better equilibrium, because it is more differentiated and integrated than a lower stage.

What we have said suggests some of the reasons why the developmentally highest stage is not universally recognized as the most adequate mode of moral thinking by either the common man or philosophers. We shall assume that most philosophers, unlike the common man, have little trouble comprehending stage-5 or 6 reasoning. They still may not recognize it as most adequate, however, because they often evaluate such moral reasoning by philosophical criteria of rationality imported from nonmoral domains. The greater structural adequacy of the developmentally more advanced, of the more prescriptive and universal, is not something that is established in terms of either scientific truth criteria or means-ends efficiency. We have said that moral judgments are not true or false in the cognitive-descriptivist sense. A higher conception of the value of life or a higher conception of moral emotion (as internal self-judgment rather than fear) is not directly truer than a lower conception. Neither can higher moral conceptions and judgments be said to be more rational by technical-economic criteria of efficiency of means to ends, that is, as better means to maximize the happiness of the self or of society.

The "natural" processes of development entail progressive organization of moral structure resolving concrete moral problems. In the context of a given dilemma it may be quite apparent that stage 6 is a more adequate, equilibrated moral solution. Stage-6 reasoning may not, however, be based on a philosophically more adequate metaethical position or even on a more elegant or "rational" formal normative ethic. Accordingly, a philosopher may judge stage 6 to be no more adequate than lower stages because it is not more scientifically true, it is not more instrumentally efficient, it need not reflect more metaethical or epistemological sophistication, and it need not reflect a tighter or more parsimonious set of normative-ethical postulates. It is, then, only the philosophical formalist who views morality as an autonomous domain with its own criteria of adequacy or rationality who is likely to evaluate moral arguments by formal moral criteria and hence to clearly recognize stage-6 reasoning as more adequate than the reasoning at lower stages.

What we have said so far provides an explanation for the fact that movement in moral thought is usually irreversibly forward in direction, an explanation which does not require the assumption that moral progression is wired into the nervous sytem or is directly caused by physical-natural forces. It also helps explain why the step-by-step sequence of stages is invariant. The sequence represents a universal inner logical order of moral concepts, not a universal order found in the educational practices of all cultures or an order wired into the nervous system. Since each new basic differentiation of each stage logically depends upon the differentiation before it, the order of differentiations could not logically be other than it is.

We have tried to show how our first basic assumption that moral judgment has a cognitive-structural core explains why there is a universal directed sequential progression in moral judgment. We shall now consider the implications of our second basic assumption, the assumption that moral stages represent the interaction between the child's structuring tendencies and the structural features of the environment. The basic set of findings explained by the assumption are that variations in the child's cognitive and social environment affect the rate and terminus of moral development, but do not define the stages as' such. In contrast to this interactional assumption, it at first seems possible to explain moral growth as resulting from exposure to higher stages of thinking presented to the child by significant figures in the child's environment. Because children reject examples of thinking lower than their own, and because they fail to comprehend examples more than one stage up, they only assimilate or take over presented messages one stage above their own (Turiel 1966, Rest 1968, Rest, Turiel, and Kohlberg 1969). If a child's parent is at the principled level, the child reaches the conventional (and principled) stage of moral judgment more rapidly than he would if his parent were at the conventional level (Holstein 1968, 1969). Passive exposure to the next stage of thinking is, however, probably neither a necessary nor a sufficient condition for upward movement. The amount of change occurring in the Turiel and Rest studies of passive exposure was extremely slight. Even where contact is presumably intense, as in the family, passive exposure does not directly account for a child's stage. If it did, conventional-stage parents would be as successful as principled-stage parents in bringing the child to the conventional level of thought. One reason why exposure is not a sufficient condition for upward movement is because a child at a given stage does not necessarily comprehend messages at the next stage up. Rest (1968, 1969) found that the only children who comprehended messages one stage above their own already showed substantial (20 percent) spontaneous usage of that stage of thought, and it was these children who accounted for all of the learning or assimilation of models at one stage up. Presumably, then, movement to the next stage involves internal cognitive reorganization rather than the mere addition of more difficult content from the outside. Following cognitive-developmental theory in general, Turiel (1969) postulates that cognitive conflict or imbalance is the central "motor" or condition for such reorganization or upward movement. To test this postulate, Turiel is conducting a series of experiments presenting children with varying combinations of contradictory arguments flowing from the same-stage structure, as illustrated by the examples in Appendix 4. These studies should provide concrete evidence for the general notion that stage change depends upon conflict-induced reorganization.

We have so far contrasted environmental influence by passive exposure to external examples of higher thought with environmental influence by the induction of conflict leading to internal reorganization, the latter clarifying our assumption of interaction. The effects of nonmoral structural features of the environment upon the child's moral thought further clarify the interactional concept; these effects are best explained by our postulate that the social-environmental determinants of development are its opportunities for role-taking. Piaget's theory (1932) has stressed the peer group as a source of moral role-taking, while other theories stress participation in the larger secondary institutions or participation in the family itself (Baldwin 1897, Mead 1934). Research results suggest that all these opportunities for role-taking are important and that all operate in a similar direction by stimulating moral development rather than by producing a particular value system. In studies in three different cultures, middle-class children were found to be more advanced in moral judgment than matched lower-class children. This was not because the middle-class children heavily favored a certain type of thought which corresponded to the prevailing middle-class pattern. Instead, middle-class and working-class children seemed to move through the same sequences, but the middle-class children seemed to move faster and farther. Similar but even more striking differences were found between peer-group participators (popular children) and nonparticipators (unchosen children) in the American sample. Studies underway suggest that these peer-group differences partly arise from, and partly add to, prior differences in opportunities for role-taking in the child's family (family participation, communication, emotional warmth, sharing in decisions, awarding responsibility to the child, pointing out consequences of action to others). In particular, Holstein (1968) found that the amount of parental encouragement of the child's participation in discussion (in a taped "revealed differences" mother-father-child discussion of moral-conflict situations) was a powerful correlate of moral advance in the child.

Why should the existence of environmental opportunities for social participation and role-taking be basic for moral advance? The answer to this question also helps answer the question, "Why are there universal features of moral judgment in all societies?" or "Why are the same thirty categories of moral judgment found in all cultures?" The answer is that there are universal structures of the social environment which are basic to moral development just as there are universal structures of physical environment basic to "pure" cognitive development. All of the societies we have studied have the same basic institutions: family, economy, social stratification, law, and government. In spite of cultural diversity in content, these institutions have universal transcultural functional meanings. Although the detailed prescriptions of law vary from nation to nation, the form of "law" and the functional value of its importance and regular maintenance are much the same in all nations with formal law.

When we try to define the universal core structures of morality, the problem is not that societies have too few core institutions in common but that they have too many. In general, when theorists attempt to extract the culturally universal essence of morality, they turn to (1) rules, (2) sympathy or concern for welfare consequences to others, and (3) justice. Developmental theory's conception of role-taking embraces all three, in the sense that all morally relevant rules and institutions are conceived of as interpreted through processes of role-taking directed by concerns about both welfare and justice. All institutions and societies are alike in the sheer fact of being societies, that is, in being systems of defined complementary roles. The primary meaning of the word "social" is the distinctively human structuring of action and thought by role-taking, by the tendency to react to others as like the self and to react to the self's behavior from the other's point of view. Essentially each of our stages defines (or is defined by) a new cognitive-structural mode of role-taking in conflict situations. To understand the development of role-taking we must consider not only the principle of empathy or "welfare," considering the effects of action upon the others involved, but also the principle of "justice," that is, of reciprocity and equality in human relations.

When we move from role-taking to the resolution of conflicting roles, we arrive at the "principle" of justice. A moral conflict is a conflict between competing claims of men: you versus me, you versus him. The precondition for a moral conflict is man's capacity for role-taking. Most social situations are not moral because there is no conflict in role-taking between the expectations of one person and another. Where such conflicts arise, the principles we use to resolve them are principles of justice. Usually expectations or claims are integrated by customary rules and roles. The principles for making rules and distributing roles (rights and duties) in any institution from the family to the government are principles of justice or of fairness. The most basic principle of justice is equality: treat every man's claim equally, regardless of the man. Equality is the principle of distributive justice, but there is another form of justice—commutative justice or reciprocity. Punishment for something bad, reward for something good, contractual exchange are all forms of reciprocity, which is equality in exchange. Arguments about what is just are either arguments about the relative claims of equality (everyone deserves a decent minimum income) and reciprocity (only those who work hard should get the rewards of hard work) or arguments about equal liberty or opportunity versus equal benefit.

The psychological unity of role-taking and justice at mature stages of moral consciousness is easily recognized. In Tillich's words, "contemporary ethical theory has strongly emphasized the person-to-person encounter as the experiential root of morality. In the case of nonpersonal reality man can make it into an object, dissect it, analyze it, or construct something new. . . . The only limit is man's own finitude. . . . There is, however, a limit . . . in the ego-thou encounter. The limit is the other person. . . . All the implications of the idea of justice, especially the various forms of

equality and liberty, are applications of the imperative to acknowledge every potential person as a person" (Tillich 1963, pp. 36–8).

If the psychological unity of empathy and justice in moral role-
taking is apparent in the stage-6 consciousness described by Tillich,
it is also apparent at the very start of the moral experience. At every
stage children perceive basic values like the value of human life and
are able to empathize and take the roles of other persons, other
living things. Even at the start the child experiences the value of his
parents' life, or of a pet dog's life, as the result of primary empathy
with other living things, of the projection of consciousness into
others. At the start, too, he has some experience of justice, since
reciprocity, too, is part of the primary experience of role-taking in
social interaction (Erikson 1950, Mead 1934; Homans 1950;
Malinowski 1929; Piaget 1932). With development, however,
basic social values and the role-taking behind them are increasingly organized in terms of moral principles of justice (as increasingly differentiated from morally irrelevant reasons for role-taking
and choice).

For example, at the age of four my son joined the pacifist and
vegetarian movement and refused to eat meat, because, as he said,
"It's bad to kill animals." In spite of lengthy Hawk argumentation
by his parents about the difference between justified and unjustified
killing, he remained a vegetarian for six months. Like most Doves,
however, his principles recognized occasions of just or legitimate
killing. One night I read to him a book of Eskimo life involving a
seal-killing expedition. He got angry during the story and said,
"You know, there is one kind of meat I would eat, Eskimo meat.
It's bad to kill animals so it's all right to eat them."

He "took the role of the seal" in the sense of empathically experiencing its predicament. This in turn implied a stage-1 sense of
justice as equality, as the equal treatment of men and seals and a
stage -1 sense of justice as reciprocity in the demand for an eye-for-
an-eye, tooth-for-a-tooth retribution on its Eskimo hunter. Such
stage-1 concepts of justice become differentiated, integrated, and
universalized with development until they eventually become Tillich's
stage-6 moral sense.

The concepts of role-taking and justice, then, provide concrete meaning to the assumption that moral principles are neither external rules taken inward nor natural ego-tendencies of a biological organism, but rather the interactional emergents of social interaction. As expressed by Piaget: "In contrast to a given rule, which from the first has been imposed upon the child from outside. . . the rule of justice is a sort of immanent condition of social relationships or a law governing their equilibrium" (Piaget 1932, p. 196).

Piaget argues that just as logic represents an ideal equilibrium of thought operation, justice represents an ideal equilibrium of social interaction, with reciprocity or reversibility being core conditions for both logical and moral equilibrium. Although the sense of justice would not develop without the experience of social interaction, it is not simply an inward mirror or sociologically prescribed forms of these relations, any more than logic is an internalization of the linguistic forms of the culture. While disagreeing with the details of Piaget's interpretation of the development of justice, we agree with his essential conception of it as an interactional emergent.

THE DEFINITION OF THE MORAL

In the preceding two sections we have attempted to show that moral stages represent an invariant series with each higher stage being more adequate structurally than its predecessors. This adequacy has been discussed from a psychological perspective, characterizing later stages as "higher," "more developed," "more differentiated and integrated," and "more equilibrated." Because a pattern of thought or action is more mature, however, it does not follow that an educator ought to stimulate the pattern of thought. Even if it be granted that the more mature is in some sense more adequate than the less mature, it does not follow that an ideal pattern of thought is to be defined in terms of a natural stage of development such as stage 6. Educators do not define ideal patterns of thought about physics in terms of natural stages of thinking about the physical world, and it is not clear that they should do so in the case of moral thought.

Therefore, to move from the "is" of natural development to an "ought" or ideal of moral education, we must consider the adequacy of our higher stages in philosophical rather than psychological terms. We have already said that the greater adequacy of higher stages is not to be evaluated by criteria of scientific truth or instrumental rationality. What, then, is the basic criterion in terms of which one stage is more adequate than another? Here we must follow those philosophers who have held to the autonomy of the moral, to the irreducibility of moral thinking or moral standards to other criteria. One can only characterize a higher stage as more moral. Moral language and moral action are *sui generis:* they cannot be evaluated except in their own terms. We shall claim, however, that only stage-6 thinking or language is fully moral, that each higher stage is a closer approximation to the characteristic which philosophers such as Hare have taken as defining distinctively moral language. In this sense, we are arguing that the educational aim of stimulating moral development to stages 5 and 6 is the aim of giving the individual the capacity to engage in moral judgment and discourse, rather than the aim of imposing a specific morality upon him.

We have claimed that higher stages of judgment are more moral than lower stages in a formal sense. Regardless of our agreement with a stage-6 judgment or the action springing from it, we are able to say it is moral. For reasons we postpone until later, it is plausible to claim that a broad view of education should include among its aims the stimulation of the child's capacity to be moral in this sense. We need to make clear, however, that our claim that stage 6 is a more moral mode of thought than lower stages is not the claim that we can or should grade individuals as more or less moral. We argue elsewhere that there is no valid or final meaning to judging or grading persons as morally better or worse. Judgments of persons as morally good or bad, or judgments of praise and blame are not justified by the existence of universal moral principles as such. At the highest stage, the principle of justice (or the principle of maximizing human welfare) prescribes an obligation to act justly (or to further human welfare), it does not prescribe a duty to blame the unjust or give us rules for meting out blame to the unjust. Although there are some rational grounds for punishment, there are no ultimately rational or moral grounds for blaming other people. From a moral point of view, the moral worth of all persons is ultimately the same, it is equal. Moral theory is not required to set up standards for evaluating the moral worth of persons, and the claim that stage 6 is a more moral way of thinking is not an assignment of higher moral worth to the stage-6 individual.

The reasons for this caveat are obvious enough to the educationist. While it is a philosophically legitimate goal for the educator to raise general intelligence, as something good, and to rejoice in a child's increase in intellectual performance, it is completely unjustified for the educator to judge a child scoring higher in intelligence as of more personal worth than one scoring lower in intelligence. While only the thoughtless teacher might make this mistake in regard to intelligence tests, it would be easy to misinterpret our tests of moral maturity as justifying such unjust moral grading.

We must now clarify in a detailed way the reasons for which we consider higher stages to be more moral than lower stages. Like most philosophers, we are claiming, but on social scientific grounds, first, that the term "moral" refers to moral judgments or decisions based on moral judgments. We will argue in the last section that the primary psychological referent of the term "moral" is a judgment, not a behavior or an affect, for example, "guilt." (The difference between fear or anxiety on the one hand and guilt on the other is provided only by a concept of moral judgments associated with the affect, not with the affect itself.) Accordingly, then, the referent of "moral" is also not sociological, for example, a rule. There is nothing in the social institutionalization of a rule that makes it moral as opposed to technological, aesthetic, etc. For one man, a prohibition of parking is a moral norm, for another a mere administrative regulation. What makes it moral is not the legislation of the rule but the individual's attitude toward it, as even the most extreme and greatest of the sociologists of morals, Durkheim, recognized.

Second, like most moral philosophers from Kant to Hare, Baier, Aiken, etc., we define morality in terms of the formal character of a moral judgment or a moral point of view, rather than in terms of its content. Impersonality, ideality, universalizability, and preemptiveness are among the formal characteristics of a moral judgment. These are best seen in the reasons given for a moral judgment, a moral reason being one which has such properties as these.

Third, we claim that the formal definition of morality works only when we recognize that there are developmental levels of moral discourse or judgment which increasingly approximate to the philosophers' forms. A developmental strategy of definition is one which isolates a function, such as intelligence, but defines this function by a progressive developmental clarification of the function. Intelligence or cognition as defined by Piaget is both something present from the start of life (in the infant's adaptive sensorimotor behavior) and something whose ultimate structure or form is given only in the final stages (e.g., the formal-operational-natural thought of the adolescent as experimenter and theorist). Similarly, in our view there is a moral judgmental function present from the age of four or five onwards in judgments of "good" and "bad" and "has to" (our stage 1), but this function is only fully defined by its final stages (principled morality).

As stated by Aiken (1952), in "Levels of Moral Discourse," moral language goes on at two levels, the conventional and the principled. (Aiken, as a nonpsychologist, ignores our preconventional level of moral discourse.) At the conventional level, moral language refers to an actual expectation or rule of the group or of particular members of the group. At this level "the moral judge functions primarily as a middleman or agent; he voices the claims of society but is not the primary source of this moral authority." As Aiken points out, however, fully moral discourse does not rest on authority but consists of reasoning based on a moral attitude or point of view which claims to be autonomously moral, that is, independent of appeals to either authority or self-interest.

Our claim that only principled-stage thinking is fully moral was concretely made earlier when we said that each stage involved a differentiation, not made at the previous stage, of moral and non-moral value; Appendix 3 illustrates this for the case of the moral value of human life.

Moral judgments are judgments about the right and the good of action. Not all judgments of "good" or "right" are moral judgments, however; many are judgments of aesthetic, technological, or prudential goodness or rightness. Unlike judgments of prudence or aesthetics, moral judgments tend to be universal, inclusive, consistent, and grounded on objective, impersonal, or ideal grounds. Statements such as "She's really great! She's beautiful and a good dancer," or "The right way to make a martini is five-to-one," involve the good and right, but they are not moral judgments since they lack the characteristics of the latter. If we say, "Martinis should be made five-to-one," we are making an aesthetic judgment: we are not prepared to say that we want everyone to make them that way, that they are good in terms of some impersonal ideal standard shared by others, or that we and others should make five-to-one martinis whether we wish to or not.

In similar fashion, when a ten-year-old at stage 1 answers a "moral should" question—"Should Joe tell on his younger brother?"—in terms of the probabilities of getting beaten up by his father and by his brother, he does not answer with a moral judgment that is universal (applies to all situations of this kind) or that has any impersonal or ideal grounds. In contrast, stage-6 statements not only specifically use moral words like "morally right" and "duty" but also use them in a moral way: "regardless of who it was," implies universality; "Morally I would do it in spite of fear of punishment" implies impersonality and ideality of obligation, etc. Thus, the responses of lower-level subjects concerning matters of moral judgment fail to be moral responses in somewhat the same sense that the value judgments of higher-level subjects concerning aesthetic or morally neutral matters fail to be moral. In this sense, we can define a moral judgment as "moral" without considering its content (the action judged) and without considering whether it agrees with our own judgments or standards. It is evident that our stages represent an increasing disentangling or differentiation of moral values and judgments from other types of values and judgments. With regard to one particular aspect, the value of life, the moral value of the person in the stage-6 argument has become progressively disentangled from status and property values (stage 1), from his instrumental uses to others (stage 2), from the actual affection of others for him (stage 3), etc.

More generally, the individual whose judgments are at stage 6 asks "Is it morally right" and means by morally right something different from punishment (stage 1), or prudence (stage 2), or conformity to authority (stages 3 and 4), etc.

MORAL PRINCIPLES

Following formalist philosophers from Kant to Hare, I have claimed that only the higher stages of moral thought have the formal features of distinctively moral judgment. We need to clarify and deepen our conception of these features of mature moral thought by clarifying our characterization of the highest stages as "principled." Many, although not all, philosophic treatments of morality view the central characteristic of adequate moral judgment as its derivation from "moral principles." It is evident enough that most of our value judgments are not directly based on principles. When we judge a martini or a painting or a scientific article as good, we do not attempt to derive our judgments from principle. If a bad painting is made according to principle, so much the worse for the principle. Nevertheless, the whole notion that there is a distinctively moral form of judgment demands that moral judgments be principled. We cited earlier Hare's characterization of the distinctive formal features of morality as "prescriptivity" and "universality" (the two in turn implying "autonomy" of moral choice or obligation). Hare's characterization echoes Kant, who defined prescriptivity as the sense of the categorical (as opposed to the hypothetical) imperative. To be categorical, an imperative must be universal: "so act as to make the maxim of thy conduct the universal will." Empirically, we have found these two features linked, so that a stage-6 judgment of a right which is prescriptive or independent of the inclinations of the self and the beliefs of others is also a judgment of a right which is right for all mankind. When an effort is made to formulate a judgment which is prescriptive and universal, the judgment almost of necessity will be made in terms of a moral principle. To understand stage-6 morality, therefore, we need to understand the nature and functioning of moral principles.

A moral principle is a universal mode of choosing, a rule of choosing which we want all people to adopt in all situations. By "principle" we mean something more abstract than the ordinary rule. Rules like the Ten Commandments are proscriptions or prescriptions of action. When conventional morality chooses to be morally pretentious, it labels such rules "principles." In regard to the drug-stealing story, conventional college students say, "The principle of loyalty to your family comes ahead of obeying the law here," or "The principle of honesty comes before helping your wife."

On the face of it, these students do not wish to universalize the rules. One cannot universalize the rule "be loyal to your family," to all people, since not everybody has a family. For the same reason, one cannot generalize it to all situations and also because it is doubtful that if one's uncle were Hitler one could claim loyalty to be a relevant or prima facie principle. One does not have to believe in situation ethics to realize that no proscription or prescription of a class of acts is universalizable. We know it is all right to be dishonest and steal to save a life because a man's right to life comes before another man's right to property. We know it is sometimes right to kill because it is sometimes just. The Germans who tried to kill Hitler were doing right because respect for the equal value of lives demands that we kill someone who is murdering others, in order to save lives. There are always exceptions to rules about classes of acts.

By "moral principle" all thoughtful men have meant a general guide to choice rather than a rule of action. Even our college student who talks of "the principle of loyalty to your family" means something like "a consideration in choosing" rather than a definite rule prescribing a class of acts. The strongest notion of principle is that defined by pure utilitarian doctrine prescribing the single principle of the "utilitarian maxim" (act always so as to maximize the greatest happiness of the greatest number) and by the Kantian doctrine prescribing the single principle of the categorical imperative. This "strong" conception of principle implies a single logically or intuitively self-evident or rational maxim for choice; from it one can deduce any concrete morally right action in a situation, given the facts of the situation as the minor premise of the deduction. Such a strong conception of principle is one which not only is universalizable to all men and all situations but also is absolutely definitive of right action in any situation. We have so far never encountered a live human being who made moral judgments in terms of principles in this sense. On the other hand, we do find people judging in terms of principles, if principles are conceived of in the weaker sense as illustrated in the writings of members of the principled-intuitionist group such as Sidgwick and Ross.

In this weaker sense, a person may consistently hold more than a single principle of moral judgment and these principles may not be definitive of choice in all situations (i.e., alternative choices may be derived from them). Such principles, however, are still to be differentiated from a collection of rules or "prima facie obligations." In our empirical work we have started by considering the term "principle" as referring to considerations in moral choice or reasons justifying moral action. They are answers to the question, "Why is it right to do such and such?" given some answer to the question, "What is it right to do?" We have found empirically that almost all these reasons easily fall into the categories outlined by principled-intuitionist philosophers, for example, Sidgwick's prudence (welfare-consequences to the self), benevolence (welfare-consequences to others), and justice (distributive equity and commutative reciprocity). The only additional category of ultimate reasons we have added is respect for authority.

Accordingly, in our detailed coding of categories of moral judgment we have the following categories of "principles": prudence (and self-realization); welfare of others; respect for authority, society, or persons; justice.

As we suggested in preceding sections, all of these "principles" or reasons are present in one form or another from stage 1 onwards, except that prudence and authority have dropped out as reasons by stage 6. From stage 1, these reasons have two characteristics. First, they are in ultimate terms, they refer to states of affairs which seem right or good in themselves and are in that sense "principles." Second, they refer to states of affairs that are involved in all moral situations and are potentially relevant to all people. There is no moral situation that does not involve considerations of people's happiness or welfare and considerations of equal treatment between people.

While benevolence and justice are used as moral reasons from stage 1 onward, they do not become genuine moral principles until stages 5 and 6. At the conventional stages, choices are made by reference to conventional rules, stereotypes, and sentiments. The reasons for conforming to these rules include considerations of benevolence and justice as well as of prudence and social authority. Where there are ambiguities, conflicts, or gaps in the rules, decisions are based on considerations of benevolence and justice. Not until stages 5 and 6, however, is there an effort to derive systematically and consistently prima facie rules or obligations from these principles or to view obligation as fundamentally directed by them, rather than by concrete rules. In this sense, the fundamental aspect of principled morality is the adoption of a lawmaking perspective. That welfare and justice are guiding principles of legislation as well as of individual moral action points to the fact that a principle is always a maxim or rule for making rules or laws as well as a maxim of individual situational conduct. This, of course, follows from the fact that if a principle is universalizable and reversible, there could not be different sets of rules for lawmakers and law-obeyers. (This is one reason why "always obey the law" does not have the status of a moral principle.) It also points out that principles are metarules—rules for the creation and evaluation of rules—rather than first-order rules.

Now it is clear that our conception of moral principle implies that one cannot ultimately separate form and content in moral analysis.

Hare has recently argued with vigor the necessity of defining truly moral judgment and "moral principles" solely in formal terms. To do so would, of course, involve a much less controversial claim for a conception of mature morality. Kant, for different reasons, insisted on a purely formal conception of principle, but to attain such a conception he made the principled form "universality" into a content, for example, into the commandment that one universalize one's actions. When one attempts a purely formal definition of principle, however, one only ends up with the old rules of conventional morality expressed in more universal and prescriptive form. Kant's claim that it was wrong to tell a lie to save a victim from a murder is a case in point. In the formalist conception, principles are still conceived of as rules of action, that is, rules prescribing classes of acts in classes of situations.

As such, their universality is always purchased at the price of ignoring unique elements of human welfare and human justice in the concrete situation. In our conception, however, principles are guides to perceiving and integrating all the morally relevant elements in concrete situations. Neither philosophers nor all the people we have interviewed have ever come up with morally relevant elements in concrete situations which are not the elements of human interests (welfare) or human rights (justice).

Now it is clear that our conception of principle implies a "situation ethic" in the sense that it reduces all moral obligation to the interests and claims of concrete individual persons in concrete situations. We take it as the characteristic logical fallacy of conventional morality that it fails to reduce the welfare and "claims" of the group as a collective abstraction to the welfare and claims of its members as individuals. Durkheim is perhaps the greatest explicit defender of the concept of obligation as directed to the group or institution rather than to the welfare and claims of its members. From our point of view there is a logical fallacy parallel to elevating the group above its members: the fallacy of treating a principle as elevated above the individuals in the situation to which it applies. Put in different terms, most of us feel a cold chill at the notion that mature moral obligation is fundamentally directed to an abstract maxim or principle, as Kant held. Moral obligations are toward concrete other people in concrete situations. The notion of a Kantian feeling obligated to the principle of the categorical imperative and so refusing to tell a lie to save a human life (i.e., refusing to modify the means for a concrete human end) is as chilling as a utilitarian Bolshevik letting ten million Kulaks starve for the greater happiness of the unborn greater number (i.e., refusing to modify the ends for the concrete human means). True principles guide us to the obligating elements in the situation, to the concrete human claims there. The case is always higher than the principle, a single human life is worth more than all the principles in philosophy to the mature man. Principles simply tell us how to resolve these concrete claims when claims compete in a situation, when it is one man's life against another's.

Perhaps the case can be made even clearer by considering the so-called "higher moral values." Just as it is possible to elevate the Ten Commandments of authoritarian (stage-4) morality into principles, so is it possible to elevate the existence of the state, or the collective goals of the state or society, into "higher moral values" or "absolutes." Said Hitler, "Our goal is that the German people should again acquire honor, again bow in adoration before its history. We recognize only two Gods; a God in heaven and a god on earth, and that is our fatherland." If Hitler had recognized only one God, the God in heaven, and held that the only absolute value was the divine will or the coming of the kingdom of heaven, the structure of his thought would have been the same. So too, the structure would have been the same if he had held up "humanity" as an absolute value, as a collective concept above the individuals involved in concrete situations, as did the Bolsheviks who let the Kulaks starve. Here is an eighteen-year-old boy who uses the "higher principle of humanity" in this disembodied and unprincipled way responding to the story about stealing the drug:

"I'd steal the drug. Whether my wife died or not, I'd feel I'd acted humanely, not just out of love, not just a personal thing between my wife and myself; I'd feel I'd done what I could for the principle of being human."
    (Even if you weren't affectionate or close to your wife?)

"Yes. If I had to kill the druggist to get the drug, I probably would, also. Because I'd be putting value on life-right, I'd kill the druggist if I had to, if there's no other way to get the drug, and suffer the consequences. It would be a personal commitment to humanity."

No wonder many mature men and astute moral philosophers reject the notion of a morality of "higher moral principles above the law" for a stage-5 relativistic insistence on democratic law and social contract and consensus.

All the misuses of the concept of moral principle thus involve a failure either to universalize a "principle" or to reduce it to a guide to the perception of the claims of persons in a moral situation. As we shall claim in the next section, when principles are reduced to guides for considering the claims of persons in concrete situations, they become expressions of the single principle of justice. The misuses of principle we have quoted immediately strike us as misuses because they are unjust, although they may be maximizations of social utility. We must now consider our rationale for reducing stage-6 moral principles to principles of justice.

THE PRIMACY OF JUSTICE

We have so far elaborated a formal conception of morality linked to principles of welfare and justice. We have not, however, differentiated clearly between stage 5 and stage 6 and the relative place of benevolence and justice in each. The core elements of stage 5 are that it is a rational legislative perspective which reduces obligations to rule-utilitarian considerations on the one hand and social contract on the other. It recognizes the arbitrary element in concrete rules and laws and derives from the obligation to obey rules the basic rational procedural principles for forming a society or for legislation. From our point of view, the core problem which stage 5 cannot resolve is the problem of the conditions under which it is morally right or obligatory to violate the law. The principles of welfare and social contract are inadequate to resolve this problem. Stage 6 resolves the problem by recognizing the primacy of justice over all other moral considerations, by recognizing that civil disobedience is justified if and only if it is preventing a legally condoned injustice.

Our major and most controversial claim is that the only "true" (stage 6) moral principle is justice. We shall claim that human welfare is always the core of morality but that, at the principled level, welfare considerations subsumed under the heading "justice" take priority over other "principles" for considering welfare whenever there is conflict between the two, and that there is no strong "principle" for deciding between the various welfare alternatives other than justice. The reason for this emphasis on justice becomes clear when we recognize that moral principles derive from, or are differentiated from, the lower stages of moral thought. We have pointed out that we take the word "justice" to mean a moral resolution of competing claims, that is, a reference to a method of distributing or defining claims. The basic rule of justice is distributive equality: treat every man equally. We recognize, however, that people also have special claims on the individual moral actor or upon the state. These claims are based on commutative justice or reciprocity, and include keeping contracts or trusts, undoing harm done, and showing gratitude as some return for service and effort. While there is no single accepted principle of justice which orders all these aspects, we generally assume a sphere of human rights in which equality takes priority over the special claims of commutative justice.

Other than justice, the only general principle seriously advanced by philosophers has been the principle variously termed utility or benevolence. It is important first to recognize that benevolence in the sense of "love, empathy, sympathy, human concern, humanism," and so on can never be a principle of choice. It is primarily another stage-3 virtue label, not a guide to action. While benevolence can be universalized in the sense of "everyone should care for the welfare of all other humans," when there is a conflict between welfares, benevolence can provide no criterion except that of quantitative maximization.

The content of moral concerns and claims is always welfare, but maximization is not a true moral principle. Concern for welfare

consequences characterizes each of our six stages; my son was concerned about "the greatest good of the greatest number" but included seals and men equally in his calculations. A clearer example
is Tommy, whose complete response to the story about stealing the
drug follows. I cite it because I defy a utilitarian to distinguish a
fundamental formal difference of principle between this stage-1
response and that of stage 6.

"His wife was sick and if she didn't get the drug quickly, she might die. Maybe
his wife is an important person and runs a store and the man buys stuff from her
and can't get it any other place. The police would probably blame the owner that
he didn't save the wife. That would be like killing with a gun or knife."
    (Would it be all right to put the druggist in the electric chair for murder?)
    "If she could be cured by the drug and they didn't give it to her, I think so,
because she could be an important lady like Betsy Ross, she made the flag. And if
it was President Eisenhower, he's important, and they'd probably put the man in
the electric chair because that isn't fair."
    (Should the punishment be more if she's an important person?)
    "If someone important is in a plane and is allergic to heights and the stewardess
won't give him medicine because she's only got enough for one and she's got a
sick one, a friend, in back, they'd probably put the stewardess in a lady's jail
because she didn't help the important one."
    (Is it better to save the life of one important person or a lot of unimportant
people?)
    "All the people that aren't important because one man just has one house,
maybe a lot of furnitire, but a whole bunch of people have an awful lot of
furniture and some of these poor people might have a lot of money and it doesn't
look it."

    Tommy thinks always in terms of the actual utility consequences
of action, even to the point of ignoring intention completely. How
bad it is to let someone die for lack of a drug depends on the
importance of the person and has nothing to do with the inhuman
attitude of the person withholding the drug. The value of the act is
determined by maximizing utility. It is true that important people
count for more than unimportant people, but it is all appraised in a
maximizing or utilitarian fashion. Only one thing is amiss—the
worth of a person's life is essentially determined by how much
furniture he owns. The moral maxim seems to be the greatest
furniture of the greatest number. Appendix 3 indicates the reasons

why Tommy's failure to differentiate the value of a person's life from the value of the furniture he owns is scored stage 1.

Our point is that concern for the welfare of other beings, "empathy" or "role-taking," is the precondition for experiencing a moral conflict rather than a mechanism for its resolution. The moral question is "Whose role do I take?" or "Whose claim do I favor?" The working core of the utilitarian principle is the principle of justice, "consider each person's welfare equally," not the maximization principle. Finally, as everyone knows, and as our studies document, the utilitarian principle of justice, "consider everyone's happiness equally," is not a working principle of justice. Our conception of justice dictates that we consider every man's moral claims equally, rather than considering every man's happiness equally. Our stage-6 subjects will say, "Steal the drug for anyone, whether it's his wife or not, every man has a right to live." But they do not advocate treating the happiness of wife and of stranger equally. Furthermore, they do not rationalize the preference for their wife's happiness on "rule-utilitarian" grounds. Instead, they speak of a marriage tie or "contract" or relationship of reciprocal trust and love, that is, a claim of commutative reciprocity, not one of utility.

At this point, I shall summarize my argument for justice as the basic moral principle. the argument involves the following steps:

1. Psychologically, both welfare concerns (role-taking, empathy, or sympathy) and justice concerns are present at the birth of morality and at every succeeding stage.

2. Both welfare concerns and justice concerns take on more differentiated, integrated, and universalized forms at each step of development.

3. However, at the highest stage of development, only justice takes on the character of a principle, that is, becomes something that is obligatory, categorical, and takes precedence over law and other considerations, including welfare.

4. "Principles" other than justice may be tried out by those seeking to transcend either (A) they do not resolve moral conflicts, or (B) they resolve them in ways that seem intuitively wrong.

5. The intuitive feeling of many philosophers that justice is the only satisfactory principle corresponds to the fact that it is the only one that "does justice to" the viable core of lower stages of morality.

6. This becomes most evident in situations of civil disobedience for which justice, but not other moral principles, provides a rationale which respects and can cope with the stage-5 contractual legalistic argument that civil disobedience is always wrong.

7. Philosophers have doubted the claim of justice to be "the" moral principle because they have looked for a principle broader in scope than the sphere of moral or principled individual choice in the formal sense (that is, they have looked for a principle for a teleological "general theory of value and decision"). For example, the maximization of welfare principle is a general principle for decision outside the area of specifically moral choice. Metaethically, then, welfare is a more ultimate principle but not in moral choice. For example, maximizing social welfare would probably be the ultimate basis for deciding that it was desirable to teach morality explicitly in the school (given that it was just, or not a violation of rights, to do so). This does not contradict the facts that the highest principle of morality to be taught is justice, or that it would be morally wrong to teach justice in the schools in an unjust way.

8. Denial of the claims of justice as the central principle of morality, then, coincides with a definition of orality which has various gaps and fallacies in terms of metaethical criteria.

FROM IS TO OUGHT: THE NATURALISTIC FALLACY

Let us consider the sense in which our description of what morality is tells us what it ought to be. To begin with, there are two forms of the "naturalistic fallacy" we are not committing. We are not equating moral judgments with cognitive-predictive judgments or with pleasure-pain statements, as do the simple cognitive-naturalistic models. Our analysis of moral judgments does not assume that moral judgments are really something else. Further, we are not assuming that morality or moral maturity is part of man's biological nature, that the biologically older is the morally better. We are, however, committing a third form of the "naturalistic fallacy" by asserting that any conception of what moral judgment ought to be must rest on an adequate conception of what it is. If all those who have Ph.D.s in philosophy showed a stage-6 concern for universal and autonomous moral principles, while all other people were Durkheimian asserters of the authority of the group or Benthamite hedonists, it would be impossible, I believe, to construct a plausible account of why men should be stage 6 or adopt a stage-6 morality. But as it turns out, neither a Benthamite nor a Durkheimian construction of what morality ought to be, based as they are on the assumptions that morality really is stage 2 (Bentham) or stage 4 (Durkheim), is viable, because both ignore the reality of what morality demonstrably is at stages 5 or 6. Every constructive effort at rational morality, at saying what morality ought to be, must start with a characterization of what it is, and in that sense commits "the naturalistic fallacy." If morality is stage 5 or 6, then what morality ought to be is either a systematized or purified version of stage 6 or else ought to be stage 7. In human history there was a time when philosophers perhaps had to create state 6 and not just systematize it. One may argue that philosophers should be defining a stage-7 morality, but I doubt if one could find any volunteers for the task. Let me be concrete about what I mean. Rawls (1963) has taken a formal set of assumptions which I term stage 5, the assumptions that society is ordered by a constitution defined by a social contract of equals. He then shows how such a society must be based upon principles of justice or of equal rights, since these are the only principles to which rational individuals in the imaginary original position could consent. These principles in turn, then, are in a sense prior to the law and social institutions and in certain conditions justify civil disobedience. In other words, Rawls has used a formal argument to derive stage-6 morality from stage 5, and to systematize stage-6 morality insofar as stage-6 morality is defined by sociopolitical choices.

My point is that Rawls is doing by formal ethical argument what "natural experience" does in development. The doctrine of a social contract and freely chosen law which must have a universal form usually rests on reference to an existing external social consensus and political process. It contains within it, however, a latent conception of autonomous principles of justice which guide both individual morality and the direction of political change. Where law or the existing social consensus is unjust, the stage-5 individual is caught in conflicts resolvable only at the stage-6 level. Let me quote an example from our longitudinal study of someone struggling between a stage-5 and a stage-6 point of view:

"We are dealing with essentially the same situation as the beginning. We have a law that says something must be done and so in disobeying this law they are doing wrong. However, it would seem that the basic law itself is morally wrong and so from a moral point of view, the right thing to do is to disobey the law."

(Why is the law morally wrong?)

"Because it is treating human beings as animals, and I said before that I do believe there is a difference."

"Here we have a situation of an individual reaching in his mind the decision that something determined by the state is wrong. Now I think this is perfectly valid that an individual can have his own feelings and opinions. However, if he makes the decision that this law is wrong and decides to disobey it, he must do so with the full realization that it is the state's prerogative to do whatever it can to uphold this law."

"I think this means that the individual must realize he is acting outside of society, so to speak, and must be prepared to take whatever consequences society is going to mete out for this."

(Would it be right to punish the people who hid the runaway slaves?)

"This is the same thing again. It is within the prerogatives of the state to uphold its laws and to punish people, again staying within the framework of the system we have now. Certainly it is right in that sense, and I think you have to stop at this point. You could say it is morally wrong because in breaking the laws the people were acting in what they thought was morally right and what I would say is morally right, but nevertheless, the action was outside the bounds of society."

(What about if its laws are morally wrong? You said slavery is wrong? Or are you saying that this is your opinion that it is morally wrong?)

"Yes. That's right. All I can say is that it is my opinion. I can't speak for anyone else."

(Do you think there are things that are morally right and wrong other than what people think are morally right and wrong? That there are some actual rights and wrongs?)

"If they are, I think they would be awfully hard to define."

(So, when you say slavery is morally wrong, you are saying it is your opinion.)

"Yes."

(At the time before the Civil War when they had slavery, was it right or wrong to have slavery? I guess I have asked this before.)

"I think it is wrong, but I think you would have to take it back to the framework of the people of that time. Dealing with a situation of ignorance and many people sincerely felt they were not dealing with human beings, maybe in that framework it was morally right from their point of view."

Our prediction is that next time we interview this subject he will assert stage-6 moral right which is right because it is ideally universalizable whether or not it is in fact universal. In any case, this man, unlike subjects at a lower stage, could profit from a conventional course in philosophic ethics.

I use Rawls's work as one "legitimate" ethical effort to show that principles of justice ought to be the ultimate basis of morality. It is legitimate in the sense that it works within the terms of moral discourse (stage 5) to clarify these terms and to show that within them implicitly there is a more fundamental set of terms (stage 6). In contrast, Durkheim attempts to use a nonmoral set of terms, those of social science, to show that stage 4 not only is but ought to be morality. The Durkheimian form of the naturalistic fallacy can be shown to be a genuine fallacy in the same sense as Benthamite reductionism was.

We maintain, then, that problems arise for stage 6 only when we ask questions of it which it cannot answer, for instance, if we try to justify the moral right in terms of the good, if we ask the question, "What good is morality?" or "What good is justice?" My claim that principles of justice are the highest developmentally, the most adequate or equilibrated, and most autonomously moral forms of moral judgment and decision-making, can be and is made without answering the question "What good is justice?" or saying that justice is better (in some all-inclusive sense) than any other form of morality. If we ask "What good is justice?" we shall immediately tend to answer it in "goal-seeking" or utilitarian terms, that is, we shall examine the consequences of just action for the individual actor's welfare or for the welfare of society or both. An evaluation in terms of welfare will be a naturalistic evaluation, that is, it will be a qualitative evaluation of the satisfaction of actual interests in some psychologically definable sense. The alternative is, of course, a definition of the goal-seeking in terms of self-realization or perfection of the individual or the group. The point I am making is that "What good is morality?" or "What good is justice?" are questions that cannot be answered by a normative ethical theory or by using moral concepts. The questions "What good is morality?" and "Why be moral?" are legitimate questions, as are questions like "What good is art?" and "Why pursue the beautiful?" Statements of what aesthetic structure or beauty are or ought to be—aesthetic "theories"— do not directly answer this question. Similarly, a theory of formal logic is a theory of what logical inference is and ought to be, but it is not a theory which answers the question "What good is logic?" or "Why be logical?" Answers to such metaethical questions are not given by a stage-6 normative ethical theory.

Now, from the educational point of view, the questions "What good is morality?" or "What good is moral development?" are extremely germane and meaningful questions, since they will determine the place we give to moral development in the definition of the aims of the school. These questions, however, are questions to be answered by "a general theory of value," not by moral theory in our sense. My own "theory of value" rests on Dewey's analysis, including an emphasis on the essential unity of scientific judgment and rational value judgment. In other words, the answer to "What good is the child's morality?" is largely a scientific statement of the functions and consequences of the child's moral development for the welfare and development of the child's personality and of his society.

In summary, my view of the various ways in which knowledge of facts and statements of value are related in the study of moral development includes the following points.

1. The scientific facts are that there is a universal moral form successively emerging in development and centering on principles of justice.

2. This Kantian moral form is one which assumes the fact-value distinction, that is, the moral man assumes his moral judgment is based on conformity to an ideal norm, not on conformity to fact.

3. Science, then, can test whether a philosoher's conception of morality phenomenologically fits the psychological facts. Science cannot go on to justify that conception of morality as being what morality ought to be, as Durkheim attempted to do. Moral autonomy is king and values are different from facts for moral discourse. Science cannot prove or justify a morality, because the rules of scientific discourse are not the rules of moral discourse.

4. Logic or nomative ethical analysis can, however, point out that a certain type of moral philosophy (e.g., stage 4) does not handle, whereas another type of morality (e.g., stage 5) can do so. Here factual investigation of men's beliefs must support internal logical analysis (differentiation and integration) of why the developmentally higher philosophy can handle problems not handled by the lower ones. In this way science can contribute to moral discourse.

5. Moral discourse between levels, then, is much like Plato's dialectical knowledge of the good. A higher-level conception of the good cannot be proved superior to a lower-level conception; it can only be "called out" by teaching or by natural moral conflict-differentiation-integration (Turiel 1966). If the individual can be brought to comprehend a higher level, he prefers it because he can then see his old lower level from the more inclusive framework of the higher level.

6. The scientific theory of why people factually *do* move upward from stage to stage, and why they factually *do* prefer a higher stage to a lower is broadly the same as a moral theory of why people *should* prefer a higher stage to a lower. In other words a psychological theory of why they move from the anal to the genital stage. It is committing the naturalistic fallacy to say that a Freudian theory of an instinctual progression is an ethical justification of why genitality is better than anality. It is here that the theory of *interactional* hierarchical stages of cognition and morality and the theory of *maturational* embryological stages are critically different in their logic, as I have discussed in detail elsewhere (Kohlberg and Turiel 1971).

7. From the moral point of view, form is absolute, the fact-value distinction is absolute, and science and ethics are different. The

proper scientific study of morality must recognize this fact. The scientific study of morality, however, must include in its scope the functions of morality for the development of the individual and the group. Here the fact-value distinction breaks down in a new way, and we get a Deweyan statement of morality, not as an autonomous absolute, as in the Kantian law or the Platonic good, but as a non-absolute part of the social life of the child, whose welfare is more important than his moral status.

A CONCEPTION OF MORAL EDUCATION

I objected earlier to the current thoughtless system of moralizing by individual teachers and principals when children deviate from minor administrative regulations or engage in behavior which is personally annoying to the teacher. I also objected to the deliberate effort to inculcate majority values. The rationale for both practices derives from the assumption of ethical relativity. Following Dewey and Piaget, I shall argue that the goal of moral education is the stimulation of the "natural" development of the individual child's own moral judgment and capacities, thus allowing him to use his own moral judgment to control his behavior. The attractiveness of defining the goal of moral education as the stimulation of development rather than as the teaching of fixed rules stems from the fact that it involves aiding the child to take the next step in a direction toward which he is already tending, rather than imposing an alien pattern upon him.

In preceding sections we have argued that the attainment of stages 5 and 6—the stages of principled judgments—is a philosophically justifiable goal of moral education. Perhaps the strongest reasons for adopting this view of moral education in the context of the public school are "negative," that is, it does not entail the violation of the child's moral freedom, which is involved in any other formulation of moral education goals. Our first statement of the respect for the child's autonomy implied in the developmental view is political and constitutional. We have argued (following Ball 1967) that the Supreme Court's post-Schempp position makes systematic conventional moral education in the public school unconstitutional (see Kohlberg 1967, for a more detailed discussion of these issues). Ball argues that it is possible to interpret the court's decision as ruling out any form of moral or ethical, as well as religious, instruction in the school. The recent court decisions define religion as embracing any articulated credo or value system, including the "Ethical Culture" or "Secular Humanism" credos which essentially consist of the moral principles of Western culture. Ball concludes that the Supreme Court is in effect prohibiting the public school from engaging in moral education since such education is equivalent to the state propagation of the religion of Ethical Culture or Secular Humanism.

Let us be concrete about the implications of what has been said. We quoted earlier the teacher who said "Don't be rude" to the child who spit in the other child's face and who had done a master's paper on the problem of social-class difference in values and the schools. She said, "I know there are class differences in values. I think politeness is important. I don't care whether it is a middle–class value or not." This, of course, was reflected in her labelling the child who spit in the other's face as "rude." We would agree that if she really systematically attempted to instill "politeness" into her pupils, she would be guilty of imposing "middle-class values," or rather her own arbitrary values, on the child. Politeness, hardly a moral virtue, may reflect a universal concern over propriety of behavior, but middle-class definitions of politeness or propriety are different from ghetto definitions of politeness. Our moral objection to spitting in another child's face is not that it is "impolite" but that it is a violation of the other's dignity, of respect for the other as a human being. An advocate of "black power" and "black values" may legitimately object to a teacher's indoctrinating children with middle-class lily-white conceptions of politeness, but he cannot object to teaching respect for the fundamental rights of other human beings. His only basis for being heard in his claims for "black values" is the basis of regard for the equal rights and dignity of blacks as human beings.

We have said that the content of moral education must be defined in terms of justice, rather than in terms of majority consensus, if the civil rights of parents and children are not to be infringed upon by such education. These claims have been made in terms of the political philosophy underlying the school as a public institution. We have argued, however, that the "official" morality of rights in our society also represents a culturally universal principled stage of moral judgment, so that the teaching of justice is also the stimulation of moral development.

The second claim for the legitimacy of the developmental approach to moral education is that the stimulation of moral development defines an educational process respecting the autonomy of the child, whereas any other definition reflects indoctrination. The constitutional issue arises from the point of view of the child's parent, who can object to the teaching of values other than the parent's own. Respect for the parent's rights is not respect for the child's autonomy, a more legitimate concern.

We have claimed that the experiences by which children naturally move from stage to stage are nonindoctrinative, that is, they are not experiences of being taught and internalizing specific content. These experiences are listed as those involving moral conflict (in the cognitive-conflict sense) and exposure to other, higher modes of thinking than one's own. Insofar as the teacher deliberately uses such experiences as her method of moral education, she is not being "indoctrinative." Expressed differently, there is little difference, from our point of view, between effective teaching "about morality" and the teaching "of morality" in the sense of the stimulation of its development.

Again, let us be concrete about this issue. A senior philosophy class in a Newton high school was used as a vehicle for the stimulation of development of moral judgment by its teacher, who was a graduate student of mine. This goal was explicitly announced and the writer's scheme of moral development was explained toward the end of the class. In order to clarify issues of indoctrination involved, a gimmick was used. The students were told that they would be post-tested on the moral judgment interview (as they had already been pretested) and that their moral level on the post-test would be used to give them a grade for the course. Only a few students objected to the procedure on indoctrination grounds. (Many did on the grounds that it was unfair because some were high levels before the course and some were not, etc.) Those who objected to this use of the test on indoctrination grounds were, needless to say, students at the principled level. The students were then encouraged to distinguish between teaching about morality and teaching of morality, in the sense of agreeing that it was legitimate to test their comprehension of stage-5 and stage-6 reasoning, but not to test their assimilation of or acceptance of this line of reasoning. The findings of the Rest, Turiel, and Kohlberg study—that adolescents do prefer, assimilate, and "believe in" the highest level reasonings which they can comprehend—were then discussed. Our efforts to get the students to comprehend stages 5 and 6 were then tantamount to getting them to accept these stages of reasoning.

Let us now be more concrete about means of moral education in the school. It is not always necessary that the matters discussed be ones of the immediate and real-life issues of the classroom. I have found that my hypothetical and remote but obviously morally real and challenging conflict situations are of intense interest to almost all adolescents and lead to lengthy debate among them. They are involving, because the adult right answer is not obviously at hand to discourage the child's own moral thought, as so often is the case. The child will listen to what the teacher says about moral matters only if the child first feels a genuine sense of uncertainty about the right answer to the situation in question. The pat little stories in school readers in which virtue always triumphs or in which everyone is really nice are unlikely to have any value in the stimulation of moral development. Only the presentation of genuine and difficult moral conflicts can have this effect.

We have mentioned that in order to stimulate development, moral communication by the teacher should, in addition to involving issues of genuine moral conflict to the child, represent cognitive elements new to him. Effective communication also involves the important problem of the match between the teacher's level and the child's. Conventional moral education never has had much influence on children's moral judgment because it has disregarded this problem of developmental match (see Hunt's paper pp. 231–51). Although children are able to understand moralizing beneath their level, they do not seem to accept it nearly so readily as comprehensible moralizing somewhat above their level. It is obvious that the teacher's implementation of this principle must start with his careful listening to the moral judgments and ideas actually expressed by individual children.

The principles just mentioned were used by Blatt and Kohlberg (1971) to develop a four-month program of once-weekly moral discussions for a class of twelve children aged eleven to twelve. Children discussed and argued hypothetical dilemmas. The teacher supported and clarified those arguments of the children which were at the average (stage 3) level, rather than those one step below that level (stage 2). When these arguments seemed understood, and could be extended to new situations, the teacher would challenge the level (stage 3) previously supported, and support and clarify the arguments of those one stage above (stage 4) the previous consensus. The children were given pre- and post-tests, using stories different from those involved in the classroom discussions (with some new stories given only for the post-test). Fifty percent of the children moved up one stage, 10 percent moved up two stages, and the remainder stayed the same. In contrast, 10 percent of a control group moved up one stage during this period, and the remainder stayed the same. One year later the relative advance was still maintained. Similar results have since been obtained by Blatt, with classes of black and white children aged eleven and fifteen in a public-school setting (Blatt 1970). The potential value of such educational efforts appears when one considers some recent longitudinal findings (on a small sample of middle-class males), which indicate that moral maturity at age thirteen is an extremely good predictor ($r=0.78$ to 0.92) of adult moral maturity (at age twenty-four to twenty-seven). This high correlation cannot be attributed to the cessation of development of moral judgment at age thirteen, for such development continues past college in most of this group. For example, while none of the thirteen-year-olds were primarily at the principled level, 36 percent of the twenty-four-year-olds in this sample were at the principled level (stages 5 and 6). Those (over 15 percent) who did not develop some such thinking by late high school, however, did not develop to the principled stage in young adulthood. In general, then, while moral development continues into adulthood, mature thirteen-year-olds retain their edge in development, presumably because development is stepwise and the advanced pupils have fewer steps to go through.

MORAL ACTION AND MORAL EDUCATION

According to Aristotle, "virtue is of two kinds, intellectual and moral. While intellectual virtue owes its birth and growth to teaching, moral virtue comes about as a result of habit. The moral virtues we get by first exercising them; we become just by doing just acts, temperate by doing temperate acts, brave by doing brave acts." Aristotle, then, is claiming that there are two spheres, the moral and the intellectual, and that learning by doing is the only real method in the moral sphere.

American educational psychology also divides the personality into cognitive abilities, passions or motives, and traits of character. Moral character consists of a bag of virtues and vices. For example, one of the earliest major American studies of moral character, conducted in the late twenties (Hartshorne and May 1928–30), included honesty, service, and self-control in the bag of virtues.

If we accept such a bag of virtues, it is evident how we should build character. Children should be exhorted to practice these virtues and should be told that happiness, fortune, and good repute will follow in their wake; adults around them should be living examples of these virtues, and children should be given daily opportunities to practice them. Daily chores should be used to build responsibility, the opportunity to give to the Red Cross should serve to build responsibility, service, altruism, and so on.

The psychologist's objection to the bag of virtues is that there is no such thing. Virtues and vices are labels by which people award praise or blame to others, but the ways people use praise and blame toward others are not the ways in which they think when making moral decisions themselves. Hartshorne and May found this out to their dismay forty years ago by their monumental experimental studies of children's cheating and stealing. In brief, they and others since have found that:

1. You cannot divide the world into honest and dishonest people. Almost everyone cheats some of the time; cheating is distributed in a bell curve around a level of moderate cheating.

2. If a person cheats in one situation, it does not mean he will or will not cheat in another. There is very little correlation between situational cheating tests. In other words, it is not a character trait of dishonesty that makes a child cheat in a given situation.

3. People's verbal moral values about honesty have nothing to do with how they act. People who cheat express as much or more moral disapproval of cheating as those who do not cheat (see Kohlberg 1963).

Once these findings were obtained, it became easy to understand the psychological mistake underlying the bag of virtues approach. Common sense tends to treat moral words as if they describe reality. However, words like honesty are actually used primarily to praise or blame other people, not to describe cognitively in the scientific sense. If people used words in the same way to praise and blame themselves and to govern their own decisions, there would be no problem. As we all know, however, behavior looks very different from the internal and external frames of reference. What is "honestly expressing your feelings" to the actor is "cruelly disregarding the other person's feelings" to the outsider. What was "conducting a scientific investigation of honesty" to Hartshorne and May was, from a different point of view, "dishonestly lying and cheating to school children" (by tempting them to cheat under the pretense of conducting intelligence tests).

What Hartshorne and May found out about honesty and the rest of the bag of virtues upsets more scientific-sounding words introduced by psychoanalytic psychology to talk about morality—for example, "superego-strength," "resistance to temptation," "strength of conscience,"etc,—just as much as it upsets common-sense treatments of moral words. When recent researchers have attempted to measure such "moral" traits in individuals, they have been forced to use Hartshorne and May's old tests of honesty and self-control and have gotten exactly the same results (Kohlberg 1963). Insofar as one can extract some general personality factor from children's performance on tests of "honesty" or "resistance to temptation," it is a factor of ego-strength, or ego-control, or will, and includes such traits as capacity to delay response, and capacity to delay gratification (Grim, Kohlberg, and White 1968). Although "ego-strength" is essential in understanding moral action, it does not take us to the core of morality or to the definition of virtue. The greatest evildoers in human history have been men with strong egos who lacked principled moral values. The capacities to pursue a goal are only positive from a moral point of view if the ego's goals are moral.

We have seen that the bag of virtues does not serve the individual very well in defining his moral goals, in spite of the obvious necessity of sometimes using virtue-labels in bringing up children. The finding that individuals do not organize their own moral behavior around a bag of virtues should be a comforting finding, however. The plight of those who try is described by the theme song of the show, *You're a Good Man, Charlie Brown.*

You're a good man, Charlie Brown,
You have humility, nobility, and a sense of honor that are very rare indeed.
You are kind to all the animals and every little bird,
With a heart of gold you believe what you're told, every single word.
You bravely face adversity, you're cheerful through the day, you're thoughtful,
    brave, and courteous.
You're a good man, Charlie Brown—
You're a prince and a prince could be king,
With a heart such as yours you could open any door—
If only you weren't so wishy-washy.

If, like Charlie Brown, we define our moral aims in terms of virtues and vices, we are defining them in terms of the praise and blame of others, and are caught in the pulls of being all things to all men and end up being wishy-washy. Virtues and vices do have a central significance to individuals at the conventional level of morality: our praise and blame of others is based on ascribing virtues and vices to them. At the preconventional level, virtues and vices have no such significance because the individual does not care about intention. The young child is not oriented to the bad as "being selfish," "Being deceitful," etc.; he is, rather, oriented to the bad as being punished (stage 1) or "not making out" (stage 2). At the stage of moral principle, the individual is oriented toward acting to create a moral state of affairs, not toward "being honest." The principled virtue, "justice," is not a "trait" like honesty; it is a concern about maintaining a just state of affairs.

What then is the place of virtues (i.e., approved "traits" of character) in defining moral education? We have said that virtues are the language of assigning praise and blame. The great believers in emotive ethics and in the irrationality of human morality—Westermarck, Freud, Nietzsche, etc.—have viewed morality as a system of blame of others (moral indignation) or self-blame (guilt and shame). The great believers in conventional morality such as Durkheim make praise and blame the core of moral education. The Russian moral education of the virtues of "self-discipline" involves the manipulation of praise and blame ("love-withdrawal") to encourage "moral character." In particular, the child is encouraged to blame other children who deviate (Bronfenbrenner 1968). The place of the virtues in moral education, then, is the place of the language of praise and blame in education.

My own uncertain answer to this question is that praise and blame are necessary parts of moral development, but should not be used to define its ends. When a child spits in another child's face, we feel it expresses a "vice" worse than "being rude." Insofar as punishment is awarded, it must be accompanied by moral blame. The "vice" of premoral (stages 1 and 2) parents and teachers is to punish instrumentally, rather than for moral reasons; they punish when there is no vice. Many a mother punishes an infant for "being

dirty" (i.e., for inconveniencing the mother) with possible detrimental effects discussed elsewhere (Kohlberg 1963). Teachers who
are not premoral, but conventional and thoughtless, do the same
thing in less severe forms. Praise and blame are inevitable in
classroom life, regardless of the teacher's moral aims. To use these
methods morally, that is, in terms of conceptions of moral virtues
and vices, is preferable to using them exclusively amorally, that is,
to praise and blame behavior, such as putting books away, which
has no moral meaning.

What then is the place of moral action in moral education?
Fortunately, moral maturity in judgment and in action are closely
related. We have already said that knowledge of the good in terms
of what Plato calls opinion or conventional belief is not virtue. An
individual may believe that cheating is very bad but that does not
entail that he will resist cheating in real life. Espousal of unpreju-
diced attitudes toward Negroes does not entail actual action to
ensure civil rights when others have shown some prejudice. However, true knowledge of principles of justice does entail virtuous
action. It appears that Plato's ancient doctrine that virtue is one and
that is justice, because virtue is based on knowledge of the good, is to
some extent true. The bag of virtues approach assumes a virtue for
every moral rule (i.e., honesty for rules of cheating and stealing, responsibility for rules about completing tasks, etc.). Because morally
mature men are governed by the principle of justice rather than by a
set of rules, there are not many moral virtues, but one. The essential
elements of justice in relation to cheating are understood by both
our stage-5 and stage-6 subjects. In cheating, the critical issue is
recognition of the element of contract and agreement implicit in the
situation, and the recognition that, although it does not seem so
bad if one person cheats, what holds for all must hold for one. In a
recent study by Krebs (1967), 100 sixth-grade children were given
experimental cheating tests and our moral-judgment interview. The
majority of the children were below the principled level in moral
judgment. Seventy-five percent of these children cheated. In contrast, only 20 percent of the principled subjects (that is, stages 5

and 6) cheated. In another study conducted at the college level, only 11 percent of the principled subjects cheated in contrast to 42 percent of the students at lower levels of moral judgment.

In the case of cheating, justice and the expectations of conventional authority both dictate the same behavior. What happens when they are opposed?

An experimental study by Milgram involved such an opposition. In the guise of a learning experiment, undergraduate subjects were ordered by an experimenter to administer increasingly severe electric shock punishment to a stooge victim. In this case, the principles of justice involved in the stage-5 social contract orientation do not clearly prescribe a decision. The victim had voluntarily agreed to participate in the experiment and the subject himself had contractually committed himself to perform the experiment. Only stage-6 thinking clearly defined the situation as one in which the experimenter did not have the moral right to ask them to inflict pain on another person. Accordingly, 75 percent of the subjects at stage 6 quit or refused to shock the victim as compared with only 13 percent of all the subjects at lower stages.

A study by Haan, Smith, and Block (1968) carries the issue into political civil disobedience. Berkeley students were faced with a decision to sit-in at the administration building in the name of political freedom of communication. The researchers administered moral-judgment interviews to over two hundred of these students. The situation was like Milgram's. A stage-5 social-contract interpretation of justice, which was that held by the university administration, could take the position that a student who came to Berkeley came with foreknowledge of the rules and could go elsewhere if he did not like them. About 50 percent of the stage-5 subjects sat in. For stage-6 students, the issue was clear-cut and 80 percent of them sat in. For students at the conventional levels, stages 3 and 4, the issue was also clear-cut and only ten percent of them sat in. However, there was another group which was almost as disposed to sit in as the stage-6 students. These were stage-2 instrumental relativists, of whom about 60 percent sat in.

We have pointed out that advance in moral judgment seems to

correlate with more mature moral action. Principled subjects both cheat much less and resist pressures by authorities to inflict pain on others much more than do less mature subjects. We do not yet know whether educational stimulation of moral-judgment advance would actually produce more mature conduct in conflict situations. In any case, in addition to stimulating the development of general moral-judgment capacities, a developmental moral education would stimulate the child's application of his own moral judgments (not the teacher's) to his actions. The effort to force a child to agree that an act of cheating was very bad, when he does not really believe it, will only be effective in encouraging morally immature tendencies toward expedient outward compliance. In contrast, a more difficult but more valid approach involves getting the child to examine the pros and cons of his conduct in his own terms (as well as introducing more developmentally advanced considerations) (Turiel 1966).

In general, however, the problem of ensuring correspondence between developing moral judgments and the child's action is not primarily a problem of eliciting moral self-criticism for the child. One aspect of the problem is the development of the ego abilities involved in the nonmoral or cognitive tasks upon which the classroom centers. For example, an experimental measure of high stability of attention (low reaction-time variability) in a simple monotonous task has been found to be a clear predictor of resistance to cheating in Hartshorne and May's tests ($r=0.68$) (Grim et al. 1968). The encouragement of these attentional ego capacities is a task not of moral education as such but of general programming of classroom learning activities.

Ego strength, however, must be considered educationally in terms of its relation to level of moral judgment. Krebs (1967) found that if children have an amoral philosophy (stage 2), they are much *more* likely to cheat if they are high on ego strength (high in attention and IQ). If children have a conventional morality (stage 4), they are much *less* likely to cheat if they are high on ego strength. In other words, high ego strength aided the preconventional hedonists in living up to their "egoistic principles" in the face of temptation and pressure to conform, whereas high ego strength aided the conventional children to live up to their "conventional principles." If children have reached the stages of principle, high ego strength is less necessary, for even those principled children who are low in ego strength do not seem to cheat. This is not surprising because it is characteristic of conventional morality to yield to (and find excuses for) behavior suggested by social pressures or by an ambiguous social situation. (In this sense, the basic virtue may be called "autonomy" as well as "justice.")

The fact that "living up to his principles" for a stage-2 child leads to cheating raises a fundamental issue for classroom moral education. In order to encourage the child's application of his values to his behavior, we need to make sure that the kinds of behavior demands we make have some match to his already existing moral values. Two major types of mismatch occur. One type, which we have already mentioned, occurs when teachers concentrate on trivial classroom routines, thus moralizing on issues that have no moral meaning outside the classroom. If the teacher insists on behavioral conformity to these demands and shows no moral concerns for matters of greater relevance to the child's (and the society's) basic moral values, the child will simply assume that his moral values have no relevance to his conduct in the classroom. It is obvious that the teacher must exert some influence toward conformity to trivial classroom rules, but there are two things he can do to minimize this sort of mismatch. The first is to ensure that he does communicate some of his values with regard to broader and more genuinely moral issues. The second is to treat administrative demands as such and to distinguish them from basic moral demands involving moral judgment and moral sanctions. This does not imply that no demands should be treated as moral demands but that the teacher should clearly distinguish his own attitudes and reactions toward moral demands from his more general conformity demands.

The second form of mismatch between the teacher's moral demands and the child's moral values arises from the fact that the teacher feels that certain behavioral demands are genuine moral demands, but the child has not yet developed any moral values that require these behaviors. This is exemplified by the fact that resistance to cheating on tests does not derive from anything like moral values in young children aged five to seven, whereas resistance to theft and aggression do correspond to more spontaneous and internal moral values at this age. Given this fact, it does not seem wise to treat cheating as a genuine moral issue among young children, whereas it may be with older children. In general, the teacher should encourage the child to develop moral values relevant to such behavior as cheating but should not treat the behavior as morally demanded in the absence of such values. It must be stressed that it is the over-concern with the conforming *behavior* characteristic of traditional approaches to moral education that lies behind most of the mistakes of educators in the moral realm.

MORAL EDUCATION AND POLITICAL EDUCATION

We have stressed the importance of defining moral education in a manner that avoids a myopic preoccupation with conformity behavior in school settings. A more balanced perspective is attained when we recognize that the development of moral reasoning is central to political or social studies education. While philosophers from Plato and Aristotle to Dewey have recognized the close relations between moral and political education, our own work is the first systematic effort to unite the two in a coherent practical way. Our efforts currently involve adapting the principles of the Blatt discussion procedures to the dilemmas that form the core of the Don Oliver "Public Issues" social studies units. Our efforts are based on research by Lockwood (1970), Fletcher and Endo (unpublished), and Bane (unpublished). These findings are:

1. Public issues of the sort used by Oliver are responded to by reliably codable moral judgment statements.

2. A student's moral level on the Oliver public-political dilemmas and on the Kohlberg moral dilemmas are correlated ($r=48$).

3. Goodness of discussion of public issues (as rated by the Oliver schema) is clearly correlated with moral level on the issues being discussed.

4. The goodness of discussion schema of Oliver, being itself a model of discussion based on a conception of constitutional democracy and philosophic rationality of value-judgment, is a model appropriate to our stage-5 and stage-6 subjects. When a stage-5 subject is engaged in "good discussion" by the Oliver criteria but is discussing with a stage-3 or stage-2 subject, the good discussion bounces off the low-stage subject.

The implications for moral education are as follows:

1. There is no clear line between effective social studies education and effective moral education.

2. The criteria of effectiveness are not essentially different. If "behavior" is exaggerated as a focus in the moral education field, it is ignored in all the rest of education. The capacity to participate in the social process is the effective sign of moral and social studies education, not either "pure knowledge" or "pure behavior."

3. The unit of effectiveness of education, insofar as it has social value is not the individual but the group. An individual's moral values are primarily important for society as they contribute to a moral social climate, not as they induce particular pieces of behavior. Whether people are for or against war in Vietnam has a social import far vaster that that reducible to indiviudal "moral" acts of Hawks and Doves. A man's moral level affects the social group and institutions to which he belongs in a myriad unspecified ways which cannot be reduced to individual acts of moral self-sacrifice or self-control. Moral discussion classes such as those of Blatt experiments are limited, not because they do not focus on moral behavior, but because they have only a limited relation to the "real life" of the school and of the child.

MORAL EDUCATION AND THE ATMOSPHERE OF THE SCHOOL

The issue of "real life" brings us to what should be a central concern of moral education, the moral atmosphere of the school

(Kohlberg 1970). To extend classroom discussions of justice to real life is to deal with issues of justice in the schools. Education for justice, then, requires making schools more just, and encouraging students to take an active role in making the school more just. Here we can only illustrate the application of our two major principles of environmental stimulation of development. The first is our conception of the enhancement of participation and role-taking opportunities. One example of the importance of social participation in moral development may be seen in the finding that children with extensive peer-group participation advance considerably more quickly through the Kohlberg stages of moral judgment than do children who are isolated from such participation (with both groups equated for social class and IQ). This clearly suggests the relevance and potential of the classroom peer group for moral education. In Russia the peer-group structure is created by the teacher (i.e., he divides the classroom into groups), and the peer group is then manipulated by punishments and rewards to impose the teacher's or the school's values upon its deviant members. If the stimulation of the moral development of the individual child is a goal, however, the role of the peer group is quite different. In the previous section we discussed the fact that classroom isolates were slower in developing moral judgment than were integrates. This suggests that inclusion of the social isolates in the classroom peer group might have considerable influence on their moral development, though not necessarily an influence on immediate conformity to teacher or school demands.

The implementation of this goal would involve various methods to encourage inclusion of isolates such as are under investigation in a research project at the University of Michigan conducted by Ronald Lippett. Some of these methods involve creating a classroom atmosphere encouraging participation rather than attempting directly to influence sociometric integrates to include isolates. Some involve a more direct appeal to integrated members of sociometric groups; an appeal to the implementation of already existing social and moral values held by these children rather than the effort to impose the teacher's values upon them by reward or punishment. The process raises many important issues and these can be potentially stimulating to the moral development of the integrates as well, for they will be coping with a new situation: "Well, we were finally nice to him and look what he did." These issues provide the teacher with an opportunity to play a different and perhaps more stimulating and open role, to act as a "moral guide" rather than as an exponent of conformity to school rules and teacher demands.

While participation in the peer group is important, the ultimate issue of participation is of course that of participation in the structure and decisions of the school itself. Here the principle of participation must be integrated with our principle of stimulation by a justice-structure one stage above the child's own. We are now studying the level of justice of schools as these are perceived by students and staff. The hypothesis is that schools with atmospheres perceived by students as at their stage or lower lead to less moral advance than do schools with atmospheres perceived at a higher stage.

In these terms we might summarize the difference in goals between a political education program and a moral education program as follows. The first might take as means and ends a community effectively run by majority vote or democratic agreement in accordance with our stage 5, whereas a moral education program might take as means and ends a community effectively and satisfactorily run by consensus. Let me give, as an example, the Friend's Meeting School in Rindge whose rules are made and discussed in a weekly business meeting. It is described by the brochure as follows:

The sense of community is most strongly felt in the weekly Meeting, consisting of faculty, their families and students. Decisions are made by consensus rather than by majority rule. This places responsibility on each member to struggle to see through his own desires to the higher needs of others and the community, while witnessing the deepest concerns of his conscience. The results of these decisions are not rules in the traditional sense, but agreements entered into by everyone and recorded as minutes.

In such meetings the student is forced to sift out where he should abide by the democratic majority and where he must uphold moral principles in spite of the majority. While institutions, as opposed to persons, can never rise above stage 5, such procedures could help in the development of a stage-6 orientation.

Ultimately, then, the issue of participation raises the issue of the social structure of the school and a complete approach to moral education means full student participation in a school in which justice is a living matter. It is clear that the educator's ability to engage in this type of education is to a considerable extent contingent on the teacher herself reaching a principled level of moral judgment.

REFERENCES

Aiken, H. D. The levels of moral discourse *Ethics* 1952 *62* 235–48

Baldwin, J. M. *Social and ethical interpretations in mental development* New York: Macmillan 1906

Ball, W. B. Religion and public education: The post-Schempp years. In Theodore Sizer (ed.) *Religion and public education* Boston: Houghton-Mifflin 1967 pp. 144–63

Berkowitz, L. *Development of motives and values in a child* New York: Basic Books, Inc. 1964

Blatt, M. Studies on the effects of classroom discussion upon children's moral development. Unpublished doctoral dissertation, University of Chicago 1970

Blatt, M., Kohlberg, L. Effects of classroom discussion on moral thought. In Kohlberg and Turiel 1971

Brandt, R. *Ethical theories* Englewood Cliffs, N.J.: Prentice Hall 1959

Bronfenbrenner, U. Soviet methods of upbringing and their effects: A social-psychological analysis. Paper read at a conference on Studies of the Acquisition and Development of Values, National Institute of Child Health and Human Development, May 1968

Child, I. L. Socialization. In G. Lindzey (ed.) *Handbook of social psychology* vol. II *Special fields and applications* Cambridge, Mass: Addison-Wesley 1954, pp. 655–92

Dewey, J. *Moral principles in education* (1909) New York: Philosophical Library 1959

Dreeben, R. *On what is learned in school* Cambridge, Mass: Addison-Wesley 1968

Durkheim, E. *Moral education: A study in the theory and application in the sociology of education* (1925) New York: Free Press 1961

Erikson, E. H. *Childhood and society* Boston: W. W. Norton & Co. 1950

Grim, P., Kohlberg, L., White, S. Some relationships between conscience and attentional processes *Journal of Personality and Social Psychology* 1968 239–53

Haan, N., Smith, M. B., Block, J. Moral reasoning of young adults: Political-social behavior, family background, and personality correlates *Journal of Personality and Social Psychology* 1968 *10* (3) 183–201

Hartshorne, H., May, M. A. *Studies in the nature of character:* I *Studies in deceit;* II *Studies in self-control;* III *Studies in the organization of character* New York: Macmillan 1928–30

Holstein, Constance. Parental determinants of the development of moral judgment. Unpublished doctoral dissertation, University of California, Berkeley 1968

Homans, G. T. *The human group* New York: Harcourt, Brace 1950

Jackson, P. W. *Life in the classroom* New York: Holt, Rinehart & Winston 1968

Jones, V. *Character and citizenship training in the public schools* Chicago: University of Chicago Press 1936

Kohlberg, L. Moral development and identification. In H. Stevenson (ed.) *Child psychology*. 62 Yearbook of the National Society for Studies in Education. Chicago: University of Chicago Press 1963

Kohlberg, L. Moral and religious education and the public schools: A developmental view. In T. Sizer (ed.) *Religion and public education* Boston: Houghton-Mifflin 1967

Kohlberg, L. Stage and sequence: The cognitive-developmental approach to socialization. In D. A. Goslin (ed.) *Handbook of socialization theory and research* Chicago: Rand, McNally & Co. 1969

Kohlberg, L. The moral atmosphere of the school. In N. Overley (ed.) *The unstudied curriculum* Monograph of the Association for Supervision and Curriculum Development, Washington D.C. 1970

Kohlberg, L., Turiel, E. *Moralization research, the cognitive developmental approach* New York: Holt, Rinehart & Winston 1971

Krebs, R. L. Some relationships between moral judgment, attention, and resistance to temptation. Unpublished doctoral dissertation, University of Chicago 1967

Lockwood, A. Relations of political and moral thought. Unpublished doctoral dissertation, Harvard University 1970

Malinowski, B. *The sexual life of savages* New York: Hilcyon House, House and House 1929

Mead, G. H. *Mind, self and society from the standpoint of a social behaviorist* Charles W. Morris (ed.) Chicago: University of Chicago Press 1934

Neill, A. S. *Summerhill: a radical approach to child rearing* New York: Hart Publishing Co. 1960

Piaget, J. *The moral judgment of the child* (1932) Marjorie Gebain (transl.) New York: Collier Books 1962

Rawls, J. The sense of justice *Philosophical Review* 1963 *72* (3) 281–305

Rest, J. Developmental hierarchy in preference and comprehension of moral judgment. Unpublished doctoral dissertation, University of Chicago 1968

Rest, J., Turiel, E., Kohlberg, L. Relations between level of moral judgment and preference and comprehension of the moral judgment of others *Journal of Personality* 1969

Ruma, E., & Mosher, P. Relationship between moral judgment and guilt in delinquent boys *Journal of Abnormal Psychology* 1967 72 122–7

Tillich, P. *Morality and beyond* New York: Harper 1963

APPENDIX 1
DEFINITION OF MORAL STAGES
I. Preconventional Level

At this level the child is responsive to cultural rules and labels of good and bad, right or wrong, but interprets these labels in terms of either the physical or the hedonistic consequences of action (punishment, reward, exchange of favors) or in terms of the physical power of those who enunciate the rules and labels. The level comprises the following two stages:

Stage 1, *punishment and obedience orientation.* The physical consequences of action determine its goodness or badness regardless of the human meaning or value of these consequences. Avoidance of punishment and unquestioning deference to power are valued in their own right, not in terms of respect for an underlying moral order supported by punishment and authority (the latter being stage 4).

Stage 2, *instrumental relativist orientation.* Right action consists of that which instrumentally satisfies one's own needs and occasionally the needs of others. Human relations are viewed in terms similar to those of the market place. Elements of fairness, of reciprocity, and equal sharing are present, but they are always interpreted in a physical, pragmatic way. Reciprocity is a matter of "you scratch my back and I'll scratch yours," not of loyalty, gratitude, or justice.

II. Conventional Level

At this level, maintaining the expectations of the individual's family, group, or nation is perceived as valuable in its own right, regardless of immediate and obvious consequences. The attitude is one not only of *conformity* to personal expectations and social order, but of loyalty to it, of actively *maintaining,* supporting, and justifying the order and of identifying with the persons or group involved in it. This level comprises the following two stages:

Stage 3, *interpersonal concordance or "good boy—nice girl" orientation.* Good behavior is that which pleases or helps others and is approved by them. There is much conformity to stereotypical images of what is majority or "natural" behavior. Behavior is frequently judged by intention: "He means well" becomes important for the first time. One earns approval by being "nice."

Stage 4, *"law and order" orientation.* There is orientation toward authority, fixed rules, and the maintenance of the social order. Right behavior consists of doing one's duty, showing respect for authority, and maintaining the given social order for its own sake.

III. Postconventional, Autonomous, Or Principled Level

At this level there is a clear effort to define moral values and principles that have validity and application apart from the authority of the groups or persons holding these principles and apart from the individual's own identification with these groups. This level again has two stages:

Stage 5, *social-contract legalistic orientation.* Generally, this stage has utilitarian overtones. Right action tends to be defined in terms of general individual rights and in terms of standards that have been critically examined and agreed upon by the whole society. There is a clear awareness of the relativism of personal values and opinions and a corresponding emphasis on procedural rules for reaching consensus. Aside from what is constitutionally and democratically agreed upon, the right is a matter of personal "values" and "opinion." The result is an emphasis upon the "legal point of view," but with an emphasis upon the possibility of changing law in terms of rational considerations of social utility (rather than freezing it in terms of stage-4 "law and order"). Outside the legal realm, free agreement, and contract is the binding element of obligation. This is the "official" morality of the United States government and constitution.

Stage 6, *universal ethical-principle orientation.* Right is defined by the decision of conscience in accord with self-chosen *ethical principles* appealing to logical comprehensiveness, universality, and consistency. These principles are abstract and ethical (the Golden Rule, the categorical imperative); they are not concrete moral rules like the Ten Commandments. At heart, these are universal principles of justice, of the reciprocity and equality of human rights, and of respect for the dignity of human beings as individual persons.

APPENDIX 2
UNIVERSAL ASPECTS OF MORALITY

Categories

Modes

Judgments of obligation	Judgments of moral value	Supportive judgments
Right	Blame	Justification
Having a right	Punishability	Nonmoral value
Duty		Descriptive and
Responsibility		definitional

Elements or principles

Teleological elements	Attitudinal elements	Relational elements
Prudential	Love	Justice as liberty
Social welfare	Respect	Justice as equality
		Justice as reciprocity

Issues or institutions

Norms	Relations and roles	Values
Social rules of norms	Authority	Life
	Civil liberties	Property

continued

Issues or institutions *cont.*

Personal	Contractual	Truth
conscience	reciprocity	Sexual
Roles of affection	Institutions of	
and welfare	punishment	

Levels

Judgment of acts	General judgments of rules	Judgments in situational conflict
		Sociopolitical judgments
		Normative and metaethical theory judgments

APPENDIX 3
SIX STAGES IN CONCEPTIONS OF THE MORAL WORTH OF HUMAN LIFE

Stage 1. No differentiation between moral values of life and its physical or social-status value.

Tommy, age 10 (III Why should the druggist give the drug to the dying woman when her husband couldn't pay for it?): "If someone important is in a plane and is allergic to heights and the stewardess won't give him medicine because she's only got enough for one and she's got a sick one, a friend, in back, they'd probably put the stewardess in a lady's jail because she didn't help the important one."

(Is it better to save the life of one important person or a lot of unimportant people?): "All the people that aren't important because one man just has one house, maybe a lot of furniture, but a whole bunch of people have an awful lot of furniture and some of these poor people might have a lot of money and it doesn't look it."

Stage 2. The value of a human life is seen as instrumental to the satisfaction of the needs of its possessor or of other persons. Decision to save life is relative to, or to be made by, its possessor. (Differentiation of physical and interest value of life, differentiation of its value to self and to other.)

Tommy, age 13 (IV Should the doctor "mercy kill" a fatally ill woman requesting death because of her pain?): "Maybe it would be good to put her out of her pain, she'd be better off that way. But the husband wouldn't want it, it's not like an animal. If a pet dies you can get along without it—it isn't something you really need. Well, you can get a new wife, but it's not really the same."

Jim, age 13 (same question): "If she requests it, it's really up to her. She is in such terrible pain, just the same as people are always putting animals out of their pain."

Stage 3. The value of a human life is based on the empathy and affection of family members and others toward its possessor. (The value of human life, as based on social sharing, community, and love, is differentiated from the instrumental and hedonistic value of life applicable also to animals.)

Tommy, age 16 (same question): "It might be best for her, but her husband—it's a human life—not like an animal, it just doesn't have the same relationship that a human being does to a family. You can become attached to a dog, but nothing like a human, you know."

Stage 4. Life is conceived of as sacred in terms of its place in a categorical moral or religious order of rights and duties. The value of human life, as a categorical member of a moral order, is differentiated from its value to specific other people in the family, etc. Value of life is still partly dependent upon serving the group, the state, God, however.)

Jim, age 16 (same question): "I don't know. In one way, it's murder, it's not a right or privilege of man to decide who shall live and who should die. God put life into everybody on earth and you're taking away something from that person that came directly from God, and you're destroying something that is very sacred, it's in a way part of God and it's almost destroying a part of God when you kill a person. There's something of God in everyone."

Stage 5. Life is valued both in terms of its relation to community welfare and in terms of being a universal human right. (Obligation to respect the basic right to life is differentiated from generalized respect for the sociomoral order. The general value of the independent human life is a primary autonomous value not dependent upon other values.)

Jim, age 20 (same question): "Given the ethics of the doctor who has taken on responsibility to save human life—from that point of view he probably shouldn't but there is another side, there are more and more people in the medical profession who are thinking it is a hardship on everyone, the person, the family, when you know they are going to die. When a person is kept alive by an artificial lung or kidney it's more like being a vegetable than being a human who is alive. If it's her own choice I think there are certain rights and privileges that go along with being a human being. I am a human being and have certain desires for life and I think everybody else does too. You have a world of which you are the center, and everybody else does too, and in that sense we're all equal."

Stage 6. Belief in the sacredness of human life as representing a universal human value of respect for the individual. (The moral value of a human being, as an object of moral principle, is differentiated from a formal recognition of his rights.)

Jim, age 24 (III Should the husband steal the drug to save his wife? How about for someone he just knows?): "Yes. A human life takes precedence over any other moral or legal value, whoever it is. A human life has inherent value whether or not it is valued by a particular individual."

(Why is that?): "The inherent worth of the individual human being is the central value in a set of values where the principles of justice and love are normative for all human relationships."

APPENDIX 4
*MOTIVES FOR ENGAGING IN MORAL ACTION**

Stage 1. Action is motivated by avoidance of punishment and "conscience" is irrational fear of punishment.

*Source: Rest, 1968

Pro—If you let your wife die, you will get in trouble. You'll be blamed for not spending the money to save her, and there'll be an investigation of you and the druggist for your wife's death.

Con—You shouldn't steal the drug because you'll be caught and sent to jail if you do. If you do get away, your conscience would bother you thinking how the police would catch up with you at any minute.

Stage 2. Action motivated by desire for reward or benefit. Possible guilt reactions are ignored and punishment viewed in a pragmatic manner. (Differentiates own fear, pleasure, or pain from punishment-consequences.)

Pro—If you do happen to get caught, you could give the drug back and you wouldn't get much of a sentence. It wouldn't bother you much to serve a little jail term, if you have your wife when you get out.

Con—He may not get much of a jail term if he steals the drug, but his wife will probably die before he gets out so it won't do him much good. If his wife dies, he shouldn't blame himself, it wasn't his fault she has cancer.

Stage 3. Action motivated by anticipation of disapproval of others, actual or imagined-hypothetical (e.g., guilt). (Differentiation of disapproval from punishment, fear, and pain.)

Pro—No one will think you're bad if you steal the drug, but your family will think you're an inhuman husband if you don't. If you let your wife die, you'll never be able to look anybody in the face again.

Con—It isn't just the druggist who will think you're a criminal, everyone else will too. After you steal it, you'll feel bad thinking how you've brought dishonor on your family and yourself; you won't be able to face anyone again.

Stage 4. Action motivated by anticipation of dishonor, i.e., institutionalized blame for failure of duty, and by guilt over concrete harm done to others. (Differentiates formal dishonor from informal disapproval. Differentiates guilt for bad consequences from disapproval.)

Pro—If you have any sense of honor, you won't let your wife die because you're afraid to do the only thing that will save her. You'll always feel guilty that you caused her death if you don't do your duty to her.

Con—You're desperate and you may not know you're doing wrong when you steal the drug. But you'll know you did wrong after you're punished and sent to jail. You'll always feel guilty for your dishonesty and law-breaking.

Stage 5. Concern about maintaining respect of equals and of the community (assuming their respect is based on reason rather than emotions). Concern about own self-respect, i.e., to avoid judging self as irrational, inconsistent, nonpurposive. (Discriminates between institutionalized blame and community disrespect or self-disrespect.)

Pro—You'd lose other people's respect, not gain it, if you don't steal. If you let your wife die, it would be out of fear, not out of reasoning it out. So you'd just lose self-respect and probably the respect of others too.

Con—You would lose your standing and respect in the community and violate the law. You'd lose respect for yourself if you're carried away by emotion and forget the long-range point of view.

Stage 6. Concern about self-condemnation for violating one's own principles. (Differentiates between community respect and self-respect. Differentiates between self-respect for generally achieving rationality and self-respect for maintaining moral principles.)

Pro—If you don't steal the drug and let your wife die, you'd always condemn yourself for it afterward. You wouldn't be blamed and you would have lived up to the outside rule of the law but you wouldn't have lived up to your own standards of conscience.

Con—If you stole the drug, you wouldn't be blamed by other people but you'd condemn yourself because you wouldn't have lived up to your own conscience and standards of honesty.

Part III

BASIC ISSUES IN THE PSYCHOLOGY OF MORAL DEVELOPMENT

Chapter 3

Developmental Psychology and Value Education

JAMES REST

INTRODUCTION

The greatest significance of the moral education programs initiated by Lawrence Kohlberg is the attempt to address the serious philosophical and psychological issues involved in such an enterprise. It is typical of value education programs to skimp on either the philosophical analysis of the enterprise or the psychological underpinnings. Some value education programs manage to skimp on both, and owe their popularity to providing teachers with concrete, ready-to-use exercises and materials. The philosophical issues of Kohlberg's approach are discussed elsewhere. The aim of this chapter is to identify the major psychological ideas on which Kohlberg's approach to moral education is based, and to summarize the status of this research in developmental psychology.

Two qualifications ought to be mentioned at the onset. First, saying that Kohlberg's educational programs are *based* on developmental psychology does not imply that the psychological research and theories are noncontroversial among psychologists. Rather this is to say that certain psychologists have operationalized the basic ideas, that they have subjected the ideas to empirical tests, and that a body of findings exists.[1] I will attempt to summarize much of the psychological research relevant to Kohlberg's approach and will indi-

101

cate which ideas have considerable support to date and which ideas have not. As in all human enterprises, you win some and you lose some.

Second, saying that Kohlberg's approach is *based* on developmental psychology does not imply that there is a one way street from lab to classroom—i.e., that truth is fixed by the academics and handed over to the practitioners to apply somehow. Rather, there should be an interaction and a dialectic between lab and classroom. Many developmental psychologists have an interest in educational projects because they provide a more naturalistic site in which to view complex human functioning (e.g., Collins, 1977; McCall, 1977; Selman, 1976)—in other words, educational programs can help basic science, as well as vice versa. Indeed, to me the most exciting prospect is that basic research will provide ideas and tools of use to educators for gathering information about their programs, which in turn will provide ideas and information about how to improve programs and improve basic theory.

THE MAJOR IDEAS FROM DEVELOPMENTAL PSYCHOLOGY

Structural Organization

Kohlberg's moral education programs are based on three major ideas of cognitive developmental psychology: "structural organization," "developmental sequence," and "interactionism."[2] The aspect of behavior of most interest to a cognitive developmentalist is a person's basic problem-solving strategies and structural organization: what stimuli are attended to; how these inputs are organized in terms of categories, concepts, or images; what integrating principles or synthesizing operations are used to formulate plans, to make decisions, etc. Jerome Bruner presented this idea in *The Process of Education* (1960), eloquently stating that education should primarily emphasize problem-solving strategies, the fundamental concepts, the basic structure of the academic disciplines, because these are the basic tools of thought for making sense out of experience and organizing plans of action and decision making. Those who acquire a basic tool of thought enhance their competence in dealing with that domain of human functioning and gain something usable outside the classroom and in a changing world. Similarly, Kohlberg has contended that moral education should not be aimed at teaching some specific set of morals but concerned with developing the organizational structures by which one analyzes, interprets, and makes decisions about social problems.

In making the person's cognitive structure the focus of value education, the developmentalist conceptualizes educational aims differently from other approaches to value education. Cognitive developmental value education differs from "socialization" or indoctrination approaches, for the cognitive developmental approach aims not at producing mere conformity with the state's, the teacher's, or the school's values, but at developing capabilities in decision making and problem solving. A cognitive developmental approach also conceptualizes educational aims differently from advocates of behavioral objectives, for cognitive structures are not specific, public performances (although, of course, their assessment is inferred from empirical data) but general, internalized conceptual frameworks and problem-solving strategies. The developmentalist also parts company with humanist psychologists who emphasize transitory affective feeling states (openness, spontaneity, joy), for the focus is upon the acquisition of structured competencies that transfer to later life. The developmentalist sees cognitive structure as the framework by which affective experiences are interpreted, and by which the strong, emotional experiences of today are translated into the commitments of tomorrow. Structure is emphasized and not the transitory awareness or feeling state. The cognitive developmental approach like the value clarification approach (e.g., Raths, Harmin, and Simon, 1966) advocates the desirability of clear thinking and explicit knowledge of one's values, but the cognitive developmentalist contends that certain problem-solving strategies are more adequate than others and that certain concepts are better tools of thought than others.

Developmental Sequence

Cognitive developmentalists are struck by the obvious fact that newly born babies lack the competencies of adults. These competencies must be acquired, and the developmentalist attempts to analyze a fully developed competence in terms of discriminations, thought operations, and rule systems that underlie the competence. Developmentalists further attempt to depict the course of how these structures are built up, i.e., which components come first and are prerequisites for the later elaborations. The developmentalist often describes in terms of "stages" the successive elaboration of more complicated and differentiated structures out of simpler ones. The developmentally earlier "lower" stages are prerequisites for the "higher" stages; the more complicated higher stages deal more effectively with the problems of wider scope and greater intricacy than do the lower stages. Hence stages are sequenced in a certain invariant order because the earlier stages are less difficult and are attainable before the later stages. Higher stages are said to be "better" than lower stages in the sense that the higher structural organizations can do a better job at analyzing problems, tracing out implications, and integrating diverse considerations.

The developmentalist is not indifferent to which cognitive structure a person ultimately ends up with, for some cognitive tools are better than others. The goal of education, then, is to stimulate development through the stages. In the case of moral education, Kohlberg contends this is not a trivial matter of trying to speed up development toward an end where all are going anyway, because very few people now reach the highest stage. There are three corollaries to this general goal: (a) the educator should be interested in facilitating development as far as possible, even in people who may never reach the highest stages; (b) even if at a certain time the educator cannot move a particular person to a new stage, he should try to prevent fixation at the lower stage and try to keep things "fluid" enough that progress may come about at a later time; and (c) the educator should strive to facilitate "horizontal" development as well as "vertical," that is, not only to push for new structures but to extend the full use of an acquired structure to new domains of activity and problem areas.

If the developmental psychologist really carries out his goal of charting the course of development of a given competence, then educators indeed have some very useful information. The characterization of the higher stage of development gives a psychological analysis of some competence—e.g., Piaget's stage of formal operations gives us an analysis of what it means to be logical; Kohlberg's "stage 6" provides a description of mature moral judgment; and the psycholinguist's characterization of the highest stage of grammatical development gives an analysis of what it takes to construct completely grammatical sentences. Note that there is much more specificity here in the characterization of cognitive structure than the honorific labels often used to define educational objectives (such as "creative," "self-actualized," "good citizen," and "well-adjusted").

Furthermore, if the educator has a step-by-step description of the development of some competence, then he has a means of ordering progress (knowing which changes are progressive), of locating people along this course of development, and therefore of anticipating the experiences to which the student most likely will be responsive and from which he will profit. The adage that the teacher should meet the student at the student's level can be given precise and operational meaning if the course of development is defined and the student's level can be assessed. Knowing the course of development enables one to optimize the match between children and curricula and also serves as a guide on how to sequence curriculum. Accordingly, at the propitious time, problems that are manageable yet challenging can be introduced which create interesting learning experiences in themselves, and at the same time serve to set up the prerequisite components for problems at the next level.

Kohlberg has criticized many moral education programs for either underestimating the sophistication of children by trying to teach a simplistic "virtue always pays morality," or by overshooting the comprehension of children with abstract and abstruse doctrines. In short, these programs ignored the notion of developmental sequence and did not match curriculum with the developmental level of the students.

Interactionism

The third fundamental idea, "interactionism," describes how cumulative, developmental change takes place and how cognitive structures are progressively elaborated. If we use the computer as an analogy to the human mind, we might say cognitive structure is the program by which people process inputs (experience) and generate outputs (behavior). The computer analogy is used by many theorists to depict human thinking, but the distinctive point of the interactionist view has to do with how these "programs" get into the head. Interactionists deny that these cognitive structures are "wired in" biologically or genetically; they also deny that these cognitive structures are simply reflections of environmental contingencies, as if people just swallow whole the organizational patterns around them. Instead, the interactionist view is that the human computer (using the analogy again) is a *self-programming* computer and new programs are developed that more adequately organize the person's experiences and that give clearer directions for action. As the child notices certain regularities in the environment and establishes behavioral patterns which interact effectively with the environment, we say that the child has built up certain cognitive structures. As the child encounters new and different experiences which cannot be understood adequately or reacted to in terms of established structures, the child seeks to revamp his or her way of thinking. The new experience interacts with previously established cognitive structures to prompt the search for more adequate structures. Once a new "program" is found which can successfully "compute" the new situation, the program becomes a part of the person's repertoire. Another way of saying this is that humans seek to establish an *equilibrium* between their internal interpretive cognitive structures and the fit of experience to these structures. Therefore, the essential conditions for the cumulative elaboration of cognitive structure are the presentation of experiences which "stretch" one's existing thinking and which set into motion this search-and-discover process for more adequate ways of organizing experience and action.

(Note that the type of changes which are of interest here are those which are fundamental, long-term, and cumulative—not changes which reflect situational fluctuations, or temporary conditions which fluctuate, reverse, and cancel out the effects of each other.)

The educational implications of "interactionism" have long been recognized by educators in terms of "discovery learning," "the Socratic method," etc. One implication of this approach has been the introduction into public schools of discussion of genuinely controversial issues. Since the teacher is no longer primarily an answer giver but a process facilitator, controversial topics in school need not entail indoctrination but can furnish a source of meaningful and spirited inquiry for students. Similarly, Kohlberg's moral education programs have not only included the discussion of controversial issues in their programs, but have made it the staple item. The chief activity of these value education programs, then, is the student's search rather than the teacher's answers.

THE RESEARCH FINDINGS

These three major ideas from developmental psychology—structural organization, developmental sequence, and interactionism—underlie all programs with a Kohlbergian approach. Various student groups, institutional settings, curricular materials, and teaching styles have emerged, and it is beyond the scope of this chapter to discuss these. The question of interest here is how research findings have supported these ideas. Since 1970 there has been an explosion of studies in moral judgment, and no current review has attempted to cover all of these. The present discussion must of necessity be undetailed and selective, but I hope not unrepresentative.

Identifying Cognitive Structures in Moral Judgment

The research operation that precedes all other operations is assessment—that is, the method for identifying what cognitive structures are present in a subject's thinking. Assessment involves devising some way of collecting information about a subject (usually by interview or questionnaire), the identification of some set of features or characteristics in terms of which a developmental analysis is made (e.g., various features of Kohlberg's stages), and methods for deriving a score for each subject (see Rest, 1979 for a detailed discussion). Kohlberg in the 1950s approached the problem by asking people to discuss how they would solve a number of hypothetical moral dilemmas. An example of one of the most often used dilemmas was given in the previous chapter, the problem of Heinz and his dying wife who needs an expensive drug. Kohlberg would interview a person, asking for judgments about such moral dilemmas and a person's reasons for making a decision one way or another. Upon examining the discussions of people on these dilemmas, Kohlberg found recurrent themes and common characteristics in what people said. These themes and characteristics seemed to cluster into six basic types, and these are the six moral stages of Kohlberg's scheme (see Appendix 1, preceding chapter). Over the years Kohlberg and his associates have been working on a scoring guide for analyzing a person's discussion of moral dilemmas (see Kohlberg and colleagues, 1978). The process involves matching what a person says with a description of stage characteristics in the scoring guide, and thereby arriving at a stage score for a subject. The method is very complicated and requires long training and has been undergoing revision since 1968. Therefore reliability and validity data are not yet available on the latest forms. However, on several earlier forms, interjudge correlations among trained judges has been in the .90s, and many interesting studies suggest that the method is extremely useful. Some psychologists have been very critical of Kohlberg for not providing a definitive set of assessment procedures along with the usual reliability and validity data (e.g., Kurtines and Greif, 1974). However, Kohlberg's own priority has been to use an ongoing longitudinal study (repeatedly retesting subjects at three-year intervals over a span of twenty years) as a basis for constructing a theoretical model of the logical structure of moral thinking (a much more ambitious goal than that of providing a procedure for moral judgment assessment). Since this work is still in progress, a definite appraisal cannot be made at this time.

At the University of Minnesota (Rest, 1976; 1979) another method of identifying a person's developmental progress has been devised that is derived from Kohlberg's basic theory of six stages but which uses a multiple-choice format and therefore can be objectively and easily scored. The new method, called the Defining Issues Test (or DIT), is based on the assumption that people at different developmental stages perceive moral dilemmas differently. Therefore if you present people with different statements about the crucial issue of a dilemma, people at different developmental stages will choose different statements as representing the most important issue. For instance, in connection with the "Heinz" story, twelve statements are presented to a subject (Table 1). The subject is asked first to rate each statement in terms of its importance in making a decision about what Heinz ought to do (on the left-hand side of the page), and secondly, a subject is asked to rank the top four choices in terms of importance (on the bottom of the page).

It turns out that people rate and rank these twelve statements very differently. Table 2 gives the percentage of subjects at different points in schooling who endorse item #3 (a stage 2 item) as a top first or second choice, and also item #8 (a stage 6 item).

As can be seen, the older, more sophisticated groups tend not to choose the stage 2 item, whereas they do tend increasingly to choose the stage 6 item. Six stories are used altogether in the DIT, each with twelve items, thus the DIT contains seventy-two items in all. The way a subject selects the most important issues in these stories yields stage scores (for stages 2, 3, 4, 5a, 5b, and 6).[3] The most often used index in research with the DIT is the combined weighted ranks of items keyed as stages 5 and 6—this is called the "P score" since it represents "principled morality" or level III in Kohlberg's scheme. The P score is interpreted as the relative importance a subject gives to principled moral considerations in making moral decisions. More recently, Mark Davison (1977; Davison & Robbins, 1978) has devised another way of indexing the DIT, using multidimensional scaling methods to derive a "D" score which is a weighted composite of all items. The D score shows some improvements over the P score.

Although an objective, multiple-choice test is obviously easier for

TABLE 1
SAMPLE DIT ITEMS BASED ON THE HEINZ STORY

GREAT Importance
MUCH Importance
SOME Importance
LITTLE Importance
NO Importance

On the left-hand side of the page check one of the spaces by each question to indicate its importance.

—— —— —— —— ——   1. Whether a community's laws are going to be upheld.

—— —— —— —— ——   2. Isn't it only natural for a loving husband to care so much for his wife that he'd steal?

—— —— —— —— ——   3. Is Heinz willing to risk getting shot as a burglar or going to jail for the chance that stealing the drug might help?

—— —— —— —— ——   4. Whether Heinz is a professional wrestler, or has considerable influence with professional wrestlers.

—— —— —— —— ——   5. Whether Heinz is stealing for himself or doing this solely to help someone else.

—— —— —— —— ——   6. Whether the druggist's rights to his invention have to be respected.

—— —— —— —— ——   7. Whether the essence of living is more encompassing than the termination of dying, socially and individually.

—— —— —— —— ——   8. What values are going to be the basis for governing how people act towards each other.

—— —— —— —— ——   9. Whether the druggist is going to be allowed to hide behind a worthless

TABLE 1, *Continued*

On the left-hand side of the page check one of the spaces by each question to indicate its importance.

GREAT Importance
MUCH Importance
SOME Importance
LITTLE Importance
NO Importance

law which only protects the rich anyhow.

— — — — — 10. Whether the law in this case is getting in the way of the most basic claim of any member of society.

— — — — — 11. Whether the druggist deserves to be robbed for being so greedy and cruel.

— — — — — 12. Would stealing in such a case bring about more total good for the whole society or not?

From the list of questions above, select the four most important:

Most important	———
Second most important	———
Third most important	———
Fourth most important	———

the researcher to score, it may appear also easier for the subject to fake or distort. Several features of the DIT help detect and/or prevent this. First of all, several items were written into the DIT to detect the tendency to endorse complex, high-sounding wording rather than choosing items for meaning. Item #7, for instance, has a complicated, pretentious ring to it, and it is not keyed to any stage, but is meaningless. If subjects choose too many of the meaningless items, the questionnaire is discarded because it appears that the subject is not paying sufficient attention to the meaning of the statements. These items are included in the DIT not so much to

TABLE 2
PERCENTAGE OF ENDORSEMENT OF DIFFERENT
ACADEMIC GROUPS ON TWO ITEMS

	Junior High	Senior High	College	Seminarians	Ph.D. in Moral Philosophy and Political Science
Stage 2 item (#3)	48	30	10	8	0
Stage 6 item (#8)	10	25	70	75	88

the basis of their apparent complexity. In fact the instructions to subjects taking the DIT clearly warn beforehand that there are high-sounding but meaningless items in the test and that the subject should choose only items that are meaningful and important. Another feature of the DIT—the consistency check—enables the identification of subjects who randomly check off their answers, or who have such a misunderstanding of the test instructions that their questionnaires are useless. If the researcher compares the ratings (the checks in the left-hand column) with a subject's rankings (the list at the bottom of the page), there should be some consistency if the subject is cooperating and understands the task. Random checkers show gross inconsistencies, and their questionnaires can be eliminated from data analysis.

McGeorge (1975) conducted an interesting study looking into whether subjects could fake high scores on the DIT. He asked subjects to take the DIT twice; on one of the times, subjects took the test under normal conditions. For the other time, some subjects were asked to fake high, and some subjects were asked to fake low. McGeorge found that subjects could fake low but not high on the DIT.

Since the DIT is easy to use and is standardized, a large body of findings have been produced in a short time. The reliability and validity of the DIT are well documented (Rest, 1979). Davison and Robbins (1978) recently summarized several reliability studies, concluding that the major indices of the DIT have internal consistencies (Cronbach's Alpha) and short-term test retest correlations in the high .70s and low .80s.

Hence of the two methods of assessment, Kohlberg's test is theoretically the more ambitious undertaking, but the DIT is easier to use and better documented. The DIT cannot be used with subjects younger than thirteen or fourteen, although the Kohlberg interview can be used with children as young as seven or eight. Studies comparing the two tests show correlations in the .60s and .70s when heterogeneous populations are used (varying in age), but much smaller correlations when the populations are homogeneous, indicating that the two tests are not equivalent. Furthermore, the DIT systematically scores a subject as developmentally more advanced than does Kohlberg's test—that is, subjects produce scores at lower stages on Kohlberg's test than they endorse as important issues on the DIT (see Rest, 1979).

Evidence for Developmental Sequence

One major hypothesis of cognitive-developmental theory is that people change over time in their moral orientation. One's type of orientation is not a permanent trait, or fixed at an early age, but undergoes successive transformations in a definite, prescribed order. Therefore one would expect that older subjects in general should show a more advanced stage of moral judgment than younger subjects. There should be developmental age trends in the usage of moral stages.

In the previous chapter, Kohlberg reported age trends among subjects at different ages: that is, the older subjects tended to show greater use of higher stages. Age trends in cross-sectional samples have also been well documented with the DIT (see Rest, Davison & Robbins, 1978). Over five thousand subjects from all over the United States at different ages and educational levels were given the DIT. Moral judgment scores are higher with increasing age and education. However, after adults finish formal schooling there seems to be a plateau effect—that is, older adults who only finished high school have DIT scores similar to current high school subjects, older adults who finished college have DIT scores similar to current college students. By and large, moral judgment seems to develop as long as people continue their education, then tends to level off. In the DIT studies the group having the highest scores were doing graduate work in moral philosophy and political science.

The studies cited so far are all *cross-sectional* studies in that they make comparisons between different groups of subjects at various ages. A more powerful kind of evidence about development is a *longitudinal* study which tests the same subjects over a period of time. At least five longitudinal studies have been reported using Kohlberg's test and as many using the DIT (see Rest, Davison & Robbins, 1978 for a review). Overall, the predominant trend is that subjects do change upward over time (where "upward" is in the direction defined as more advanced by theory). This is not to say that *all* subjects move upward. Adults tend to stay pretty much the same over two- to three-year intervals; a small portion of subjects actually moved downward; and developmental change is much clearer over longer intervals of time (four years) than over shorter intervals (two years or less). Nevertheless, among junior and senior high school subjects tested at three- to four-year intervals, about two-thirds of them show upward movement and only 6–7 percent of them show downward movement: so the ratio is 10 to 1 in favor of upward change.

These findings favor a conclusion somewhere between two extremes. On the one hand, some psychologists have argued that there is no evidence that development takes place in moral judgment (Bandura & Walters, 1963; Kurtines & Greif, 1974). With the evidence now in hand (which was not available to these critics when they wrote their statements), I can't imagine them accepting any claim in psychology if they don't accept this one. On the other hand, the evidence has not been strong or clear enough to support Kohlberg's claim that *all* subjects move step by step through the sequence of stages without a single reversal. I think the limits of our methods of assessment have to be acknowledged as involving a certain degree of error. Also, we have not fully accounted for many factors which affect performance on a test. The conclusion that does seem warranted, however, is that over the years, young people's moral judgments tend to shift from low-stage thinking to higher-stage thinking. There is a natural order of change in the way moral thinking progresses.

Evidence that Moral Judgment is Cognitive

Even if we accept the claim that moral judgment does change in certain ways with age, what evidence is there that upward movement represents greater social-moral understanding, better problem solving, or more equilibrated cognitive structures? How do we know that moral judgment reflects predominantly *cognitive* processes rather than affective processes? Isn't morality more a matter of the heart than of the head?

The earliest research on this question presented correlations of IQ measures with moral judment (Kohlberg, 1964). It was argued that significant correlations with IQ indicated that moral judgment development was largely cognitive rather than a matter of acquiring mindless habits or conditionings, identifying with parents, getting in touch with inner feelings, or increasing one's capacity for guilt.

A more recent line of research, the Comprehension Test, involves developing a test of the capacity to comprehend moral concepts which is different from Kohlberg's test or the DIT. Note that Kohlberg's test and the DIT are essentially tests of what concepts a subject chooses to use in making a moral decision—they do not give direct evidence about what concepts a subject has the capacity to use. It is within the realm of possibility that a subject with a low score on Kohlberg's test or the DIT actually could have used a high-stage concept, but for some reason just decided to give a low-stage answer. The purpose of the Comprehension Test is to inventory what concepts a subject is capable of understanding, regardless of which concept the subject uses to make a moral decision. Therefore, the Comprehension Test makes possible the following research strategy: If moral judgment (as measured by Kohlberg's test or the DIT) is largely governed by cognitive processes and largely reflects the upper limits of a person's capacity to understand the social-moral order, then moral judgment should be highly correlated with the Comprehension Test. Several studies with Kohlberg's test and quite a few with the DIT show that this is a consistent finding (see Rest, 1979). Comprehension correlates with moral judgment up to the .60s in several studies. Furthermore, in longitudinal studies, as subjects improve on the Comprehension Test, so also do they increase on DIT. Of the subjects who increased on the DIT, 81 percent also increased on the Comprehension Test.

The Comprehension studies indicate the following: 1) as people *can* comprehend higher moral concepts, they tend to *use* them in making moral decisions; 2) moral comprehension puts an upper limit on what statements are intelligible to a person—if a message presupposes too high a level of comprehension, the argument will not be understood or seen as very important; 3) even though subjects understand the statements of stages below the level that they use in decision making, subjects reject the lower statements as too simplistic and inadequate.

Another corroborating line of research on this issue has already been mentioned: the "fakability" study by McGeorge (1975). When subjects were encouraged to raise their moral judgment scores above their "natural" levels (to "fake good"), there was no significant increase; however, when subjects were asked to "fake bad," their scores significantly decreased. This suggests that DIT scores usually represent a subject's upper limit of conceptualization and that subjects deliberately avoid less adequate forms of thinking.

A third line of evidence relating moral judgment to *cognitive* processes comes from examination of the patterns of correlations of the DIT with many other variables (Rest, 1979, chapter 6). Looking at 50 correlations of the DIT with various cognitive measures (IQ, intellectual aptitude, achievement tests, school grades, Piagetian Formal Operations, Perry's scale, Loevinger's test, etc.) shows that the correlations are usually significant and mostly in the .20s to .50s range. In contrast, looking at about 150 correlations of the

DIT with "affective" or personality measures (locus of control, Allport-Vernon-Lindzey Test of Values, Tennessee Self Concept, anxiety tests, etc.) indicates that the correlations are usually nonsignificant or inconsistent, very rarely as high as .50.

In the mid-1950s when Kohlberg began his research in moral judgment, there was vociferous opposition to the idea that any aspect of morality had much to do with cognitive processes. Morality belonged in the "affective domain" and not in the "cognitive domain." Since then, the study of cognition has flourished in psychology. Humans are viewed as active operators on their experiences and organizers of their environments, and hence, behavior has to be analyzed in terms of the internal organizational systems of the subject. This change in psychology is dramatized, for instance, by noting that Walter Mischel and Alfred Bandura (major critics of Kohlberg) now refer to their positions as "*cognitive* social learning" theories, whereas in the 1960s such a label was virtually a contradiction in terms (Mischel & Mischel, 1976; Bandura, 1977). The claim that moral judgment is linked to cognitive development is today not nearly so controversial, partly because of the accumulated evidence and partly because psychology in general has become more cognitivist. However, the debate has shifted ground and there are now at least three areas of contention:

(1) While the general notion has been accepted that cognitions are important and that they develop, there is debate over whether the best way to portray cognitive development is by using the stage concept. John Flavell, a noted Piaget interpreter, suggests giving up the notion and instead portraying development in much more specific terms which make less stringent claims about invariant sequences (1977). Various types of cognitive structures other than "stages" have been proposed: scripts, frames, self-schemata, plans, goals, themes, etc. The arguments and evidence in this debate are too involved to go into here, and their relevance to moral judgment research are detailed in Rest, 1979, chapter 3, which proposes a reconceptualization of the stage concept. Again, at issue is not whether there are cognitions or whether they develop, but whether cognitive structures are best represented by the stage concept.

(2) Another debate centers on Kohlberg's specific definitions of developmental features (c.f. Damon, 1977; Eisenberg-Berg, 1978; Gilligan, 1976; Haan, 1978; Hogan, 1970; Holstein, 1976; Lee, 1971; Rest, 1979). The most serious charge is *not* that Kohlberg's descriptions of development are entirely erroneous, but that the descriptions are not entirely generalizable, complete, or final. Given the fact that so much research has produced significant findings using Kohlberg's scheme, I believe that there has to be some truth in his characterizations, at the very least. Furthermore, it is easy to say there might be alternative schemes, and far more difficult to specify exactly what these alternatives are and to document their superiority to Kohlberg's scheme. Nevertheless, I think that refinements, additions, and realignments of developmental schemes will continue.

(3) A third controversy is over the distinctiveness and importance of moral judgment as assessed by Kohlberg's test or the DIT. Mischel and Mischel (1976), for instance, argue that what people say (including their moral judgment verbalizations) has a very tenuous relationship with what they do, and furthermore, development in moral judgment is simply a reflection of general cognitive and linguistic development. The Mischels say that it is no surprise that older people with more education talk in more complex and fancier ways than younger people—but this only means that the more advanced people have developed fancier patterns of language or thinking-in-general, and doesn't entail anything about their morality. They say, "It would not be parsimonious to believe that the latter (moral judgment) reflects more than the growth of cognitive competencies interacting with socialization practices" (1976, p. 97).

There are two questions here: First, is moral judgment any different from verbal development or cognition-in-general? Second, how is moral judgment related to the way people actually behave and to general personality organization? I will discuss the second question in the next section. With regard to the first question on the distinctiveness of moral judgment, there is supportive correlational and experimental evidence. Although cognitive developmentalists want to claim that moral judgment development is *part* of general cognitive development, they want to maintain it is a distinguishable part and deserves special study. One line of evidence in support of the cognitive developmental view is that measures of moral thinking are more highly correlated among themselves than with measures of general cognitive development (Rest, 1979, chapter 6). Another line of evidence is that moral judgment has significant and unique predictive power to behavior even when IQ and other variables are controlled or statistically partialled out (G. Rest, 1978; McColgan, 1975). A third line of evidence comes from the distinctive effects of different educational interventions. Panowitsch (1975) pre- and post-tested a college ethics class and a logic class on the DIT and on a logic test. He found that the ethics class tended to move students up on the DIT but not on the logic test; the logic class tended to move students up on the logic test but not on the DIT. Therefore there must be something distinctive about moral reasoning and what the DIT measures because the different interventions produced different effects.

I think the evidence shows that the "parsimony" of treating moral judgment as indistinguishable from general cognitive development is simplistic.

Moral Judgment, Values, and Behavior

The crux of this issue is whether high development in moral judgment (as assessed by Kohlberg's test, the DIT, or similar measures) only reflects fancier talking, or whether it reflects something more than that. Some views of the Mischels have already been mentioned, but their most bizarre suggestion is that there might be a negative correlation between moral judgment and morality (1976, pp. 107).

History is replete with atrocities that were justified by involving the highest principles and that were perpetrated upon victims who were equally convinced of their own moral principles. In the name of justice, of the common welfare, of universal ethics, and of God, millions of people have been killed and whole cultures destroyed. In recent history, concepts of universal right, quality, freedom, and social equity have been used to justify every variety of murder including genocide.

It seems to follow that if we find genocide distasteful, we ought to devise educational programs that *prevent* development in moral judgment; if the murderers were without their highest principles, perhaps millions of people and whole other cultures would still be with us!

In pursuing the role that moral judgment plays in human functioning, we should be clear about the kind of psychological construct that moral judgment is. I find it useful to think of a moral judgment test as having some similarities with a mathematics test or a German test: under controlled conditions, a person is presented with a hypothetical problem (a math problem, a language translation problem, a moral problem), and the purpose of the test is to determine not only the adequacy of the solution but also to determine the problem-solving strategies and interpretive framework of the subject. It is true that a subject's performance in a math exam may or may not reflect how he as an engineer actually begins a bridge; likewise, performance in a German exam may or may not reflect how a student visiting Germany actually converses with the native shopkeeper; and similarly, the way that a person structures moral problems in a test may or may not be the way a person structures his thinking in actual social decision making. But in each of these cases, we elicit samples of problem solving and look for basic competences in the way a subject goes about structuring an answer. Note that the mathematics teacher does not test for mathematical competence by asking subjects to rate themselves on a one-to-five scale on the item, "I know mathematics." Rather, samples of mathematical problem solving are collected. Similarly, the moral judgment researcher does not ask subjects to rate themselves on a one-to-five scale on the item, "I am honest," or "I would not steal." Unlike many self-report personality tests, such as the MMPI or CPI, a moral judgment test does not ask a subject to give an estimation or prediction about himself, but collects samples of his ways of solving problems. Therefore, the observation that people often promise one thing but actually do another is a little beside the point. The real question is whether the problem–solving capacities displayed in an artificial test are representative of the problem capacities utilized in nonartificial situations, and how differences in ways of problem solving affect decisions. Likewise, it is irrelevant to moral judgment assessment what fancy language or catch words are used. It is not the invoking of "high principles" that credits a subject with high-stage thinking, but rather the way that a subject sets up the problem and deals with the claims of all participants in a dilemma. The higher stages are not defined in terms of what verbal garnish a subject uses but in terms of the basic logic of the cooperative scheme presupposed in a solution of a social problem (see Rest, 1979, chapter 2). And so, even though a Nazi stormtrooper may invoke words like "justice," "universal ethics," etc., to justify the operation of a concentration camp, that does not entail that the justification satisfies the logic of higher stages of moral judgment. Therefore, in conclusion, moral judgment deals with the kinds of considerations that are taken into account in making a moral decision, and the kinds of prioritizing and integrating principles that are used to come down in favor of one line of action or another.

In considering the evidence, first let us look at the relation of moral judgment (the basic ways that moral problems are structured) to the decisions or subjective value positions that people take (what line of action they advocate). Sometimes people have referred to this issue as the relation between structure and content. Cognitive developmentalists have emphasized strenuously that structure cannot be equated or reduced to content. This, however, has led some people to infer that structure ought to have nothing to do with content, that measures of moral judgment ought to be empirically independent of decision-outcomes or people's values (e.g., Martin, Shafto & VanDeinse, 1977). This is to confuse the nature of the distinction between content and structure, and in effect asserts that the way a person construes a situation and goes about making a decision will have nothing to do with the final decision. The evidence is clear that the mode of structuring a moral situation *is* related to decision making and value positions; level of moral reasoning is related to the choice of action that is advocated (e.g., Kohlberg, 1958; Rest, 1976), and is related to people's stands on controversial public issues (Candee, 1976; Fishkin, Keniston &

MacKinnon, 1973; Fontana & Noel, 1973; Kohlberg & Elfenbein, 1975; Rest, et al., 1974; Rest, 1975—see Rest, 1979 for review). Therefore moral judgment is not a value neutral, a bloodless and purely cerebral style of intellectualizing, but is connected with values and decision outcomes.

The objection may be raised here that these studies are only linking one measure of subjective thinking with another measure of subjective thinking. What about the relation of moral judgment to *behavior?* Although the term "behavior" is difficult to define, I would propose these two criteria: (1) information about a subject's activity that is public, that is not an inferred inner state or subjective disposition, but something that independent observers can say did or did not happen; (2) an activity of a subject which has a potential effect on the flow of events in the real world, not some indication of the subject to an experimentor in an artificial situation contrived only for the purpose of research.

A great variety of studies have linked moral judgment to many types of behavior: cheating, helping, promise keeping, delinquency and antisocial behavior, the distribution of goods, voting in elections, student protests, abortion decisions, etc. (See Kohlberg, 1969 and Rest, 1979 for partial reviews.) In general these studies have shown positive but only modest relationships. It seems clear that moral judgment is related to behavior, but it is also clear that other variables are complicating, mediating, or modifying that relationship. In some multiple regression studies, moral judgment is shown to contribute unique and significant predictability to behavior, but in other studies moral judgment is too confounded with other variables.

I think the evidence leads us to reject two extreme positions: on the one hand, that moral judgment has no substantial or interesting relation to behavior; and on the other hand, that knowing a subject's moral judgment score (from one of the usual tests of moral judgment) affords us a fairly complete picture of the inner world of the subject and how the subject is likely to organize his or her life. Between these extreme views, moral judgment can be viewed as an important factor in real—life decision making, but its interaction with other factors complicates the relationship such that simple, linear correlations cannot be expected. A review of the literature (Rest, 1979, chapter 6) suggests that there are at least seven kinds of other factors to consider: "ego strength" or a self–regulation factor (e.g., Krebs, 1967; Mischel, 1974); situational and performance factors (e.g., Huston & Korte, 1976; Latane & Darley, 1970); other values besides moral values (e.g., Damon, 1977); the distinction between operative and reflective planes of thought (Piaget, 1932; Aronfreed, 1976); deliberate misrepresentation, and other factors. All of these factors have to be considered simultaneously in order to have any hope of powerful prediction to behavior—and this is an undertaking which we are only just beginning.

Educational Interventions

Can moral judgment be affected by experimental or educational intervention? The answer to this question is closest to home for the educator, because if no one can do anything to change moral judgment, then it is hardly worth developing programs for that goal.

The early work of Turiel (1966) seemed to give an unambiguous "Yes!" to the question of whether change was possible, and many subsequent researchers and educators cite this study as giving the green light to intervention efforts. The conclusion that many drew from this study was that change was possible by modeling for a subject the stage of thinking directly above his own ("+1 modeling"). In retrospect, I think this study posed intriguing questions, explored them in an ingenious way, and, offered many provative ideas—however, the results of the study are really very ambiguous (see Hoffman, 1970; Kurtines & Greif, 1974). Subsequent studies have contradicted the conclusions (see Turiel, 1973), and many researchers now (including Turiel) have second thoughts about the meaningfulness of attempting to change a subject's moral judgment stage by a half-hour intervention. Some researchers continue to do short-term (an hour or less) intervention studies, but the results are confusing and inconsistent. Is it reasonable to expect that mild interventions that last an hour or less can alter the fundamental way a person thinks about moral issues, especially considering that it takes over five years on the average for one of Kohlberg's longitudinal subjects to move one stage?

The first longer intervention programs (9 to 12 weeks) were conducted by Blatt (1969; Blatt and Kohlberg, 1973). Blatt's first study turned out to have the greatest gains of any program done in the 10 years since then. It was conducted with only 30 children in a Jewish Sunday school, aged 11–12 years, meeting for an hour a week over 12 weeks to discuss controversial moral problems based on biblical situations. Using Kohlberg's test, 9 out of 11 subjects tested showed upward movement between the pre-test and the post-test (a gain of 66 points on the Moral Maturity Scale, or the equivalent of 2/3 of a stage) in contrast to several comparison groups drawn from other studies which did not show significant gains. Furthermore, on a follow-up testing one year later, Blatt's discussion group had essentially stabilized their gains made during the intervention.

Blatt's second study was an expansion and replication of his first and of the three dozen or so studies that I have seen since then, it remains one of the best designed and executed studies. Variations explored in this study included two age levels (6th grade and 10th grade), two socioeconomic groups (lower middle class and lower class) associated with race (white and black), and different "curriculum" (a teacher-led discussion group versus a peer-led discussion group). In addition, the study contained a comparison group from the same schools and much more adequate sample sizes (46 subjects in the teacher-led treatment, 41 in the peer-led treatment, and 40 in the control condition). Blatt met with subjects in the teacher-led condition in groups of 8 to 12 subjects, over 18 sessions held twice a week for 45 minutes each. Again, the format was the discussion of moral dilemmas. The teacher-led discussion group showed average increases in Kohlberg's Moral Maturity Score of 34 points (1/3 of a stage) while the other groups showed a 7-point gain and a 15-point drop, respectively. In a follow-up testing one year later the teacher-led group maintained its lead over the other groups.

Blatt's findings created a great deal of enthusiasm in educational-researcher circles because they indicated that educational intervention programs could be devised to produce significant shifts in an important variable, moral judgment. A large number of educational programs have followed Blatt's lead, although not always replicating Blatt's findings. Lockwood (1977) and Lawrence (1977) have reviewed over two dozen value education projects which had as a major goal the facilitation of moral judgment development. As is common in educational research, the experimenters did not always have much control over the schools or students and also there are many shortcomings in the designs and execution of the studies as pieces of scientific research. Some of the problems that made conclusions difficult are the following: (1) only some of the studies had random assignment of students to treatment conditions, and some did not have control groups at all; (2) few studies performed adequate statistical analyses comparing gains of the experimental groups with gains of control groups; (3) in some studies, students were exposed to and directly taught Kohlberg's stage theory, thereby making it difficult to interpret the post-test gains; (4) some studies reported that subjects were resistant to taking the tests or did not fully understand the tests; (5) most of the interventions were taught by inexperienced teachers (mostly doctoral students doing their dissertations) who were trying out the program for the first time; (6) many of the studies had inadequate sample sizes; (7) many studies did not include follow-up testings to demonstrate the stability of the findings.

Nevertheless in many of the studies, the changes from pre-test to post-test were much greater in the experimental groups than would be expected by regular, natural development. I get the following impressions from the studies: (1) interventions that have an explicit and heavy emphasis on moral reasoning (rather than focusing on psychological growth in general or on broad cultural exposure) are the ones more likely to produce change in moral judgment; (2) there is no evidence that "+1 modeling" is the effective condition for growth; (3) interventions shorter than several months are unlikely to produce significant changes; (4) even when there is change it tends to be slight—no study produced students whose scores looked like those of a group of moral philosophy students; (5) it is likely that directly teaching Kohlberg's theory in the intervention biases the post-testing; (6) it is unclear which pedagogical practices are generally most effective or even which practices work best with which students (e.g., how much peer-group discussion is optimal, versus outside practical experiences, versus reading and formal study); (7) it is unclear whether the curricula themselves are developmentally sequenced (i.e., that one experience lays the groundwork for the following more difficult experience, etc.).

Currently there is much effort directed at devising richer curriculum materials and exploring various educational settings and formats. While these efforts as yet have not fully demonstrated their effectiveness and usefulness, they are grounded on a psychological variable, moral judgment, that has demonstrated its empirical reality. In fact it is my view that in the whole field of personality and social development, there is currently no psychological construct that is in better shape than moral judgment in terms of its theoretical richness, practical implications, and empirical validation. Preliminary results of program evaluations indicate that educational intervention in this area is possible. Furthermore, by being grounded in a solid research base, various programs and innovations can be tested—and need not depend solely on their surface plausibility or the salesmanship of their proponents. Hopefully new program ideas will keep pace with ideas about how to gather information on program effectiveness, such that successive rounds of educational decisions will be self-correcting and make optimal use of intuition as well as empirical data. In turn, developmental psychology has much to learn from educational interventions, and both stand to gain from an alliance.

NOTES

1. This is in contrast, for instance, to the lack of psychological theory and research on the most basic ideas in the value clarification approach. For example, what psychological tests exist for determining the degree of values clarification in

specific people or for determining who is in a state of "clarified values" and who is not? What empirical evidence is there that people with clarified values are markedly more positive, purposeful, enthusiastic, and proud than other people?

2. Portions of this section first appeared in Rest, 1974.

3. No single item by itself is a reliable guide to assessing moral judgment, and the scores that are used are based on seventy-two items from six stories.

REFERENCES

Aronfreed, J. Moral development from the standpoint of a general psychological theory. In T. Lickona (Ed.), *Moral development and behavior.* New York: Holt, Rinehart & Winston, 1976, 54–69.

Bandura, A. *Social learning theory.* Englewood Cliffs, N.J.: Prentice-Hall, 1977.

Bandura, A. & Walters, R. H. *Social learning and personality development.* New York: Holt, Rinehart & Winston, 1963.

Blatt, M. Studies on the effects of classroom discussion upon children's moral development. Unpublished doctoral dissertation, University of Chicago, 1969.

Bruner, J. *The Process of Education.* Cambridge: Harvard University Press, 1960.

Candee, D. Structure and choice in moral reasoning. *Journal of Personality and Social Psychology,* 1976, *34,* 1293–1301.

Collins, W. A. Counseling interventions and developmental psychology: reactions to programs for social-cognitive growth. *The Counseling Psychologist,* 1977, *6* (4), 15–17.

Damon, W. *The Social World of the Child.* San Francisco: Jossey-Bass, 1977.

Davison, M. L. On an undimensional, metric unfolding model for attitudinal and developmental data. *Psychometrika,* 1977, *42,* 523–548.

Davison, M. L. & Robbins, S. The reliability and validity of objective indices of moral development. *Applied Psychological Measurement,* 1978, in press.

Eisenberg-Berg, N. The relationship of prosocial moral reasoning to altruism, political liberalism, and intelligence. Unpublished manuscript, Arizona State University, 1978.

Fishkin, J., Keniston, K. & MacKinnon, C. Moral development and political ideology. *Journal of Personality and Social Psychology,* 1973, *27,* 109–119.

Flavell, J. *Introduction to cognitive development.* 1977.

Fontana, A. & Noel, B. Moral reasoning at the university. *Journal of Personality and Social Psychology,* 1973, *3,* 419–429.

Gilligan, C. In a different voice: women's conceptions of the self and of morality. *Harvard Educational Review,* 1977, *47* (4), 418–517.

Haan, N. Two moralities in action contexts: relationships to thought, ego regulation, and development. *Journal of Personality and Social Psychology,* 1978, *30,* 286–305.

Hoffman, M. Moral development. In P. Mussen (Ed.), *Carmichael's manual of child psychology.* Volume II. New York: Wiley, 1970, 261–359.

Hogan, R. A dimension of moral judgment. *Journal of Consulting and Clinical Psychology,* 1970, *35,* 205–212.

Holstein, C. B. Irreversible, stepwise sequence in the development of moral judgment: a longitudinal study of males and females. *Child Development,* 1976, *47,* 51–61.

Huston, T. L. & Korte, C. The responsive bystander: why he helps. In T. Lickona (Ed.), *Moral development and behavior.* New York: Holt, Rinehart & Winston, 1976, 269–283.

Kohlberg, L. The development of modes of moral thinking and choice in the years 10 to 16. Unpublished doctoral dissertation, University of Chicago, 1958.

Kohlberg, L. Development of moral character and moral ideology. In M. L. and L. W. Hoffman (Eds.), *Review of child development research.* Volume I. New York: Russell Sage Foundation, 1964.

Kohlberg, L. Stage and sequence: the cognitive-developmental approach to socialization. In D. Goslin (Ed.), *Handbook of socialization theory and research.* Chicago: Rand McNally, 1969, 347–480.

Kohlberg, L. & Colleagues. Moral stage scoring manual. Cambridge: Center for Moral Education, Harvard Graduate School of Education, 1978.

Kohlberg, L. & Elfenbein, D. The development of moral judgments concerning capital punishment. *American Journal of Orthopsychiatry,* 1975, *45* (4), 614–640.

Krebs, R. L. Some relations between moral judgment, attention, and resistance to temptation. Unpublished doctoral dissertation, University of Chicago, 1967.

Kurtines, W. & Greif, E. The development of moral thought: review and evaluation of Kohlberg's approach. *Psychological Bulletin, 81* (8), 1974, 453–470.

Latane, B. & Darley, J. Group inhibition of bystander intervention. *Journal of Personality and Social Psychology,* 1968, *10,* 215–221.

Lawrence, J. A. Moral judgment intervention studies using the Defining Issues Test. In J. Rest (Ed.), *Development in judging moral issues—a summary of research using the Defining Issues Test.* Minnesota Moral Research Projects, *Technical Report #3,* 1977. (ERIC Document Reproduction Service No. ED 144 980.)

Lee, L. C. The concomitant development of cognitive and moral modes of thought: a test of selected deductions from Piaget's theory. *Genetic Psychology Monographs,* 1971, *83,* 93–146.

Lockwood, A. L. *The effects of values clarification and moral development curriculum on school-age subjects: a critical review of recent research.* Unpublished manuscript, University of Wisconsin, 1977.

Martin, R. M, Shafto, M. & Van Deinse, W. The reliability, validity, and design of the Defining Issues Test. *Developmental Psychology,* 1977, *13,* 460–468.

McCall, R. B. Challenges to a science of developmental psychology. *Child Development,* 1977, *48* (2), 333–344.

McColgan, E. Social cognition in delinquents, pre-delinquents and non-delinquents. Unpublished doctoral dissertation, University of Minnesota, 1975.

McGeorge, C. The susceptibility to faking of the Defining Issues Test of moral development. *Developmental Psychology,* 1975, *11,* 108.

Mischel, W. Processes in delay of gratification. In L. Berkowitz (Ed.), *Advances in social psychology,* Vol. VII. New York: Academic, 1974.

Mischel, W. & Mischel, H. N. A cognitive social learning approach to morality and self-regulation. In T. Lickona (Ed.), *Moral development and behavior.* New York: Holt, Rinehart & Winston, 1976, Chapter 4.

Panowitsch, H. R. Change and stability in the Defining Issues Test. Unpublished doctoral dissertation, University of Minnesota, 1975.

Piaget, J. *The moral judgment of the child* (M. Gabain, trans.). New York: The Free Press, 1965. (Originally published, 1932.)

Raths, L. E., Harmin, M. & Simon, S. B. *Values and teaching: working with values in the classroom.* Columbus, Ohio: Merrill, 1966.

Rest, G. J. Voting preference in the 1976 Presidential Election and the influences of moral reasoning. Unpublished manuscript, University of Michigan, 1977.

Rest, J. R. Developmental psychology as a guide to values education: a review of "Kohlbergian" programs. *Review of Educational Research,* 1974, *44* (2), 241–259.

Rest, J. R. Longitudinal study of the Defining Issues Test: a strategy for analyzing developmental change. *Developmental Psychology,* 1975, *11,* 738–748.

Rest, J. R. New approaches in the assessment of moral judgment. In T. Lickona (Ed.), *Moral development and behavior.* New York: Holt, Rinehart, & Winston, 1976, 198–220.

Rest, J. R. *Development in judging moral issues,* Book in press, 1979.

Rest, J. R., Cooper, D., Coder, R., Masanz, J. & Anderson, D. Judging the important issues in moral dilemmas—an objective test of development. *Developmental Psychology,* 1974, *10* (4), 491–501.

Rest, J. R., Davison, M. L. & Robbins, S. Age trends in judging moral issues: a review of cross-sectional, longitudinal, and sequential studies of the Defining Issues Test. *Child Development,* 1978, *49* (2), 263–279.

Selman, R. Toward a structural analysis of developing interpersonal relationship concepts: research with normal and disturbed preadolescent boys. In A. Pick (Ed.), *Tenth Annual Minnesota Symposium on Child Psychology.* Minneapolis: University of Minnesota Press, 1976.

Turiel, E. An experimental test of the sequentiality of developmental stages in the child's moral judgments. *Journal of Personality and Social Psychology,* 1966, Vol. III, No. 6, 611–618.

Turiel, E. The effects of cognitive conflicts on moral judgment development. Unpublished manuscript, Harvard University, 1973.

Chapter 4

Moral Stages and the Development of Faith

JAMES FOWLER

INTRODUCTION

In 1974 Lawrence Kohlberg published an article entitled "Education, Moral Development and Faith."[1] Originally an address to the
National Catholic Educational Association, this paper represents a
rather direct statement of the central themes of Kohlbergian
"faith." It expresses Kohlberg's commitment to a Platonic understanding of justice as the central and unitary moral virtue.[2] It states
his claim that justice is a naturalistic virtue, emerging in children
(at differing rates and with differing points of final equilibration) in
all cultures as a result of their interaction with other persons and
with social institutions. It affirms that the capacity for discerning
the requirements of justice has an ontogenetic history, recapitulated
at varying rates in individuals and their societies, but essentially
common to all persons. It claims that moral education can be pursued in public schools without reference to the contents of students'
particular beliefs, attitudes, or values. To fulfill this possibility,
public education must meet the following imperatives: according to
Kohlberg, (1) justice must be embodied in the *modus operandi* of the
school; (2) moral thinking must be stimulated by attention to real
and hypothetical moral dilemmas; and (3) students must be exposed
to moral arguments on these issues one stage beyond their own. If

these significant conditions are met, Kohlberg believes, growth in individuals' capacity to discern the requirements of justice should occur. Further, if the social environment encourages children and youth to take the personal and social perspectives of others, the expansion of moral imagination eventually required for principled moral reasoning will be nurtured.

Underlying these elements of Kohlbergian faith is a conception of moral development which Kohlberg appropriated from J. Mark Baldwin, John Dewey, Jean Piaget, and others. This tradition rejects theories of moral development centering in the teaching of multiple virtues or moral ideals. Instead, it argues that moral judgment and action arise out of a person's way of constructing (knowing) situations requiring moral choice. The key to moral development, and therefore to moral education, lies in the cognitive operations by which persons "know" their social environments. Moral development requires progress in the ability accurately to take the perspectives of others, their needs and rights, and to see one's own claims and obligations with similar balance, detachment, and accuracy. Following the path of cognitive development more generally, moral judgment—cognitive operations as applied to questions of rightness, goodness, obligation, duty, and responsibility—also exhibits a developmental trajectory.

Kohlberg's stage theory sets forth the developmental trajectory he finds in persons' moral thinking. Claiming both empirical validation and logical-philosophical justification for the stage sequence,[3] Kohlberg has provided a powerful heuristic model against which to examine patterns of moral reasoning in individuals and groups.

"Education, Moral Development and Faith"either assumes or explicitly restates most of the elements of the Kohlbergian faith I have just enumerated. But it also does more. Kohlberg begins the article in an interesting way:

While moral development has a larger context including faith, it is possible to have a public moral education which has a foundation independent of religion. We believe that the public school should engage in moral education and that the moral basis of such education centers on universal principles of justice, not broader religious and personal values.[4]

The references to "faith," "religion," and "broader religious and personal values" signal an agenda to which Kohlberg returns later in the article.

In a section headed "Moral Development and Education as Centered on Justice," he points to Socrates and Martin Luther King, Jr. as great moral teachers whose lives and teachings manifested their centering commitments to principles of justice. For Kohlberg, the principle of justice held by both these men derived from their considering "social justice, or the nature of an ideal society."[5] The principle of justice, this suggests, is a transcendent ideal, a universal norm arising from the vision of a just society. With this point Kohlberg circles back to the themes promised in his opening sentences:

We have stressed so far the place of universal principles of human justice as central to moral development, principles which can be defined and justified without reference to a specific religious tradition. We need now to note that while Socrates and Martin Luther King died for principles of human justice, they were also deeply religious men. What, then, is the relation of the development of religious faith to the development of moral principles?[6]

At this juncture in his 1974 text, Kohlberg introduces the fledgling work on stages of faith development of his then Harvard colleague James Fowler, myself. He quoted an early version of our stage theory *in extenso,* but without any attention to what we mean by "faith." In order to discuss some of the relations between moral development and faith, and between stages of moral judgment and possible stages in faith, let me present an introduction to the focus of our work in its present form.

THE FOCUS ON FAITH

I begin with three brief case synopses.
Case Number 1:

A woman in her mid-twenties tells her story. "The years from seventeen to twenty-two were my lost years, the years I searched and tried everything, but accomplished nothing. I tried sex, illicit drugs, Eastern religions, the occult, everything. I filled myself with vain knowledge, but gained nothing as far as my real spiritual hunger was concerned." At twenty-two, eight months after "an extraordinary experience on L.S.D.," and after having two persons close to her witness to the lordship of Jesus Christ, she accepted him as her Lord. Her story of the next five years resembles those of many in her generation: movement from one new Christian, true church movement to another; submission to the often conflicting authority of self-appointed Christian elders and to the disciplines of neo-Christian group life. She suffered the psychological violence inflicted by newly converted folk who, in radically denying their own pasts and affirming their new beings in Christ, projected much of the horror and guilt of what they denied in themselves onto others. Her odyssey carried her through at least four such groups before she found one led by mature Christians. At the encouragement of one ill-prepared leader, she had married a man she hardly knew, and for two years "submitted" to horrendous marital anarchy and degradation. Through it all, she affirms, "The Lord never left me bereft. He was leading me, teaching me, shaping me." Though raw and hurting, her faith in the Lord more than ever occupies the center of her efforts to discern what she should do next and to know how to think of herself. "I just pray that the Lord will show me the ministry he has for me."

Case Number 2:

A small-town merchant pours six long days a week into the management of his clothing store. A kind man with a friendly and helpful attitude, his business flourishes. He belongs to a local church and contributes generously. He belongs to a local civic association and gives modestly of his time to its projects. He is a respected member of the town's Chamber of Commerce, and is admired as a progressive force in the refurbishing of Main Street. One day his son, intending it as a joke, gives the attentive observer a frightening clue: "Daddy," he says, "doesn't have a thing except Mama that he wouldn't sell if the price were right!" And this was true. It would be too extreme to speak of money in his case as a fetish, but clearly his son had named the center of the father's value system. And the other involvements and extensions of self—even to the extent of caring financially for an alcoholic brother—served this central devotion to enlarging his "estate."

Case Number 3:

The fourth of ten children born to an Irish-Italian marriage, Jack grew up in "the Projects." "There were so many of us boys that people never knew our first names. They just called us 'Seely' (not the real name). My voice sounded so much like my brothers that sometimes even I got confused." Under the influence of the Sisters in parochial school he became, during his late childhood and early adolescence, a faithful churchgoer. "One year," he said, "I made mass every day and did two novenas, which was hard. I got up early every day and went over there; I never sat on the bench, but always stayed on my knees. I felt like I was one of Jesus' special kids. I liked it, and I kind of made a bargain that I would do all this for him if he would sort of straighten my dad's drinking out a little bit. He would go out on Friday, Saturday, and Sunday nights and come back drunk. Sometimes he beat mother when they argued." At the end of his seventh grade year Sister called him up to the front of the room and publicly recognized him as the only boy who had been faithful in attending mass daily throughout the spring. "She should'na done that," he said. "They got me then, the bullies. They gave me a hard time for the next two years. I quit going to church. But I guess it was just as well. The old man didn't ease up on the drinking. In fact, he started going out on Thursday nights too!" Today, near thirty, still out of church, he lives in a nice but confining low-cost private housing project. Every thirty seconds during most of the day the large jets taking off or landing at the nearby airport shake the windows in their apartment. He and his wife lead the Tenants Association in its struggle against rent-gouging landlords. They have helped organize tenant groups all over their part of the city, and, for their troubles, have two separate $1 million suits against them initiated by landlord associations. His $12,000 per year job and her nightly work as a waitress keep them both very busy. "Blacks and poor white people need to get together here. We've been pitted against each other, to *their* advantage, for too long. I don't know much theory; I can't talk about Hegel and philosophy, and I don't know Marx too good. But I do know my class and I know we're getting stepped on. Me and my wife want to give everything we got to giving poor folks a break. And while we do it, we gotta remember that there are people under us too, people worse off. We may be in the alley fighting, but down below in the cellar somewhere they are fighting for a chance to breathe, too. We gotta be careful not to step on them."

These are vignettes on faith; windows into the organizing images and value patterns by which people live. The stories let us in on their life wagers. They give us access to the ways three persons are pouring out their life energies—spending and being spent in the service of valued projects, in light of which their own value and worth as persons seek confirmation.

In this way of thinking, faith need not be approached as necessarily a religious matter. Nor need it be thought of as doctrinal belief or assent. Rather, faith becomes the designation for a way of leaning into life. It points to a way of making sense of one's existence. It denotes a way giving order and coherence to the force-field of life. It speaks of the investment of life-grounding trust and of life-orienting commitment.

Now let us look at these matters a little more systematically. This way of approaching faith means to imply that this phenomenon is a human universal. That is to say, as members of a species burdened with consciousness and self-consciousness, and with freedom to name and organize the phenomenal world, we nowhere can escape the task of forming tacit or explicit coherent images of our action-worlds. We are born into fields of forces impinging upon us from all sides. The development of perception means a profound limiting and selection of the *sensa* to which we can consciously or unconsciously attend. The development of cognition—understood here in its broadest sense—means the construction of operations of thought and valuing in accordance with which the *sensa* to which we attend are organized and formed. Composition and interpretation of meanings, then, are the inescapable burdens of our species. Consciously or unconsciously, in this process, we invest trust in powerful images which unify our experience, and which order it in accordance with interpretations that serve our acknowledgment of centers of value and power.

We encounter this force-field of life in the presence of others. From the beginning others *mediate* in our interaction with the conditions of our existence. Somatic contact, gestures, words, rituals from other persons—all serve to link us with aspects of the surrounding environment. And before we can think with words or symbols, primitive images or pre-images of felt "sense" begin to form in us. Therefore we must think of even our earliest steps toward interpretation and meaning as shared, as social.

Reflection on this social character of even our earliest moves toward construction of meaning points to another important feature of faith. Our investment of reliance upon, or trust in, interpretative images does not occur apart from our investment of reliance upon or trust in the significant others who are companions or mediators in our acts of meaning construction. Faith involves, from the beginning, our participation in what we may call tacit, covenantal, fiduciary relationships. Put another way, our interpretations of and responses to events which disclose the conditions of our existence are formed in the company of co-interpreters and co-respondents whom we trust and to whom we are loyal. Faith is a relational matter. As we relate to the conditions of our existence with acts of interpretative commitment, we do so as persons also related to and co-involved with companions whom we trust and to whom we are loyal. This means that the interpretative images by which we make sense of the conditions of our lives inevitably implicate our companions. It also means, reciprocally, that our experiences with these companions in interpretation have decisive impact on the forming and re-forming of our interpretative images and for the values and powers they serve.

Let us designate those images by which we holistically grasp the conditions of our existence with the name *images of the ultimate environment.* And let us point out that such images of the ultimate environment derive their unity and their principle of coherence from a center (or centers) of value and power to which persons of faith are attracted with conviction. Faith then, is a matter of composing an image of the ultimate environment, through the commitment of self to a center (or centers) of value and power giving it coherence. We do this in interaction with communities of co-interpreters and co-commitants. And our commitments so made with the interpretative impacts they carry, become occasions for the re-ordering of our loves and the re-directing of our spending and being spent.

We have intended in these paragraphs on faith to present it as a dynamic phenomenon. Faith is an ongoing process. It is a way of being and of leaning into life. Crises, disclosure-events, the fulfillment or failure of hopes, betrayals and experiences of fidelity in the force-field of life continually impact a person's image of the ultimate environment and his or her commitment to the value-, or power-center(s) sustaining it. Conversion or re-conversion in small or large ways can be precipitated without conscious desire or intent. Confusion, doubt, and the conflicts of double or multiple pulls to commitment represent inherent dynamics of faith. And for most of us our controlling image of the ultimate environment is likely to be as much an aspiration to worthy and true faith as it is an accomplished and integrated reality of faith. Competing master images of the ultimate environment contend for loyalty in societies and cultures, and within individual human breasts.

Let us try to bring this introductory characterization of faith into summary focus. Faith, we may say, is

—a disposition of the total self toward the ultimate environment

—in which trust and loyalty are invested in a center or centers of value and power

—which order and give coherence to the force-field of life, *and*

—which support and sustain (or qualify and relativize) our mundane or everyday commitments and trusts

—combining to give orientation, courage, meaning, and hope to our lives, and

—to unite us into communities of shared interpretation, loyalty, and trust.[7]

FAITH AND MORAL REASONING

Before we go on to the matters of stages of faith in relation to stages of moral reasoning we should examine some conceptual and phenomenal relations between faith and moral reasoning. I am claiming that we human beings necessarily engage in constructing frames of meaning for our lives, and that we do this, with others, by making tacit and/or explicit commitments to value-and-power centers which promise to sustain our lives and meanings. This activity I call faith. Faith is a valuing and a committing; it is axiological and volitional. But it is also a knowing—a composing, a construing, an interpreting. Faith, like moral judgment, has an important epistemological dimension.[8]

Kohlberg recognizes this in the latter parts of "Education, Moral Development and Faith." There he introduces—for the only time in published form that I am aware of—reference to a metaphorical, nonmoral "stage 7." He introduces this intriguing notion after having reiterated his belief that moral principles can be formulated and justified without reliance upon faith or religion. He says:

> In some sense, however, to ultimately live up to moral principles requires faith. For this reason, we believe, the ultimate exemplars of stage 6 morality also appear to be men of faith.... I believe then, like Kant, that ultimate moral principles, stage 6 morality, can and should be formulated and justified on

grounds of autonomous moral rationality. Such morality, however, "requires" an ultimate stage of faith and moves men toward it. The faith orientation required by universal moral principles I call stage 7, though at this point the term is only a metaphor. This faith orientation does not basically change the definition of universal principles of human justice found at stage 6, but it integrates them with a perspective on life's ultimate meaning.[9]

In other writings Kohlberg has held that the critical question, "Why be moral?" is answered from within the logic of stages one through five. In "Moral Stages and Moralization," for example, he includes a chart which provides one of the most recent accounts of stage specific "reasons for doing right."[10] At stage 1 the person "does right" in order to avoid punishment and because of the superior power of authorities. At stage 3, one is moral because of "the need to be a good person in your own eyes and those of others. . . . " Adherence to the requirements of justice at stage 5 derives from "a sense of obligation to law because of one's social contract to make and abide by laws for the welfare of all and for the protection of all peoples' rights."[11] Kohlberg nowhere claims that these motivational factors *exhaustively* account for persons' adherence to the requirements of right or justice. But clearly he wants to avoid any suggestion that moral judgments are essentially dependent upon the particular contents of a person's or group's values, attitudes, world view, or religious orientation.

At stage 6, however, Kohlberg sees no rationale inherent in universal moral principles by which to answer the question, "Why be moral?" The answer to this question at stage 6, he has often said in public discussions, is always a religious answer. In "Education, Moral Development and Faith," he puts it this way:

I have argued that the answer to the question, "Why be moral?" at this level entails the question, "Why live?" (and the parallel question, "How face death?") so that ultimate moral maturity requires a mature solution to the question of the meaning of life. This, in turn, is hardly a moral question per se, it is an ontological or religious one.[12]

"Solutions" to these ontological or religious questions, Kohlberg points out, cannot be reached on purely logical or rational grounds.

They represent ways of seeing the human situation in relation to a more transcending framework of meaning and value. In Kohlberg's language:

The characteristic of all these stage 7 solutions is that they involve contemplative experience of a nondualistic variety. The logic of such experience is sometimes expressed in theistic terms of union with God but it need not be. Its essential is the sense of being a part of the whole of life and the adoption of a cosmic, as opposed to a universal humanistic "stage 6" perspective. [13]

He turns then to an example of stage 7 faith constituted by the Stoic, mystical resignation of the *Meditations of Marcus Aurelius*.

In private, and in a brief published statement, [14] I have expressed my agreement with Kohlberg in his claim that moral stage 6 implies an accompanying faith vision and faith commitment. I am glad for his recognition that commitment to principled morality is part of a more comprehensive stance or disposition toward the ultimate conditions of our lives. But this recognition, I contend, does not go far enough. The question, "Why be moral?" cannot be answered adequately within the terms of *any* of Kohlberg's stages without reference to a person's commitments to a wider frame of meaning and value. There is a faith context—as I characterize the term faith—informing and supporting a person's consistent adherence to justice, the right or the good, as discerned through the logic of *any* of the stages of moral reasoning.

Let us consider a few examples. In stage 1, Kohlberg tells us, the child's reason for doing good is to avoid punishment and to be rewarded. Also there is deference—presumably a mixture of fear and respect—for the superior physical power of authorities. I am inclined to believe Kohlberg is right as regards the epistemology of moral judgment at this stage. Children do determine what is right by reference to the punishment and reward responses of parents or parentlike adults. But surely the issue of why the child wants to be good, or is interested at all, requires us to go further. My own research with children leads me to suggest that because of ties of dependence and affection, and because of the preoperational child's imitative interest in adult behaviors and values, there is already forming by stage 1 what I call a rudimentary loyalty to the *child's construction* of her or his family's "ethos of goodness." For punishment and reward to make any sense to the child, and for it to contribute to moral growth, it must be linked to a framework of shared meaning and value, no matter how primitively construed by the child. Otherwise we have no way to account for the generalization of experiences of punishment and reward into "improved behavior" across the board, or for the child's countless adoptions of desirable behavior patterns for which there have been no specific occasions of positive or negative sanction. Moral decision or choice for the preschool and early school child, I am arguing, is already beginning to be lodged in a framework of meaning and value, and is part of the child's way of participating in the faith ethos of his or her family or family surrogate.

At moral stage 2, Kohlberg tells us, persons are moral "To serve one's own needs or interests in a world where you have to recognize that other people have their interests too."[15] Stage 2's instrumental hedonism, with its reciprocity of perspectives and its recognition of others' claims, represents the child's first constructions of "fairness." Surely with these insights Kohlberg contributes something extremely valuable to our understanding of the epistemology underlying the child's conception of fairness. But as an account of why the child becomes committed to fairness as a normative principle, it is plainly incomplete. It sheds very little light on why the child feels that some ligament of the universe has been torn if he or she, or a friend, or even a stranger, is treated unfairly. Here again, I submit that the child's adherence to fairness as a valued and respected norm bespeaks a broader frame of meaning and value through which the child finds coherence in life and maintains a sense of worthy membership in a valued group.

In other writings[16] I have followed theologian H. Richard Niebuhr and philosopher Josiah Royce in claiming that any lasting human relation or association has a fiduciary or faith structure. By this I mean initially that as selves we maintain our identities through relations of reciprocal trust in and loyalty to significant others. Our mutual investments of trust and loyalty with these others, however, are deepened, stabilized, and prevented from having to bear more moral weight than they can sustain, by our shared trusts and loyalties to centers of value and power of more transcendent worth.

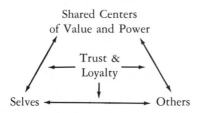

Kohlberg's stages of moral judgment, *especially* through stage 4 and the conventional level, are inexplicable as regards moral motivation and accountability apart from a self's valued membership in groups or communities joined by commitments to meaning frames centering in shared values and images of power.[17]

The stages of faith development to which I now wish to turn, represent our effort to describe a series of stagelike "styles" in which persons participate in the activity of meaning-making and in communities of shared meaning and value. From this perspective, faith stages are to be understood as formal (i.e., content-free) descriptions of the operations of knowing and valuing underlying a person's composing and maintenance of a meaning-value perspective. As such, a faith stage includes and contextualizes a form of moral reasoning such as that characterized in the corresponding Kohlberg stage. After examining the overview of faith stages, we will look briefly at some theoretically predicted and empirically determined relations between the faith stages and stages of moral reasoning.

STAGES OF FAITH

We are going to examine here stages of faith development as we have identified them in the course of seven years of research. Our research procedure has been described in detail elsewhere.[18] Briefly, we employ a semiclinical, open-ended interview of one to three hours (somewhat briefer with children) in which the respondent is asked to share aspects of his or her life history and to express in detail his or her feelings and attitudes regarding a cluster of universal life-issues with which faith must deal. (The list of issues: death and afterlife; the limits of knowledge; causation and effectance in personal and historical life; evil and suffering; freedom and determinism; power and agency; meaning of life; ideal manhood or womanhood; the future; grounding of ethical and moral imperatives; communal identifications and belongings; bases of guilt and shame; central loyalties and commitments; locus of transcendent beauty, value, or power; objects of reverence or awe; grounds of terror or dread; sin and violation; religious experiences, beliefs, and practices; specific meaningful religious symbols.) This list is uniformly pursued in each interview. Respondents are encouraged to share concrete experiences and crises out of their own lives, and to address the faith issues experientially whenever possible. Though respondents often voluntarily answer in specifically religious terms, religion as an issue and context is not explicitly introduced until the last one-third of the interview. An effort is made to test espoused beliefs, values, and attitudes against self-reports of performance and choice in actual situations.

These interviews are then transcribed. Analysis for structural features is carried out by trained scorers. The formulations of position and outlook in relation to the faith issues are regarded as the *contents* of the person's faith. A thematic or content analysis can be carried out and systematized in order to understand the person's faith or belief system. Structural analysis, however, aims to go "under" the content elements to "liberate" the deeper structural operations of knowing and valuing which underlie, ground, and organize the thematic content.

We have conducted and analyzed about 380 interviews of the type just described. The sample has been cross-sectionally balanced for age from four to eighty. It includes slightly more females than males, includes Protestants, Catholics, Jews, atheists, and agnostics (in representative numbers), several Western adherents of Eastern traditions, and has a reasonable range of educational, social class, and ethnic variations. We have begun to follow a select longitudinal sample at five-year intervals, but have only limited longitudinal data so far. We have not conducted cross-cultural investigations. Therefore the stage descriptions we offer here must still be considered as provisional.

In this context, what do we mean by the term "stage"? In contemporary usage this word has a lot of meanings. Here we intend by it the following: *one of a sequence of formally describable "styles" of composing an ultimate environment, of committing the self to centers of value and power, of symbolizing and expressing those commitments, and of relating them to the valued perspectives of others.* We speak of stages rather than of types because we believe that the stage sequence we have identified is invariant. That is, we believe the stages come in the order presented here and that persons do not skip over a stage. Please notice that we say "formally describable." This means that a stage is not defined by a particular *content* of belief or valuing. Rather, a stage is a particular *way* or organizing, composing, or of giving form to the contents of beliefs or values. Stage descriptions focus on the *how* of faith rather than on the *what* or the content of faith.

Stages are not "there" like a set of stair-steps to climb up. To make a transition from one stage to another is to undergo the often painful process of giving up one's familiar and comfortable ways of making meaning and sustaining commitment. Transition means a kind of coming apart as well as a new construction. Periods of transition can be protracted over several years.

Let me make one other potentially confusing matter clear. Many stage theories, such as Erikson's "Eight Ages of the Life Cycle,"[19] tie the movement from one stage to another directly to chronological age and biological maturation. Particularly in the earlier stages which, for Erikson, are most directly psycho-sexual stages, maturation sets the pace and precipitates the movement from one stage to another. Our stages, like Piaget's and Kohlberg's, are dependent upon age and maturation in that these factors provide some of the *necessary* conditions for stage transition. But they are not *sufficient* conditions. Other factors, such as the richness and stimulation of the environment, the availability of models of the next "place," and "catch" a subject as to correct a test-taking set to choose items on the person's encounter with crises or dilemmas which shake up his or her faith outlook, play significant roles in determining the rate and timing of stage changes. To show what this means, it is not too unusual to find normal persons who are chronologically and biologically adult, but whose patterns of faith can best be described by our stage 2. This is a stage that typically arises during the years from seven to eleven. We are suggesting that "normal" persons may equilibrate or arrest in faith growth at any of these stages from the second stage on. Certain factors in maturation must occur before the school child is ready for transition to stage 3, but maturation and age, by themselves, do not guarantee readiness for the next stage.

Now we are ready to examine an overview of this sequence of stages. The description of each stage will include a general characterization. This will be followed by a somewhat more detailed elaboration. Then, briefly, we will suggest some of the signs of transition to the next stage.[20]

Undifferentiated Faith

The preconceptual, largely prelinguistic stage in which the infant unconsciously forms a disposition toward its world.

> Trust, courage, hope, and love are fused in an undifferentiated way and contend with sensed threats of abandonment, inconsistencies, and deprivations in the infant's environment. Though really a prestage, and largely inaccessible to empirical inquiry of the kind we pursue, the quality of mutuality and the strength of trust, autonomy, hope, and courage (or their opposites) developed in this phase, underlie (or undermine) all that comes later in faith development.

Transition to stage 1 begins with the convergence of thought and language, opening up the use of symbols in speech and ritual play.

Stage 1. Intuitive-Projective Faith

The fantasy-filled, imitative phase in which the child can be powerfully and permanently influenced by the examples, moods, actions, and language of the visible faith of primal adults.

The stage most typical of the child of three to seven, it is marked by a relative fluidity of thought patterns. The child is continually encountering novelties for which no stable operations of knowing have been formed. The imaginative processes underlying fantasy are unrestrained and uninhibited by logical thought. In league with forms of knowing dominated by perception, imagination in this stage is extremely productive of long-lasting images and feelings (positive and negative) which later, more stable and self-reflective valuing and thinking will have to order and sort out. This is the stage of first self-awareness. The "self-aware" child is egocentric as regards the perspectives of others. Here we find the first awarenesses of death and sex, and of the strong taboos by which cultures and families insulate those powerful areas.

The emergence of "concrete operational" thinking underlies the transition to stage 2. Affectively, the resolution of Oedipal issues or their submersion in latency are important accompanying factors. At the heart of the transition is the child's growing concern to *know* how things are and to clarify for himself or herself the bases of distinctions between what is real and what only "seems to be."

Stage 2. Mythic-Literal Faith

The stage in which the person begins to take on for himself or herself the stories, beliefs, and observances which symbolize belonging to his or her community. Beliefs are appropriated with literal interpretations, as are moral rules and attitudes. Symbols are taken as one-dimensional and literal in meaning.

In this stage the rise of "concrete operations" leads to the curbing and ordering of the previous stage's imaginative composing of the world. The episodic quality of intuitive-projective faith gives way to a more linear, narrative construction of coherence and meaning. Story becomes the major way of giving unity and value to experience. This is the faith stage of the school child (though we sometimes find its structures dominant in adolescents and in adults). Marked by increased accuracy in taking the perspective of other persons, stage 2 composes a world based on reciprocal fairness and an immanent justice based on reciprocity. The actors in its cosmic stories are full-fledged anthropomorphic "personalities." Those in this stage can be affected deeply and powerfully by symbolic and dramatic materials, and can describe in endlessly detailed narrative what has occurred. Stage 2 does not, however, step back from the flow of its stories to formulate reflective, conceptual meanings. For this stage the meaning is both carried and "trapped" in the narrative.

The implicit clash or contradictions of stories leads to reflection on meanings. The transition to "formal operational" thought makes such reflection possible and necessary. Previous literalism breaks down; new "cognitive conceit" (Elkind) leads to disillusionment with previous teachers and teachings. Conflicts between authoritative stories (i.e., Genesis on creation vs. evolutionary theory) must be faced. The emergence of mutual interpersonal perspective-taking ("I see you seeing me; I see me as you see me; I see you seeing me seeing you") creates the need for a more personal relationship with the unifying power of the ultimate environment.

Stage 3. Synthetic-Conventional Faith

The person's experience of the world now extends beyond the family. A number of spheres demand attention: family, school or work, peers, street society and media, and perhaps religion. Faith must provide a coherent orientation in the midst of that more complex and diverse range of involvements. Faith must synthesize values and information; it must provide a basis for identity and outlook.

> Stage 3 typically has its rise and ascendancy in adolescence, but for many adults it becomes a permanent equilibration. It structures the ultimate environment in interpersonal terms. Its images of unifying value and power derive from the extension of qualities experienced in personal relationships. It is a "conformist" stage in the sense that it is acutely tuned to the expectations and judgments of significant others, and as yet does not have a sure enough grasp on its own identity and autonomous judgment to construct and maintain an independent perspective. While beliefs and values are deeply felt, they typically are tacitly held—the person "dwells" in them and the meaning world they mediate. But there has not been occasion to reflectively step outside them so as to examine them explicitly or systematically. At stage 3 a person has an "ideology," a more or less consistent clustering of values and beliefs, but he or she has not objectified it for examination, and in a sense is unaware of having it. Differences of outlook with others are experienced as differences in "kind" of person. Authority is located in the incumbents of traditional authority-roles (if perceived as personally worthy) or in the consensus of a valued, face-to-face group.

Factors contributing to the breakdown of stage 3 and to readiness for transition may include any one or more of the following: serious clashes or contradictions between valued authority sources; marked changes, by officially sanctioned leaders, of policies or practices previously deemed sacred and unbreachable (e.g., in the Catholic church, changing the mass from Latin to the vernacular, or no longer requiring abstinence from meat on Friday); the encounter with experiences or perspectives that lead to critical reflection on how one's beliefs and values have formed and changed, and on how "relative" they are to one's particular group or background.

Stage 4. Individuative-Reflective Faith

The movement from stage 3 to stage 4 is particularly critical, for it is in this transition that the late adolescent or adult must begin to take seriously the burden of responsibility for his or her own commitments, lifestyle, beliefs, and attitudes. Where genuine movement toward stage 4 is underway, the person must face certain unavoidable tensions: individuality vs. being defined by a group or group membership; subjectivity and the power of one's strongly felt but unexamined feelings vs. objectivity and the requirement of critical reflection; self-fulfillment or self-actualization as a primary concern vs. service to and being for others; the question of being committed to the relative vs. struggle with the possibility of an absolute.

This stage most appropriately takes form in young adulthood (but let us remember that many adults do *not* construct it and that for a significant group it emerges only in the mid-thirties or forties). This stage is marked by a double development. The self, previously sustained in its identity and faith compositions by an interpersonal circle of significant others, now claims an identity no longer defined by the composite of one's roles or meanings to others. To sustain that new identity it composes a meaning frame conscious of its own boundaries and inner connections, and aware of itself as a "worldview." Self (identity) and outlook (worldview) are differentiated from those of others, and become acknowledged factors in the reactions, interpretations, and judgments one makes on the actions of the self and others. The self expresses its intuitions of coherence in an ultimate environment in terms of an explicit system of meanings. Stage 4 typically translates symbols into conceptual meanings. This is a "demythologizing" stage. The self is likely to attend minimally to unconscious factors influencing its judgments and behaviors.

Restless with the self-images and outlook maintained by stage 4, the person ready for transition finds him/herself attending to what may feel like anarchic and disturbing inner voices. Elements from a childish past, images and energies from a deeper self, a gnawing sense of the sterility and flatness of the meanings one serves—any or all of these may signal readiness for something new. Stories, symbols, myths paradoxes from one's own or other traditions may insist on breaking in upon the neatness of the previous faith. Disillusionment with one's compromises, and recognition that life is more complex than stage 4's logic of clear distinctions and abstract concepts can comprehend, press one toward a more dialectical and multileveled approach to life-truth.

Stage 5. Paradoxical-Consolidative Faith

This stage involves the integration into self and outlook of much that was suppressed or evaded in the interest of stage 4's self-certainty and conscious cognitive and affective adaptation to reality. This stage develops a "second naivete" (Ricoeur) in which symbolic power is reunited with conceptual meanings. Here there must also be a new reclaiming and reworking of one's past. There must be an opening to the voices of one's "deeper self." Importantly, this involves a critical recognition of one's *social* unconscious—the myths, ideal images, and prejudices built deeply into the self-system by virtue of one's being nurtured within a particular social class, religious tradition, ethnic group, or the like.

Unusual before midlife, stage 5 knows the sacrament of defeat and the reality of irrevocable commitments and acts. What the previous stage struggled to clarify, in terms of the boundaries of self and outlook, this stage now makes porous and permeable. Alive to paradox and the truth in apparent contradictions, this stage strives to unify opposites in mind and experience. It generates and maintains vulnerability to the strange truths of those who are "other."

Ready for closeness to that which is different and threatening to self and outlook (including new depths of experience in spirituality and religious revelation), this stage's commitment to justice is freed from the confines of tribe, class, religious community, or nation. And with the seriousness that can arise when life is more than half over, this stage is ready to spend and be spent for the cause of conserving and cultivating the possibility of others' generating identity and meaning.

Stage 5 can appreciate symbols, myths and rituals (its own and others') because it has been grasped, in some measure, by the depth of reality to which they refer. It also sees the divisions of the human family vividly because it has been apprehended by the possibility (and imperative) of an inclusive community of being. But this stage remains divided. It lives and acts between an untransformed world and a transforming vision and loyalties. In some few cases this division yields to the call of the radical actualization that we call stage 6.

Stage 6. Universalizing Faith

This stage is exceedingly rare. The persons best described by this stage have generated faith compositions in which their felt sense of an ultimate environment is inclusive of all being. They become incarnators and actualizers of the spirit of a fulfilled human community.

They are "contagious" in the sense that they create zones of liberation from the social, political, economic, and ideological shackles we place and endure on human futurity. Living with felt participation in a power that unifies and transforms the world, universalizers are often experienced as subversive of the structures (including religious structures) by which we sustain our individual and corporate survival, security, and significance. Many persons in this stage die at the hands of those whom they hope to change. Universalizers are often more honored and revered after death than during their lives. The rare persons who may be described by this stage have a special grace that makes them seem more lucid, more simple, and yet somehow more fully human than the rest of us. Their community is universal in extent. Particularities are cherished because they are vessels of the universal, and are thereby valuable apart from any utilitarian considerations. Life is both loved and held to loosely. Such persons are ready for fellowship with persons at any of the other stages and from any other faith tradition.

MORAL STAGES AND THE DEVELOPMENT OF FAITH

As I conceive them, the faith stages are more comprehensive constructs than are the Kohlberg stages of moral reasoning. A faith
stage is meant to integrate operations of knowing and valuing which
underlie and give form to the contents of a person's system of
meaning. As such, faith stages represent modes of knowing, commitment, and action, in which thought and emotion, rationality and passionality, are held together. This does not mean, as some
critics have suggested, that faith is an irrational or a'rational matter.[21] It does mean, however, that the logic of faith is more comprehensive than the logic of rational certainty characterizing
Piaget's and Kohlberg's cognitive theories. Faith employs images
and ontological intuitions. It relies on historical and present experiences of disclosure and "revelation." Faith works with elements of
religious, philosophical, and ideological traditions. The culture of
myths, symbols, and ritual are part of its media. These elements
faith interrogates by means of rational operations testing for sense
and consistency. The resulting "logic of conviction" (as I have called
it elsewhere)[22] is open to ongoing tests for existential validity,
generalizable truth, and reflective equilibrium. To recognize that
the logic of conviction has this dialectical character in no way renders it a'rational or irrational. This recognition simply reminds us
that a logic of rational certainty alone cannot resolve ontological and
axiological questions.

Kohlberg's only published response to the stage theory of faith
development in "Education, Moral Development and Faith" seems
uncertain as to how to regard the relation of faith stages to stages of
moral reasoning. In some passages he writes as though faith and
moral judgment stages are two comparable strands of a larger developmental process, such as ego. In other passages he seems to recognize the kind of claim I make here, that faith stages are broader
constructs aiming to comprehend and contextualize stages of moral
judgment. Finally the choice between these options is less important for him than the issues of whether moral judgment stages
precede faith stages (both logically and chronologically) in de-

velopment, and whether faith stage development is *caused* by moral stage change rather than vice versa. Kohlberg—because of his deep concern for the foundations of a nonsectarian approach to moral education in the public schools of the United States—wants to demonstrate that moral reason requires faith rather than that morality derives from faith. In his words,

We may then expect a parallel development of faith stages and moral stages. The critical question, both psychologically and philosophically, is whether moral development precedes (and causes) faith development or vice versa. The data on this question is not yet available. We hypothesize, however, that development to a given moral stage precedes development to the parallel faith stage. Psychologically I believe that it takes a long time to work out a moral stage in terms of its elaboration as an organized pattern of belief and feeling about the cosmos which Fowler calls a faith stage. Philosophically I incline to Kant's solution that faith is grounded on moral reason because moral reason "requires" faith rather than that moral reason is grounded on faith.... Universal moral principles cannot be derived from faith because not all men's faith is, or can be, the same.

Moral principles, then, do not require faith for their formulation or for their justification. In some sense, however, to ultimately live up to moral principles requires faith.[23]

Consistant with my understanding of faith stages as the more comprehensive constructs, inclusive of moral judgment making, and drawing on our interview data, my associates and I have distinguished seven structural "aspects" of each faith stage. I have tried to suggest in my longer writings how these aspects undergo transformations from stage to stage.[24] Among these aspects I have included the patterns of cognitive development as identified by Piaget. I have included the stagelike levels of social-perspective taking as researched by Robert Selman.[25] Kohlberg's stages of moral reasoning have been included, showing the broad parallels he predicted, and which we have found, between moral and faith stages. In addition to these three aspects, we have distinguished four others in the integrated operations of a faith stage. They are: (1) the locus of authority, (2) the bounds of social awareness, (3) the form of world coherence, and (4) the role of symbols.[26] In Table 1 we suggest the correspondences we find between these aspects in the faith stages.

Notice that our data supports Kohlberg's prediction that there

TABLE 1: FAITH STAGES BY ASPECTS
(FROM "FAITH AND STRUCTURING OF MEANING")

Aspect / Stage	Form of Logic (Piaget)	Role-Taking (Selman)	Form of Moral Judgment (Kohlberg)	Bounds of Social Awareness	Locus of Authority	Form of World Coherence	Role of Symbols
0			Undifferentiated combination of basic trust, organismic courage, premonitory hope with admixtures of their opposites—preconceptual, prelinguistic mutuality.				
1	Preoperational.	Rudimentary empathy (egocentric).	Punishment—reward.	Family, primal others.	Attachment/dependence relationships. Size, power, visible symbols of authority.	Episodic.	Magical-numinous.
2	Concrete operational.	Simple Perspective taking.	Instrumental hedonism (reciprocal fairness).	"Those like us" (in familial, ethnic, racial, class and religious terms).	Incumbents of authority roles, salience increased by personal relatedness.	Narrative-dramatic.	One-dimensional; literal.
3	Early formal operations.	Mutual Interpersonal.	Interpersonal expectations and concordance.	Composite of groups in which one has interpersonal relationships.	Consensus of valued groups and in personally worthy representatives of belief-value traditions.	Tacit system, felt meanings symbolically mediated, globally held.	Symbols multidimensional; evocative power inheres in symbol.

Opera-tion. (Di-chotomi-zing)	self-selected group or class (social).	spective; Reflective Relativism or class-biased universalism.	compatible communities with congru-ence to self-chosen norms and insights.	ment as informed by a self-ratified ideo-logical perspective. Authorities and norms must be con-gruent with this.	conceptually medi-ated, clarity about boundaries and inner connections of system.	from symbolized. Translated (reduced) to ideations. Evoca-tive power inheres in *meaning* conveyed by symbols.
5 Formal opera-tions. (Dialec-tical)	Mutual with groups, clas-ses and tradi-tions "other" than one's own.	Prior to society, prin-cipled higher law (universal and critical).	Extends be-yond class norms and in-terests. Dis-ciplined ideo-logical vul-nerability to "truths" and "claims" of out-groups and other traditions.	Dialectical joining of judgment-exper-ience processes with reflective claims of others and of various expressions of cumulative human wisdom.	Multisystemic sym-bolic and concep-tual mediation.	Postcritical rejoin-ing of irreducible symbolic power and ideational meaning. Evocative power in-herent in the reality in and beyond sym-bol *and* in the power of unconscious pro-cesses in the self.
6 Formal opera-tions. (Synthe-tic)	Mutual, with the common-wealth of being.	Loyalty to being.	Identification with the species. Trans-narcis-sistic love of being.	In a personal judg-ment informed by the experiences and truths of previous stages, purified of egoic striving, and linked by dis-ciplined intuition to the principle of being.	Unitive actuality felt and participated unity of "One be-yond the many."	Evocative power of symbols actualized through unification of reality mediated by symbols and the self.

will be a close parallel between moral and faith stages. Variations come around stages 3 and 4, however. Up to and through faith stage 3, the parallels are exact. Some faith stage 3s, however (usually men), are best described by moral stage 4. Most faith stage 4s are best described by a position which Kohlberg, for a time, would have called moral "stage 4½," a transitional position exhibiting a relativistic outlook.[27] These persons take account of the need for occasional departures from law or the rules governing systemically defined roles in the service of the "greater good." However, they lack a consistently principled basis for shaping and justifying actions on these occasions. We call this position "reflective relativism" or "class-biased universalism." The latter reference is to persons who recognize higher law principles and claims, but in applying them fall into a pattern of distorting the interests and well-being of other persons and groups by assimilating them to their own, resulting in a kind of moral pseudo-stage 5.

This latter point indicates that moral stage 5, as an intellectual or cognitive construct, is possible at faith stage 4. But a moral stage 5 which integrates and forms a person's consistent moral action appears to be unlikely apart from a faith stage 5. Faith stage 5, we believe, can exhibit either moral stages 5 or 6 with authentic comprehension. Our data on faith stage 5 is far more limited than our studies of faith stages 3, 3(4), 4(3), and 4; therefore, our claims about the relations between faith and moral stages 5 and 6 are more speculative than our claims about the middle stages.

Considerably more detailed data, testing the issue of precedence and cause of development between moral judgment and faith stages, are found in the doctoral dissertation completed by Eugene J. Mischey at the University of Toronto, in 1976.[28] "Faith Development and Its Relationship to Moral Reasoning and Identity Status in Young Adults" is the title of this study. Mischey used the Fowler faith development interview and scoring procedures. He tested for identity status with Marcia's (1966) interview format. In addition he administered Kohlberg's moral dilemmas in a written form, Faulkner and Dejong's Religiosity Scale, and Rotter's Internal-External Locus of Control Scale. His subjects were 30 young adults between the ages of 20 and 35. While we must observe some caution about the adequacy of relying upon pencil and paper measurement of response to Kohlberg's moral dilemmas, Mischey's findings about the relations between faith and moral stages of his respondents are quite interesting. Of the 30 subjects, only 4 showed a level of moral judgment more developed than their faith stage. Interestingly, these 4 were not randomly distributed throughout the sample, but were clustered together in the group Mischey scored as faith stage 3(2). Each of the four scored this way showed a somewhat more fully developed moral judgment stage than faith stage. Nine of his respondents, this time representing faith stages 3, 4(3), 4, and 4(5), showed directly parallel development in faith and moral stages. Surprisingly, 17 of his subjects reflected faith stages more developed than their moral stages.

Most striking in this study are Mischey's findings about the relations between the faith and moral stages and the identity status of his respondents. The 4 subjects whose moral stages exceeded their faith stages in development were the lowest of the sample on both stage scales. In addition, all 4 reflected a *diffuse* pattern of identity. Of those who showed either direct stage parallels (9) or more developed faith stages (17), 4 were described as "mixed" in identity status and 7 showed characteristics of identity "foreclosure." The remaining 15, the most developed by both faith and moral measures, all reflected Marcia's "identity achieved" status. This represents an important independent corroboration of the faith theory's findings about faith stage 4 and individuating identity. It also provides significant light on the question of precedence in faith and moral growth, and concerning the "causes" of the development. Mischey summarizes these implications:

If the present sample of young adults can be considered "random" to the extent that it is not "deviant" in any form or fashion, then it seems that Kohlberg's contention that development to a given moral stage precedes development to the parallel faith stage is open to question. It seems ironical that not *one* individual, who has achieved an identity for himself, tends to score higher on morality than on faith. Consequently it is imperative to ask whether it is truly possible that this sample of individuals fails to provide at least *one* example of where an identity-achieved person is found to be in the process of "working out a moral stage in terms of its elaboration as an organized pattern of belief and feeling about the cosmos which Fowler calls a faith stage." In terms of Kohlberg's perspective it would stand to reason that the present sample should exemplify individuals scoring higher in moral reasoning and in the midst of formulating a parallel faith stage since, as he notes, the faith element is a wider, more comprehensive system of constructs requiring more time and experience; this latter situation would then predicate a lower faith score. The results of the present study, however, show no evidence to validate such an assumption.[29]

Mischey himself acknowledges that while his data provide a basis for questioning Kohlberg's theoretical prediction that moral stages will precede faith stages, and in some sense "cause" them, much more research on these issues is needed. Of most significance is his relation of moral and faith stage to identity formation. Mischey's work supports my claim, made earlier, that forms of moral judgment at each stage are anchored in and supported by the larger frames of meaning and value we call faith. Mischey's work suggests that in young adults who have exercised some choice about the kind of persons they intend to be—and have formed ways of seeing the world and leaning into life that express those intentions—forms of moral judgment which are congruent with these value and belief choices then emerge. He writes:

. . . (T)he present results indicate that ontological issues and perspectives are an integral part of the "developing personality" and that these perspectives significantly contribute to the structuring of one's moral reasoning and behavior. . . . (I)t seems that an individual initially seeks out answers to questions surrounding his existence as a human being and the general purpose of his life before he realizes the *need* to be ethically responsible in society. It seems that if individuals do not find answers or, at the very least, do not come to some general understanding of ontologically based questions, then the incentive or motivation to be morally inclined may be placed in a precarious position. . . . [30]

Clark Power, a research associate of both Kohlberg and Fowler, undertood a careful study of 21 protocols which included both faith and moral dilemma interviews.[31] Power's careful paper delineates the separable but integrally related domains of morality and faith as they appear in these interviews. His sample included Jews,

Catholics, Protestants, and Orthodox (Eastern) representatives, as well as agnostics and atheists. Ten females and 11 males were included, and the interviews were distributed from stages 1–5. Power was only incidentally interested in the question of precedence. He found "a hundred percent agreement between the major faith stage and the major moral stage through stage three. At stage four I found moral stage four only with faith stage four, but moral five with both [faith] stages four and five."[32] Power's paper represents an original clarification of the interrelatedness of moral and faith stages, but is too substantive and nuanced for brief summary. For our purposes his conclusions about the moral and faith domains can be presented and placed alongside those of Mischey.

Referring to faith as a kind of relatedness of human beings to the ultimate conditions of our existence, Power speaks of six functions faith plays in supporting and informing moral judgment. First, faith constitutes an "onlook"—a way of seeing, a mode of interpreting a moral situation. "An onlook can provide an interpretation of a situation which can motivate action."[33] Second, faith represents a sense of commitment. The experience of one's contingency or finitude gives rise, Power argues, to a renewed sense of purpose: "I must be here to do something." Third, faith impacts ethical sensitivity. As Power puts it, "If the order of the universe is sensed as being lawful or loving then we feel that we should conform our spirit so as to be at one with all that is." (I might point out that conversely, and in a less benign sense, a faith vision that sees the universe as ultimately indifferent or hostile would also have powerful determinative impact on moral judgment.) Fourth, faith can offer "the reassurance that ethical actions in an unjust world are not fruitless, that they (may) have some eternal or eschatological significance."[34] Faith requires a complementarity with being, which relativizes the tendency of persons to center their meanings in themselves. Finally, Power suggests, faith functions "to support human action especially in the ambiguities of life when one cannot control or predict the outcomes of one's actions."[35] As a summary of his claims Power writes,

The role of faith in relation to moral judgment would seem to be that of providing the very condition for the possibility of making any moral judgment. That is, in every moral judgment there is an implicit future judgment that the activity of moral judging is in fact necessary. . . . It is the very ground to our ethical judgment which I hold to be the province of faith.[36]

CONCLUSION

Kohlberg has so far opted not to develop a theory of the moral self or of the development of virtue.[37] He has aimed instead to restore that dimension of the natural law tradition which affirms that there is a rational core to moral decision making and action, and that this rational core is universal. Further, he has had a passionate commitment to the development of an approach to moral education which avoids dependence upon specific religious or ideological traditions which could not meet the constitutional requirements regarding separation of church and state. While Kohlberg has been clear that his developmental stages focus upon and are limited to the structures of moral reasoning, he has frequently—especially in connection with his educational writings—propounded a commitment to justice as the unitary virtue (or comprehensive value) in a faith-like moral ideology. His writing about "stage 7" is, in a sense, his owning of a faith vision which sustains and is the culmination of the moral stage sequence.

The faith development theory conceptually and empirically offers a way of broadening Kohlberg's account of moral development. I have suggested here that each moral judgment stage implies and requires anchorage in a more extensive framework of belief and value. We have examined the research of Mischey and Power which corroborates and extends this claim. Our stage theory attempts to describe this sequence of structural approaches to the forming and maintenance of faith visions in formal, non-content-specific terms. I hope Kohlberg and his followers will consider whether the faith theory opens a way to expand the focus of moral development research without jettisoning its heuristic power. I hope those Kohlberg critics who find his research and educational approaches too narrowly cognitive[38] may see in the faith stages a more adequate, though still formally descriptive and normative, model for investigating and sponsoring moral development.

NOTES

1. In *Journal of Moral Education,* Vol. 4, No. 1, pp. 5–16. Cited hereafter as Kohlberg, 1974.

2. See also Kohlberg, "Education for Justice: A Modern Statement of the Platonic View," in Nancy F. and Theodore R. Sizer, Eds., *Moral Education.* Cambridge, Mass.: Harvard University Press, 1970, pp. 57–83.

3. See Kohlberg, "From Is to Ought: How to Commit the Naturalistic Fallacy and Get Away with It in the Study of Moral Development," in T. Mischel, Ed., *Cognitive Development and Epistemology.* New York: Academic Press, 1971, pp. 151–284.

4. Kohlberg, 1974, p. 5.

5. Ibid., p. 10.

6. Ibid., p. 11.

7. For other, more detailed discussions of our understanding of faith, see Fowler, "Stages in Faith: The Structural-Developmental Perspective," in Thomas Hennessy, Ed., *Values and Moral Development.* New York: Paulist Press, 1976, pp. 173–179, and Fowler and Keen, *Life Maps: Conversations on the Journey of Faith,* Waco, Texas: Word Books, 1978, pp. 14–25.

8. See Fowler, "Faith and the Structuring of Meaning," to be published by Silver Burdett as part of a Symposium on Moral and Faith Development in 1980, James W. Fowler, Ed.

9. Kohlberg, 1974, p. 14.

10. In Thomas Lickona, Ed., *Moral Development and Behavior.* New York: Holt, Rinehart and Winston, 1976, pp. 34–35.

11. Ibid.

12. Kohlberg, 1974, pp. 14–15.

13. Ibid. p. 15.

14. See Fowler, "Stages in Faith: The Structural Developmental Perspective," in Hennessy, op.cit., pp. 207–211.

15. Kohlberg in Lickona, op.cit., pp. 34–35.

16. Fowler in *Life Maps* and "Faith and the Structuring of Meaning."

17. See Fowler, *To See the Kingdom: The Theological Vision of H. Richard Niebuhr.* Nashville, Tenn.: Abingdon Press, 1974, especially Ch. 5.

18. Fowler, "Stages in Faith: The Structural Developmental Perspective," in Hennessey, op.cit., pp. 179–183.

19. Erik H. Erikson, *Childhood and Society* (Second Ed.). New York: WW Norton, 1963, Ch. 7.

20. For more detailed accounts of the structural features of the stages and for examples from interviews, see *Life Maps,* pp. 39–95.

21. See the critical perspective of Ernest Wallwork in this volume.

22. See"Faith and the Structuring of Meaning."

23. Kohlberg, 1974, p. 14.

24. *Life Maps;* "Stages in Faith . . . "

25. Robert L. Selman, "The Developmental Conceptions of Interpersonal Relations." Publication of the Harvard-Judge Baker Social Reasoning Project, December, 1974, Vols. I and II. See also Selman, "Social-Cognitive Understanding," in T. Lickona, Ed., *Moral Development and Behavior.* New York: Holt, Rinehart and Winston, 1976, pp. 299–316.

26. For explications of these categories see *Life Maps* and "Faith and the Structuring of Meaning."

27. Kohlberg, "Continuities in Childhood and Adult Moral Development Revisited," in P. B. Baltes and K. W. Schaie, Eds., *Life-Span Developmental Psychology: Personality and Socialization.* New York: Academic Press, 1973, pp. 179–204.

28. Eugene J. Mischey, *Faith Development and Its Relationship to Moral Reasoning and Identity Status in Young Adults.* Unpublished doctoral dissertation, Department of Educational Theory, University of Toronto, 1976.

29. Ibid., pp. 227–28.

30. Ibid., p. 235.

31. Clark Power, Unpublished and untitled paper prepared for presentation at the American Psychological Association Convention, Section 36, San Francisco, August 26, 1977.

32. Power, p. 4.

33. Ibid., p. 47.

34. Ibid.

35. Ibid.

36. Ibid., pp. 47–48.

37. See indications of the promising ways in which he could move in these directions in "Stage and Sequence: The Cognitive-Developmental Approach to Socialization," in David A. Goslin, Ed., *Handbook of Socialization Theory and Research,* Chicago: Rand-McNally, 1969, pp. 347–480. See especially parts 5–10, pp. 397–433.

38. The most helpful of these constructive critiques are those by Paul J. Philibert, "Kohlberg's Use of Virtue," in *International Philosophical Quarterly,* Vol. 15, No. 4, 1975, pp. 455–479; and Andre Guindon, "Moral Development: Form, Content and Self. A Critique of Kohlberg's Sequence." Unpublished paper, 1978.

Chapter 5

Cognitive-Developmental Theory of Moral Development: Metaethical Issues

BRENDA MUNSEY

INTRODUCTION

Lawrence Kohlberg's work on moral judgment has had a major impact on the shape of recent psychological research on morality. His particular metatheoretical presuppositions are undoubtedly the dominant paradigm for cognitive developmentalism's study of moral judgment. This chapter examines cognitive developmental psychology's program for studying moral judgment from the standpoint of its metaethical presuppositions. The issues will be addressed in terms of a comparison of Kohlberg's treatment of the phenomena with an alternative approach to be described in this chapter. Kohlberg's work is guided by a fundamentally different type of normative ethical theory from the pragmatically grounded ethics underlying this proposed alternative. The specific metatheoretical issue to be addressed is the question of whether to tie cognitive developmental psychology's treatment of the development of moral judgment to an ethical rule theory, as does Kohlberg, or to an ethical act theory, as proposed herein. The nature of the act theory/rule theory distinction in ethical theories will be explained in the first section of the chapter, followed by an examination of its

161

significance for cognitive developmental accounts of moral judgment.

Any coherent psychological account of the development of moral judgment is committed to specific philosophical positions regarding the nature of sound moral judgment. A psychologist's claim that an individual's moral judgment has "developed" or "matured" implies that the individual's current moral judgments better fulfill valid normative ethical criteria than did his judgments at some previous reference point. For example, Lawrence Kohlberg's account depicts the process of cognitive moral development as a hierarchy of six stages, the normative structure of each later stage better fulfilling the criteria of formalistic ethics than did that of any previous stage. This process is thought to culminate in stage six, when an individual's moral judgment exemplifies the Kantian-Rawlsian normative ethics which Kohlberg believes best fulfills these formalistic criteria.

Since a satisfactory defense of the normative ethical presuppositions of psychological theories of moral development is based on metaethical criteria, that task must be carried out in the field of moral philosophy. A philosophical claim that a certain normative ethical theory provides the soundest means of handling moral problems is defended in the same general way as is a claim that a certain scientific theory provides the soundest means of handling the particular scientific problems falling under it. Each such theoretical proposal is argued on the basis of the appropriate criteria for assessing when a problem has or has not been adequately resolved; metaethical criteria in the case of normative ethical theories and metascientific criteria in the case of scientific theories. Furthermore, just as we look to the community of scientists for authoritative assessments of the adequacy of a particular theory of physics, so also do we look to the community of moral philosophers for authoritative assessments of normative ethical theories.[1]

The normative ethical presuppositions of Kohlberg's analysis of moral judgment fall within the formalist tradition of ethical theories. Thus Kohlberg's ethics, like all formalistic theories, is an ethical rule theory. However, a rival type of ethical theory, an act theory, could also provide a coherent ethical analysis of the data of cognitive developmental psychology. In this chapter it will be argued that the goals of cognitive developmental psychology would be better served if based on an ethical act theory, rather than rule theory, interpretation of moral development. A brief analysis of the act theory/rule theory issues in ethics will be given below, followed by an examination of their significance for cognitive developmentalism's treatment of moral judgment.

NORMATIVE ETHICS: ACT THEORY AND RULE THEORY

The primary task of a normative ethical theory is to enable persons to make justified singular moral judgments. *Rule theorists* suppose that moral rules are required to justify singular moral judgments; that a necessary part of the evidence one must have to make a warranted moral judgment is a moral rule. In contrast, *act theorists* hold that moral rules are *not* a required part of the evidence justifying the singular judgments falling under them. Rather, justified singular moral judgments can be made merely on the basis of the relevant particular facts involved in a given moral dilemma. General considerations (i.e., moral rules) are not required. The identification of the morally relevant particular facts, while facilitated by moral rules, is logically independent of moral rules.

In this regard, rule theorists would agree with act theorists that making a justified judgment requires knowing the relevant particular facts involved in a given moral dilemma. But unlike act theorists, they believe that knowledge of such particulars, though necessary, is not sufficient for the exercise of sound moral judgment. According to rule theory the morally relevant facts cannot even be identified without moral rules, since it is such rules which make them relevant.[2] In contrast, act theorists hold that the relevant *particular facts* can be identified without moral rules, and that ascertaining the truth of such purported facts is a sufficient justification for singular moral judgments.

Although (according to act theory) moral rules[3] are not a necessary condition for *justifying* moral judgments, they are nevertheless an extremely important part of moral deliberation. They are moral generalizations derived from summarizing our knowledge of the morally relevant particular factors which warranted our past moral judgments. Such "summary" moral rules function as "starting points" in subsequent deliberations and are implicit in our "spontaneous" identification of certain factors as relevant to a justified resolution of a present moral dilemma. However, they do not define our reflective identification of *all* morally relevant factors. It is always possible to recognize *novel situational factors* as relevant to a justified resolution, factors which may not be adequately covered by a present structure of summary moral rules (no matter how "generally" adequate it might be).[4]

This issue concerning the nature of moral rules can be understood as the issue of whether valid moral rules (whatever they are thought to be) are constitutive rules or summary rules. If moral rules are taken to be constitutive rules, then they are thought to define moral reasoning. They would be a set of a priori rules which could not admit of exception. If an exception were admitted to a set of rules regarded to be constitutive, then the set would necessarily have to be regarded as inadequate. A set of constitutive moral rules purportedly specifies *all* categories of facts which are relevant to making a justified moral judgment. Thus, if a justification were given for a certain moral judgment which did not fit into one of the acknowledged categories of morally relevant reasons, it would be *logically impossible* to regard it as a "moral" justification.

If, on the other hand, a set of moral rules is taken to be a set of summary rules, then they could admit of exception. They would be a set of empirical generalizations purportedly identifying the categories of facts which have *tended* to be relevant in making justified moral judgments. Such rules would summarize the content of moral reasoning but would not purport to *define* (a priori) moral justification. Thus, if a justification were given for a certain moral judgment which did not conform to a present set of summary moral rules, it would still be *possible* to call it a "moral" justification.

Given that a set of summary rules "summarize" but do not exhaust all possible moral reasons, then the fact that certain particular considerations do not fall neatly within some preferred structure of morally relevant categories (such as "don't steal," "don't kill," "don't lie," "maximize welfare," "maximize equality," etc.) does not rule out their being identified as "moral grounds" for resolving novel moral dilemmas.

As noted earlier, based on their view of the nature of moral rules, normative ethical theories can be divided into rule theories and act theories. According to rule theories, *there are valid constitutive moral rules,* while according to act theories, *all valid structures of moral rules are summary rules.* Lawrence Kohlberg is a rule theorist, believing that his stage 6 justice structure defines moral justification. The stage 6 structure is taken to be as an a priori criterion for distinguishing *justified* moral judgments from *unjustified* moral judgments—there are no exceptions.[5] In those cases in which justice considerations conflict with other sorts of purportedly relevant facts, an adequate resolution of the dilemma would necessarily give priority to justice. Justice, according to Kohlberg, is "constitutive" of moral justification.

In contrast, ethical act theorists such as John Dewey or Bernard Rosen (see chapter 8) treat all moral rules as summary rules. There are no moral rules which are a priori criteria for distinguishing those facts which are always morally relevant from those which are never morally relevant. Valid summary rules help us identify facts in a situation which are likely to be morally relevant. But actually identifying the particular facts which bear on a justified resolution of a moral dilemma or disagreement must be done situationally.

To avoid a possible confusion, act theory does not say that moral disputes are merely factual disputes (the so-called "naturalistic fallacy") but rather that particular moral disputes are *grounded* in particular factual disputes. The autonomy of morality is preserved. Moral disputes are about moral judgments, about the "moral rightness" of certain acts, about "moral duties" and "moral rights," etc. My position is not that moral claims are *logically* equivalent to scientific claims, but rather that singular moral claims are justified by appeal to *particular* factual matters—rather than by appeal to *general* factual matters, as rule theorists suppose. Let us grant that there is a logical distinction between moral claims, on the one hand, and scientific (factual) claims, on the other. *Both* rule theorists (e.g., W. D. Ross, J. Rawls, or L. Kohlberg) and act theorists (e.g., Bernard Rosen or John Dewey) would agree that moral judgments *are justified by appeal to factual claims.* The difference between them is that rule theorists believe they can specify, a priori, the basic *types of facts* which are relevant to justifying singular moral judgments. Act theorists, on the other hand, believe that any specification of the types of morally relevant facts constitutes a set of a posteriori generalizations about the factors which have tended to be relevant in sound moral judgment.

COGNITIVE-DEVELOPMENTAL PSYCHOLOGY: METATHEORETICAL ASSUMPTIONS

A basic assumption of cognitive-developmental psychology's approach to the genesis of human behavior is the Deweyan assumption that "man is by nature an active organism." Thus, a developmental moral psychology would assume, but would not have to explain, the existence of a first (identified) structure of moral judgment. In other words, a developmental account would *begin* with the first structure of that activity which researchers are able to identify, and the theoretical task would be to try to explain "changes in that initial structure," as well as changes in any subsequent structures. This does not mean that the first structure cannot be explained. For example, genetics or some other branch of psychology might undertake that task. Rather, all that is implied by this assumption is that such is not the task of cognitive-developmental moral psychology.

Lawrence Kohlberg's research on moral judgment, like the Piagetian work on which it is based, exemplifies the cognitive-developmental approach. By analyzing the verbal responses of children to a series of moral dilemmas, Kohlberg specified a "first moral structure." Then by presenting these same and related dilemmas to such subjects at regular intervals through adulthood (and analyzing their responses), Kohlberg concluded that there are five additional structures which emerge. His data purportedly showed that the sequence of the six identified stages is invariant and culturally universal.

There is one additional metatheoretical assumption of cognitive-developmental accounts of moral judgment of special interest for the concerns of the present chapter. Namely, psychologists like Kohlberg assume that there are objective criteria available for assessing the philosophical adequacy of each identified cognitive structure as a mode of resolving moral dilemmas and disagreements. For this purpose, Kohlberg adopted the set of metaethical criteria which he thought provided moral philosophers with a "neutral" basis for determining the better of competing normative ethical theories (e.g., Kantian ethics versus Deweyan ethics). As a result of examining the sequence of structural changes in light of these purportedly objective criteria, he concluded that each new cognitive structure provided a more adequate method of resolving moral dilemmas than did any of the individual's previous structures. From stages 1 through 6, each structural transformation is upward toward increasingly more adequate normative ethical theories.

An analogy with Piaget's study of cognitive scientific development might help to clarify the nature of this moral epistemological assumption. In explaining his data showing structural changes in the growing child's mode of resolving scientific problems, Piaget assumed that there were valid objective criteria available for assessing the relative adequacy of each of the emergent scientific structures he was able to identify. Thus, he used the philosophical criteria thought to be employed by the scientific community to assess the relative merits of competing scientific theories (e.g., to show that Einsteinian physics is better than Newtonian physics).

A psychological account of how individuals develop new modes of moral judgment would not necessarily presuppose that the later structures are more philosophically adequate than their predecessors. For example, a structural transformation might be explained as a function of contingencies of reinforcement with no implication that the new structure provides a sounder moral basis for judgment (than did the former structure). However, suppose purportedly sound philosophical criteria are applied to each of the emergent structures (as did Kohlberg), and it is found that the later structures are also more philosophically adequate. Then that fact would itself become data about cognition, in need of psychological explanation. Then psychology would have to explain not merely how and why a cognitive structure changes, but also how and why such a structure changes into a philosophically better structure. Kohlberg explains this datum by the hypothesis that individuals are "natural philosophers." That is, not only can an individual recognize that another justification is better than one he himself would "spontaneously" give; he tends to prefer the better one, and his present structure gets reconstructed accordingly.[6]

Given the above assumptions, together with their "data to be explained," we can now formulate the theoretical question asked by cognitive-developmental psychologists as follows: *Given that each successive change in an individual's structure of moral deliberation is toward a more (philosophically) adequate structure, how and why do such changes occur?*

According to Kohlberg, the emergence of each new normative structure is to be explained as a function of transactions between an individual's present structure and the objective features of the moral dilemmas actually arising in his or her social environment. Kohlberg claims that an individual's present moral structure largely determines the form of reasoning used in resolving present moral problems. However, he also claims that individuals sometimes recognize when their own proposed arguments are an inadequate basis for resolving present moral dilemmas. Specifically, Kohlberg's account grants that it is possible for individuals at stages 1 through 5 to deliberate about the objective features of particular moral dilemmas, with a degree of independence of their present moral structure. (The possibility of objectively examining and judging the soundness of proposed moral arguments, including one's own, is the possibility of doing moral philosophy.)

Data showing that individuals at times specify morally relevant grounds for resolving dilemmas with a degree of independence of their present moral structures are part of Kohlberg's (psychological) explanation of their construction of new and better structures. According to Kohlberg, individuals at the first five stages can, upon reflection, recognize the relative inadequacy of their own proposals for resolving specific moral dilemmas.[7] Through a process in which they encounter and recognize the greater adequacy of alternative proposals for resolving given moral problems, individuals ultimately construct new structures of moral norms which cover those arguments "perceived to be better" than their own. Given that it is possible for an individual who has attained any one of the first five stages to recognize "as better" a moral argument not yet covered by his or her own present structure, then none of those structures could be said to *define* that individual's (present) "perception of moral reasons." It would be logically inconsistent to hold that an individual could appreciate particular justifications not yet covered by her present moral structure, while holding that her present structure *defines* her perception of moral justification. If a given normative structure were to function as a definition of moral judgment, it would not merely summarize an individual's past moral reasoning (and her "unreflective" response to present dilemmas), it would exhaust her perception of all possible sound moral reasons.

Given the assumed hierarchal nature of cognitive moral stages, the capacity to recognize that a proposed moral argument is better than one's own spontaneous proposal could not be sufficiently explained in terms of an individual's present moral structure (since that acquired structure presumably does not cover the "better" argument). Rather, if would have to be explained in terms of the "yet to be constructed" new structure which the individual is presumed to be "building." An adequate analysis of the process whereby an individual "stands apart from his own acquired structure of moral rules" and assesses whether a particular judgment based on those norms is as warranted as is a judgment made on some other basis, presupposes sound metaethical criteria. Moreover, the fact that individuals tend to prefer philosophically more adequate arguments over their own spontaneous proposals can be taken as evidence that sound metaethical criteria underlie their preferences and are implicit in their assessment process.

In keeping with the tenets of cognitive-developmental psychology, Kohlberg's account assumes that some such "objective" criteria are operant in individuals' active reconstruction of their present moral stage.[8] He claims that the "deep structure" of this process parallels the "deep structure of systems of normative ethics." However, the difficulty with the purportedly "neutral" metaethical theory Kohlberg adopts as a basis for interpreting the greater adequacy of each successive stage, is that it is hardly neutral! The metaethical criteria which he identifies as the "deep structure" of moral philosophy turn out to be criteria agreeable to only one tradition of normative theories in moral philosophy, namely ethical rule theories.

Kohlberg apparently arrived at his particular ethical analysis of moral stages in the following way. He adopted what he thought to be the "neutral" metaethical criteria employed by philosophers in assessing whether one normative ethical theory is better than another. Given that applying these philosophical criteria to his identified stages showed that each successive structure better fulfills the criteria than did the previous one, Kohlberg concluded that these very criteria must be implicit in the psychological process of constructing each new structure. In short, by successfully applying the purportedly neutral criteria of moral philosophy to the observed sequence of structural changes, Kohlberg inferred that the "deep structure" of cognitive moral development parallels the "deep structure" of moral philosophy. The fact that he happened to adopt formalistic philosophical criteria to interpret this psychological process meant that the inferred "deep structure" of cognitive moral development would parallel formalistic moral philosophy.

Use of "formalistic" criteria such as "universality" would not be equally acceptable to ethical act theorists (see chapter 8). While the formalistic metaethics adopted by Kohlberg might well be a "neutral" basis for assessing the relative adequacy of competing normative rule theories (e.g., Kant's, W. D. Ross's, or Kohlberg's own

Kantian-Rawlsian theory), it would be a "loaded" criterion if one of the competitors turned out to be an act theory. For example, in a philosophical assessment of the relative merits of the act theory of John Dewey and the rule theory of John Rawls, exclusive employment of "formalistic" criteria would seriously bias the outcome in favor of Rawls and against Deweyan normative ethics.

Kohlberg appears not to appreciate that there are metaethical theories besides formalism which might have been adopted by cognitive-developmental psychology to interpret the sequence of cognitive moral change. (If he is aware of viable alternatives, he does not acknowledge them or address the metatheoretical issues raised herein.) For example, adoption of pragmatic metaethics would also enable cognitive-developmental psychologists to interpret and justify their basic assumptions that individuals are rational; that they are "natural moral philosophers" (preferring better moral arguments) capable of philosophical assessments of their own singular moral judgments. Like formalism, pragmatic metaethics would also enable psychologists to demonstrate that a later emerging postconventional morality (of some sort) is more adequate than was a prior conventional moral stage. However, the implications of a pragmatic account would be radically different from those of a formalistic account regarding such basic issues as what it is for individuals to be "rational," or what it is for them to make "philosophical assessments" of singular moral judgments, or what it means to say that a given postconventional morality is "better" than a given conventional morality. Finally, a pragmatic account would entail an essentially different interpretation of the nature of "cognitive moral maturity" from the formalistically grounded formulation Kohlberg calls stage 6.

Assuming that cognitive-developmental psychology's data on the development of moral judgment can be given a pragmatic metaethical interpretation, we could then challenge Kohlberg's theoretical conclusions about the nature of that process. It could just as well be argued that a pragmatic, rather than formalistic, criterion is the "deep structure" of cognitive moral development. Inevitably, a metaphilosophical criterion of some sort must be used to interpret the psychological process of cognitive moral development, but the existence of viable alternatives ought to be acknowledged. For example, John Dewey's psychological analysis of moral development incorporates a pragmatic metaethics and an ethical act theory. In contrast, Kohlberg's psychological account is based on a formalistic metaethics and an ethical rule theory.[9]

The major goal of this chapter is to criticize Kohlberg's formalistic interpretation of moral development and to defend an alternative pragmatic interpretation. As noted earlier, a fundamental difference between these two sorts of interpretations focuses on the question of whether or not the structure of a "highest" cognitive moral stage can be described as a *definition* of sound moral judgment. As an ethical rule theorist, Kohlberg assumes that an adequate normative ethical theory is a definition of sound moral judgment. Consequently, any structure he identifies as the highest stage of moral judgment would presumably constitute a definition of sound moral judgment. In adopting this position about a "highest" stage, Kohlberg in effect rules out the possibility of further progressive reconstruction beyond stage 6. If the stage 6 structure were a definition of sound moral judgment, it would not, indeed could not, have any exceptions. Given Kohlberg's psychological assumption that individuals' "intuitive" recognition of valid exceptions to their own present structure is a necessary condition for their building a better structure, "true" stage 6 persons could not possibly build a better "stage 7."

A proposal that a certain normative structure *defines* sound moral judgment can be interpreted either as an empirical claim or as a philosophical claim. I believe that Kohlberg is making both sorts of claims about stage 6. In order for him to establish the philosophical claim, he would have to show that the stage 6 structure provides the best of all possible modes of resolving moral problems (since it purports to be *the* definition of sound moral judgment). On the other hand, justification of the empirical hypothesis would require empirical data showing that persons known to have acquired this "highest" stage do not in fact perceive exceptions to their present structure. If the stage 6 structure defines the subsequent moral reasoning of those who attain that stage, then, by hypothesis, they would acknowledge no cases wherein some other proposed consideration would be a better basis for resolving a moral dilemma than would their own "spontaneous" stage 6 proposal. If, contrary to this hypothesis, some of the subjects are found to accept the validity of an occasional exception to their present stage 6 structure, then it would be empirically false that the stage 6 structure defines their perception of sound moral reasoning.[10]

In short, Kohlberg's metaethical assumption that sound moral reasoning has a certain a priori form means that the moral norms of individuals who have attained that highest stage of moral judgment would not be open to revision in light of further moral experience. Although Kohlberg's account of the development of moral judgment assumes that the epistemological relationship of the first five moral structures to the particular judgments falling under them is a posteriori (i.e., these structures are subject to revision in light of subsequent moral experience), stage 6 is purportedly a structure of constitutive moral rules. Hence, the epistemological relationship of the stage 6 normative structure to the particular judgments falling under it is a priori. If cognitive-developmental psychology accepts that the normative structure of a highest stage of moral judgment is a priori, then it would not, because it could not, entertain the question of its possible reconstruction in light of an individual's continuing moral experience.

As a result of his adoption of formalistic metaethics, Kohlberg portrays the whole of cognitive moral development as a quest for the "true" definition of moral judgment. In claiming that stage 5 is better than the first four moral stages, he means that it is a priori better. Similarly, he argues in terms of merely formalistic criteria (i.e., universality, correlativity of "rights" and "duties," etc.) that the stage 6 structure is a better definition of moral judgment than either of an individual's first five "attempts" to construct such a definition. The fact that valid exceptions to each of the first five normative structures can be identified is interpreted as evidence that none of these "attempted definitions" is *the* true definition of sound moral judgment. Finally, in arguing that his own "preferred definition" (in terms of Rawlsian justice) is the best of the alternative definitions proposed by formalistic moral philosophers, he means that it is a priori best (on grounds that it better fulfills the established formalistic criteria for the acceptability of normative ethical theories).

Kohlberg's exclusive employment of formalistic metaethical criteria presupposes that a formally best normative ethical theory is *the* best normative theory. In terms of psychological theory, this presupposition means that Kohlberg's own claims about the philosophical superiority of stage 6 would not be open to a posteriori counterarguments. (A successful a posteriori challenge would presumably be a case in which a moral judgment implied by the stage 6 structure is acknowledged to be "counterintuitive.") In contrast to Kohlberg, some ethical rule theorists reject the sufficiency of a merely formal justification of a proposed set of moral norms, openly acknowledging that their own proposed definition of morality is subject to a posteriori challenges. For example, according to W. D. Ross,[11] the fact that a given normative structure better fulfills formal criteria, does *not* entail that it is the best normative ethical theory. On the contrary, he believes that his own proposed definition of moral reasoning is subject to correction if found to be inconsistent with our mature intuitions about particular cases. Ross's proposed definition was itself the result of explicating the grounds found to be implicit in countless clear cases of justified moral judgment. Although Ross's hypothesis that there are six basic categories of moral reasons (i.e., six prima facie moral rules) is *about* the a priori structure of all justified moral judgments; the hypothesis itself is not treated as a priori. He assumes that his hypothesis about the definition of morality is (in principle) a posteriori. In contrast, Kohlberg's hypothesis about the a priori structure of sound moral judgment is treated as an a priori hypothesis, defended in terms of merely formal criteria and presumably subject to merely formal counterarguments.

Because he acknowledges the insufficiency of a merely a priori determination of a best definition of morality, Ross's ethical rule theory is closer to the pragmatic position being defended in this paper than is Kohlberg's rule theory. Kohlberg claims that the stage 6 structure is *the* definition of sound moral judgment solely because it is the formally best normative ethical theory. Given this position, a posteriori cases showing that this stage 6 structure implies some admittedly "counterintuitive" moral judgments would appear to be irrelevant.

PRAGMATIC METAETHICS AND COGNITIVE-DEVELOPMENTAL PSYCHOLOGY

Our discussion has thus far centered on issues in moral epistemology as they relate to certain issues in cognitive-developmental theory of moral judgment. The goal has been to compare metaethical formalism with metaethical pragmatism as contrasting bases for cognitive-developmental moral psychology. I would like to extend this analysis a bit further by pursuing the contrasting interpretations likely to issue from each tradition of a psychological phenomenon already explored above: namely, the fact that individuals sometimes favor resolving a moral dilemma on the basis of reasoning not yet covered by their present moral norms. According to Kohlberg's own data, individuals tend to prefer moral arguments at a stage or so higher than their present stage.

Our pragmatic interpretation of this phenomenon would coincide with Kohlberg's formalistic analysis on at least one crucial point. Namely, both suppose that an adequate ethical analysis of an individual's acknowledging a "better" argument "as better"—when it is not yet covered by his or her present structure of moral norms— entails our referring to another structure of norms which does cover that "better" argument. However, in contrast to pragmatic ethics, Kohlberg's analysis supposes that a sufficient philosophical account of these valid "exceptions" (to the norms of a given moral stage) requires not merely our referring to a "higher" structure of norms which would cover those particular justifications; but rather referring to a "highest" structure of norms, one which would cover all possible moral justifications. Thus, Kohlberg's philosophical explanation of the resolution of particular dilemmas not adequately re-solvable at given lower stages refers to a certain definition of moral justification, that is, the stage 6 structure. Pragmatic accounts of this phenomenon in terms of a "higher" structure of norms would in no way imply that the structure in question is the best of all possible normative structures.

Kohlberg's account grants that individuals at stages 1 through 5 can recognize exceptions to their present normative structure—even when they cannot yet fully articulate why a proposed moral argument "perceived to be better" than their own spontaneous argument is better. As noted above, giving a satisfactory philosophical account of the inadequacies of one's own present normative ethical structure would be possible only after one had constructed a more adequate structure of norms. However, it is possible for one to acknowledge the (relative) inadequacy of his or her own argument, as compared to another, without yet being able to explain why it is less adequate. Again, Kohlberg's own psychological account assumes that subjects can "intuitively" identify particular examples of "better moral reasoning" even though they have not yet constructed a normative structure enabling them to explain (philosophically) why those "better reasons" are better.

In order for Kohlberg (who is presumably at stage 6) to be able to give a sufficient philosophical account of the possible exceptions to his stage 6 structure, he must have already constructed a stage 7. Yet Kohlberg's actual construction of a stage 7 (according to his own psychological account of cognitive reconstruction) is contingent on his retaining the capacity to recognize particular cases in which another proposal for resolving a dilemma is better than his own spontaneous stage 6 proposal. However, given the merely formal grounding of Kohlberg's claim that stage 6 defines moral justification, he does not even acknowledge the possibility of identifying such a posteriori exceptions to his present structure.[12] Hence, for Kohlberg, the question of opening his present stage 6 structure of norms to correction on the basis of further moral experience is "inconceivable." His stage 6 is not an a posteriori structure; rather, it is a structure of constitutive moral rules specifying what it means to judge morally.[13]

Stage 6 is what it means to judge morally. If you want to play the moral game, if you want to make decisions which anyone could agree upon in resolving social conflicts, stage 6 is it.[14]

In contrast, the pragmatic assumption that any structure of moral norms consists of summary rather than constitutive rules means that it is at least possible to identify a posteriori exceptions "to the rules." In terms of the process of cognitive moral development, if such an exception were encountered by an individual, his present structure of norms would tend to be subtly modified in ways which tended to make it a more adequate summary of his particular moral experience. It is precisely this possibility of further structural revision based on particular, novel features of moral situations which rule theorists like Kohlberg explicitly rule out—by interpreting cognitive moral maturity in light of norms said to define sound moral judgment.

Given the example of the historical progression of science, one might have expected a psychological paradigm for studying cognitive moral development to at least leave open the question of the possible reconstruction of a "highest" identified cognitive moral stage. As argued above, the explanation for Kohlberg's not doing so was his adoption of a rationalistic epistemology.[15] In contrast, if pragmatic assumptions were the basis for interpreting the sequence of cognitive development, the possible revision of a "highest" identified structure would be taken for granted. Pragmatic metaethics would enable cognitive-developmental psychology to accomplish a presumably requisite task, i.e., to understand how certain later emerging postconventional structures are better than earlier conventional or preconventional modes of resolving moral problems.[16] However, on the basis of pragmatic assumptions, a philosophical defense could not be given for a claim such as Kohlberg's that a certain postconventional structure is the *definition* of moral reasoning and hence, by implication, the best of all possible systems of moral norms.

Moving to a related point, it now becomes obvious why a pragmatic metaethical framework for cognitive developmental psychology would necessitate drawing conclusions very different from Kohlberg's, about the nature of "mature moral judgment." If a pragmatic line of argument were used to establish that a certain cognitive structure is better than certain others, it would be logically inconsistent to then argue that this "best" structure is also a *definition* of justified moral judgment. A basic premise of pragmatic metaethics is that the identification of a particular exception to any one of the rival normative ethical theories being assessed is at least logically possible. Given this premise, it would be incoherent to argue that a "pragmatically" best normative ethical theory is also the "definition" of moral justification. Put in terms of cognitive moral stages, it would be incoherent to argue that a "pragmatically" highest stage is also the definition of singular moral judgment.

A pragmatic philosophical interpretation of cognitive moral development would entail the existence of a logical distinction between each emergent structure of moral norms and the singular moral judgments falling under them. A pragmatic argument that a given normative structure is better than another would be based on a direct appeal to the particular justified judgments purportedly summarized by such structures. This presupposes that it is at least logically possible to identify particular exceptions to such a structure—or else its adequacy could not be tested by appeal to particular cases. For example, suppose we were considering the hypothesis that Kohlberg's stage 6 normative structure is better than W. D. Ross's structure of 6 prima facie moral rules. The soundness of this hypothesis could be assessed on the basis of each structure's consistency with particular justified moral judgments (purportedly covered by each), only if we assume that it is possible to identify such judgments without thereby implying one of the two competing structures.

Once a certain structure is identified as the *definition* of moral judgment and, by implication, implicit in every justified moral judgment, then trying to demonstrate its inadequacies by an appeal to particular counterexamples becomes problematic. There would then be an a priori prejudice against a theorist's acknowledging proposed exceptions to his own preferred normative theory. In identifying something as a "justified moral judgment," that theorist would be implying that it is consistent with the very normative structure in question. Unless it is acknowledged that a preferred structure of moral rules and the particular cases falling under it are logically independent, it would be an a priori impossibility to identify an exception. A theorist's preferred structure of moral norms could be successfully challenged by appealing to his perceptions (or, if you like, his "intuitions") about particular dilemmas only if we assume that his perceptions are somewhat "neutral" in such matters.[17]

To summarize, given that cognitive-developmental psychology's use of the term "development of moral judgment" presupposes a particular moral philosophical analysis of sound moral judgment, this chapter examined the impact of adopting either of two contrasting sets of philosophical assumptions on cognitive-developmental theories of moral judgment. Lawrence Kohlberg's interpretation of developmental stages of moral judgment was said to presuppose a Kantian-Rawlsian ethical rule theory. We assessed Kohlberg's metapsychological understandings in this regard and argued that psychology's effort to explain the development of moral judgment would be better served if guided by a normative act theory (rather than rule theory) conception of sound moral judgment and by a pragmatic (rather than formalistic) metaethical conception of sound normative ethical theories.

NOTES

1. The psychological fact that Einstein's theory of relativity was not implicit in the "physical" reasoning of all but a handful of scientists in the early twentieth century did not warrant claiming that Einstein's physics was an inadequate means of resolving physical problems. Rather, it was the fact that Einstein's physics was judged by the scientific community to better satisfy its metascientific criteria than did the established Newtonian physics which warranted claiming that it provided the more adequate framework for handling physical problems.

2. Thus, a sufficient justification of a singular moral judgment would require our knowing the relevant set of moral rules, along with knowing that the *particular facts* fall under them. Knowledge of the particular factors is necessary for identifying a given dilemma as an *instance* covered by the relevant moral rules—and to thereby be able to derive a warranted singular judgment.

3. A distinction is sometimes drawn between moral principles and moral rules, based on their level of abstraction. However, the term "moral rules," as used in this chapter, refers to both types of moral rules.

4. For a more extensive philosophical treatment of the sort of act theory adopted in this chapter and of the "method of moral negotiation," see chapter 8. Also see Bernard Rosen, "Rules and Justified Moral Judgments," *Philosophy and Phenomenological Research,* Vol. XXX, No. 3, March 1970; "Moral Education and Moral Theory," *Teaching Philosophy,* Vol. I, No. 4, Fall 1976; and *Strategies of Ethics* (Boston: Houghton Mifflin, 1978).

5. Other rule theorists make a more limited claim. For example, W. D. Ross regards his proposed definition of morality as merely an a priori criterion for distinguishing morally relevant grounds from morally irrelevant grounds. Ross's position is that there is no a priori criterion for distinguishing justified singular moral judgments from unjustified moral judgments. Ross acknowledges the relevance of situational variables in determining which of his six basic categories of moral grounds has priority, in cases wherein they conflict. Thus Ross's rule theory position is much closer to an act theory view than is Kohlberg's.

6. On the other hand, if a psychologist tended toward a behavioral paradigm, he might claim that an "adequately resolved" moral dilemma is itself a positive reinforcer (or else a means to attaining reinforcement), and this fact is what explains an individual's development of increasingly more adequate modes of resolving moral problems.

7. Kohlberg's research supports this hypothesis. That is, he reports that individuals tend to regard as inadequate examples of reasoning which are at stages lower than their present stage and to give their highest rating to examples of reasoning at a stage (or so) higher than their own present stage.

8. L. Kohlberg, "From Is to Ought: How to Commit the Naturalistic Fallacy and Get Away with It in the Study of Moral Development," *Cognitive Development and Epistemology,* T. Mischel (ed.), New York: Academic Press, 1971, p. 224.

9. "Postconventional" rule theorists (like Kohlberg) and "postconventional"act theorists (like Dewey) could agree that "conventional morality" is not an *adequate* way of resolving moral problems. However, in grounding their agreement, each would be implying radically different things about conventional and postconventional morality as a result of their basic differences regarding the nature of moral judgment and moral justification.

10. Suppose we were to find such a subject. If Kohlberg responded to this datum by claiming that the fact that such a subject accepts the validity of an exception to his present structure means that he had not fully attained stage 6, then we would be warranted in concluding that Kohlberg's apparent "empirical" hypothesis about the stage 6 structure's being *the* definition of stage 6 moral reasoning is, after all, empirically unfalsifiable.

11. W. D. Ross, *The Right and the Good,* Oxford: The Clarendon Press, Inc., 1930.

12. I would of course claim that it is possible for any man, Kohlberg included, to recognize exceptions to his present structure. The fact that Kohlberg mis-

takenly (in my view) believes that he cannot do so might, however, explain the psychological fact that he does not do so.

13. If there were exceptions, they would have to be identified by means of an a priori argument establishing that some other definition better fulfills the formalistic criteria than does his own stage 6 structure.

14. Kohlberg, pp. 217–218.

15. What is so puzzling about the "philosopher" Kohlberg's a priori stance in ethical theory is the fact that, as a developmental psychologist, he assumes the possibility of structural transformation "upward" for all but stage 6. It just seems "unscientific" for him to rule out even the possibility that a "higher" stage 7 might be constructed, by his a priori claim that "true" stage 6 persons could not acknowledge particular cases wherein their present structure is inadequate. Why doesn't he at least leave open that logical possibility?

16. As well as enable us to show why a given postconventional morality is better than certain alternative postconventional moral theories.

17. Because ethical rule theorists believe that sound moral reasoning is defined by a best structure of moral rules, they tend to assume that a philosophical hypothesis about *the* best such definition could not be successfully challenged a posteriori, by appealing to our mature "intuitions" about proposed counterexamples. If each theorist's own preferred structure of moral norms did in fact *define* his own present moral deliberations, it would in effect rule out his recognition of potential counterexamples. Perhaps appreciating this psychological difficulty, ethical rule-theorists have tended to rely on formalistic criteria to decide on the best of competing definitions of morality.

Part IV

BASIC ISSUES IN MORAL PHILOSOPHY

Chapter 6

The Rawls Connection

DWIGHT BOYD

INTRODUCTION

In discussing philosophical questions concerning his theory of
moral development, Lawrence Kohlberg has repeatedly made reference to John Rawls's theory of justice.[1] These references vary both
in terms of their content and in terms of their relative clarity. The
starting assumption of this paper, however, is that they point to an
important aspect of Kohlberg's theory which has been understood
only partially, as is evidenced by numerous critical but vague references in the literature to Kohlberg's "liberal bias," but one which
warrants further clarification and examination.[2] Kohlberg's most
direct claims about Rawls are essentially that Rawls's theory represents a good example of the stage 6 form of moral judgment or, more
precisely, that Rawls's theory is a theoretical derivative from and an
attempt to justify the "natural structure" of stage 6, which is the
end point of Kohlberg's developmental scheme: " . . . the central
achievement of Rawls's theory is that it represents the first clear
systematic justification of the principles and methods of decision we
call 'Stage 6,' principles and methods of decision only partly articulated by Kant."[3] Kohlberg's discussion of this claim points to the
"common roots" of both theories (in Kant and in the Piagetian
notion of equilibration of functional forms) and attempts to argue
that Rawls's notions of the original position combined with reflec-

tive equilibrium is a theoretical construct reflecting a basic concern for justice as reciprocity which is present at all levels of development, but only fully equilibrated at stage 6.

This paper will not be a direct explication and critical analysis of Kohlberg's claims concerning Rawls. Although Kohlberg does not always express his ideas with the kind of precision, clarity, and consistency that satisfies philosophers, I have tried not to let that get in my way in this paper. That is, I have assumed (and, to be honest, do believe) that there are core ideas in Kohlberg's work worthy of recognition and development; and indeed some of the problems with precision, clarity, and consistency should be taken, in part, as indicators of this substance. What I will try to do is to express and develop systematically some of those core ideas in a way which I think is faithful to what Kohlberg might *want* to say. It should also be acknowledged that I will not try to avoid expressing what *I* want to say. I will seek to support my interpretation by citing passages from Kohlberg's writings, on which it is based. But I will not be unduly worried by passages which seem to support a different interpretation. The point will be to develop as coherently as possible at least the gross outlines of a position which seems to me both correct and a plausible interpretation of Kohlberg's comments about Rawls. If I am wrong from Kohlberg's point of view, then that much at least can soon be made clear.

As suggested, I will attempt only to outline what I see as the most basic connection between Kohlberg and Rawls. In doing this I will have to assume the reader's familiarity with the essential claims and terminology of both Rawls's theory of justice and Kohlberg's theory of moral development. Similarly, because of the complex nature of both theories, I will have to ignore many interesting but more problematic points of connection, under the assumption that these can be adequately analyzed only from within the general framework elaborated in this paper. I will try to establish this framework by elucidating several interrelated points of connection. I will argue that the first basic point of connection has to do with their common entry point into the moral realm or, if you will, the conceptual focus and deontological orientation of both theories.

Then I will turn to their shared emphasis on the concept of justice and try to show how their substantive conceptions of justice are quite similar, the similarity depending in the end on how both use the notion of respect for persons. Finally, I will argue that their shared concern for justice as analyzed rests on a conception of persons which links both theories in at least three ways. The first two of these are touched on only briefly and involve noting the congruence between this conception of persons and the nature and methodologies of their respective theories. The third way this link is manifested, I will argue, is both the most important and the most problematic. Thus I will end by arguing that the legitimacy of the Rawls connection in Kohlberg depends ultimately on a clarification of Kohlberg's description of stage 6 in a way which accords with a "constructive" interpretation of how judgments of justice are made, one which "does justice" to the considered conception of persons as agents of mutual respect.

THE "RIGHT" BEGINNINGS

At the first level of connection, Kohlberg and Rawls share a common entry point into the moral realm which shapes their respective theories in similar ways. Both Kohlberg and Rawls approach moral questions through a focus on the concept of the right, that is, in terms of that aspect of morality dealing with (at least the potentiality of) interpersonal conflict and having an adjudicatory function. Conceptions of the good and ideals of human perfection are by no means unimportant for either Kohlberg or Rawls. But they do not constitute the essence of morality, nor adequately circumscribe the proper entry point into moral questions.[4] For both, pursuit of the good and human perfection is subordinated as a concern to adjudicating *differences* among individuals on how the good and human perfection are to be defined, furthered, and distributed. One cannot understand this entry point unless one understands that they assume that individuals do and will differ in this way. This presumption of human conflict rests on a more fundamental belief that the good, even for *one* individual, is not one but pluralistic. As Rawls says, "human good is heterogeneous because the aims of the self are heterogeneous" (p. 554). This idea has been expressed most eloquently by Isaiah Berlin in his "Two Concepts of Liberty." His discussion points not only to the pluralistic conception of human ends, but also to the inevitability of conflict in the way that it functions for both Kohlberg and Rawls.

> The world that we encounter in ordinary experience is one in which we are faced with choices between ends equally ultimate, and claims equally absolute, the realization of some of which must inevitably involve the sacrifice of others. . . . If, as I believe, the ends of men are many, and not all of them are in principle compatible with each other, then the possibility of conflict— and of tragedy— can never wholly be eliminated from human life, either personal or social. The necessity of choosing between absolute claims is then an inescapable characteristic of the human condition.[5]

In other words, both Kohlberg's and Rawls's theories start from the premise that no one view of the good can be taken as overriding. Choice of the good is seen as fundamentally subjective and pluralistic, and the moral point of view is seen as objectivity seeking, interpersonal, and adjudicatory. They both start, I submit, from what Strawson has called a "minimal interpretation of morality" as a public convenience "of the first importance as a condition of everything that matters, but only as a condition of everything that matters, not as something that matters in itself."[6]

Although Rawls seeks to avoid letting anything hang on analysis of the concepts of right or morality, the conceptual boundaries of his theory are clearly established throughout the book via the careful use of language, and quite specifically identified when he elaborates "the formal constraints of the concept of right." The original position is identified, in part, in terms of embodying certain characteristics of the concept of the right.

> The situation of the persons in the original position reflects certain constraints . . . which I refer to as the constraints of the concept of right since they hold for the choice of all ethical principles and not only for those of justice. (p. 130)

Then after elaborating these constraints and arguing for their acceptability, Rawls summarizes:

Taken together, then, these conditions on conceptions of right come to this: a conception of right is a set of principles, general in form and universal in application, that is to be publicly recognized as a final court of appeal for ordering the conflicting claims of moral persons. Principles of justice are identified by their special role and the subject to which they apply. (p. 135)

Kohlberg is not always so consistent in his use of moral language, but it is clear that he intends to delimit his sphere of concern in roughly the same way. Thus when he speaks of a "moral" conflict, he means ". . . a conflict between claims of men: you versus me, you versus him."[7] Whether or not it constitutes linguistic fiat, it should be clear that Kohlberg limits the referent of the term "morality" to the arena of interpersonal conflict calling forth the concept of right. ". . . The problem of morality is justice, the problem of considering and choosing between the *claims* or rights of other persons. Stated otherwise, the sphere of morality is the sphere of duty or obligation. . . . "[8] The dilemmas upon which Kohlberg's data-gathering procedure is based all exemplify this notion of morality as involving adjudication of competing claims or interests in an interpersonal context.

But Kohlberg also goes further than this, in much the same way as Rawls, by specifying a metaethical point of view from which questions of the right are to be considered.

. . . morality is a unique, *sui generis* realm. If it is unique, its uniqueness must be defined by formal criteria, so our metaethical conception is *formalistic*. Like most deontological moral philosophers since Kant, we define morality in terms of the formal character of a moral judgment, method, or point of view, rather than in terms of its content. Impersonality, ideality, universalizability, preemptiveness, etc., are the formal characteristics of a moral judgment. These are best seen in the reasons given for a moral judgment, a moral reason being one which has these properties.[9]

I think this further refinement in the characterization of Kohlberg's starting assumptions can best be approached through his reference to "deontological" moral philosophers. This identification should not be taken as referring to some mysterious capacity of moral agents to judge the rightness of moral acts independent of *any* consideration of the consequences of those acts. On the contrary, I submit that Kohlberg shares this orientation with Rawls in precisely the way Rawls explicates it. A deontological theory is "one that either does not specify the good independently from the right, or does not interpret the right as maximizing the good. . . . Justice as fairness is a deontological theory in the second way" (p. 30). It should be noted that simply specifying the constraints on right does not by itself differentiate the deontological orientation from the teleological; utilitarians undoubtedly would accept them also. Rather, as we will see, it is the priority of the principles of the right and the way this is expressed in the original position as a decision procedure that most adequately characterizes a deontological theory such as Rawls's, one which accepts and seeks to help us understand "our intuitive conviction of the primacy of justice" (p. 9).[10]

THE SEVERAL SIDES OF JUSTICE

So far I have drawn the commonality between Kohlberg and Rawls in terms of a narrowness of their foci and the deontological lens which tints what they see. What they see within these boundaries is justice, but their conception of justice is, paradoxically, far broader than many other philosophers'. It is clear, first of all, that both see justice as the central moral concept. Rawls describes "justice as fairness" as trying to account for our intuitive convictions of the primacy of justice, as expressed most eloquently in the opening sentence of *A Theory of Justice:* "Justice is the first virtue of social institutions, as truth is of systems of thought" (p. 3). And as we have already seen in the passages quoted above, Kohlberg sometimes simply identifies "morality" with justice, arguing elsewhere that "if the function of moral principles is to resolve conflicting claims, in some sense these principles must be principles of justice or fairness."[11] I doubt that many would disagree with this conclusion, given the premise. As John Orr has claimed:

Persons who define morality as social rules will inevitably concern themselves with the origin and authority of those rules, and also with the more abstract principles in terms of which conflicts can be mediated. Ultimately the argument will be about the shape of justice. There is no other way to move.[12]

However, Kohlberg and Rawls are also linked by a much broader conception of justice than is manifested in most interpretations of this concept. For them the shape of justice is outlined by their initial foci and by the deontological lens through which they view it. At first glance we might say that justice is an umbrella concept for them, covering concerns of liberty, equality, and respect for persons. But this is far too simple a metaphor. It suggests merely that other things are included under "justice." But the shape of their conception is more complicated than that. It is perhaps more closely approximated by the following. Justice is at the same time the cell of living moral concern and the nucleus which controls the cell. That is, justice does not simply "cover" liberty, equality, and respect for persons, but in fact is the essential unit of moral concern constituted by their interrelationships. And it is via the just decision that liberty, equality, and respect for persons have their primary manifestations in social life.

That Kohlberg interprets justice broadly and as some kind of combination of other principles is easy to believe: every third paper he issues seems to "define" justice in terms of yet another substantive moral principle, or at least to point out a different interrelationship among principles. For example, one can easily find the following range of assertions:

(i)   Justice . . . is a matter of equal and universal human rights.

(ii) At advanced stages, the most basic principle of justice is equality: treat every man's claim equally, regardless of the man.

(iii) As a reason for action, justice is called respect for persons.

(iv) In one sense, justice is itself content-free; that is, it merely prescribes that principles should be impartially applied to all. However, we have also argued that the stage 6 form implies justice as equity, that is, as a treatment of persons as morally equal. . . . Second, we have argued that it also implies commutative justice as reciprocity, contract, and trust.

(v)   The primary substantive principle stage 6 holds is the *respect for persons* principle: Treat each human being as an end in himself, as of ultimate worth. This also implies the following subprinciples: a) *Liberty* . . . , b) Equality or justice . . . , c) The greatest good or utility. . . . The ultimate stage 6 principle of respect for persons, then, is the principle of justice.

(vi) At heart, these [stage 6 principles] are universal principles of *justice*, of the *reciprocity* and *equality* of human *rights*, and of respect for the dignity of human beings as *individual persons*.[13]

Although the variations are often puzzling and would take more space than is available in this paper to explicate and examine for coherence, I think there is a core idea running through all of them. This core idea runs as follows. Justice is the general moral perspective through which competing claims of persons should be resolved. It is not simply an empty abstract formula requiring mechanistic application, but rather it identifies substantive ways of conceiving persons and their interactions in situations of competing interests. It is a perspective which does not dictate certain, final answers but rather structures a framework for a process of resolving conflicts (or potential conflicts) in a way acceptable to all parties. The central lines of this structure consist of an integration of two things: (i) a conception of persons as equal vis-à-vis their right to formulate their own ends and their agency as rule-following creatures, and (ii) a reciprocity of intention of persons to afford each other as much freedom as possible in furthering those ends. The motivational "heart" of this structure is summarized in the attitude and principle of respect for persons—of recognizing and acknowledging the other as an equally unique subject of his or her own experience, *including* the experience of myself and my ends, and of acting toward each other as if the other's interests and ends were my own.

It is one thing to string together a few nice-sounding phrases as expressing a "core idea," but quite another to flesh it out, showing not only what the parts mean and how they can be integrated, but also how the total conception coheres in a way which strengthens our basic intuitions and provides a plausible defense of them. I submit, however, that it is essentially this task which Rawls has tackled in *A Theory of Justice,* and that his efforts are expressive of essentially the same core idea as that which I am suggesting makes the most sense of Kohlberg's various assertions. Certainly it is not hard to argue at least part of this. First of all, it is clear that Rawls does not rest with the simple formal components of justice, but intends to offer a substantive conception of justice (see pp. 58–59). Furthermore, as he says in many places throughout the book, it is the total picture which should be taken as his conception of justice: how the substantive parts fit together is to be understood as part of the conception, and its strength is to be tested by this rather than by the strength of any of the parts taken independently. It is also clear that equality in the sense suggested above is one of the essential parts of the overall conception:

> . . . the purpose of [the conditions which characterize the original position] is to represent equality between human beings as moral persons, as creatures having a conception of their good and capable of a sense of justice. The basis of equality is taken to be similarity in these two respects. Systems of ends are not ranked by value; and each man is presumed to have the requisite ability to understand and to act upon whatever principles are adopted (p. 19).

Further, if persons so conceived as equal would seek to embody this mutual equality in the structure of their most basic social institutions through which they interact, they would, so Rawls argues, be most concerned with reflecting it in the priority of a principle of equal liberty.

It is at this point of emphasis that any argument for a direct parallel between Kohlberg and Rawls becomes more tenuous. On the one hand, Kohlberg merely nods to the "subprinciple" of liberty in passing, whereas Rawls salutes the priority of liberty as the central organizer of his theory of justice. On the other hand, Rawls frames the notion of respect for persons as only an interpretative side door to the maze of his argument, whereas Kohlberg spotlights it to the center stage of our attention. How much should we make of this apparent difference if we are examining the similarity of their core conceptions of justice? In this context, I think one can argue that the difference is more apparent than substantive.

First of all, that liberty gets emphasized in Rawls, indeed argued for as the lexically prior principle of justice, is a function of the fact that he restricts his immediate attention to the basic structure of society as an organized whole. Rawls notes that justice is a normative concern, not just with regard to aspects of social systems, but also to a wide range of other things, including actions, decisions, judgments, implications, attitudes, dispositions, and persons themselves (p. 7). His focus is restricted, however, to one essential part of this general concern.

Our topic, however, is that of social justice. For us the primary subject of justice is the basic structure of society, or more exactly, the way in which the major social institutions distribute fundamental rights and duties and determine the division of advantages from social cooperation. By major institutions I understand the political constitution and the principal economic and social arrangements (p. 7).

The important point to note here is that Rawls does not claim that the conception of justice outlined in *A Theory of Justice* applies without modification to all problems of justice considerations, but only "directly to the most important case, the justice of the basic structure" (p. 11).[14] In fact, he very carefully notes that "there is no reason to suppose ahead of time that the principles satisfactory for the basic structure hold for all cases," although he does expect that the theory arrived at in this context "should provide the key for some of these other questions" (p. 8). Since Kohlberg is clearly talking about justice in a far broader context, namely, any kind of judgment called forth in the context of adjudicating interpersonal claims, it is thus hardly surprising that Kohlberg's conception of justice organizes a similar set of principles in a slightly different way. What is a bit more problematic is the almost total absence of argument about the place of a "subprinciple" of liberty, and how it must be an integral part of a conception of justice when one is *not* dealing with the basic structure of society.

I think an argument of this sort can be given, but only in the context of the other apparent difference between Kohlberg and Rawls noted above, the relative emphasis placed on the principle of respect for persons. Indeed, within this context we can also see that the first difference is less substantive than it might seem and that both differences may be accounted for by differing levels of specificity of the problem when justice is our concern.

As noted above, Kohlberg seems to be more explicit than Rawls about the centrality of respect for persons in his conception of justice. Although sometimes it appears to be equated with justice, while other times it is *conjoined with* justice, respect for persons is consistently acknowledged by Kohlberg as the most basic principle of his most mature stage. However, nowhere does Kohlberg provide us with a systematic articulation of what he is referring to, beyond the identification of the principle as requiring that one "treat each human being as an end in himself, as of ultimate worth" (see quote "v" above). I wish to claim, however, that *if* Kohlberg were to elaborate a more systematic articulation, it would be along the lines of that provided by Downie and Telfer. There are several points at which their analyses seem to parallel and illuminate Kohlberg's claims;[15] for the purpose of this paper, I can only draw attention to two points developed by them which are not explicitly made by Kohlberg, but which seem to contribute to a more complete and coherent picture of Kohlberg's claims about justice.

The first point is that "respect for persons as ends" can, according to Downie and Telfer, refer to both an attitude and a principle of action. And more importantly, they argue that the attitude is both logically and morally basic:

> The attitude is *logically* basic in that the principle has to be explained in terms of it; it is the principle which logically must be adopted (other things being equal) by someone who has the attitude of respect. But it is also *morally* basic in that it includes in its scope modes of feeling and thinking as well as of acting; and that which is morally fundamental is a total quality of life rather than a principle of action in the narrow sense.[16]

I think this attitudinal side of respect for persons is what Kohlberg must be getting at when he characterizes a principle as a *"mode* of choosing," or as a "general guide to choice rather than a rule of action."[17] In this sense a stage 6 conception of justice consists primarily of a way of *regarding* persons, which in turn entails a way of *treating* them according to certain principles of action. Failure to understand this attitudinal underpinning of stage 6 has led, I suspect, to the many misinterpretations of Kohlberg as "excessively rationalistic." It is this attitudinal underpinning which I was anticipating by referring to respect for persons as the motivational heart of Kohlberg's core conception of justice (see the discussion earlier in this section).

The second point important for the purposes of this paper consists of Downie and Telfer's analysis of the components of this attitude of respect for persons. They clearly identify two sides to this attitude,

where Kohlberg is (mistakenly) thought to see only one. Downie
and Telfer summarize:

> In so far as persons are thought of as self-determining agents who pursue objects
> of interest to themselves we respect them by showing active sympathy with them;
> in Kant's language, we make their ends our own. In so far as persons are thought
> of as rule-following we respect them by taking seriously the fact that the rules by
> which they guide their conduct constitute reasons which may apply both to them
> and to ourselves. In the attitude of respect we have, then, two necessary compo-
> nents: an attitude of active sympathy and a readiness at least to consider the
> applicability of other men's rules both to them and to ourselves. These two
> components are independently necessary and jointly sufficient to constitute the
> attitude of respect which it is fitting to direct at persons, conceived as rational
> wills.[18]

Reversing the order of these two components, I think it is relatively
clear that Kohlberg's conception of justice incorporates the second
attitude constituting respect for persons. In theoretical contexts it
surfaces in his concern for universalizability and reversibility, and it
lies at the heart of his developmentalism. In practical activities it
manifests itself in the emphasis on consensual democratic community as a necessary condition of development. (Its relative clarity also
contributes to the "excessively rationalistic" misinterpretations
mentioned above.) However, I also want to claim that the attitude
which Downie and Telfer identify as "active sympathy" is equally
integral to Kohlberg's conception of stage 6 justice. The support for
this claim is more indirect than that for the first because as far as I
know Kohlberg never talks explicitly about an attitude of "active
sympathy," but he comes very close to this occasionally when he
discusses role taking as a necessary component of moral judgment,
and refers to a "psychological unity of empathy and justice in moral
role taking."[19] Two additional points of indirect support can also be
noted. The first is that Downie and Telfer clearly see the attitude of
active sympathy as an interpretation of the Kantian formulation of
the categorical imperative to "always treat another as an end in
himself, never solely as a means"; and this is precisely that part of
Kant to which Kohlberg refers us for a deeper understanding of his
own views.[20] (He *seldom* refers to the other facets of Kant which, by
themselves, might lead to a legitimate charge of excessive

rationalism.) Second, the notion of active sympathy seems to me a necessary part of the metaphor of "moral musical chairs" which Kohlberg uses to explicate his understanding of stage 6 judgment:[21] The aim of the metaphor, in part, is to express the notion of approaching decisions affecting others *as if* their ends of inclination are equally as important as one's own. The "constructive" nature of this conception of principled moral judgment will be discussed in the following section of this paper, but the relevant point here is that it should not be understood as some sort of purely cognitive mechanistic calculation. On the contrary, Downie and Telfer claim "that active sympathy is one form of 'creative emotional response,' and that it is a response to a conception of persons as self-determining agents pursuing ends of inclination. As such it is a necessary component in the attitude of respect."[22] Indeed, they go on to identify the whole attitude of respect for persons as the species of love known as *agape*.[23]

If we assume that the above is a plausible interpretation of Kohlberg's understanding of respect for persons, how is it different from Rawls's? As far as I can tell, there is no difference in the way Rawls interprets this notion; as suggested above, the possible difference lies more in the function it has in their respective conceptions of justice. Rawls notes a possible objection to his theory that because the original position does not "explicitly" include the notion of respect for persons his argument might be thought unsound. His answer is that although the principles of justice cannot be *derived* from the notion of respect for persons, the whole theory can be seen as giving more definite meaning to it:

I believe . . . that while the principles of justice will be effective only if men have a sense of justice and do therefore respect one another, the notion of respect or of the inherent worth of persons is not a suitable basis for arriving at these principles. It is precisely these ideas that call for interpretation. . . . Once the conception of justice is on hand, however, the ideas of respect and of human dignity can be given a more definite meaning. . . . The theory of justice provides a rendering of these ideas but we cannot start out with them (pp. 585–586).[24]

However, it can be argued that although the two principles are not in any rigorous sense derived from respect for persons, this notion is assumed implicitly by Rawls as the very basis of the original position. First of all, Rawls does explicitly acknowledge that *self*-respect (or self-esteem) is "perhaps the most important primary good" (p. 440). The "primary goods" in Rawls's theory are, of course, those things which everyone is said to want *whatever else* he or she wants, and they represent the only specific pieces of knowledge about their conceptions of the good which persons assuming the original position are allowed to have. But then because people in the original position are deliberating from an initial position of equality and from behind the veil of ignorance which prevents them from knowing anything which would permit identification as a *particular* person, persons are for the purpose of this kind of deliberation indistinguishable. It follows that respect for self is also indistinguishable from respect for "other" persons. Respect for persons is in this sense at the heart of Rawls's theory, as well as of Kohlberg's. As Rawls says, "the principles of justice manifest in the basic structure of society men's desire to treat one another not as means but as ends in themselves" (p. 179). Dworkin has argued in a similar way that the fundamental concept which is assumed in the design and working of the original position is the "abstract right to equal concern and respect." He concludes:

We may therefore say that justice as fairness rests on the assumption of a natural right of all men and women to equality of concern and respect, a right they possess not by virtue of birth or characteristic or merit or excellence but simply as human beings with the capacity to make plans and give justice.[25]

We can at this point return to the general question of the noted differences between Kohlberg and Rawls in the shape of their respective conceptions of justice. As suggested above, the difference can now be seen as less substantive than apparent as a result of a more delimited focus of attention in Rawls's theory. In order that this can be seen, I have tried to show that a shared understanding of respect for persons lies at the heart of both Kohlberg's and Rawls's theories. If this is correct, then the differing emphasis on liberty must be interpreted against this common background. Since Kohlberg is concerned with all institutions of human interaction calling out principles of justice, he focuses more explicitly on the general notion of respect for persons. Liberty gets acknowledged as a "subprinciple" because it points to a context within which respect for persons becomes particularly problematic. As Downie and Telfer note, "the principle of liberty is . . . the principle of respect for persons expressed in a context where the importance of self-realization is being weighed against that of achieving a harmonious and cooperative society."[26] That is, it is in the context of individual persons' dealings with large numbers of others and with the demands of the collective that, in Berlin's words, "how many doors are left open to me/you" becomes a salient concern. And it is this limited context within which Rawls is formulating a conception of justice as fairness, so that liberty is the natural focus of attention against an assumed background of respect for persons. It has already been noted above (earlier in this section) how Rawls cautions his readers with respect to the generality of his conception of justice (and this might be applied to Kohlberg). However, Rawls is not entirely unequivocal about this, acknowledging that there might be a "key" in his theory which should fit a wider range of justice problems (p. 8), and tantalizing us with views of a more general theory of "rightness as fairness" (p. 17). It seems to me that this "key" is not to be found in the two principles of justice and their expressed priority of liberty, but rather in the constructive use of the original position as a way of interpreting respect for persons in different contexts. And it should be noted that it is this notion of Rawls that Kohlberg seeks to develop through such metaphors as "moral musical chairs." In fact, when we concentrate less on the shape of their conceptions of justice and more on what underlies their shared concern for justice, a more fundamental level of connection is revealed. It is this kind of connection to which I will now turn.

PERSONS AS SUBJECTS OF RESPECT

So far it has been argued that respect for persons constitutes common ground between Kohlberg and Rawls, within which their conceptions of justice are shaped. How the several substantive, constitutive principles are balanced and interrelated represents differences in the specificity of problems addressed rather than in the common ground itself. As I have suggested through the use of Downie and Telfer's analysis, the attitude of respect toward entities of a certain sort is the pivotal normative concept in this common ground. What makes respect the appropriate general attitude—and justice the main concern in situations of conflicting claims—is how the objects of that attitude are conceived. In short, it is the characterization of persons as self-determining and rule-following agents that forms the most fundamental and pervasive link in the Kohlberg-Rawls connection.[27] As Rawls puts it, "Moral persons are defined as persons that have a conception of the good and a capacity for a sense of justice."[28] This link is manifested in different ways and at different levels of abstraction throughout their respective theories.[29] For reasons of space I will mention three, but develop only the third, which I consider to be the most important and problematic one.

First of all, that human beings are persons in the sense of individual, self-determining, and rule-following agents concerned with mutual respect is an assumption which differentiates Kohlberg's theory from other kinds of psychological theories and differentiates Rawls's theory from other kinds of philosophical theories. Kohlberg makes this assumption about his psychological subjects and then as a result is concerned with identifying the different patterns through which such subjects seek to understand interactions with others in the context of conditions of justice; by contrast, he does not concern himself with the way in which societies seek stability through the inculcation of fixed values into the consciousness of new members. Similarly, Rawls makes this assumption about the parties in the original position as a way of elaborating and legitimating our intuitions of the primacy of justice; in doing so he also seeks to contrast his theory with others, such as utilitarianism, which extend principles of choice appropriate for one person's conception of the good to questions concerning the regulation of associations of many persons (pp. 19, 28–29).

The second way in which this link is manifested is related to the first, but yet distinct. That is, it would be possible to embrace a set of assumptions about the nature of persons and then proceed to ignore them in one's methodology. However, it seems to me that in the cases of Kohlberg and Rawls there is a healthy congruence between their normative anthropological assumptions and how they go about developing, testing, and validating their respective theories. For Kohlberg this congruence is perhaps reflected most prominently in what he has recently referred to as a "boot-strapping" method of longitudinal interviews combined with an ongoing, theoretical interpretation of those interviews. The data which are elicited and interpreted are not predetermined, quantifiable choice responses, but rather, systematic attempts of one person trying through dialogue to understand the qualitative structure of how another person seeks to organize and make sense of certain aspects of a shared social world.[30] Although Rawls is clearly engaged in the philosophical task of elaboration and justification of a theory of justice rather than in the scientific task of verification of a psychological theory about how a mature sense of justice develops, there is a similar kind of congruence between his deep theoretical assumptions about persons and the way he characterizes the interaction between his ideas and those of his readers. This is so seldom noticed that it is worth quoting here:

> . . . If we should be able to characterize one (educated) person's sense of justice, we would have a good beginning toward a theory of justice. We may suppose that everyone has in himself the whole form of a moral conception. So for the purposes of this book, the views of the reader and the author are the only ones that count. The opinions of others are used only to clear our own heads (p. 50).

I think Rawls should be taken seriously when he says that "for the purposes of this book, the views of the reader and the author are the only ones that count." It reflects, I believe, a radical expression of faith in philosophical method as a rational dialogue between two equal, self-determining, and rule-following agents.

There are two further points which I wish to note briefly in the context of this second link. The first is in the nature of a qualification, and the second points out an interesting parallel between Kohlberg and Rawls which results. First of all, it is difficult to know how much Rawls sneaks in through the parenthetical qualification "(educated) person's" in the passage quoted immediately above. He obviously intends this to rule out certain kinds of views as counting in the same way. But what kind? How much of what kind of education is necessary before the reader's views are counted on equal terms with those of the author? If the claims of developmental theories such as Kohlberg's are even partially correct, they would seem to suggest that the conceptions of justice that older people have may differ qualitatively from those held by younger people, and perhaps even from those held by older, but relatively uneducated, persons. Whether Rawls can endorse his radical methodological stance vis-à-vis *all* persons, or only some who have achieved a certain level of maturity, is thus problematic.[31] And I suspect it is this problem which Rawls finds distasteful to acknowledge, but does so, reluctantly, in the qualifier "(educated)." But if we do accept this qualification and its implications, an interesting parallel between Kohlberg and Rawls can then be noted more clearly. In the construction of the original position, Rawls places explicit limits on the kinds of views which will count as legitimate proposals of "justice." Among these limits are the constraints of the concept of right mentioned above and the veil of ignorance behind which the parties in the original position must deliberate as indistinguisable persons. Now if one were to take account of the psychological complexities and interrelationships between various aspects of these two kinds of limits in the process of convincing people not already in it to assume the original position, then it strikes me that Kohlberg's developmental theory is not far off as an account of how it might be done. The differing patterns in differentiating and integrating various constraints of the right together with different kinds of information irrelevant to decisions of justice are exactly what Kohlberg is identifying as stages towards or steps into the original position. How much of this should be characterized as a problem of education toward the capacity to assume the original position is a problem which Rawls never discusses.[32]

Finally, there is yet a third way in which a conception of persons can be seen as forming the strongest link in the Kohlberg-Rawls connection. I find that it is the hardest to describe and the most problematic as an interpretation of what Kohlberg says, but I am convinced that it is also the most important from the point of view of what these two theories together help us to understand about our sense of justice. The shortest way of saying it is to say that in both theories principled judgments of justice are seen as the constructive emergents of a dynamic process of interaction among persons conceived as self-determining and rule-following agents. In this view, "justice" refers to, as Edmond Cahn has argued, "not a state, but a process; not a condition, but an action. 'Justice' means the *active process* of remedying or preventing what would arouse the sense of injustice."[33] In the context of justice in this sense, judgments of principle do not derive their validity from an epistemological status of certainty attributed to the principles referred to, but rather from their being viewed as what all parties could agree to when conceived of as persons seeking to regulate their interactions fairly. Rawls's original position and Kohlberg's "ideal role-taking" must be seen primarily as ways of entering moral argument; they are procedural interpretations of how persons of a certain sort seek a provisional, dynamic state of reflective equilibrium with each other about questions concerning their interactions in a world of a certain sort. In what follows I will try to explicate what all this means by focusing on the "constructive" aspect of principled judgments of justice. It will be relatively clear that this interpretation accords with Rawls's expressed views. It will, by contrast, be more problematic as an interpretation of Kohlberg. However, I want to argue that the legitimacy of the Rawls connection hangs, in the end, on whether or not Kohlberg's descriptions of stage 6 can be clarified in this way.

In his paper "The Original Position," Dworkin has cut to the core of Rawls's theory in a way which illuminates what is at issue in this last point. Dworkin elaborates two philosophical positions which give differing accounts for the way in which our ethical theories can be thought of as relating to our basic moral intuitions. He calls one the "natural model," and the other a "constructive model."

[According to the natural model] theories of justice, like Rawls's two principles, describe an objective moral reality; they are not, that is, created by men of societies but are rather discovered by them, as they discover laws of physics. The main instrument of this discovery is a moral faculty possessed by at least some men, which produces concrete intuitions of political morality in particular situations, like the intuition that slavery is wrong. . . . The second model is quite different. It treats intuitions of justice not as clues to the existence of independent principles, but rather as stipulated features of a general theory to be constructed, as if a sculptor set himself to carve the animal that best fit a pile of bones he happened to find together. This "constructive" model does not assume, as the natural model does, that principles of justice have some fixed, objective existence, so that descriptions of these principles must be true or false in some standard way. . . . It makes the different, and in some ways more complex, assumption that men and women have a responsibility to fit the particular judgments on which they act into a coherent program of action, or, at least, that officials who exercise power over other men have that sort of responsibility.[34]

Dworkin then examines the fit between each of these models and Rawls's conception of "reflective equilibrium." Although I cannot go into his argument here, I believe he argues convincingly that because in the natural model moral intuitions have the status of absolutely certain perceptions of moral reality, it is only the constructive model which can account for the "two-way feature of equilibrium."[35] For our purposes here the essential point, if we accept Dworkin's claim about Rawls, is that the two models reflect different conceptions of persons insofar as they make claims of justice which impinge on others. As Dworkin notes,

The natural model, we might say, looks at intuitions from the personal standpoint of the individual who holds them, and who takes them to be discrete observations of moral reality. The constructive model looks at these intuitions from a more public standpoint; it is a model that someone might propose for the governance of a community each of whose members has strong convictions that differ, though not too greatly, from the convictions of others.[36]

In the terms of this paper, it is the constructive model which conceives persons in such a way as to render mutual respect a viable, overriding attitude/principle. Persons are not thought of as independent, isolated "rule followers," with greater or lesser direct access to moral truth, but rather as rule-followers-in-relation who must construct and continually reconstruct through public dialogue the perspective from which rules governing their interaction have validity.

Now when we examine Kohlberg's claims in the light of this analysis of Rawls, the connection becomes more problematic at this point. As we have seen, Kohlberg wants us to believe that Rawls can be taken as providing a good example of an argument representing the stage 6 form. If this is so, and if the above interpretation of Rawls is correct, then what Kohlberg says about stage 6 should be congruent with the constructive model. The problem is that there are two possible lines of interpretation of what Kohlberg says about stage 6, only one of which supports this argument, and this one is by far the more inferential.

The first line of interpretation draws its support from the short descriptions of the stages which Kohlberg has used in numerous articles. If one concentrates exclusively on these descriptions, it would appear that stage 6 represents a good example of the "natural model," and, indeed, any "constructive" elements are exactly what is transcended in the move from stage 5 to stage 6. Thus stage 5, called "the social-contract legalistic orientation," emphasizes a kind of embeddedness in a community and procedures for dealing with differences within the community:

Right action tends to be defined in terms of general individual rights, and standards which have been critically examined and agreed upon by the whole society. There is a clear awareness of the relativism of personal values and opinions and a corresponding emphasis upon procedural rules for reaching consensus.[37]

By contrast, stage 6 is called "the universal ethical principle orientation" and appears to place more emphasis on the individual and his or her direct perception of moral truth:

Right is defined by the decision of conscience in accord with these self-chosen *ethical principles* appealing to logical comprehensiveness, universality, and consistency.[38]
The reason for doing right is that, as a rational person, the stage 6 individual has seen the validity of principles and has become committed to them.[39]

One gets the impression from this kind of short description that what distinguishes someone at stage 6 from someone at stage 5 is that the former has somehow transcended his or her ties to any real

community of others and needs only to consult an internal, infallible "faculty" of conscience in order to "see" or "discover" universally valid moral principles. In this interpretation, stage 6 reduces
to a "natural" position of "In your heart you know what's right"
dressed up in psychological and philosophical jargon.[40] It would
clearly be inconsistent with a "constructive" interpretation of
Rawls, and would to that extent make Kohlberg's use of Rawls
puzzling, to say the least.

However, there is a second possible line of interpretation which is
not well articulated in the short descriptions of the stages, but is
embedded in Kohlberg's several attempts to address the question of
"why stage 6 is better." Although it is less easily supported by
specific references, I believe it is both the correct interpretation and
the only one which supports the Rawls connection at this crucial
point. It depends, first of all, on noting the understanding of conscience which is common to both Kohlberg and Rawls. Thus, contrary to what seems to be implied in the short descriptions of stage
6, Kohlberg does not count reference to one's conscience as sufficient evidence for identifying the form of sound moral judgment.

To count as post-conventional such ideas or terms [as "conscience"] must be used
in such a way that it is clear that they have a foundation for a rational or moral
individual whose commitment to a group or society is based on prior principles.[41]

Although this seems to me an awkward way of putting it, I think
what Kohlberg is getting at here is, by implication, what Rawls
notes very bluntly: "A person's conscience is misguided when he
seeks to impose on us conditions that violate the principles to which
we would each consent in [the original position]" (pp. 518–519). In
other words, the soundness of moral judgment does not reside in an
individual's conscientious commitment or result from an infallible
faculty of conscience which somehow "discovers" moral truth in the
form of abstract moral principles; rather it is something that is
"constructed" through an equilibrium with principles arrived at in a
certain way.

For both Kohlberg and Rawls justice is the result of a dynamic, constructive decision procedure of a certain kind. Although there are some important differences with implications beyond the scope of this paper, the commonality which anchors these differences rests in a formally similar interpretation of how a conception of persons is embodied in decisions of justice. For Rawls this interpretation is reflected in the now familiar notion of the original position in which persons are thought of as deliberating about the choice of principles to regulate their interaction, a deliberation which is fair because it starts from a condition of "equality between human beings as moral persons, as creatures having a conception of their good and capable of a sense of justice," and procedurally "excludes the knowledge of those contingencies which sets men at odds and allows them to be guided by their prejudices" (p. 19). For Kohlberg, this interpretation is reflected in his description of stage 6 in terms of individuals seeking complete "reversibility" of judgment through "ideal role-taking" (or, more whimsically, "moral musical chairs"):

We call the process by which a reversible moral decision is reached, "ideal role-taking." Stage 6 moral judgment is based on role-taking the claim of each actor under the assumption that all other actors' claims are also governed by the Golden Rule and accommodated accordingly. . . . . . . Ideal role-taking is the decision-procedure ultimately required by the attitudes of respect for persons and of justice as equity recognized at higher stages. . . . . . . A decision reached in that way is in "equilibrium" in the sense that it is "right" from the point of view of all involved insofar as they are concerned to be governed by a moral attitude or a conception of justice, i.e., insofar as they are willing to take the roles of others.[42]

As Kohlberg suggests here (and has tried to develop more fully in a recent paper[43]), the kind of equilibrium sought through justice is not the sort of thing that can be conceived from the point of view of persons in isolation (as the natural model would suggest). Rather, it is a provisional point of hypothetical agreement resulting from a way of entering moral argument and seeking fair adjudication of competing claims of persons, where persons are conceived as agents of mutual respect. If I am correct in this interpretation of Kohlberg, it is at this point that the Rawls connection is most clearly revealed and legitimated.

NOTES

1. See, for example, Lawrence Kohlberg, "From Is to Ought: How to Commit the Naturalistic Fallacy and Get Away with It in the Study of Moral Development," in *Cognitive Development and Epistemology,* ed. Theodore Mischel (New York: Academic Press, 1971), pp. 151–235; also, Kohlberg's "The Claim to Moral Adequacy of a Highest Stage of Moral Judgment," *Journal of Philosophy* 70 (October 1973): 630–646. The references to Rawls are to *A Theory of Justice* (Cambridge, Mass.: Belknap Press, 1971); in this paper, unless otherwise noted by footnote, references to Rawls will be to this source, with page numbers identified in the text.

2. See, for example, E. V. Sullivan, *Kohlberg's Structuralism: A Critical Appraisal,* Monograph Series, no. 15 (Toronto: Ontario Institute for Studies in Education, 1977).

3. Lawrence Kohlberg, "Justice as Reversibility," manuscript of a chapter to be included in a forthcoming collection edited by P. Laslett and J. Fiskin (London: Blackwell), p. 46.

4. For a good discussion of what is at issue here, see Charles Fried, *Right and Wrong* (Cambridge, Mass.: Harvard University Press, 1978); for Rawls's most concise discussion of these conceptual distinctions, see Section 68 of *A Theory of Justice;* for a discussion of the distinctions and their application to Kohlberg, see Dwight R. Boyd, "The Moralberry Pie: Some Basic Concepts," *Theory into Practice* 16, no. 2 (April 1977): 67–72.

5. Isaiah Berlin, *Four Essays on Liberty* (London: Oxford University Press 1969), pp. 168–169.

6. P. F. Strawson, "Social Morality and Individual Ideal," in *The Definition of Morality,* ed. G. Wallace and A. D. M. Walker (London: Methuen & Co., 1970), p. 103.

7. Lawrence Kohlberg, "Stages of Moral Development as a Basis for Moral Education," in *Moral Education: Interdisciplinary Approaches,* ed. C. M. Beck, B. S. Crittenden, and E. V. Sullivan (Toronto: University of Toronto Press, 1971), p. 51.

8. Lawrence Kohlberg, "Why a Higher Stage Is a Better Stage," in *Collected Papers on Moral Development and Moral Education,* vol. 2, edited by Kohlberg and disseminated by the Center for Moral Education (Cambridge, Mass.: Harvard University Press, 1975).

9. Kohlberg, "Is to Ought," p. 215.

10. See Ronald Dworkin, "The Original Position," in *Reading Rawls.* ed. Norman Daniels (New York: Basic Books, 1976), pp. 40–46. Although he is concerned with characterizing Rawls's theory as a political theory, and is thus using "right" in this context, Dworkin has made this point about Rawls quite clearly, arguing that the centrality of the contract in Rawls's methodology indicates that his theory must be "right-based," rather than either "goal-based" or "duty-based."

11. Kohlberg, "Why a Higher Stage is a Better Stage," p. 27.

12. John B. Orr, "Cognitive-Developmental Approaches to Moral Education: A Social Ethical Analysis," *Educational Theory* 24, no. 4 (Fall 1974): 367.

13. Lawrence Kohlberg, (i) "Education for Justice: A Modern Statement of the Platonic View," in *Moral Education,* ed. Nancy F. Sizer and Theodore R. Sizer (Cambridge, Mass.: Harvard University Press), p. 69; (ii) "Is to Ought," p. 192; (iii) "Education for Justice," p. 70; (iv) "Is to Ought," p. 221; (v) "Why a Higher Stage Is a Better Stage," pp. 11–12; (vi) "Is to Ought," p. 165, Table 1.

14. Given the proclivity of some to criticize Rawls for having a narrow or restricted view of social interaction, I might also note that neither does Rawls claim that justice is the only normative principle that matters, but simply that it may be the most important part of any more general conception of a "social ideal" which deals with "all the virtues of the basic structure" and their interrelationships (p. 9).

15. R. S. Downie and Elizabeth Telfer, *Respect for Persons* (New York: Schocken Books, 1970). One of the more interesting points is their metaethical speculations and their relation to Kohlberg's claims in "Is to Ought" about how developmental theory interacts with the naturalistic fallacy. See also Dwight Boyd and Lawrence Kohlberg, "The Is-Ought Problem: A Developmental Perspective," *Zygon* 8, nos. 3–4 (September–December 1973): 358–372.

16. Downie and Telfer, *Respect for Persons,* p. 17.

17. Kohlberg, "Stages of Moral Development," p. 58.

18. Downie and Telfer, *Respect for Persons,* pp. 28–29.

19. Kohlberg, "Is to Ought," pp. 190–193.

20. Kohlberg, "Is to Ought," pp. 208–213.

21. See Kohlberg, "Claim to Moral Adequacy," p. 644, and "Justice as Reversibility," pp. 15–16.

22. Downie and Telfer, *Respect for Persons,* p. 27.

23. Ibid., p. 29. If I am correct here, then part of Sullivan's critique of Kohlberg (*Kohlberg's Structuralism*) may be aimed at a straw man: he wants to characterize stage 6 as "impersonal," but it is hard to imagine a more personal attitude than love! It might also be noted that, although Michael Pritchard has recently faulted Rawls for not utilizing the capacity for sympathy in his conception of moral development, Rawls also sees a close tie between his conception of justice and love, claiming at one point that " . . . the sense of justice is continuous with the love of mankind" (p. 476). See Michael S. Pritchard, "Rawls' Moral Psychology," *Southwestern Journal of Philosophy* 8 (Winter 1977).

24. In fact, consistent with this discussion, Rawls has acknowledged (personal communication) that he finds little wrong with Downie and Telfer's analysis of respect for persons; he simply thinks that they do not get very far because they start in the wrong place.

25. Dworkin, "The Original Position," p. 51.

26. Downie and Telfer, *Respect for Persons,* p. 58.

27. This, of course, even when spelled out should not be taken as their complete conception of persons, but rather that *part* which is relevant under the conditions of justice.

28. John Rawls, "Fairness to Goodness," *The Philosophical Review* 84 (1975):

539, footnote. See also Rawls, "The Independence of Moral Theory," *Proceedings of the American Philosophical Association* 47 (1974–75): 18.

29. Although I do not have space here to elaborate, I suspect that the failure to keep these ways and levels differentiated leads to many of the interpretations of both Kohlberg and Rawls which I would argue are just mistaken, e.g., the criticism that self-interest still reigns as the chief motivation in Kohlberg's stage 6 and Rawls's well-ordered society. A criticism of Kohlberg on this point can be found in Elizabeth Morelli, "The Sixth Stage of Moral Development," *Journal of Moral Education* 7, no. 2: 97–108. References to criticisms of Rawls on this point, as well as his reply, can be found in "Fairness to Goodness" and "The Independence of Moral Theory." In the latter Rawls replies in a way which I think also accords with Kohlberg's position: " . . . a basic form of moral motivation is the desire to be and to be recognized by others as being a certain kind of person" (p. 13).

30. Lawrence Kohlberg, "The Meaning and Measurement of Moral Development," paper delivered to the American Psychological Association, Toronto, Canada, September 2, 1978. Although the recent changes in Kohlberg's scoring methodology discussed in this paper may have answered some of the more serious psychometric challenges coming from critics, I would argue that insofar as this has been accomplished through a rigid standardization of the interview format and the way in which responses get interpreted, a serious weakening of the very sort of congruence that I am noting here may be the not insignificant price.

31. And whether the latter can be done in a noncircular way is, in turn, one of the central philosophical problems which plagues a developmental theory such as Kohlberg's.

32. When he does elaborate his own theory of moral development (see chapter 8), Rawls does so in the context of the stability problem, *not* as a problem cutting to the core of his mode of justification.

33. Edmond Cahn, *The Sense of Injustice* (Bloomington: Indiana University Press, 1964), p. 13.

34. Dworkin, "The Original Position," pp. 27–28.

35. Ibid., p. 34.

36. Ibid., p. 31.

37. Kohlberg, "Is to Ought," p. 165.

38. Ibid.

39. Lawrence Kohlberg et al., *Assessing Moral Stages: A Manual*, Part I (Cambridge, Mass.: Center for Moral Education, Harvard University, 1978), p. 28.

40. As I have argued in "An Interpretation of Principled Morality," *Journal of Moral Education* 8, no. 2 (1979), this interpretation characterizes something closer to a rule orientation of conventional morality than one of principled moral judgment. This argument is now supported at least operationally in Kohlberg's coding methodology. In the new *Assessing Moral Stages: A Manual* (p. 26) this perspective is characterized as the "B/C Transitional Level"—"postconventional but not yet principled," and one of the subpositions of this level is defined as the "obligation to our conscience orientation."

41. Kohlberg, *Assessing Moral Stages* p. 21.

42. Kohlberg, "Claim to Moral Adequacy," pp. 643–645.
43. Kohlberg, "Justice as Reversibility."

REFERENCES

Aron, Israela Ettenberg. "Moral Philosophy and Moral Education: A Critique of Kohlberg's Theory." *School Review* (February 1977): 197–217.

———. "Moral Philosophy and Moral Education II. The Formalist Tradition and the Deweyan Alternative." *School Review* (August 1977): 513–534.

Baier, Kurt. "Moral Development." *The Monist* 58, no. 4 (October 1974): 601–615.

Bates, Stanley. "The Motivation to Be Just." *Ethics* 8, no. 1: 1–17.

Berlin, Isaiah. *Four Essays on Liberty.* London: Oxford University Press, 1969.

Boyd, Dwight. "An Interpretation of Principled Morality." *Journal of Moral Education* 8, no. 2 (1979).

———. "The Moralberry Pie: Some Basic Concepts." *Theory into Practice* 16, no. 2 (April 1977): 67–72.

Boyd, Dwight, and Kohlberg, Lawrence. "The Is-Ought Problem: A Developmental Perspective." *Zygon* 8, nos. 3–4 (September–December 1973): 368–372.

———. "Medical Ethics: An Antidote for Sophomoritis." In *Teaching Biomedical and Health Care Ethics to Liberal Arts Undergraduates.* pp. 38–49. Edited by H. Bradley Sagen. Chicago: Associated Colleges of the Midwest, 1977.

Bunzl, Martin. "The Moral Development of Philosophers." *Journal of Moral Education* 7, no. 1: 3–8.

Cahn, Edmond. *The Sense of Injustice.* Bloomington: Indiana University Press, 1964.

Cranor, Carl. "Justice, Respect, and Self-Respect." *Philosophy Research Archives* 2, no. 3 (1976): 89–110.

Crittenden, Brian. *Form and Content in Moral Education.* Monograph Series, no. 12. Toronto: Ontario Institute for Studies in Education, 1972.

Daniels, Norman, ed. *Reading Rawls: Critical Studies of "A Theory of Justice."* New York: Basic Books, 1976.

Darwall, Stephen L. "A Defense of the Kantian Interpretation." *Ethics* 86, no. 2: 164–170.

———. "Two Kinds of Respect." *Ethics* 88, no. 1: 36–49.

Downie, R. S., and Telfer, Elizabeth. *Respect for Persons.* New York: Schocken Books, 1970.

Fried, Charles. *Right and Wrong.* Cambridge, Mass.: Harvard University Press, 1978.

Gibbs, John. "Kohlberg's Stages of Moral Development: A Constructive Critique." *Harvard Educational Review* 47, no. 1 (1977).

Hall, Robert, and Davis, John. *Moral Education in Theory and Practice.* Buffalo: Prometheus Books, 1975.

Johnson, Oliver A. "The Kantian Interpretation." *Ethics* 85, no. 1: 58–66.

Kohlberg, Lawrence. "The Claim to Moral Adequacy of a Highest Stage of Moral Judgment." *The Journal of Philosophy* 70 (October 1973): 630–646.

————. "Education for Justice: A Modern Statement of the Platonic View." In *Moral Education.* Edited by Nancy F. Sizer and Theodore R. Sizer. Cambridge, Mass.: Harvard University Press, 1970.

————. "From Is to Ought: How to Commit the Naturalistic Fallacy and Get Away with It in the Study of Moral Development." In *Cognitive Development and Epistemology,* pp. 151–235. Edited by Theodore Mischel. New York: Academic Press, 1971.

————. "Justice as Reversibility." Manuscript of a chapter to be included in a forthcoming collection edited by P. Laslett and J. Fiskin. London: Blackwell.

————. "Stages of Moral Development as a Basis for Moral Education." In *Moral Education: Interdisciplinary Approaches,* pp. 23–92. Edited by C. M. Beck, B. S. Crittenden, and E. V. Sullivan. Toronto: University of Toronto Press, 1971.

————. "The Meaning and Measurement of Moral Development." Paper delivered to the American Psychological Association, Toronto, Canada, September 2, 1978.

————. "Why a Higher Stage Is a Better Stage." In *Collected Papers on Moral Development and Moral Education,* Vol. II. Edited by Lawrence Kohlberg and disseminated by the Center for Moral Education. Cambridge, Mass.: Harvard University Press, 1975.

Kohlberg, Lawrence; Colby, Anne; Gibbs, John; Speicher-Dubin, Betsy; and Power, Clark. *Assessing Moral Stages: A Manual.* Cambridge, Mass. Center for Moral Education, Harvard University, 1978.

Morgan, Kathryn. "Philosophical Problems in Cognitive-Moral Developmental Theory: A Critique of the Work of Lawrence Kohlberg." *Philosophy of Education 1973:* Proceedings of the Twenty-ninth Annual Meeting of the Philosophy of Education Society.

O'Neil, Richard A. "On Rawls' Justification Procedure." *Philosophy Research Archives* 2, no. 2 (1976): 196–209.

Orr, John B. "Cognitive-Developmental Approaches to Moral Education: A Social Ethical Analysis." *Educational Theory* 24, no. 4 (Fall 1974): 365–373.

Pritchard, Michael S. "Rawls' Moral Psychology." *Southwestern Journal of Philosophy* 8 (Winter 1977): 59–72.

Raphael, D. D. "The Standard of Morals." Presidential Address read before the 96th Session of the Aristotelian Society. *Proceedings of the Aristotelian Society* 75 (1974–75): 1–12.

Rawls, John. "The Basic Structure as Subject." *American Philosophical Quarterly* 14, no. 2 (April 1977): 159–165.

————. "Fairness to Goodness." *The Philosophical Review* 84 (1975): 536–554.

————. "The Independence of Moral Theory." *Proceedings of the American Philosophical Association* 47 (1974–75): 5–22.

————. "Reply to Alexander and Musgrave." *The Quarterly Journal of Economics* 88 (November 1974): 633–655.

————. *A Theory of Justice.* Cambridge, Mass.: Belknap Press, 1971.

Sichel, Betty. "A Critical Study of Kohlberg's Theory of the Development of Moral Judgments." *Proceedings of the Thirty-second Annual Meeting of the Philosophy of Education Society* (1976): 209–220.

Singer, Marcus G. "The Methods of Justice: Reflections on Rawls." *Journal of Value Inquiry* 10, no. 4 (1976): 286–316.

Strawson, P. F. "Social Morality and Individual Ideal." In *The Definition of Morality*, pp. 98–118. Edited by G. Wallace and A. D. M. Walker. London: Methuen & Co., 1970.

Sullivan, E. V. *Kohlberg's Structuralism: A Critical Appraisal.* Monograph Series, no. 15. Toronto: Ontario Institute for Studies in Education, 1977.

Wren, Thomas E. "Rightness and the Formal Level of Action." *Ethics* 83, no. 4 (July 1973): 327–337.

Chapter 7

Philosophical Difficulties and "Moral Development"

JOHN WILSON

INTRODUCTION

As a character in one of Iris Murdoch's novels somewhere re marks, when a philosopher says, "I don't understand," he may often mean, "You're not clear," or even "That's not sense." The general tenor of what I want to say lies somewhere in the middle of these. If what is said by Lawrence Kohlberg and other developmental psychologists about "stages of development," "moral judgments," and other things is clear, it is not clear to me (I don't understand it); and while of course it *may* make sense, or sense might be made of it by some well-wisher, my guess is that it does not.

By "make sense" I do not, of course (being a philosopher), mean "fit the facts." That is, in part at least, an empirical matter; and if the distinction between empirical and conceptual (philosophical) questions is lost, this sort of enquiry might as well be abandoned altogether. I mean rather that the various *concepts* and *descriptions* used by such psychologists are unclear and may be incoherent (that is, internally contradictory). To take an obvious, and naturally debatable, example: it is not clear to me in what sense, if any, a person's mind, or his understanding of the appropriateness of a certain kind of reason, or even his willingness to use that kind of

214

reason in decision making and/or in action, can be said to *develop*. Brains, busts, and biceps may develop or be developed in a sense in which minds and moral understanding logically cannot. If now someone says that "develop" is being used in a different, perhaps more general or looser, sense—very well. But then I want to know exactly what that sense is and what it implies. (Clearly there is some sense in which I develop my mind, or my mind is developed, by my being taught mathematics. But this sense, whatever it is, equally clearly carries no implication that teaching and learning are in any way opposed to or even different from "development.")

It may be as well to say at the start that muddle and incoherence in psychology and "social science" (whatever that may be) are wholly unsurprising phenomena. We are not dealing with a physical world in which, by and large, there are plenty of discretely observable entities whose descriptions may give us no trouble. But those psychologists who live up to the root-meaning of their title by being concerned with the human mind—not the brain or the body— would naturally expect conceptual or philosophical difficulties right at the beginning of their work. For how they describe the phonomena, or what they call "a fact," is immediately controversial. Somebody says something in a certain situation ("That's wrong," "I'd do such-and-such," or whatever)—is that a *judgment?* Is it a *moral* judgment? Well, what counts as a "judgment"? And what counts as "moral"? It is no use trying to pretend either (a) that we all know the answer to such questions (if we did, there would be no such enquiry as the philosophy of mind or ethics), or (b) that it doesn't matter whether we know what we mean by them (for if we don't, how can we know what we are talking or doing psychology *about.*).

No sophisticated person, then (and certainly no philosopher), can suppose that progress on this front can be anything but slow and arduous. Nor can he or she believe that we are yet anywhere near being able to formulate anything to be called a "theory of moral education," indeed, I myself would not know what such a phrase meant. Apart from whatever philosophical clarity may already have been achieved, we are surely in the early taxonomic stage of any empirical enquiry; a stage at which we need to look very hard at what lies open to observation and match it with appropriate linguistic descriptions—all this before we can start even stating "the facts," let alone "theorizing" about them.

Most of this paper will consist of an (inexhaustive) account of some of the problems which crop up in this area; this in order to show, at least, just what sort of problems they are. However, I also have some more positive suggestions to make (based on common sense, backed by a little conceptual clarity): (1) about the kind of approach and set-up required for further progress in research, and (2) about what can here and now be done in practical moral education, without the benefit (or the impediment) of developmental psychology. I ought perhaps to add that, though I shall refer often to Kohlberg, I am not trying to "demolish Kohlberg's theory" or to score points off him. What I say applies to empirical work in this field generally. My personal opinion is that the ground-level data that Kohlberg has produced are a good deal more interesting than anything we have had so far, and certainly worth pursuing. It is when the data—what various children or other subjects actually say and do—are too hastily built up into a "theory" ("model," etc.) that things go wrong.

DIFFICULTIES AND OBSCURITIES

The problems to be examined overlap, but may be (brutally) placed under three headings: "morality," language, and stages.

"Morality"

The initial question for all researchers in this field is not "What is morality?" in the sense of "What does morality consist of (what is its essence, how does it function)?" but rather "What are we going to count as 'moral' or 'morality'—what are we going to mean by these terms?"

Usually the assumption has been made that "morality" must have a particular *content*. Researchers have assigned (usually unconsciously) some such content to "morality" and proceeded to conduct their empirical inquiries on this basis. Very often they have done this with extreme naiveté, and tacitly defined "morality" in terms of what is considered to be "moral" in their own society. Thus Havighurst and Taba[1] inquired into five "moral traits"—honesty, responsibility, loyalty, moral courage, and friendliness. Not all the items on this list would commend themselves to, for instance, a Japanese samurai, Machiavelli, or members of a tough teenage gang. The point comes out more strongly in their assessment methods: the researchers derived *reputation ratings* from peers, day-school teachers, Sunday school teachers, youth leaders, and employers. In other words, "moral" is to mean "what is thought to be good by the society (or the official 'establishment' of the society)." The same point applies to other studies, such as Hartshorne and May,[2] Peck and Havighurst,[3] and others too numerous to mention—indeed, to almost all work in this field.

A determined, though also confused, attempt to use a logical or formal criterion is apparent in Kohlberg's work.

> . . . Like most [?] moral philosophers from Kant to Hare, Baier, Aiken, etc., we define morality in terms of the formal character of a moral judgment or a moral point of view, rather than in terms of its content. Impersonality, ideality, universalizability, and pre-emptiveness are among the formal characteristics of a moral judgment. Unlike judgments of prudence or aesthetics, moral judgments tend to be [?] universal, inclusive, consistent, and grounded on objective, impersonal or ideal grounds. This enables us to define a moral judgment as "moral" without considering its content (the action judged) and without considering whether it agrees with our own judgments or standards.[4]

However, it is not really clear what this criterion is supposed to be. Our suspicions are aroused when Kohlberg outlaws statement like "It's not right to steal because you'll get put in jail" claiming that these are "not moral judgments."[5] The dismissal of "judgments of prudence or aesthetics" suggests that Kohlberg is in fact using a criterion in terms of the *kind of reasons given*. The picture is of a class of "moral" reasons (derived from or connected with justice, in Kohlberg's view) alongside a class of "prudential" or "aesthetic" reasons which are impersonal, based on an ideal, and universalized (whatever the best interpretation of these terms may be). For instance, I may govern my behavior and think that others should govern theirs by some kind of egoism, or by an "honor ethic." *Any* kind of reasons *can,* in point of strict logic, be used to back whatever behavior I think it right for myself and others to engage in—though it does not follow that all reasons are equally good.

We shall see later the effect that this confusion has on Kohlberg's assessment procedures. But we can already guess that his picture of morality (whether intentionally adopted or not) is, in fact, not content-free. It is a utilitarian picture based on justice—roughly, a basic "social morality." Hence, we are not surprised at such remarks as "The most fundamental values of a society are termed moral, and the major moral values in our society are the values of justice,"[6] "A moral obligation is an obligation to respect the right or claim of another person,"[7] "A moral conflict is a conflict between competing claims of men,"[8] and so forth. Despite Kohlberg's flirtation with a formal, content-free criterion, the content is plain enough.

It is possible to see fairly clearly how this restricted picture of morality affects the assessment methods commonly used by researchers. First, the selection of assessment methods—Kohlberg's stories, for instance—will naturally be dictated by the (tacit) definition of morality in terms of a particular content. They will not necessarily tap the subject's (S's) overriding principles, which may fall outside that content. This obviously sets a limitation on the assessments: they cannot serve us if we are concerned to find out what are S's most important values, principles, or behavior-generating rules. (Already we feel tempted to say "S's morality," a temptation to which we ought to yield.)

But this is more than a limitation. If we do not know what S's overriding principles are, how can we select the stories fairly? I mean this: It might be said, by Kohlberg and others, that all we want to know in this research is how S stands in relation to "social morality" (justice and so forth). So we pick stories designed to elucidate this and see how S rates on these stories, what "stage of development" he has reached. But how much *weight* S puts on this "social morality" will depend on what the counterattractions are, on the "pulls" or distractions from other kinds of principles—principles of honor, guilt, self-advantage, or whatever. Now unless we have a clear idea of what these other "pulls" are, we cannot construct stories which incorporate them satisfactorily; and if we do not incorporate them, we cannot measure how S stands in relation to "social morality." We cannot tell what S really thinks he or anybody else ought to do in a "justice" situation unless we build in possible conflicts produced by other "pulls"—I would say, other kinds of morality.

It might be argued that the stories themselves (and, more plausibly, the lengthy interviews and other data that precede the story construction) determine what the "pulls" are. But this is not convincing. First, if we conceive of "morality" as "social morality," this will inevitably prejudice our collection of data, for we will perceive various "pulls" *only as connected with* this social morality. Thus, the description of the supposed "stages" is nearly always in terms of an S failing to get, or partly getting, or wholly getting the hang of social morality. For example, S is concerned with "performing good or right roles" (a case of partly getting the hang). The "pulls" are not done justice to in their own right. Secondly, there will be "pulls"—other overriding principles or types of morality—which may not conflict at all with social morality. "Honor" may usually coincide with "justice," or "honor" may operate in areas where there is no possible conflict. The former case can be taken care of by a close inspection of the reasons for choice. Does S think that the debt should be repaid because it is honorable, or because it is just? But the latter case is more difficult. Suppose S's overriding concerns (morality) are with "honor" or some other ego-ideal in an area which rarely or never conflicts with social morality: for instance, in the area of religious observance, dress, various food taboos, etiquette, or sex, and so forth? It might be hard here even to think of ways of measuring this concern against the concerns of social morality, particularly if S is a hermit or a "dropout" or in some other way disconnected from society. We need, initially, a much more open and theory-free approach.

Language

There are also very serious problems about the language used in the assessments. I am not now referring to whether test stories are constructed in the first or third person, or to the children's verbal ability, or to similar methodological (rather than conceptual) difficulties. I refer to the obvious fact that *we do not know what S means* when he uses words like "right," "ought," "should," and so on, and that we cannot assign a "stage" or type of reasoning to S unless and until we do know.

Thus, for one S, "right" may actually mean "approved by adults" or "approved by peers"; for another, "ought" may mean "serving my own advantage"; for another, "good" may mean "in accordance with the rules." So if we ask these Ss what is right, or what they (or another) ought to do, or what is good, we are already loading the responses (for each S) with an inbuilt demand for a certain mode of reasoning. Now it might be thought that this hardly matters, that we are eliciting his or her mode or style of moral reasoning anyway—and if philosophers choose to describe this as "finding out what Ss mean by moral language," who cares? But this will not do; for there is no necessary connection between what any S means by (say) "ought" and "right," on the one hand, and what S's own moral values actually are on the other. To take an extreme case: a teenage S might give very satisfactory answers to questions about what was "right" or what "ought to be done," in terms of the reasons given by adults at stages 5 or 6; but, on further investigation, this may only mean that the teenager is good at playing this particular language game on demand. "Ought" and "right" for him mean "what sophisticated adults tell me"; he does not personally *value* those reasons, and his own moral judgments may be expressed in quite different language—that is "with it," "trendy," "groovy," or whatever the current slang may be.

This last point, like the others, stems partly from the restricted picture of morality we have been criticizing, but it has a broader application. To enlarge on this point, we may consider research which seems prima facie to fit a wider picture of morality.

Williams[9] used interviews to classify children's "moral thinking," without overtly loading the dice in favor of a particular kind of morality or a particular content. For much of the interview the child was allowed to respond freely to what he thought "good," "bad," "right," or "wrong," and was asked to say why he thought this. The responses of the children were then classified under a number of "modes of thought" (originally more than ten).

Roughly, then, when the child or interviewer has given an example of something "wrong" or "bad," the child is asked, "Why is that wrong (bad)?" and replies, "Because . . . " Now, what ambiguities are there here? First, there are at least five things the child may understand by "wrong." The child may understand (i) what *other people think or say* is wrong or ought not to be done; (ii) what *other people actually avoid doing* is wrong; (iii) what *he thinks* (in a general way) is wrong or ought not to be done; (iv) what *he* actually avoids doing is wrong; (v) what he thinks *he himself ought* not to do is wrong. (If we wanted to, we could make more distinctions still. For instance, we have not considered S's feelings about rightness and wrongness, which are distinguishable both from S's beliefs and S's actions.)

Secondly, when the child says "Because . . . " he appears to be proffering a reason, but the child may think that the "reason" is (be proffering the reason *as*):

(a) a *good* reason, or just *a* (possibly bad) reason;

(b) a reason which is "ultimate" (stands on its own feet), or which assumes a background of higher-level reasons;

(c) a reason which the child would use (have in mind) when acting, or which the child knows of but would not use;

(d) a reason which would be also the cause of the child's behavior and which he or she approves of, or a reason which would cause the child's behavior and which he or she does not approve of (a reason or cause which, in some sense, operates against the child's better judgment).

This last possiblity (d) reminds us that we at least have to draw some distinction between "reasons" and "causes"—more precisely, between responses which are meant as justifications and those meant only to explain. Of course these interconnect in complicated ways; but many responses do not, prima facie, even look like reasons in the sense of attempts to justify. They look more like admissions of psychological compulsion, descriptions of emotion or feeling states, or attempts to render intelligible the kind of "pulls" which an S is moved by. These differences connect, obviously enough, with different senses or implications that words like "wrong," "ought," etc., may have for different Ss. The position is further complicated by the fact that different "pulls" or syllogisms may operate at different levels of S's mind. One part of S, we may be tempted to say, pulls one way, and another part pulls another. At a given time S may express one "pull" in his response, at another time another "pull," and at a third time S may stand back from both "pulls" and in some sense adjudicate between them.

To appreciate these (elementary) distinctions is to gain a distant view of the extent of our own ignorance. Pursuing the linguistic points a little further, we can see the need for listing a number of possible words and phrases which may figure in our questions. Along these lines:

Would it be *wrong/right* to . . . ?

What *ought you/he/one* to . . . ?

What *should you/he/one* . . . ?

Would it be *good* (bad, better, worse, best, worst) to . . . ?

What *is he* to . . . ?

Would it be *mistaken/correct* to . . . ?

What is your *duty* . . . ?

What are you *obliged* to . . . ?

These variations are not trivial, insofar as it may be the case that different words and phrases generate or induce different answers. Are we even clear ourselves about the conceptual/linguistic differences in "normal" English usage—let alone the differences that affect the responses of children and adolescents?

Nor is this all; for (as always in philosophy) we are concerned with English usage only in order to establish conceptual, language-free distinctions, and we cannot be certain that these and other particular English phrases give us all the differences that are possible, and hence that are possibly in the minds of our respondents. What responses would we get if we asked French-speaking children, *"Que faut-il faire?"* or *"Que devez-vous . . . ?"* or *"Que devriez vous . . . ?"* What distinctions are incorporated in the German modal verbs *sollen, müssen*, etc.? The point here is not that, as good internationalists, we are concerned with other people besides those of the Anglo-Saxon races. The point is that we cannot even begin to evaluate a "response" unless we are absolutely clear what the respondent means, and that this is a long and difficult business.

In this light, even the research title of "moral judgment" seems questionable. By what right do we describe all the responses that we get from children (or indeed adults) as *judgments?* Many expressions or sentences could not properly be called judgments or beliefs at all. It is obvious, for instance, that if I respond to talk of homosexuality or pork-eating by saying "Ugh! How foul!" or something of that kind, I have not necessarily made a judgment at all; I may have merely expressed my feelings. Further, the linguistic form may mislead here. Although, when doing philosophy, we can distinguish between "It's disgusting" and "It disgusts me," or between "It's right" and "I like it," many people may mean the one when they say the other.

It seems plain that many linguistic expressions, particularly in the areas of morality and religion, do not represent beliefs at all, or, at least, they do not represent supposed *truths* to which the speaker is wedded (or even thinks that he or she is wedded) via the *evidence.* The expressions represent, rather, feelings or fantasies or pictures of some kind to which the speaker is indeed firmly wedded; but it is some emotion that has made the marriage, not any consideration of evidence. When we consider such notions as "taboo," "dislike," "disapproval," "guilt," "ego-ideal," and "shame," it is clear that many responses are not judgments at all, although the linguistic forms (usually forced on Ss in test stories or interviews) may appear in the indicative mood. We cannot tell what a response means without further investigation. One Jew may say, "It's wrong to eat pork," and mean that to eat pork is, in fact, a moral mistake, incorrect, unreasonable in terms of whatever reasons he may have in mind.

Another may say just the same, but mean no more than "Ugh!" or "Not for me!"

On the other hand, if we are at all interested in what might generally be called S's moral *commitments,* then it is fairly clear that we cannot satisfactorily determine these without adequate data about S's feelings and *behavior.* For we should then be interested in those senses of S's response words ("wrong," "ought," etc.), or those speech acts of S, which involved some tendency or commitment to *action* on S's part. And we should not accept the words or speech acts as sincere, fully "meant," or wholehearted unless, in fact, S did characteristically take such action, or take it "under normal circumstances" (however this phrase may be construed). To use a philosopher's term, we should not know whether S's judgments of certain things as "right," "wrong," etc., were genuinely *prescriptive,* unless we had checked these judgments against S's behavior.

Stages

I have little to say under this heading that amounts to any more than an expression of total bafflement on my part. Given a clear answer to the question "What are the stages supposed to be stages *of?*" I might have more to say. But I have found no one to give me such an answer. "Moral development" ("moral judgment," etc.) seems to me no answer at all, for plainly, on any account, the morally educated ("developed?" "mature?") person requires a considerable number of *different* attributes. I shall mention later at least sixteen, and no doubt more distinctions are to be made. Thus it is part of what it means to be morally educated that one (1) has the concept of a person, (2) aims at using a principle of action based on the wants and interests of people (rather than on honor, selfishness, or whatever), and (3) genuinely accepts this principle, in that one has some investment of feeling in it—that one does not just accept it in theory, so to speak. There are also attributes less uniquely concerned with morality, such as determination, alertness, emotional insight, and so on. Now it is surely quite clear that a person's "development" or progress may be—almost certainly will be—different in respect of these different attributes. Each person might, I suppose, have a set of "stages" or milestones, but each would not have the same set. This is why it seems vague to the point of meaninglessness to talk blandly of "stages of moral judgment" (". . . development").

Secondly, one would need to know whether the stages are supposed to be logically necessary or only empirically (contingently) the case. Is it like having to grasp (in chess) the concept of a king before the concept of check, and the concept of check before the concept of checkmate? Or does it just happen to be the case that some, most, or all human children move from one stage to another in a certain order? Peters[10] thinks that the Kohlbergian stages (like at least some of Piaget's) are logical; I myself am not clear, because it is not clear what the stages are stages of. It is worth noting, perhaps, that if they are purely contingent then presumably they can be altered. New methods of pedagogy or upbringing or new kinds of societies and experiences could, in fact, change the whole picture. Any very serious impossibility of missing out stages, or reversing their order, would have to depend on the stages being logically necessary.

I do not myself see that the logic of morality—the structure of the concepts involved and their complexity—is particularly difficult. What makes morality difficult, as surely we know quite well, is not that people are not clever or "intellectual" enough but that we yield to temptations and muddle. I should be surprised if the central notions of morality involved a great deal of intellectual ("cognitive") sophistication, though of course our understanding of what constitutes people's interests in complex cases, or of their and our own emotions, is often inadequate. So I doubt if anyone could show any very elaborate structure of thought or concepts—anything analogous, say, to the structures involved in mathematics or science— inherent in which were many complicated "stages" of a logical kind.

SOME POSITIVE REQUIREMENTS

As I see it, no strategy in moral education or development— whether for research or practical teaching or anything else—can be regarded as serious unless it begins by listing the attributes or qualities of a morally educated (mature, developed, etc.) person: that is, what must (logically) count as such. Without such a list, we cannot know what we mean by "properly educated," "having made (good or optimum) progress," "being properly developed," etc., in morality. The best I myself have done along these lines so far is the following list:

PHIL(HC)	Having the concept of a "person."
PHIL(CC)	Claiming to use this concept in an overriding, prescriptive, and universalized (O,P, and U) principle.
PHIL(RSF)(DO & PO)	Having feelings which support this principle, either of a "duty-oriented" (DO) or a "person-oriented" (PO) kind.
EMP(HC)	Having the concepts of various emotions (moods, etc.).
EMP(1)(Cs)	Being able, in practice, to identify emotions, etc., in oneself, when these are at a conscious level.
EMP(1)(Ucs)	Ditto, when the emotions are at an unconscious level.
EMP(2)(Cs)	Ditto, in other people, when at a conscious level.
EMP(2)(Ucs)	Ditto, when at an unconscious level.
GIG(1)(KF)	Knowing other ("hard") facts relevant to moral decisions.
GIG(1)(KS)	Knowing sources of facts (where to find out) as above.
GIG(2)(VC)	"Knowing how"—a "skill" element in dealing with moral situations, as evinced in verbal communication with others.
GIG(2)(NVC)	Ditto, in nonverbal communication.
KRAT(1)(RA)	Being, in practice, "relevantly alert" to (noticing) moral situations, and seeing them as such (describing them in terms PHIL, etc., above).

KRAT(1)(TT)	Thinking thoroughly about such situations, and bringing to bear whatever PHIL, EMP, and GIG one has.
KRAT(1)(OPU)	As a result of the foregoing making an overriding, prescriptive, and universalized decision to act in people's interests.
KRAT(2)	Being sufficiently wholehearted, free from unconscious countermotivation, etc., to carry out (when able) the above decision in practice.

If this list is not philosophically acceptable (I have argued at length for it elsewhere)[11] I invite the reader to costruct his own. I dare say it will not be radically dissimilar, so long as the reader (a) sticks to plain English (avoiding terms like "authoritarian," "utilitarian," etc.), (b) avoids vagueness ("a responsible attitude," "emotional maturity," etc.), and (c) sets out to be nonpartisan rather than sectarian ("a Christian attitude to life," "democratic values," etc.).

From this list, or any similar list, two practical desiderata seem to follow:

1. It will be clear that research should be conducted on the basis of such a list. This means, among other things, that we must abandon once and for all the idea that morality or moral development (competence, etc.) consists of someone attribute, as if it were like being red-blooded or fair-haired. We have to produce assessment methods (obviously different ones in each case) for the attributes, then conduct experiments—if that is not too strict a word for the much looser kind of work that will probably be appropriate to determine what factors generate these attributes in what types of people. (Some may perhaps be already obvious in the light either of logic or of common sense and common knowledge.) I do not say that research which is not based on some such list is worthless. The point is, rather, that we cannot say how much it is worth (or even what it really tells us about morality or moral development) unless and until it is related to an adequate and clear picture of the kind that such a list tries to paint. (Just as research in, say, "scientific" education or progress or development would be

hopeless unless we already knew, and agreed about, what counted as "good science" or "a competent scientist."

I hope also to have said enough to show that there is little hope of really solid progress in this field unless we pay serious attention to the language, descriptions, and conceptual distinctions involved. This must surely mean some kind of teamwork. A lot of the business is really a matter of what J.L. Austin described as "linguistic phenomenology," and is properly the task of analytic philosophers. (Austin wrote *How to Do Things with Words,* Oxford University Press, 1962.) But the work of such philosophers, if left by themselves in ivory towers, is liable to generate no sort of practical action or even empirical research. Indeed, analytic philosophers are for the most part not even listened to or understood, as the recent history of educational research shows. Some of them, at least, have to be put to work, and that means operating as members of a team involving other disciplines. It is not at all clear, actually, which other disciplines or forms of enquiry are peculiarly relevant to moral education. I myself would put more money on the clinical (post-Freudian) psychologists or psychiatrists than on developmental psychologists, and more money on both than on those psychologists who might merit such terms as "behaviorist" or even "experimental." (The Skinnerian fantasy is one of the main obstacles to progress.) But whether this is right or wrong, a team of this kind seems essential. For without it no solid and impartial work can really be done at all. Inevitably the field is at the mercy of different groups or gangs run by people of quite different disciplines (or of no disciplines at all, "educationalists"), between whom communication is difficult or impossible.

2. Secondly, an overgeneralized notion of "moral development" masks what seems to me to be the clear fact that *some* of the attributes of the morally educated person can be straightforwardly *taught* to children, and reasons for them given. It can be explained to children what a person is (insofar as they do not know this already), and they can be told that in behavior what ought to count is the interests of people—that reasons relating to those interests are appropriate, and other reasons (what they feel like doing, what all

their friends do, what some "authority" tells them to do, etc.) are inappropriate. Children can also be shown why the former are good reasons and the latter bad (or not really reasons, in the sense of justifications, at all). Indeed, parents frequently do this, when they say things like "How would you like it if *your* toys were smashed?" (". . . if *you* were hit?")—that is, they remind children of what, in a sense, they know already (just as, when they remain sane, adults also know)—that they are not to make special cases of their own interests, that they are not the only pebbles on the beach, that other people count.

If there are "stages" through which children must pass before being able to learn this, either they occur very early or I am not clear what they are. All that seems to be required is some reasonably satisfactory concept of a person, and some concept of interests, of things being nice and nasty for people. I would guess that most children have the relevant concepts at a very early age. Certainly the intellectual machinery required seems much simpler than that which we expect children to use in, for instance, reading or writing or elementary mathematics. So this can and should be taught to them. Of course this per se will not make them always want to use these reasons in daily life. That is another matter, and requires different attributes. But at least they can be brought to see what reasons they ought to be using, how they ought to be thinking in the field of morality and practical action. That is far from unimportant. If backed by persistent training, practice, habit forming, and whatever other means of reinforcement we can find, it may be that this teaching (plus the reinforcement) will carry the children a long way in practical action as well as in theoretical understanding. This too I have discussed elsewhere.[12]

Why does this not happen? Most new subjects or departments of life have been put on the map, not by waiting for developmental psychologists to give us a "model" or a "theory" of (for instance) children's "scientific development," but by bringing persons to understand what science is and what attributes are required by the person who is going to answer questions about the physical world seriously. That understanding, communicated to teachers and the general public, allowed us to teach a lot of science and communicate a great deal of the scientific attitude before psychology (in the modern sense) got going at all. Not only our intellectual understanding but also our practical behavior was very greatly affected. The same seems to me true, by and large, of morality. The hold-up is not due to the lack of strictly empirical research or of some general "model" or "theory," but to the failure to understand and agree on the methodology or principles which are appropriate to moral thought and action.

What we can do in practical moral education—and it extends far beyond teaching the relevant concepts and principles (the methodology)—seems so entirely obvious that I incline to ascribe our failure to do it (at least in any public and coherent form) largely to the operation of fantasy, rather than inertia, stupidity, or genuine intellectual disagreement. That, however, is a matter for (philosophically competent) psychiatrists. It would be interesting to know more about the kinds of prejudices and fantasies which inhibited the understanding and teaching of other forms of knowledge. History and science might offer useful parallels. Morality may be more liable to the irruption of fantasy than nearly every other department of life (I suppose religion and personal relationships might beat it to the post); and much might be gained, in educating ourselves as well as our children, by recognizing and trying to combat this enemy.

Perhaps I might usefully conclude by instancing one symptom of fantasy. It is characteristic of human beings that when there is no solid agreement on some matter we tend to divide into gangs, "schools of thought," each with its particular line of goods, and often headed by some well-known name or "authority." The absurdity is, of course, that our enquiries are often too little advanced to talk as if there were clear questions on which opinions were divided. The questions are not clear, and all we can do is mutually to try and get clearer. But we find this too much like hard work; it is better to run up flags, support or demolish "theories," be for or against people. We start playing politics, at times almost religion, instead of patiently enquiring. The original enquirers themsleves are often caught up in this process through no fault of their own. This has happened to Larry Kohlberg (I can, I think, say this without prejudice, since—in a smaller way and in somewhat different circles—it has happened also to myself). But the way in which to honor those who produce interesting work is to submit that work to serious examination, from the ground floor upwards: not to take sides.

NOTES

1. R. J. Havighurst and H. Taba, *Adolescent Character and Personality* (New York: Wiley 1949).

2. H. Hartshorne and M. A. May, *Studies in the Nature of Character* (New York: Macmillan 1928–30).

3. R. H. Peck and R. J. Havighurst, *The Psychology of Character Development* (New York: Wiley 1960).

4. L. Kohlberg, 'Stages of Moral Development as a basis for moral education', in *Moral Education,* ed. C.M. Beck *et al.* (University of Toronto Press 1971).

5. L. Kohlberg, 'The Development of Moral Character and Moral Ideology', in *Review of Child Development Research,* ed. M. L. and L. W. Hoffman (New York: Russel Sage Foundation 1964), p. 405.

6. L. Kohlberg, 'Education for Justice', in *Moral Education,* ed. N. F. and T. R. Sizer (Cambridge, Mass.: Harvard University Press, 1970), p. 67.

7. Ibid., p. 70.

8. Kohlberg (1971), p. 51.

9. N. Williams, *The Moral Development of Children* (London: Macmillan 1970).

10. R. S. Peters, 'Moral Development: A plea for pluralism', in *Cognitive Development and Epistemology,* ed. T. Mischel (New York: Academic Press 1971).

11. See my *The Assessment of Morality* (N.F.E.R., Slough, Bucks., U.K.: 1973).

12. See my *Practical Methods of Moral Education* (London: Heinemann 1972).

Chapter 8

Moral Dilemmas and Their Treatment

BERNARD ROSEN

INTRODUCTION

Lawrence Kohlberg and his followers assign an important place to moral dilemmas and their treatment in a program of moral education.[1] In light of this it is surprising that there are so few discussions of the nature of moral dilemmas, either by the Kohlbergians or their critics. This paper is an attempt to give an account of moral dilemmas that is neutral with respect to any ethical theory or theory of moral education.[2] The treatment of moral dilemmas by two rival ethical theories, act and rule theories, will be presented. I shall then provide a detailed act theoretical account of dilemmas, along with additional comparisons with the rule theory orientation of Kohlberg. The paper will have the following sections:

1. The nature of moral dilemmas.
2. Act and rule theory accounts of moral dilemmas.
3. A step-by-step approach to the treatment of moral problems and dilemmas: an act theoretical treatment.
4. The act and rule theory treatments of moral problems and dilemmas compared.

THE NATURE OF MORAL DILEMMAS

Among the ancient Greeks the form of dilemma was first stated: there are two apparently equally acceptable conditional statements and two apparently equally acceptable antecedents (or two equally acceptable negations of consequents). The apparently acceptable antecedents are usually thought to exhaust the possibilities. Sometimes the claims in the antecedent or the consequent are the same claim, and sometimes they are different claims. Some examples will help to make all this abstract talk clear. Students who have not studied for an examination sometimes face the following dilemma: If they take the test, then they will flunk. On the other hand, in many courses if they do not take the exam, they will flunk. Since they either must take the exam or not, they flunk. Suppose we partially symbolize this argument as indicated.

p = John (a student who has not studied) takes the exam.
q = John flunks the exam.
   If p then q
   if not-p then q
   p or not-p
   ―――――――――
   Therefore, q[3]

The form of a moral dilemma is that of a dilemma; there will be three premises, two of which will be conditional. For most, the consequents of the two conditional statements will be competing moral judgments. In the third premise will be a disjunction of the antecedents or a disjunction of the denials of the consequents. Some common dielmma forms are:

If p then q	If p then q	If p then q	If p then q
If r then s	If r then s	If r then s	If p then r
Either p or r	Either not-q or not-s	Either p or r	Either not-q or not-r
―――――――	―――――――	―――――――	―――――――
Therefore, either q or s	Therefore, either not-p or not-r	Therefore, q	Therefore, not-p

Sometimes, as in the third form, there are but three distinct statements, with the same statement or its negation in both antecedents or both consequents.[4]

There are at least two relevant senses of *or* that can be used in the third premise. A statement with two components connected by the inclusive sense of *or* is true when at least one of the components is true, and false only when both are false. "He is either very sick or very drunk," "We have cream or sugar," are two examples. The first one is more unusual, for it would be rare to have someone stagger about who is both drunk and ill, but it does sometimes happen. If the person was, instead, an actor, though, the statement would be false.

A statement with two components connected by the exclusive sense of *or* is true when exactly one of them is true. When both are false and when both are true, then the statement is false. "Either Columbus or Cincinnati is the capital of Ohio," and "The plane figure is either a triangle or it is not," are examples of such statements.[5]

No doubt there are times when one sense is used in a dilemma and other times when the other is used. If the premises are set up carefully, the items in the antecedent and in the consequent will be at least contraries, and hopefully contradictories. If the items in the antecedent are contradictories then the *or* has the force of exclusive disjunction even when you use inclusive disjunction as the connective.[6]

Moral dilemmas are not troublesome because they can be represented in a certain argument form, they are troublesome either because the third premise, the disjunctive one, causes a problem or because the conclusion causes a problem. (The *or* in the last sentence is inclusive.) In the first instance we usually have an epistemic problem; we do not know which of the disjuncts is true or acceptable, while we feel quite confident about the acceptability of the two conditionals. So, while we know that one of the consequents represents an acceptable moral judgment, perhaps a claim about what we ought to do, since we don't know which of the antecedents is true we don't know what our actual obligation is. This is represented in the following example.

If racial tension is decreased by busing (. . .) then busing is right.
If racial tension is not decreased (is perhaps even increased) by busing . . . then busing is not right.
Either racial tension is decreased by busing or it is not.

Therefore either busing is right or it is not.

There is nothing troublesome about the conclusion as such, for it represents an uninteresting logical truth. The problem is in the third premise, for we do not know which of the disjuncts is true. If we are committed to doing the right thing, we will be in distress because we do not know what to do. The ellipses indicate that many other things would, of course, go into the antecedent. Those items would add to the difficulty of determining what is the right thing to do. We do not know what is the right thing to do because we do not have sufficient evidence to affirm just one of the antecedents. This is true, usually, because there is evidence on both sides or not enough evidence about what will occur in the future.

Another explanation of why something is a moral dilemma is that the conclusion represents an option, or two options, that are morally unacceptable, and yet the premises appear to be true or acceptable. Another made up and simplified example will illustrate this. Suppose a sensitive student makes a claim that involves a mistake commonly made by students in philosophy. Correction will put the student off and thus cause alienation, but failure to correct the student requires you to mislead the rest of the class.

If John is corrected and thus alienated then you have done what is wrong.
If John is not corrected and thus the rest of the class misled then you have done what is wrong.
Either you correct John or you do not.

Therefore, you do what is wrong.

There appears to be no set of facts here to determine; the opposite seem to be true. You think that the facts are in, and the only two options both result in a morally unacceptable outcome. Continuing in the noncomparative mode, we can claim that the first premise is not acceptable. It may be true that some harm is created by correcting John, but one doesn't have to be a utilitarian to point out that more harm is avoided and more good done by correcting than not. Furthermore, it is not clear that we want to accept John's sensitivity without attempting to do something about it. A turn to the comparative mode will reveal this point more clearly. To do this, though, requires an explanation of what the comparative mode is.

A comparative judgment of value would have the form, "x is better than y," or, "x has more intrinsic value than y." A noncomparative judgment of value would have the form, "x is intrinsically valuable." A noncomparative judgment about the moral worth of actions would have the form, "x is right," or "x is obligatory." The comparative judgment would be, "x is more right than y," or "x is more obligatory than y." Pacifists sometimes claim that killing is wrong, but when opposing slavery or Hitler it is sometimes more obligatory to kill than not because it is more obligatory to prevent slavery or Hitler from taking power than to abstain, in that set of circumstances, from killing.[7] When philosophers use prima facie they are, in my view, capturing this sense. It is prima facie obligatory, they tell us, not to kill, but it is also prima facie obligatory to fight against the Nazis. In this instance, such philosophers tell us, the prima facie obligation to fight against the Nazis is stronger than the prima facie obligation not to kill.

When we apply the comparative mode to the problem of the sensitive student, we can construct a different statement.

> If John is corrected and thus alienated, but the rest of the class enlightened, then correcting John is more right than wrong. If John is corrected and thus alienated, and the rest of the class is not (particularly) enlightened, then correcting John is more wrong than right.

Some may not want to use "right" and "wrong," but some value terms such as "better" and "worse" to describe the *situation* that results from correction or lack of correction. It doesn't matter bacause the reason the person supposes there is a moral dilemma remains; the person finds the options available morally unacceptable. In the comparative mode, though, the third premise and the claim in the conclusion now become:

> Either John is corrected and thus alienated, but the rest of the class is enlightened, or John is corrected and thus alienated, and the rest of the class is not (particularly) enlightened.

> Therefore, correcting John is more right than wrong or correcting John is more wrong than right.

Now we have a dilemma of the first type, where the concern is over which of the disjuncts in the third premise is true. I have no general argument to show that all the moral dilemmas of the second type, where there is a conclusion that contains a morally unacceptable claim derived from apparently acceptable premises, can be "reduced" to ones of the first type. This is my hunch, but more evidence will have to be sought.

To conclude: while moral dilemmas are dilemmas, they aren't problems because of the logical form. They are problems either because we cannot determine which of two competing disjuncts is acceptable, or because we suppose that either disjunct leads to something morally unacceptable. The claims about the few, most common, forms are supposed to apply to all the others. If not, additional comments will have to be supplied.

Thus far there has been no crucial mention of any normative ethical theory. Now we shall turn to a comparison of types of normative ethical theory.

COMPARISON OF ACT AND RULE THEORY ACCOUNTS OF MORAL DILEMMAS

Normative ethical theories, whatever else they do, provide a device for arriving at singular moral judgments. These are judgments that apply to individual actions, states of affairs, and such. A singular moral judgment is, "It was wrong of Nixon to lie about Watergate." An appropriate general judgment in the same area might be, "It is wrong to lie," or "If any action is one of lying then it is wrong." All normative theories aim to provide some way of arriving at singular moral judgments. Rule theories are those normative theories that suppose some general moral claim, a rule or principle, is required to arrive at the justified singular moral judgments. Act theorists deny that claim. Such theories offer a method for arriving a singular moral judgments, but that means does not require the use of any moral rules or principles.

Some rule theories propose a one-step process of arriving at singular moral judgments: we apply a rule to a situation and arrive at a moral judgment. For example, suppose that the rule adopted is "If any action maximizes the good for the greatest number, then that action is obligatory to perform." Suppose further that the action that would maximize the good for the greatest number is abandoning neighborhood schools in favor of busing for the purpose of racial balance within school districts. We would then conclude, directly via the rule, that busing is obligatory.

> If any action maximizes the good for the greatest number then that action is obligatory.
> Busing maximizes the greatest good for the greatest number.
> _____
> Therefore, busing is obligatory.

Since the moral rule is applied directly to the proposed action, this sort of rule theory is called a *direct rule theory*. Other theories, though, propose rules or, as some call them, principles, that apply not directly to actions (persons, things, or whatever) but to rules that do apply directly. For example, one indirect rule might be, "If any proposed direct moral rule, when acted upon, maximizes the good for the greatest number, then proposed DMR_1 (direct moral rule 1) is a direct moral rule." When someone puts forward an indirect moral rule, then usually the direct moral rules are such as "Lying is wrong." If we wish to show how such an ethical theory works to arrive at singular moral judgments, we need to use two steps.

If any proposed direct moral rule, DMR_1, when acted upon, maximizes the good for the greatest number, then the proposed DMR_1 is a direct moral rule.

"Lying is wrong" is a proposed direct moral rule which is such that when acted on maximizes the greatest good for the greatest number.

Therefore, "Lying is wrong" is a direct moral rule.

Lying is wrong.

Telling the bank clerk on the telephone that you did not receive $20 more than you were entitled to is lying.

Therefore, telling the bank clerk on the telephone that you did not receive $20 more than you were entitled to is wrong.

If any action is an instance of lying, then it is wrong.

Telling the bank clerk on the telephone that you did not receive $20 more than you were entitled to is lying.

Therefore, telling the bank clerk on the telephone that you did not receive $20 more than you were entitled to is wrong.

This procedure can be made to look more like the direct rule one when we realize that "Lying is wrong" is usually thought to be the claim that all lying is wrong. This, in turn, is rendered by "If any action is an instance of lying, then it is wrong." This would enable us to replace the first premise of the second step with an equivalent statement that has a conditional statement form.

It should be realized that we would have more questions for any indirect theorist to answer. We would want to know if there was any provision for exceptions. We would want to know if the claim is that when everyone always acts on that direct moral rule the greatest good is maximized, or some other claim is being made.[8]

Cutting across the distinction between direct and indirect rule theories is the distinction between categorical and prima facie rules. The former are rules whose consequents hold, once the antecedent is affirmed, no matter what else is true of the situation or thing being judged. We usually classify deductive reasoning rules as of this sort, but games are another example. "If any plane figure is enclosed and has three straight sides, then it is a triangle." "If a fielder catches a fly ball hit by a batter before it hits the ground, then the batter is out." No matter what else is true of the plane figure, e.g., that it is drawn in chalk or has sides one centimeter long, it is a triangle given that it has the characteristics mentioned in the antecedent. The batter may have hit a long fly ball or popped the ball up in the infield; no matter, he is out. The categorical imperative of Immanuel Kant is a good example of an indirect categorical rule.

... I ought never to act except in such a way that I can also will that my maxim ought to become a universal law. . . .

. . . I can indeed will to lie, but I can by no means will a universal law of lying; for by such a law there could properly be no promises at all, since it would be futile to profess a will for future action to others who would not believe my profession or who, if they did so over-hastily, would pay me back in like coin; and consequently my maxim, as soon as it was made a universal law, would be bound to annul itself.[9]

Kohlberg holds a version of this kind of theory.

Right is defined by the decision of conscience in accord with self-chosen *ethical principles* appealing to logical comprehensiveness, universality, and consistency. These principles are abstract and ethical (the Golden Rule, the categorical imperative); they are not concrete moral rules like the Ten Commandments.[10]

The maxims Kant mentions are the direct moral rules, the ones that are tested by the indirect moral rule. The usual theory with indirect moral rules has one such rule and a number of direct moral rules. If there are many such rules, there is the problem of what to do if there is a conflict.

A prima facie rule is one of a number of rules of the same type, whether direct or indirect, such that the rules have no fixed relative weight. That is, in some circumstances one of the rules is stronger than or overrides another, but in other circumstances the other will override the one. Here is how W.D. Ross describes such rules.

I suggest 'prima facie duty' or 'conditional duty' as a brief way of referring to the characteristic (quite distinct from that of being a duty proper) which an act has, in virtue of being of a certain kind (e.g., the keeping of a promise), or being an act which would be a duty proper if it were not at the same time of another kind which is morally significant. Whether an act is a duty proper or actual duty depends on all the morally significant kinds it is an instance of.[11]

Since this is not a work in ethical theory, the interested reader will have to look elsewhere to find more details about these theories. Those who wish to find the main arguments, from an act theory point of view, against the various types of rule theories, as well as to find more extensive discussion of them, can see the items in footnote 2.

There are at least two different kinds of act theory. One view, perhaps represented by G.E. Moore, holds that we somehow "intuit" a moral property such as *good*. The other view, professed by the vast majority of those who are in the act theory tradition, holds that our moral knowledge, if that is the term to use, is dependent upon or connected with some nonmoral information.[12] The way to understand this more clearly is to contrast the view with the rule theory view about the "bottom line" of justification. According to every normative theory, at a certain point we reach a basic justified moral unit—one that can justify other units but that does not itself require justification. For the direct rule theorist this comes when we reach the direct moral rule, and for the indirect moral rule theorist this comes when we reach the indirect moral rule that generates the direct moral rule. When we have reached a unit within the area of morality that is used to justify other units within that area, but itself does not require justification, then we have reached a basic unit. The basic units of the rival theories, act and rule, in their most general form appear in this way:

rule	act
If any x is F then x is M	If this x is F then x is M
$(x) (Fx \rightarrow Mx)$	$Fa \rightarrow Ma$

There are questions that people typically ask of basic units, some of which are sensible and others of which are not. We can sensibly ask if the basic unit is reducible to some other area, but not what the required justification for it is within the very area of which it is the basic unit. We can ask whether the basic unit is necessarily true or contingent, or whether it is fixed or is changeable. We may ask for the justification of the choice of this rather than that as the basic unit. We can ask why we should prefer an act theory type of basic unit and not that of a rule theory. We can ask why we should prefer an indirect rather than a direct rule as the basic unit. There are many questions of this sort that are asked in moral philosophy about these issues. These, though, are not the questions that concern us here, so no stand is taken on the issues raised. We are concerned to contrast rule and act theory accounts of moral dilemmas.

The act theory that will be discussed here is my own view, so I can speak with great confidence about the analysis of dilemmas. One kind of dilemma occurs when there is agreement or acceptance of two conditionals, one of which contains a certain moral judgment, Ma, and the other of which its denial, not-Ma, and there is no way to justify the choice of one antecedent over the other. Another occurs when the consequents are the same, Ma, but the antecedents are contradictories, and Ma, for whatever reason, appears to the person not to be acceptable.

If Fa then Ma	If Fa then Ma
If not-Fa then not-Ma	If not-Fa then Ma
Fa or not-Fa	Fa or not-Fa
Therefore, Ma or not-Ma	Therefore, Ma

The first of these is perhaps more typical of moral dilemmas. The arguments are valid, so we are concerned, especially in the first argument, with the truth of premises. The force of the dilemma comes not from the form of the argument but from the human condition of not being able to determine which of the disjuncts in the third premise is true or acceptable, and the need, sometimes moral, to take a stand. To offer a simplified version of an earlier example, suppose that Ma is "It is morally required to have quotas for racial minorities." Fa could then be, again simplified, "The use of race or minority status for jobs and admissions will significantly reduce racial tension." Many people think that using race or minority status as a criterion will not reduce tension at all, but will instead increase it.

It is very difficult, given the evidence now available and likely to be gathered, to determine which of the alternatives is so. Since we must suppose that one of them is so, that quotas will bring about a change as indicated or they won't, we know what our obligations are conditionally. We also know that we must take a stand, for the issue is pressing and failure ever to take a stand is itself not morally acceptable. So, the form of the dilemma is captured by the logic, but the moral pressure comes from the inability to determine what is so and the pressing need to take a stand.

In the second sort of delemma we usually have a Ma that represents an unacceptable moral stand. In my view there are no actual dilemmas of this form with all true premises. That is, either the conclusion does not represent an unacceptable moral position, or at least one of the three premises is not true. Suppose, as our example, that Ma is "It is morally unjustified to institute quotas for educational programs." For our antecedents suppose Fa is the complicated claim that quotas lead to a significant reduction in academic standards through the selection of the educationally disadvantaged.

If you choose the educationally disadvantaged in the quota system you are choosing the only group that can legitimately claim the need for a quota, but educational standard are thus lowered. If you choose a group from a minority population whose admission to the educational program would not lower standards, then you are not choosing the educationally disadvantaged. We can put all that by claiming that either you choose the educationally disadvantaged in your quotas or you do not. In either case, so the argument goes, the quotas are then morally unjustified.

It may very well be, of course, that the conclusion is justified, but it is not justified on the basis of this argument. In this instance I would consider the first two conditional premises not adequate to represent the conditional agreement needed. Another way to put this is to say that there are better conditionals that represent the positions. When these conditionals are represented, then the argument changes its form.

While the conditionals could be in either the comparative or the noncomparative mode, a better set can be constructed in the comparative mode.

> If the use of quotas would not significantly lower educational standards, and we can thereby provide minority exemplars, and increase the quality of professional services in minority communities, and even granting that some noneducationally disadvantaged minority members will be included as a result of the quota, then the use of quotas is more right than wrong.
>
> If the use of quotas would significantly lower educational standards, and even if we increase the number of minority examplars we would have a significant number of such persons who were substandard, and at least half of those who get in on the quota would not be educationally disadvantaged, even granting that the quality of professional services in minority communities will be improved somewhat, then the use of quotas is more wrong than right.

Even these more complicated conditionals no doubt leave out some of the items that many of you would want to include. How this is to be handled by the rival act and rule theories will be seen shortly.

The two conditionals are made more dramatic by talking about pre-Bakkean quotas and not post-Bakkean use of race as a criterion, but the same points in the antecedent, suitably modified, could be made in the criterion discussion. Finally, since more descriptive material has been put in the antecedent, even the noncomparative mode can be used now to capture the claim that people want to make in the consequent. We can now say, "The use of quotas is morally justified" in one consequent and its negation in the other. Of course, the use of that phrase, "morally justified," is not common outside discussions among academics. Perhaps, though, if we persist we can spread it more widely.

A STEP-BY-STEP APPROACH TO MORAL DISAGREEMENT AND DILEMMAS

In this section will be described a method, the method of moral negotiation, that according to the act theory can be used to resolve moral dilemmas and to conduct moral discussions between persons who morally disagree.

According to the act theory, the first step is to identify the two conflicting moral judgments in such a way as to capture both the moral concerns of the parties to the dispute, or the two competing judgments of a person, and to have two *contradictory* moral claims If necessary, and especially with comparative judgments, it would be permitted to have two contrary moral claims, but for reasons that should become clearer as we proceed, this is not a very fruitful manner of setting up the two competing noncomparative moral positions. When we are concerned with race as a criterion for jobs and education, the two competing moral judgments are, "The use of race as a criterion for jobs and admission to educational programs is morally justified," and "The use of race as a criterion for jobs and admissions to educational programs is not morally justified." We could use, "We have an obligation to use race as a criterion," and "We have an obligation not to use race as a criterion," but these two are not exhaustive since they are not contradictories. It may turn out that we have no obligations to use race as a criterion, though it might be morally permissible to do so. For the same reason, since it is morally permissible, it is not true that we have an obligation not to do so. Each of us is morally permitted, in most circumstances, to whistle the theme from the movie *Star Wars*, but we have no obligation, in most circumstances, to do so. We also seem not to have an obligation not to whistle the theme in most circumstances.

The two claims are related as contraries, for both claims can be false even though not both claims can be true. What is most useful for clear discussions is to have moral judgments, what will appear in the consequent, that are contradictories. That is. when one of the claims is true and the other is false.

To get to the point of having contradictory moral judgments, it is usually necessary to allow a few minutes of unstructured discussion so as to see what each side wishes to claim. The leader of the discussion will have to ask clarifying questions. "Is it your claim that the use of race as a criterion is not morally acceptable?" In every dispute there is a pair of contradictory moral judgments that can be set forth, though it may be that the parties are not familiar with that way of putting it. If the parties do not feel comfortable with my way of stating the moral issue as a pair of contradictory claims, I am willing to state the issue as a pair of contrary claims. Since both of the views can turn out to be false or unacceptable, this does not allow us to assert that one of the parties is correct, though it does allow us to say that not both are correct. If the moral judgment is comparative, as noted, contraries are almost certain to be used.

The second step is to find the items to put in the antecedents so that all parties to the dispute will agree with both conditional statements. If there is one person involved in a dilemma, then the task is to find the items that capture the person's reasons for being drawn to each of the contradictory or contrary moral judgments. The task is the same, from the point of view of logic; the only difference is the one between an internal dialogue and a public dialogue. For this first task I always ask people to present everything they can think of that has been said on the issue, whether it is their point of view or not. This has an additional benefit, especially in a group setting, of "loosening" people up. Many of the items that are included in the antecedents in this second step are normative. For example, if the question is whether to use race as a criterion or not, one of the items will revolve around the claim of whether or not we will have a better society if we use race as a criterion. If racial criteria for jobs and educational admissions will reduce racial tension and lead to a better society (plus a number of other items), then their use is morally justified. If such criteria will increase racial tension and lead to a worse society than we now have (plus a number of other items), then their use is not morally justified. The tendency is to have value times in the antecedent when we have an evaluation of actions in the consequent, and vice versa. The first situation, though, is much more common than the second. More on this sort of situation later.

After the second step the discussion leader asks whether there is agreement on both of the conditionals. If it is an individual considering a dilemma, the person asks himself or herself whether both conditionals are acceptable. Depending on the person or the audience, there will be some people who think they disagree with one of the conditionals because they think that one or more parts of the antecedent or one of the consequents is false. This has to be handled on an individual basis. When I ask if people disagree with one of the conditionals, and someone does, I ask if they can say why they disagree. If it is because they disagree with the moral judgment in the consequent, then I go over the nature of conditional statements again. This seems to be sufficient. If the person does not agree because there are some items they think are essential, these are then added to the appropriate antecedent.

Given the nature of my act theory there are two different conditions, besides the simple misunderstandings mentioned above, that account for disagreement with one of the conditionals. One has to do with abnormality and the other with a certain kind of use of an ethical theory. If a person is unable to make a range of judgments, e.g., about time or events not present, as a result of some disability, usually psychological, then that person may not be able to understand and agree with one or both of the conditionals. This can include the data that Piaget gives us about when children are able to understand conditional statements, and it may turn out that some subjects (e.g., agricultural economics) cannot be understood by most children until the age of twelve. Insofar as any of those subjects needs to be understood in order to understand and thus agree with one or both conditionls, then the person will not agree. The test for such understanding cannot be, of course, a moral test. We cannot build a moral requirement into the conditions without constructing a circular specification of when persons will agree with the conditionals.

The second defeating condition concerns a certain use of some normative ethical theory. If a person holds that ethical egoism is correct and (probably falsely) that ethical egoism justifies quotas, then we might have trouble. We can include the claim of ethical egoism in one of the antecedents and simply evaluate the theory along with the other claims in the antecedent when we attempt to affirm one of them. This is no problem.

If ethical egoism is correct and quotas will not maximize my (speaker's) benefit, and . . . (lots of other things), then quotas are not morally justified.

When we attempt to affirm the antecedent, we will have to determine if ethical egoism is an acceptable normative ethical theory. This theory is mentioned because philosophers are generally agreed that it does not fare very well in competition with other normative ethical theories. The methods for choosing the best ethical theory from among the competitors is an interesting subject about which there is considerable theoretical disagreement, though in practice most philosophers do many of the same things in their evaluations. It will be assumed that everyone has some method to evaluate normative ethical theories, though if they do not or if they have doubts about the existence of such methods of evaluation, a good deal of literature exists on that.[13]

The overwhelming number of discussions and individual considerations of moral problems do not involve bringing to bear some normative ethical theory. In using conditional agreement as part of the method of moral negotiation, the discussion leader should not try to bring in such theories, though if they come up they can be added to one or the other of the antecedents at the beginning of the discussion in step two.

The third step in the method of moral negotiation consists of paring down the items in the antecedents to the actual reasons that persons holding the position have for holding those very moral claims. If the discussion is about the moral acceptability of using race as one criterion for hiring and admission to educational programs, someone might offer, "The use of race as a criterion for hiring will lead to an invasion by the Venusians that will wipe out the entire human race," as an item in the antecedent. We would probably all agree that if that were true, and the other items were held constant, it would support the claim that the use of such a criterion was not morally justified. So, the claim is relevant in that if it were true then it would support the consequent. However, it is not relevant in that it is not a reason that any actual person has. If there is someone who takes this as an actual reason, then it should be included.

What is an actual reason? It is not the same thing as a true statement, for the person may think the claim is true when it is not. It is, though, something the person thinks is one of the items that has some likelihood of being true. It is one of the items that a person presents when asked to present his or her reasons for that particular moral claim.

To make this clearer, consider a person who wishes to prevent the method of moral negotiation from working within a group and sets about to sabotage the procedure. This person can add many items to the antecedents that he or she does not think are actual reasons for holding the position described in the consequent. "Racial criteria for hiring will lead to the enslavement of humans by Venusians," is a claim that if true would be relevant to the acceptance of a conditional. In light of this danger, some might be tempted to add, as one of the conditions of moral negotiation, that the persons involved be of good will. This is not needed, but we do have to make sure that the items actually included in the antecedent represent views of persons involved in the discussion.

The fourth step is to identify and treat, as needed, the normative items in the antecedent. In almost all moral discussions about what action to choose, some claim about the value of a result of the proposed action will be given as a reason for performing or not performing the action.

If slavery will result in a better life for the slaves, then slavery is morally justified.
If slavery will result is a worse life for the slaves, then slavery is not morally justified.

The comparison is between a free life and the life of a slave. What does the value notion *better* mean? In almost every instance there are additional nonvalue predicates that people have in mind when they make such claims; more pleasure, the one true religion, protection against the elements that the slaves cannot provide for themselves, protection against those who would rob and cheat the simpleminded (who are the slaves), and so on. All of these supposed facts about slaves would be in the antecedent of another conditional whose consequent would be the value claim. If there is a serious lack of clarity about the value claim, then it should be set into its own pair of conditionals. Usually the value claim is put comparatively— slavery is better than freedom or freedom is better than slavery. The comparative judgment (to repeat a point) can both be false, for freedom and slavery may be equally good or bad. There may even turn out to be a third condition, perhaps something akin to being a serf, that is better than either condition. Since in comparative value disputes the parties usually have two contrary options in mind, this is reflected in the example provided.

In most instances the parties to the dispute, or the one person involved in a moral dilemma, will be able to note the value claim in the antecedent and simply continue the negotiation until conditional agreement is reached. That is, there is usually agreement on what constitutes *better*. Perhaps this is really an implicit conditional agreement, and so the discussion on whether we ought to repeal the slave laws, or whatever, continues in this context.

A more awkward situation occurs when there is another claim about the morality of actions, for example, a claim about what ought to be done. This has to be treated by exposing it and, if there is not agreement on what, in this instance, constitutes an obligation to act, it has to be treated by placing it in a set of conditionals of its own.

A fifth step consists of attempting to locate subsets of items in the antecedent that themselves allow acceptance of the conditional statements.

If Fa & Ga & Ha then Ma
If Fa & Ga then Ma
If Fa & Ha then Ma

Suppose the first of the conditional statements is agreed to by the individual or all parties to the dispute. However, let us also suppose that each of the other conditionals is also agreed to by the individual or all parties to the dispute. This is a sort of overdetermination of the moral question, a situation that is not particularly unusual. We may find that slavery is morally acceptable when it prevents a childlike race from being victimized and provides the slaves with the one true religion. We may also find that slavery is morally acceptable when it prevents a childlike race from being victimized and provides the slaves with employment that they would not otherwise be able to find. The situation becomes easier to manage if we find that Ga or Ha is not believed to be true or acceptable by anyone. This would enable the person or group to drop it from consideration and attend only to the third of the conditionals listed above.

A more interesting situation occurs when we find that we have acceptance of the first two conditionals but not of the third. In this instance you would abandon the third conditional and work with the second. In a group the only difficult situation of this sort would be a slightly different arrangement of the agreements and disagreements.

Person 1 holds: (If Fa then Ma) and (not-(If Ga then Ma))
Person 2 holds: (If Ga then Ma) and (not-(If Fa then Ma))
Persons 1 and 2 agree that: If Fa & Ga then Ma

This situation divides into three different arrangements.

A.   Person 1 supposes that G is not relevant to M and person 2
     supposes that F is not relevant to M.

B.   Person 1 supposes that G is negatively relevant to M but
     when a is both F and G it continues to be M because of the
     greater strength of F. Such a person would also then think
     that "If Ga then not-Ma," is true. Similar remarks hold of
     person 2 and F.

C.   Person 1 supposes there is some H that is relevant to M that
     is the important or primary reason for holding not-Ma. This
     H in conjunction with G supports not-Ma. "If Ga and Ha
     then not-Ma," is the claim that is actually in the mind of
     the person.

The last arrangement shows that the second step was not fully
carried out, for there is some additional relevant characteristic that
was not added to the list. Once it is added then the situation reverts
to one of the earlier stages and the negotiation can continue. In the
second situation we should make clear what is actually held by
constucting the appropriate conditionals.

     If Fa and not-Ga then Ma
     If not-Fa and Ga then not-Ma

These conditionals, though, would turn out to be too simple, for
they do not include the other reasons that people would have.
However, that would require us, again, to have fulfilled stage 2
more fully.

The first arrangement returns us to the question of relevance. If
an item is truly thought not to be relevant by a person, then its
inclusion is justified only when another in the group does consider it
relevant. No harm is done since the irrelevant item is simply extra
baggage for one person. However, when the relevant item for one

person is true and the relevant item for the other is not, then we have to look for other items or restructure the conditionals to show that. If a single person is concerned with a dilemma, he or she should include only those items believed relevant. This is not to say there should be no concern with searching out additional relevant items—indeed that is the very strong advice given.

Almost all the possibilities listed in this stage and the other stages, for that matter, are fictional—they are possibilities springing from the mind of a philosopher concerned with what might happen. It is better to cover such possibilities, though, than to allow them to arise and then consider what to do. These practical suggestions are offered for situations that are not likely ever to arise, but having a stock of solutions to problems is a good way to increase the chances that you will be able to solve any problem when it arises as a real one.

The last stage is one in which an attempt is made to determine the truth or falsity of an antecedent's consequent. If this stage is completed, we will suppose that the person or all parties to a group discussion will accept a consequent or the denial of one of the antecedents. This should lead to unconditional acceptance of one moral judgment. In practice, of course, many persons will then look around for more reasons for their moral view. This is not a bad thing to do in the area of morality, and it is done in every other area of human concern. When you think a view is correct and someone shows your reasons to be defective, quite frequently you will look for additional reasons for your view rather than give it up right at that time.

THE ACT AND RULE THEORY TREATMENT OF DILEMMAS COMPARED

Typical moral dilemmas are moral problems in which, to repeat what was said at the beginning, the person cannot determine which of two competing antecedents are true, though both conditionals are accepted or the consequents contain one or two morally unacceptable items. Only the simple form will be considered, though any comments made about it will apply, with suitable alterations, to the other forms of dilemmas. This treatment of dilemmas makes use of a valid argument form, and places the puzzling part of the dilemma either in (a) the inability to affirm one of the antecedents in preference to the other or in (b) the moral unacceptability of the consequents. However, since I already have argued that the latter situation is best rendered as the former, when properly understood, only the former will be directly discussed.

In the previous section a step-by-step procedure for using the method of moral negotiation was provided, most of it described in terms of group discussion or an individual's dilemma. A group can have a dilemma, though we usually have in mind a single individual who has posed, or imposed, a moral problem that is difficult. All the methodologies provided in the last section, accordingly, were seen to apply to the account of dilemmas. Instead of a group discussion leader following the directions, we would have one person being given advice or following the advice on his or her own.

The act theorist would claim that a dilemma is of the form described. In addition, though, there is some valuable information that is forthcoming from that theory. Each of the conditionals represents what is, according to that theory, a purported basic unity of morality. There is no further justification of either of the conditionals from some general rule or principle. We can also account, on the act theory view, for why there is agreement on the conditionals. On the supposition that the theory describes the way people, except those corrupted by mistaken ethical theories, actually do reason, then we find that people agree with what is taken by people to be basic. Let this sound like the ravings of a mad man, it can be noted that philosophers have long made the claim that people do actually reason morally in the way their own theory supposes. For example, let me quote Kant and secondly J.S. Mill.

... bare conformity to universal law as such ... is what serves the will as its principle, and must so serve it if duty is not to be everywhere an empty delusion and a chimerical concept. The ordinary reason of mankind also agrees with this completely in its practical judgments and always has the aforesaid principle before its eyes.[14]

It would, however, be easy to show that whatever steadiness or consistency these moral beliefs have attained, has been mainly due to the tacit influence of a standard not recognized. . . . the principle of utility . . . has had a large share in forming the moral doctrines even of those who most scornfully reject its authority.[15]

It is not my view that agreement on what is a basic unit is the same thing as having reached a basic unit. It is my view that we approximate the truth insofar as we engage in dialogue with others and internal dialogue with ourselves, and elicit from others and ourselves the items that are to go in the antecedent. There is no "proof" that we have included all the relevant items, but that is the same situation that prevails for any empirical claim to know. A physician with a set of symptoms offers a disease as a hypothesis to explain them. Additional evidence, additional symptoms, may be identified and the physician may reject the former diagnosis. However, the way to reach a correct diagnosis is to gather the information and subject it to scrutiny. Do this also for moral matters. Be prepared to be mistaken as revealed by the results of future investigation. For those who wish to have a definition of absolute truth, an opinion that would remain fixed no matter what further investigation took place, that can be provided.

The opinion which is fated to be ultimately agreed to by all who investigate, is what we mean by the truth. . . . [16]

I do not countenance subjectivism or relativism, though the exact form of my normative and metaethical theory will have to be sought elsewhere.[17] Enough has been said, I think, to contrast the act theory with the more usual and more familiar rule theory approach to dilemmas. On the supposition that I have described the form of dilemmas correctly, we should distinguish between the treatment of dilemmas by direct and indirect rule theories. Consider, first, direct rule theories with one (categorical) rule. We have been considering both egoism and utilitarianism as our sample theories. In those views the materials in the antecedent would take the following form for one of the dilemma forms discussed.

If action A should maximize my good (good for the greatest number) them A is obligatory.

If action A should not maximize my good (good for the greatest number) then A is not obligatory.

A maximizes my good (good for the greatest number) or it doesn't.

Therefore, A is obligatory or it is not.

Perhaps you think that this kind of argument is extremely uninteresting, and there is something to that reaction. However, suppose the question is whether or not Heinz, in the famous example Kohlberg provides, ought to steal the drug for his wife.

In the Heinz dilemma, Heinz must imagine whether the druggist could put himself in the wife's position and still maintain his claim and whether the wife could put herself in the druggist's position and still maintain her claim. Intuitively we feel the wife could, the druggist could not. As a result, it is fair for the husband to act on the basis of the wife's claim.

For the purpose of solving individual moral dilemmas, we do not want to assume that the individual is ignorant of the probabilities of outcome of a given decision to each person involved, only that he is ignorant of the probability of being any particular person in the situation, i.e., that he is likely to be any particular person in that situation.

Returning to the stealing-the-drug situation, let us imagine someone making the decision under the veil of ignorance, i.e., not knowing whether he is to be assigned the role of husband, wife, or druggist. Clearly, the rational solution is to steal the drug; i.e., this leads to the least loss (or the most gain) to an individual who could be in any role. This corresponds to our intuition of the primacy of the woman's right to life over the druggist's right to property and makes it a duty to act in terms of those rights. If the situation is that the dying person is a friend or acquaintance, the same holds true. Here a solution achieved under the veil of ignorance is equivalent to one obtained by ideal role-taking.[18]

If we listened to Hobbes, Mill, Kant, or Kohlberg for that matter, all the rule theorists would be telling us something about how to subsume what occurs in the antecedent under the proper rule (perhaps chosen with the aid of an indirect rule), or, as a nonexclusive alternative, telling us that following the guidance of the rule or principle we should look for certain evidence. The Kohlberg method of treating dilemmas is a typical rule theorist method, though we are given very little direction about how we actually affirm one of the antecedents. In the passage cited we are given the Rawlsian "rational" solution involving the mini-max principle. Obviously this is a solution only when this is the best normative ethical theory. The criticisms of Rawls's ethical theory are, at this time, so numerous that everyone would agree that there are at least problems with his view.

Is there a right to life and another right to property such that the first has "primacy" over the second? Well, obviously this depends on the nature of the claims and the theory supporting them. In the act theory view there is no kind of situation or characteristic of a person or situation which in all its instances is also an instance of a moral kind. This is the claim that there are no moral constitutive rules. In a prima facie rule theory, such as Rawls and Kohlberg hold, each of the kinds imparts a prima facie right (or obligation or whatever). The actual right (or obligation) is "stronger" in a given instance. All those who hold a prima facie theory make use of something called "intuition" or "perception" finally to decide which of the applicable rights (or obligations) is stronger. If Milton Friedman is correct, then we should ignore our "intuitions" and opt for property rights, for they are essential for freedom.[19] T. Hobbes and J.S. Mill, among others, would not be impressed by Kohlberg's "intuition."

In the Kohlberg view of dilemmas, one of the conditionals or antecedents is not acceptable. This is probably because it incorporates a "lower" stage of moral reasoning. It may very well be that those who disagree with us morally do so because of a structural difference in reasoning, but in the act theory we need not assume this for adults or children. The analysis is that there are nonmoral notions, such as love, betrayal, and fidelity, that are not fully understood until certain ages. This would prevent the understanding of some conditionals until a certain age, but even this is subject to empirical investigation. It is not a matter of a priori speculation. It is not a matter of assuming that some ethical theory is correct, that all others are incorrect, and that testing must then be done within the context of that ethical theory. The method of moral negotiation does not assume the correctness of an act theory, for example, so testing can be done to see if the claims concerning the method are justified—at least partially independently of any ethical theory. This is not obviously true of Kohlberg and his claims.

Kohlberg thinks he has a solution to the Heinz dilemma because of his ethical theory, but in my view he thinks this also because of what I consider to be an unrealistic idea of what a moral problem is. Does Kohlberg think that a life right always overrides or has primacy over a property right? If he does, then we can provide him with numerous counterexamples. Suppose we are guarding the border against terrorists and a terrorist violates our property. Certainly it seems that the protection of our property in that instance (usually) overrides that of the life right of the terrorist. It will do no good to say that we are concerned about our own or another's life right, for we can imagine a situation is which the guard is in no danger. You can say, to continue the inevitable dialectical development, that the lives of others are in danger. Well, imagine that the terrorist wears the unmistakable costume of the Zorro sect that maims but never kills its victims. It would seem there is reason to suppose the guard is justified in acting in that circumstance on the property right.

What about poor Heinz? Suppose he really wonders what to do and looks for help from the various theories that are available. My advice to him, as an act theorist, is to find out more about the situation—certainly more than we are told in Kohlberg's little story. Is the druggist a wealthy millionaire? Does Heinz's wife want to die? Is Heinz's wife a biologist on the verge of discovering how to prevent aging? Will Heinz gradually pay the total amount after he gets the drug? Will one dose of the drug cure Heinz's wife?

We all know there are numerous additional details that would swing the decision one way rather than another. Suppose Heinz was a sadistic physician at the concentration camp in which the druggist was forced to develop the drug in order to save Heinz's wife. Several people suffered acute agony, though none died, in the course of the development process. Heinz is now living under a different identity and the druggist cannot prove his part in the suffering caused by the forced experimentation. One suspects that this additional fact would do a great deal to Kohlberg's "intuitions." Suppose the wife has contemplated suicide for years and wishes to die with dignity now. Hienz wants her to stay alive because he and she live off the interest of a trust fund set up in her name. The druggist is the brother of the wife, knows his sister's intentions, and while he legally would have to sell the drug to Heinz if the latter had the money, he uses the legal excuse not to sell the drug in order to allow his sister to carry out her own ends.

We would have to know much more about Heinz, the druggist, the wife, the society they live in and many more relevant items, in order to construct our conditionals. To suggest that one has a dilemma on the basis of a few descriptive phrases is, to the act theorist, ludicrous. Moral dilemmas are real problems, faced by real people in a real setting. It is no test of an ethical theory, or of the moral reasoning of people for that matter, to pose artificial problems. The problems, note, are not artificial primarily because they are fictional. They are artifical because they do not represent realistic situations with all their complexity. Perhaps we should let the poets and the novelists describe the moral problems for the tests and not philosophers and psychologists. The problems would be more difficult to solve, but at least they would be relevant to the real problems that human beings have.

If I were a utilitarian, I would want to say much more about dilemmas. I would want to give some practical advice such as has been provided for an act theory. It might be said that the dilemma of the Heinz case is not knowing which action, stealing the drug or not, would lead to the greatest good for the greatest number. The fact-finding component would look very much like the one the act theory proposes, though it would be directed to one determined characteristic, maximizing the good of the greatest number. In this view of what dilemmas are, the utilitarian would also claim that dilemmas are problems primarily because of a lack of knowledge, and not because of logic. One would also have to allow, of course, that there are times when one genuinely cannot determine what the facts are, whether this course of action or that will maximize the greatest good for the greatest number.

The rule theorist's strategy of appealing to rules, either directly or indirectly, contrasts quite strongly with the act theory appeal to conditional statements. In either instance one usually "solves" the dilemma by finding, depending on the form of the dilemma, that this antecedent rather than that is justified. Why the conditional statement is acceptable requires, according to the rule theorist, another step. That step consists of appealing to the appropriate rule or principle. If the rule is direct, the conditional is an instance of it, and if it is indirect then the conditional is an instance of a direct rule that is justified by the indirect rule. The act theory claims that the conditional is of the form of what is a basic unit within the area of morality. The rule theorist claims that the basic unit within the area of morality is a rule. How one goes about justifying the one proposed basic unit rather than another is a matter for philosophical argument, though philosophy should accept whatever evidence is relevant from any other areas such as psychology.

One final substantive word about "intuitions." Obviously I must be very much concerned about this to put the term in scare quotes almost every time it is used. Frequently rule theorists criticize act theories on the grounds that they do not justify the conditionals. The act theory response is that the conditionals are the basic units, so they cannot have a justification within the area of ethics. This is true of whatever the basic unit is taken to be. A moral rule, if it is the basic unit, cannot have a justification within the area of ethics. So far the act and rule theories are on the same footing. The act theorist then says that you affirm an antecedent in order to determine what is right or obligatory or valuable. Those who hold a prima facie rule theory, though, tell us that we not only have to have a basic unit in the form of a series of prima facie moral rules, but we then have to have a way to determine in a given set of circumstances which of the rules is strongest. This is primarily the role of "intuition." Notice that this totally mysterious step is not required by an act theory. It might be claimed that the awareness of the basic unit is intuitive, so that the act theory has an intuition of its own. This is not my view,[20] but even if it were, we would still have the act theory with one mystery and the prima facie rule theory with two.

SUMMARY

In this paper my concern was to explain the nature of moral dilemmas as moral problems expressed in a certain logical form, the dilemma, and to consider the fact of lack of knowledge concerning which of two competing antecedents or negations of consequents was true. Some people suppose that there are dilemmas in which both of the consequents are morally undesirable, e.g., we act unjustly whether or not we bus, and whether or not we use race as a criterion for jobs and admission to educational programs. My view is that we choose, in such instances, the best situation, the action that is most right or the thing or situation that is better than the alternatives. A comparison of act and rule theory treatments of dilemmas shows how the methodology of act theories, moral negotiation, fits in a most natural way the structure of moral dilemmas. Rule theories, too, can be used to describe moral dilemmas, though my own view is that they do not do so as fruitfully. Following this discussion I presented a description of how one would proceed, step by step, using the act theory format when engaged in moral disputes or in the attempt to solve moral dilemmas. The typical rule theory treatment of such problems was then compared with the act theory as laid out. I did not present a great deal of detail for the rule theory treatment, both because it is more familiar to people than the act theory, and also because such detail should be provided by the people who hold such theories. Some suggestions were made concerning the ways in which an act theory approach is preferable to a rule theory approach, though this was certainly not the main purpose of this paper. Those who are interested in criticisms of rule theories and further descriptions of act theories have been referred elsewhere.

NOTES

I would like to thank Peter Horn and George Peters for their many helpful critical comments.

1. See, for example, L. Kohlberg, "From Is to Ought: How to Commit the Naturalistic Fallacy and Get Away with It in the Study of Moral Development," T. Mischel, ed., *Cognitive Development and Epistemology* (New York: Academic Press, 1971).

2. To see the kind of view I hold you can look at B. Rosen, "Moral Education and Moral Theory," *Teaching Philosophy*, Fall, 1976, and B. Rosen, *Strategies of Ethics* (Boston: Houghton Mifflin, 1978). For the statement of my own normative ethical theory see especially chapters 5 and 6.

3. Some of you think that moral dilemmas are best captured by some other dilemma form. Nothing critical hangs on which form is used or how they are arranged. Here for example, ia an arrangement that George Peters supplied.

I. A.	If p, then q	B.	If p, then q	C.	If p, then q
	If not-p, then r		If r, then s		If r, then s
	p or not-p		p or r		not-q or not-s
	——————————		——————————		——————————
	q or r		q or s		not-p or not-r

II. A.	If p, then q	B.	If p, then q	C.	If p, then q
	If not-p, then q		If r, then q		If p, then r
	p or not-p		p or r		not-q or not-r
	——————————		——————————		——————————
	q		q		not-p

4. We do not need to have the same statement in both consequents, of course, as is indicated in a different example. If John takes the exam without cheating, then John flunks. If John takes the exam and cheats, then John is immoral. Either John takes the exam without cheating or he takes the exam and cheats. Therefore, either John flunks or he is immoral. You may think, of course, that one or more of the premises is false, but to find true premises is not one of the aims, it is only to find examples that illustrate what a dilemma is. Moral dilemmas are of the same logical type, though the content is what is of primary interest. Two contemporary dilemmas faced by many Americans involve busing and racial criteria for employment and admission to educational programs. The latter issue is a dilemma in that the use of race or other minority status as a criterion for admission to educational programs and for employment violates a sense of equal treatment, whereas the fact that many of the persons in those minority groups have not been treated equally in educational opportunities and thus are handicapped in the competition for admission and jobs also violates a sense of equal treatment. Putting this into the same format as the nonmoral dilemmas, we have:

p = We use race as a criterion for admission to educational programs and for employment (as apparently approved by the Bakke decision).

q = We violate a sense of fairness.
If p then q
If not-p then q
Either p or not-p

Therefore, q

In stating the dilemmas there has been, obviously, an immense simplification of the moral issues. The dilemma concerning race as a criterion will be taken up again.

5. A truth table shows the difference visually:

Inclusive	Exclusive
p or q	p or q
T T T	T F T
T T F	T T F
F T T	F T T
F F F	F F F

This column under the term *or* gives the truth value for the whole statement while the columns under the p and q give the truth values for the component parts. The inclusive *or* has Ts in every line but the last, while the, exclusive *or* has F in the first and lst line, but T in the middle two.

6. If the premise is "Either p or not-p" and you use inclusive disjuntion in a truth table, you have:

Inclusive

p or not-p
T T F
F T T

This is the same, notice, as the middle two lines of exclusive *or*.

As long, then, as the items in the antecedent are contradictory, you don't have to worry about whether you use inclusive or exclusive disjunction. Furthermore, it is advisable, given the method of the act theory, as will be explained, to use antecedents and consequents that are contradictory. Secondly, even if the components of the antecedent and the consequent are contraries, the need to make a decision as to whether the connective is inclusive or exclusive can be avoided for most instances. Contraries are claims that both can be false but not both can be true. "The light is either green or it is red." is false when it is neither. The two senses of *or* would both have it that way. The first line of the table, where the exclusive sense would have the statement false when both of the consequents are true, cannot arise for contraries.

When as argument depends on the exclusive sense of *or* that should be noted, otherwise it will be assumed that the sense is inclusive. Consider this constructed example.

Janice has just asked you how she looks as you prepare to leave for the opera. You think she looks terrible, but know that if you say so, she will want to change and you will be late. You have to say she looks fine or that she doesn't, for failure to say that she looks fine will be taken as the claim that she looks terrible. Janice suffers greatly when she finds out that she looks terrible at public places, and she usually finds out from her enemy, Gladys, who will be at the opera. You, on the other hand, suffer greatly when you arrive at the opera late. . . .

The soap opera fan can fill in additional details as needed for our dilemma to be made even more explicit. The part we wish to draw attention to is the third premise.

Either you tell Janice she looks fine or you tell her she looks terrible.

This seems to be a clear instance in which the connective cannot be inclusive disjunction, for, by hypothesis, you cannot tell her both that she looks fine and that she looks terrible. To capture this premise, if we let it stand as the way to capture the concern, we would have to use exclusive disjunction. This, as indicated, is all right as long as it is made clear. However, one could also translate the third premise in a different manner.

Either you tell Janice she looks fine or you do not.

This gives us a pair of contradictories, so no decision need be made as to whether this is exclusive or inclusive disjuntion. The statement can be treated as though it were inclusive disjuntion without any distortion of the situation. Should thie ever not be so, though, then use exclusive disjunction.

7. During the autumn of 1977 I taught a philosophy segment to a group of fourth to sixth graders at a Columbus, Ohio, public school. The three-month, once-a-week, mini-course started with concerns about general reasoning. (I think that Matthew Lipman is right in his emphasis on reasoning and logic as the foundation of doing any philosophy with children.) I then introduced normative concerns. We discussed the question of whether pets should be allowed to choose their own diets. (We proposed to place kibbles in one bowl, fatty meat in another, and canned dog food in a third, and so on. We would then feed the dog whatever it preferred.) After the students told me about the awful results of doing that we then asked the same question about young children (younger than fourth graders) choosing their own diet. Sure enough, the "slippery slope" finally led them to claim that adults, especially those with children who were dependent on them, should not be allowed to choose their own diets. We invented the Diet Police, fines for dread crimes such as eating too many potato chips or drinking too much beer, and finally prison for those who were unable to control their forbidden foods lust. At this point the group decided that something had gone wrong and retraced the steps whereby we reached the unacceptable conclusion. They decided on a version of Mill's principle concerning *harm;* people should be allowed to do what they want as long as it doesn't hurt other people in some direct or serious manner. Children should be allowed to make their own decisions

as soon as possible, though we all agreed that it was difficult to draw the line.

The discussion was almost entirely within a comparative mode. The students would say, "It is more right than wrong to allow a parent to eat potato chips." It was I, not the children in the group, who resisted this mode. Finally, I gave in and joined in with the comparative mode talk.

8. *Strategies of Ethics,* pp. 17–18, 134–138. These passages should give a better idea of what indirect rule theories are and how they are to be evaluated.

9. I. Kant, *Groundwork of the Metaphysics of Morals,* trans. by H.J. Paton, (London: Hutchinson University Library, 1948), pp. 69–71.

10. Lawrence Kohlberg, "The Claim to Moral Adequacy of a Highest Stage of Moral Judgment," *Journal of Philosophy,* Vol. LXX, No. 18, October 25, 1973, p. 632.

11. W.D. Ross, *The Right and the Good* (Oxford: The Clarendon Press, 1930), p. 19.

12. See chapters 5 and 6 or *Strategies of Ethics* for a complete description of an act theory of obligation and value. There are some criticisms of rule theories in chapter 4, and additional arguments in 5 and 6.

13. If you look at what William K. Frankena does in *Ethics* (Englewood Cliffs, N.J.: Prentice-Hall, 1973), or what Bernard Gert does in *The Moral Rules* (New York; Harper & Row, 1973), you will find that they both test normative ethical theories by their ability, among other things, to account for what we think are clear instances of justified judgments. This is a standard method used by Mill and Kant as well as contemporary writers. There is enough in common among most writers to agree when something is a criticism, though it is more difficult to agree that something counts as positive evidence.

14. I. Kant, *Groundwork of the Metaphysics of Morals,* p. 70.

15. J.S. Mill, *Utilitarianism in John Stuart Mill: A Selection of His Works.* ed., J.M. Robson (New York: Odyssey Press, 1966), p. 153.

16. C.S. Peirce, *Philosophical Writings of Peirce,* ed., Justus Buchler (New York: Dover Publications, 1955), p. 38.

17. A summary of the metaethical positions relevant here is to be found in chapter 7, "Meta-ethics", of *Strategies of Ethics.*

18. Lawrence Kohlberg, "The Claim to Moral Adequacy of a Highest Stage of Moral Judgment," p. 644.

19. See, for example, Milton Friedman, *Capitalism and Freedom* (Chicago: The University of Chicago Press, 1962), chapter 2. In this chapter, though he does not specifically put the discussion in terms of property, he does seem to suppose that the control of property by individuals is critical for having a free society.

20. See B. Rosen, "A Meta-Theory for Ethical Theories," *The Journal of Value Inquiry,* Vol, IX, No. 1, Spring, 1975.

Part V

BASIC ISSUES IN RELIGION AND RELIGIOUS EDUCATION

Chapter 9

Morality, Religion, and Kohlberg's Theory

ERNEST WALLWORK

INTRODUCTION

No recent scientific theory of morality has sparked as much interest on the part of religious ethicists and educators as Lawrence
Kohlberg's work. Among several reasons for this attention, four are
sufficiently important to warrant brief summary at the outset of this
critique of Kohlberg's views on the relationship between religion
and morality.

First, Kohlberg identifies morality, and thereby implicitly defines it, using the ordinary terms that laymen and moralists themselves employ. Unlike many recent psychologists, Kohlberg does
not attempt either to "reconstruct" or "reform" our ordinary understanding of morality with technical concepts, like the "superego" or
"conditioned avoidance reaction" (Eysenck, 1961; Kohlberg, 1971:
152). The trouble with these reformulations, Kohlberg realizes,
is that they include a wide range of phenomena not generally
thought to be moral—like spontaneous, unconscious anxieties.
Properly understood, morality is that language game in which we
use concepts like right, wrong, good, bad, ought, just, and unjust
to consistently prescribe or commend human conduct. Kohlberg
similarly orders his research, using familiar general types of normative judgment—ranging from hedonism through utilitarianism and

269

rational contractarianism—that have been repeatedly identified historically as the most basic and consistent ethical options. With Kohlberg, the man on the street is on recognizable moral terrain, as is the philosopher or theologian. For the educator, Kohlberg deals with decisions that can be taught or at least elicited, given appropriate age, stage, and circumstances. To the ethicist, Kohlberg uses the distinctions of ordinary moral discourse that are his own specialty to define what it is that the human scientist should be researching.

Secondly, Kohlberg avoids the usual scientific reductionism that blithely ignores the revolution in the analysis of moral language wrought by G.E. Moore's *Principia Ethica* (1903). What Moore discovered is that the meaning of moral terms, such as "good," cannot be exhaustively reduced to nonethical terms. Moore referred to all such reductionist translations as "the naturalistic fallacy." Moore himself thought that ethical terms could not be analyzed into nonmoral constituents, because they are propositions that refer to simple unanalyzable, nonnatural properties. Few contemporary linguistic analysts agree with this latter aspect of Moore's theory, but his point is generally granted that moral terms are sui generis. Following Austin's *How to Do Things with Words* (1962) and R.M. Hare's (1952; 1963) analysis of the prescriptive usage of moral utterances, it is now widely believed that moral terms are nonreducible by virtue not of *what* they refer to, but *how* they are used. In saying "good" and "ought," we do something in a speech-act that we do not do with descriptive terms; that is, we prescribe or commend. The meaning of ethical terms resides largely, if not wholly, in their peculiar prescriptive or commendatory force. Kohlberg's developmental theory preserves this autonomy of moral language by providing a causal account of changes within the moral language game, instead of reducing the distinctively moral to the nonmoral.

Thirdly, Kohlberg offers to resuscitate the ailing natural law tradition, which has served as the major vehicle for religious ethical thought in the West at least since the Stoics. According to this tradition, all essential ethical principles are knowable by persons of "sound reason," apart from special revelation. In the Rabbinic literature, non-Jews often simply are assumed to know the difference between right and wrong, whereas an explicit natural law tradition was developed in Christianity, beginning with St. Paul (Rom. 2:14–15). Kohlberg offers a new variant of the natural law theory in ethics when he claims to move "from is to ought," that is, from a description of moral development to an ethical justification of normative standards. Reason and role taking are the necessary and sufficient conditions respectively, Kohlberg argues, for discovering that stage 6 alone is ethically adequate, with its truly universalizable ethical prescriptions. This new version of natural law, together with Kohlberg's stage 6 justification of Judeo-Christian respect for all persons as ends in themselves apart from idiosyncratic capacities and accomplishments, is unquestionably a major source of his appeal to religiously knowledgeable persons. Roman Catholics, for example, tend to respond most favorably to Kohlberg's work, presumably because the natural law tradition is more alive for them than for Protestants and Jews, who are often unfamiliar with this part of their own religious traditions. Whether Kohlberg's claim to move "from is to ought" is consistent with the autonomy of moral language just discussed under the second observation is an issue which is too complex to discuss here. It is sufficient for our purposes to note that Kohlberg does not really move "from is to ought," in the sense of moving from description to prescription. Rather, he attempts to explain why, given his definition of morality, only one type of ethical judgment, stage 6, is "universalizable."

Finally, Kohlberg's stages provide teachers, parents, and clergy with practical ways to identify the moral judgment levels of their charges and to intervene helpfully in a highly sensitive aspect of life. He has accomplished this by taking traditional normative theories, like hedonism and utilitarianism, out of academic treatises, laying them end to end, and showing why it is plausible to believe that we develop through these positions in sequence. Ethical theory is thus made more directly relevant for child rearing and education than it has been since the Victorian era. These practical advantages naturally are put in the limelight by educators, but the pragmatic suggestions are plainly parasites of the hypotheses framed by the preceding assumptions, particularly the autonomy of morality in the first two points which underlie Kohlberg's entire enterprise. Hence, the alleged autonomy of morality will receive the primary focus of attention in this essay.

ANALYSIS AND CRITIQUE

Paradoxically, Kohlberg's assumption about the autonomy of morality, which is a primary source of his appeal to informed religious persons, is also the source of their greatest difficulty with his work. For Kohlberg's defense of the independence and self-sufficiency of morality from the nonmoral phenomena studied by other psychologists (e.g., the oedipal complex) includes its autonomy from religion. And this is scarcely an uncontroversial claim. Indeed, it is safe to conclude from public discourse and the testimony of social scientists that most Americans believe morality to be dependent on religion, in some sense. One thinks, for example, of the numerous parents, clergy, and educators, not to mention politicians, who advocate religious instruction as the firmest foundation of morality. Certainly many religious believers provide impressive personal testimony to the deep anchorage of the moral life in religious convictions. Converts always provide the most dramatic examples, as R.M. Hare makes clear in the following observation:

What was it that happened to St. Paul when he stopped being an ordinary Jew and became a Christian? There may be a more recondite answer to this question; but . . . one obvious thing that happened to him was that his ideas about what he ought to do (his principles of action, or, in a wide sense, his moral principles) changed radically. And this is also true of lesser converts. Part of what it means to stop being a drunkard or a cannibal and become, say, a Methodist, is that one stops thinking it right to consume gin or human flesh. (Hare, 1957: 179–80)

Many social scientists further confirm that morality is dependent on religion. Emile Durkheim, for example, argues the common socialization thesis that morality depends causally and logically on religion, because it is only after one has come to respect something as sacred that it is possible to understand the ways in which moral principles cohere around that which society takes as its ultimate center of value. James Fowler represents a similar position within the developmental tradition of Jean Piaget and Kohlberg, although, in doing so, he breaks with one of its cardinal assumptions regarding the independence of morality.

Unfortunately, it is often by no means clear what people mean when they profess the dependence of morality on religion. More often than not, and Fowler is a clear example of this, they seem to imply several very different possible relationships at once.[1] Some advocates, for instance, seem content with the relatively modest observation that morality often *motivationally* depends upon some buttressing from religion. Thus religion is said to provide sanctions against immoral acts and support for altruistic behavior. (The considerations of self-interest involved in some theories of motivation cannot be viewed as "moral reasons" here without justificatory issues becoming confused with motivations. Motivations are seen more clearly if one thinks of the nonrational, frequently unconscious, effects of symbols, myths, and stories.) For those who think primarily in terms of motivational influences, whether completely nonrational or self-interested in a nonmoral sense, Kohlberg's work poses no genuine problems. For he clearly acknowledges that religious convictions often encourage people, against self-interest, to do what they know independently to be the right course of action. Because Kohlberg does not consider self-interest alone a sufficient moral reason, he has no difficulty recognizing that motivation may include conscious self-interested reasons for action, e.g., the expectation of heavenly rewards for virtuous behavior.

Other statements advocating the dependence of morality on religion focus on a necessary *metaphysical* relationship. Morality, it is said, depends on God or a ground of being, like everything else that exists. This is really a relatively weak claim regarding the dependency of morality, although it is an admittedly strong assertion against the beliefs of atheists and agnostics. No more is implied than that God's existence is as necessary for morality as it is for the rest of the universe, i.e., for planets, oceans, plants, animals, and

persons. Nothing is implied about knowledge of God being required for the form or content of moral standards. Plants do not
need to believe in God or the ground of being without which they
would not exist and neither do men in order to moralize. To say that
morality depends on God for its existence is not to say that it rests
logically on any theological beliefs whatsoever.

Still other statements refer to the *causal* dependence of morality
on religion. Children, for example, are often thought to need religious supports for morality in their formative years, before they can
understand the real reasons why they ought to be moral. Clearly,
this causal interpretation as to why persons become moral with the
aid of religion differs from any claim about the possibility or necessity of deducing or deriving morality from religion. Something like
religious awe of parents could be a necessary causal step in moralization, but this fact would scarcely make it always necessary or sufficient to derive or infer morality from religion.

Far more important than any of the preceding claims is the claim
regarding the *logical* dependence of morality on religion. Most
heated debates over the autonomy of morality center on this issue.
For we really do care about whether we can justify our moral judgments by deducing, inferring, or deriving them from religion. In
reflecting on this issue, it is useful to distinguish two broad types of
logical relations that are possible. The first is that beliefs are *sufficient* to justify logically some or all ethical principles. Religious
beliefs are sufficient if some or all ethical judgments can be justified
by being logically inferred, deduced, or derived from religious
premises. The second claim is that religious beliefs are *necessary* for
the justification of all ethical judgments. Religion is necessary if
ethical judgments can be justified only by being derived logically
from religious ones. As Frankena rightly observes, both logical
relations imply that moral terms can be "defined by reference to
(derived from or analyzed into) those, of religion" (Frankena,
1973:298). Hence, the definitional issue will loom large in the
following analysis of why Kohlberg's fundamental thesis about the
autonomy of morality is right.

One of the strongest arguments against the thesis that religious beliefs *suffice* to establish moral judgments logically is the familiar Humean dictum, "no ought from an is." No ethical conclusions can be derived, by the canons of formal deduction, from nonethical premises. In other words, no ethical conclusion follows from a proposition like "God loves all persons" or "God commands us not to fornicate." In order to derive ethical conclusions from theological premises like these, a second, specifically ethical premise is required, as in the following syllogism:

(1) God loves all persons.

(2) We *ought* to love anyone whom God loves.

(3) Therefore we ought to love all persons.

The ethical conclusion here follows logically from (1) together with the ethical premise (2), but not from (1) alone. The theological premise is not sufficient to justify logically the ethical judgment in (3). And this insufficiency holds for all strictly factual theological propositions. None alone or in combination can justify by logical entailment an ethical judgment.

One reason theologians are often untroubled by logical demonstrations of this familiar sort is their expansive understanding of religious propositions. Fowler, for example, includes an ethical commitment to an ultimate center or centers of value in his understanding of "faith-knowing." With moral evaluation built into religious judgments in this way, it *is* logically possible to infer ethical conclusions, using ordinary logic. The problem is that this move does not really establish the logical dependence of morality on religion as much as it underscores the autonomy of the moral element within religion, from which the ethical conclusions are being drawn. If the moral element within religion is distinguished from factual, theological beliefs, it once again becomes impossible logically to infer moral conclusions from nonmoral premises. That there is a form of nonmoral theological "evaluation" from which moral judgments can be deduced is a proposition that theologians and philosophers of religion have yet to demonstrate successfully.

The more frequent theological move in defense of the dependence of morality on religion, given the is-ought split, is to *define* ethical terms and judgments by reference to religious concepts or

categories. It is sometimes held, as, for example, by Emil Brunner
that "Good consists in always doing what God wills in any particular moment" (Brunner, 1947:   ). Here, "we ought to love all
persons" follows logically from "God commands us to love
everyone," not as an "ought" from an "is," but because "ought"
means "commanded by God." No violation occurs of "no ought from
an is without an ethical premise," because the additional premise
here is a semantical, rather than an ethical, statement. The principal
justification of this approach is the believer's conviction that what
she and fellow believers mean by "ought" is adequately translated
by "commanded by God." Whatever sense this translation makes
for some persons within the linguistic community of faith, it runs
into the problem of making mere tautologies out of some of the
other things believers themselves very much want to say. If
"ought," "duty," and "right" in a moral context mean just "commanded by God," it becomes nonsense to ask why God commands
one thing rather than another. What would be the point of doing
so? His commanding alone makes whatever he commands obligatory or right. "God commands it because it is right" becomes "God
commands it because God commands it." But the first sentence is
not a tautology; it means that God's commands are based on good
reasons, not simply on the fact of his decrees. It also becomes
senseless for believers to say, "I ought to obey God's command," if
"what I ought to do" and "what God commands" mean exactly the
same thing. But "Should I obey God's commands?" appears to be a
meaningful, open question (see Nielsen, 1973:ch.1).

The strongest and most obvious grounds for denying the divine
command translation of "ought," "duty, "right," and other moral
terms is the violence it does to what nonreligious persons mean
when they use these terms, without any reference to God's command, love, or any other theological concept. "It is your duty" as
used in ethical contexts by many people does not mean what the
divine command theory says it must, since those using it make
perfectly good sense without believing in God's existence. When
these people say "torturing innocent people is wrong," they do not
mean that there is a God, and it is against his will to torture the

innocent. And believers understand what is being said by non-believers, without translating their moral utterances into statements about divine commands. Thus, the divine command theory cannot be an analysis of what "duty," "obligation," "wrong," and so forth, always mean in moral contexts.

The plausibility of the divine command theory derives from some very specific Judeo-Christian assumptions about "God" as a moral being. "God is good" is often assumed to be an analytic statement or truth about language. Goodness is assumed to be true of godhood by definition, whatever one might say to the contrary about the spirits, ghosts, and gods, with a small "g," of nonmonotheistic religions. But this analytic assumption is incorrect. The word "God" does *not* have the same meaning as the word "good." To say "God is good" is not to utter the tautology that "God is God." And "God" cannot be substituted for "good." "How good of you" clearly does not mean "How God of you."

If the analytic equation fails, it is still true that the predicate "goodness" partially defines "God" in Western thought. But this partial definitiveness in no way establishes that God is a criterion for goodness. As Kai Nielsen observes in this connection, "God is good" is a truth of language like "puppies are young" and "triangles are three-sided." Goodness is partially definitive of godhood, just as youngness is partially definitive of puppyhood and three-sidedness is partially definitive of triangularity.

We could not understand the full religious sense of what is meant by God without knowing that whatever is denoted by this term is said to be good; but, as "young" or "three–sided" are understood without reference to puppies or triangles though the converse cannot be the case, so "good" is also understood quite independently of any reference to God. We can intelligibly say, "I have a three-sided figure here that is most certainly not a triangle" and "colts are young but they are not puppies." Similarly, we can well say "conscientiousness, under most circumstances at least, is good even in a world without God. . . . " Such linguistic evidence clearly shows that good is a concept which can be understood quite independently of any reference to the deity, that morality without religion, without theism, is quite possible. (Nielsen, 1973: 9–10)

In fact, to say "God is good" requires an independent understanding of goodness. Just as a prior understanding of "young" is required to understand the sentence "Puppies are young," so, too, we require an independent understanding of "good" to apply it correctly to God. To claim that God is a moral being, moral concepts have to be defined prior to and independently of God. One way of proceeding along this line is to provide a *formal* account of why God's commandments are good, say, because they conform to the criteria of the ideal observer theory in ethics.[2] But, then, we must know independently that these criteria are good ones for moral decision making.[3] Another procedure is to say God's will is good according to a certain definition of the content of morality. God is good because he is loving, merciful, just, and so on. But, then, God's will is a moral will not by virtue of being his, but because it expresses love, justice, and mercy. If God did not possess these and other moral qualities, he would be God in the sense of creating heaven and earth, being omnipotent, etc. But he would not be a morally good being. For either the formal or substantive procedure to hold up, morality must be defined independently of God. And, this, of course, is precisely the point of the claim that morality is independent of religion.

If moral concepts cannot be deduced from or translated by religious terms, there may still be a wider sense of "justification" that would make religious presuppositions logically *necessary* for the support of ethical judgments. Fowler takes this tack when he makes the justification of moral principles dependent on faith in something ultimate. In sharp opposition to Kohlberg's views on the autonomy of morality, Fowler writes, with the logical supremacy of his own faith stages in mind:

The nub of my theoretical and conceptual difference with Kohlberg can be put this way: I think it is a mistake to assume that faith is or must be a posteriori derivative of or justification for morality. . . . In fact, I would argue conversely, that every moral perspective, at whatever level of development, is anchored in a broader system of beliefs and loyalties. Every principle of moral action serves some center or centers of value. Even the appeals to autonomy, rationality and universality as justifications for Stage Six morality are not made *prior* to faith. Rather they are expressions of faith—expressions of trust in and loyalty to the valued attributes of autonomy and rationality, and to the valued ideal of a universal commonwealth of being. (Fowler, 1976:209)

Faith for Fowler is obviously not something in addition to morality, as it is for Kohlberg. In this passage, faith appears to be *always necessary* for the justification of an ethical position. Fowler's appreciative nods to Kohlberg's developmental theory notwithstanding, he turns on its head Kohlberg's basic philosophical thesis regarding the relationship between morality and religion. Kohlberg's developmental work on morality shrinks to a mere theme in the larger drama of faith development, as indicated by Fowler's very recent use of the Kohlbergian stages as one among several other "windows" on faith. And Kohlberg's central philosophical argument that normative judgments can be rationally justified independently of religion is rejected. In its place, ethical judgments are made dependent on largely nonrational faith-commitments, at least insofar as the affective element predominates in faith knowing (Fowler, 1974:4). Whether this means anything whatsoever can be justified as a moral standard by virtue of a nonrational act of faith is left obscured by Fowler's continued use of Kohlberg's stages of moral development, as if he believed in their restricted range of justifiable normative options. Yet, it would seem that in principle one could commit oneself nonrationally to virtually any central value as the ultimate ground of ethics, within Fowler's formal faith stages, including the most advanced. Fowler himself seems to imply this in the above relegation of stage 6 universal respect for persons to an ideological faith commitment over which men presumably disagree.

Fowler's wider justification of morality by faith tends to befriend religion at the expense of ethics, Fowler's personal intention to do justice to both notwithstanding. If we need considerably more than Kohlberg's universalizable prescriptions to justify moral judgments, serious questions arise as to the accessibility of that which we do require. If I take a few paragraphs to criticize Fowler's controversial justification of ethics through faith, it is primarily to illustrate the types of problems posed by such broad concepts of religious justification in ethics. I choose Fowler's work, because he gives expression among developmentalists to a powerful American theological tradition (most recently represented by H. Richard Niebuhr and his disciples) which is apt to be wrongly invoked against the autonomy of morality, upon which Kohlberg's work rests. I believe Fowler is wrong not only on philosophical grounds, but for jettisoning classical theological supports for natural law theory in ethics.

The first of several critical points that need to be made by way of criticizing the approach Fowler represents on the justification of morality by religion is that "faith" is defined so broadly that everyone is assumed to possess it. In Fowler's inclusive definition, faith is an affective and cognitive construing or interpreting that "fixes on the relatedness of a person or a community to those sources of power and values which impinge on life in a manner not subject to personal control" (Fowler, 1976:175). In theological language, the ultimate environment is apprehended as the transcendent. But all sorts of historical and unconscious forces also may be construed by persons as transcendent in the broad sense of being beyond personal control. Fowler uses the term in this latter sense. Even the most blatantly antireligious views become forms of faith on this reading. From such a broad definition, however, it no longer follows that ethics depends upon a "religious" worldview in any traditional sense. And the sort of dependence of morality on religion that many people are most intent upon demonstrating, in this area goes by the board. What is being alleged is only the formal point that there are ideological commitments (beliefs and loyalties) that always enjoy a supremacy over and, therefore, enter into the justification of ethical judgments.

At the same time that this broad interpretation is given so as to include everyone, Fowler tucks in an extensive list of very specific claims that make it empirically unlikely that everyone has all these elements tied up in an ideology of some sort. For example, faith is said to be a cognitive–affective construing of "sources of power and values" that impinge on the self from beyond the self. The emotions are particularly central in this construing of the ultimate conditions of existence. "One trusts, gives loyalty, loves and admires the beauty of the Transcendent" (Fowler, 1974:3). That which is construed is further assumed to form a "coherent pattern" which unifies the "total self," conscious and unconscious. Given the centrality of the emotions or affective dispositions in this theory, one wonders whether this coherence is not falsified by the radically discordant and inconsistent affective experiences of such "powers and values" that psychoanalysis uncovers in quite normal people. There does not seem to be much "coherence" in situationally specific anxiety reactions to the same reality as a "whole" that on other occasions appears quite benign. Even assuming that we consciously identify with a cognitively coherent world, however we affectively experience it, the additional notion that the conscious and unconscious are harmoniously integrated by an act of faith is a contradiction of terms, at least within the psychoanalytic tradition that Fowler cites. The dynamically repressed unconscious is defined precisely by its opposition to, and conflict with, conscious thoughts and intentions. Additional considerations along these lines could be brought forward (see Wallwork, 1980), but enough has been said to raise some doubts about whether everyone has faith in Fowler's sense. Indeed, I question whether anyone does. These doubts are relevant, because a large part of Fowler's claim on behalf of faith's justification of morality rests upon the empirical fact, if it is one, that everyone has such a larger justificatory scheme. If this is not the case, questions arise as to whether faith is indeed necessary to justify morality.

Fowler also assumes that some or all of the transcendent constitutes a center of ultimate value. In faith, he writes, "the self makes a bid for relationship to a center of value and power which is adequate to ground, unify and order the force field of life taken in its totality" (Fowler, 1977:5). This identification of the transcendent with the ultimate good, by definition, has already been explored when the transcendent is taken as the God of the Judeo-Christian tradition. Further questions arise with Fowler's broadening of the range of phenomena that count as transcendent powers. One wonders, for instance, about the religions of nonliterate peoples in which spirits, ghosts, and gods, though certainly transcendent beings beyond human control, are variously viewed as evil, disinterested in human affairs, frequently immoral, or, at least, never perfectly good. What examples of sacred beings from the religions of nonliterate peoples point to is Fowler's tendency to merge moral and religious elements in his understanding of faith, so that the distinguishing features of each are lost. It is difficult to see how Fowler's assumption that the transcendent powers are ultimate values can account for the following example of quite mundane ethical values being used to criticize a religious commandment:

Thus there is a tradition that the men of Purka clan were once faced by their clan-gods' demand for human sacrifice, but rather than comply with this gruesome command they rushed to the nearest river, and threw the sacred whisk symbolizing the female clan-deity into the water, and hence have performed the sacrificial rites only with the symbol of the male god who accepts the sacrifice of a goat and a cow. (Furer-Haimendorf, 1967:146)

Most modern believers would probably refuse similar divine commands for human sacrifice, against Kierkegaard's teleological suspension of the ethical, in the name of superior ethical standards.

Fowler might try to deal with this type of example by claiming that any supreme moral value in a society, no matter how mundane, belongs *by definition* within the realm of faith. But he cannot save his position in this way without sacrificing his central assumption that the supreme values are always transcendent. In my opinion this sacrifice would be a move in the right direction, since moral values generally protect mundane interests in personal well-being and harmonious interpersonal relationships. Morality is distinguished not only by its prescriptive force, but also by its substantive concern with the fundamental needs, interests, and wants of persons, the self, and others (Wallwork, 1979). However, recognition of this substantive content would force Fowler to distinguish morality from religion in ways that would argue for the autonomy of morality.

Another problem with defining moral standards as faith-values whenever they are supreme is that this victory for religion turns out to be a hollow one. The supremacy of faith over morality is achieved by a sleight-of-hand redefinition of the most basic moral standards. Every fundamental moral commitment becomes a religious act of faith by definition. But this makes an ethical conviction of the supremacy of a moral value like Bentham's utilitarian pleasure principle a type of religious faith. Yet it is "patently odd," as Little and

Twiss put it (in Outka and Reeder, ed., 1973:68), to refer to Bentham's principle as an object of religious faith. The reason it is odd, they go on to point out (in a more careful treatment of the distinction between religion and morality than Fowler provides) is that while the utilitarian principle displays two common features of religious objects in being both "authoritative" (in the sense of being normatively determinative) and "of special prominence" (in "standing out" or being unusually significant in the world of human affairs), the utilitarian principle cannot be understood as satisfying the third criterion for a religious act of faith, that of constituting a "scope of reality" beyond human control. Fowler, of course, wants to claim for the object of faith this broad scope. But, if he holds to this criterion, he cannot elevate every supreme moral standard into the realm of faith. Some "center or centers of value" do not belong to religion at all, but to morality.

What this latter point highlights is that religion or faith cannot be held by definition to be necessarily superior, in the sense of overriding the moral, as the ground and source of the moral. As the story of the men of the Purka clan indicates, moral standards sometimes override in importance religious claims. Fowler is thus wrong in asserting in his critique of Kohlberg that faith in an "ultimate environment" always enjoys a normative superiority that enables it to justify strictly moral principles. Sometimes moral standards override constructs of faith, frequently on the mundane grounds of human interests. In fact, if criticism of religion by morality were not fairly commonplace, it is hard to imagine how it would be possible progressively to revise religious and ideological worldviews either developmentally or historically. Unless morality had a certain degree of autonomy, criticism of this sort would not be possible.

Fowler's postulate that morality is always justified by a broader worldview has the additional disadvantage of making implausible assumptions about what we have to know in order to justify moral principles like noninjury of others, promise keeping, truth telling, beneficence, gratitude, reparation, and fairness. Sir David Ross may have been incorrect in assuming that these prima facie principles are self-evident intuitions, but he was right in saying that we do not need to get a number of large metaphysical questions settled in order to know—at least in the abstract—that these prima facie principles are right. If some large picture of man's place in the universal scheme of things is required to justify these quite ordinary, but basic, moral principles, Fowler must tell us precisely how each major element of faith-knowing relates by way of justification to specifically moral judgments.

One has the impression that Fowler views commitment to a "center of values" as the principal way in which faith justifies morality. But this proposal has the disadvantage of resting ethics upon nondemonstrable, possibly even arbitrary, nonrational foundations. If we can posit any center of value we happen to choose within Fowler's formal stages, we not only make up our own minds about specific moral questions, we also make up the grounds upon which we are willing to argue morally. R.M. Hare (1963) argues much the same line, although he has a much clearer understanding than Fowler of the types of considerations that constitute a moral judgment. But Hare has been taken to task severely by a long string of critics (e.g., Warnock, 1971; Little and Twiss, 1973), who have pointed out that only certain substantive arguments—like those having to do with fundamental human needs and interests—count on behalf of moral standards. In other words, morality itself imposes restrictions on what kinds of considerations support a distinctively moral judgment. The fact that individuals decide to adopt a certain ultimate value does not make it one of their moral standards unless they adopt it because they think action in accordance with that principle is required by morality. For a principle to be moral, a person must *suppose* it satisfies the fundamental needs, interests, or wants of *some* persons (Wallwork, 1979). Factual mistakes may be made, but the supposition is necessary.

In sum, there are very good reasons for agreeing with Kohlberg, against theologians like Fowler, that religion is neither necessary nor sufficient for the justification of morality. (See the Afterword for further discussion of Fowler's work.) This is true, whether religion is defined in terms of classical theism or faith in the ultimate conditions of existence. If this conclusion seems to challenge traditional assumptions, it is only because Americans have lost touch with the classical natural law tradition of both Judaism and Christianity. Within both these religions, it has been assumed widely that morality can be justified by reason alone, apart from special revelations to chosen communities. It is thus a very traditional claim that I have been defending against modern apologists for faith.[4]

The preceding arguments for the logical autonomy of morality should not be taken as implying that religion has no role to play in the justification of moral principles. To the contrary, sincere religious conviction profoundly affects how persons go about justifying moral judgments, although the precise nature of this influence tends to be misconstrued as a consequence of confusions over the logical connections discussed earlier. It is to these positive religious influences, which Kohlberg ignores and Fowler vaguely intuits, that I would like to turn now. Unfortunately, the length restrictions on this essay permit no more than a summary account of several positive points of contact.

Kohlberg would undoubtedly be led by his own theory to say that I am concerned here with how religion provides "content" for the formal structures of his moral stages. (For an application of this approach to Christian morality, see Duska and Whelan, 1975:80–99.) But I differ with Kohlberg in believing that religion provides something more than mere content. Positively, religion offers practical reasons that contribute to the justification of both the form and the content of moral judgments. Kohlberg himself has not provided much insight into the practical moral reasons that may be offered in defense of his stages, presumably because he believes reason and role-taking experience together provide sufficient support. But moral justification involves more complex considerations of practical reasoning, and these may include some religiously grounded reasons for action. Gene Outka (1972), for example, brings forward theological grounds for adhering to stage 6 universal respect for persons, while Rawls (1971), Downie and Telfer (1970), and Gewirth (1978) provide differing rational grounds in support of this moral attitude. The fact that theological considerations may be included among the practical reasons favoring a moral position in no way detracts from my previous argument that religion is neither a necessary nor sufficient justification of the most basic, universal ethical principles. On this point, I am in agreement with Kohlberg. But I disagree with him over the sufficiency of the grounds he provides for justification of his ethics of stage 6 in "From Is to Ought" (1971). In addition to reason and role-taking experience, a theory of practical moral reasoning is required to bring off the justification Kohlberg wants to make. Assuming that practical moral reasoning is essential, I now wish to show that religion may provide believers with: (1) additional arguments on behalf of ethical principles that are also rationally justifiable, (2) alternative perspectives on, and weightings of, morally relevant facts, and (3) distinctive religio-moral obligations that are required only of believers.

First, religion offers an additional source of reasons informing practical moral judgments. These additional reasons may not be necessary for the justification of any basic moral standards, but they do provide the believer with other "considerations," to use J.S. Mill's words, "capable of determining the intellect to give its assent." For example, most moral principles—like promise keeping, gratitude, honesty, and beneficence—are given a further justification when they are said not only to serve the fundamental interests of other persons, but also to be in accordance with the will of God. The deity's interests are thus added, as it were, to those of human beings in support of basic moral obligations. Of course, it is possible, as we previously observed, for the deity's commands to conflict with moral obligations, but where there is harmony, the faithful have additional religious reasons supporting basic moral obligations. James Gustafson (1975) refers to cases of this type as being justified by "two distinctive but 'overlapping' reasons" (p. 175). Calvin argued similarly when he claimed that the second table of the Decalogue could be known by all persons of sound reason, but Jews and Christians enjoy an additional clarification of the divine will in the written words of the scriptural Decalogue. What these theologians realize is that identical basic moral principles are held by believers and nonbelievers alike. But the believer has religious as well as moral reasons for accepting these principles, whereas the nonbeliever has only a moral justification.

Religious convictions also influence the justification of normative judgments through the interpretation of morally relevant facts. Among these, the interpretation of human nature set forth by most religions is especially significant, because it identifies and ranks the fundamental human interests with which morality is also concerned. Although there are limits set by human nature itself as to what religions may say about basic human needs and interests, there is also considerable room for varying degrees of emphasis and comparative weighting. If life is short in a world without God, health and psychological well-being are apt to receive greater emphasis than in a religious doctrine that views man's true *telos,* fulfillment, and happiness as everlasting communion with God. In comparison with this end, mere earthly health and serenity may seem almost trivial.

Religious (and secular) assumptions about human interests play a more significant role in justifying moral judgments than Kohlberg's theory supposes. The equilibrated role reversal that Kohlberg talks about only results in interpersonal moral agreement if there is a prior consensus about the relative importance of the fundamental interests of the parties involved. If there is disagreement about these interests—say, among Brahmins, Confucians, Catholic Christians, and Marxists—equally rational, universally impartial and emphathic stage 6 judges will not reach the same conclusions. No determinate moral judgments are generated by the application of rationality to reversible role-taking without making some substantive assumptions about the hierarchy of human interests. Kohlberg believes Rawls most faithfully represents stage 6 among contemporary philosophers, but this presupposes acceptance of Rawls's restricted list of primary goods. There are good reasons supporting Rawls's list. But they include acceptance of general facts about human nature and social institutions provided hypothetical persons in the original position. These facts include the importance of self-esteem in fulfilling a life plan and the interdependence of persons in societies. These may be reasonable doctrines, but they are not uncontroversial claims. In other words, reason and role-taking alone are not sufficient to advance toward Kohlberg's highest stages. Some conception of fundamental human interests is required, and this calls for a conception of human nature, like those offered by traditional religions.

If Kohlberg wants to avoid assumptions about human nature, by consigning such considerations to "content," he will have to further purify his own stages in a formalist direction. This cannot be done, however, without extracting the normative judgments currently embedded in what are described as "formal" stages. To move in this direction would seem to require acceptance of a variety of equilibrated reversible role-taking ethical theories at stage 6, depending upon the doctrine of human nature embraced. This change would seem to have a lot to recommend it to a cross-cultural theorist of moral development. Presumably, a more strictly formal model would pick up forms of equilibrated role-taking among Buddhists, Hindus, Moslems, and Marxists that are not currently tapped by the liberal content built into postconventional stages 5 and 6. But this cross-cultural advantage would be purchased at the high price of abandoning the liberal or Rawlsian normative implications of the developmental theory. Personally, I do not see how Kohlberg can exclude concepts of human nature, which are admittedly variable, on the grounds of "content," while proceeding, at the same time, to use stages that presuppose a particular concept, unless he can show that his view is more reasonable on some basis.

Religions also influence morally relevant facts by their interpretations of the wider context within which moral action takes place. These interpretations have a less direct effect upon what Kohlberg calls the "form" of moral judgment than doctrines of human nature. But assessments of how actions promote or frustrate human interests obviously are influenced by religious or secular interpretations of the forces at work in the world, that is, by some sort of implicit or explicit cosmology. These alleged "facts" about reality do not directly entail normative conclusions, and an elaborate metaphysics certainly is not required. But acceptance of a religious "picture" of the world, in Wittgenstein's sense, enters into one's assessment of the powers that may be working for or against one's practical moral goals, and, hence, into how one ought to behave. If justice is the major premise in an Aristotelian practical syllogism, it makes a difference whether the minor, factual premise holds that God is providentially governing the world through traditional political institutions or that he is working to liberate the oppressed by revolutionary means.

Finally, religion influences moral judgment by adding distinctive obligations and virtues to those required of the faithful. Jewish requirements regarding charity are a case in point, as are the strenuous obligations of the Sermon on the Mount. Whether these additional obligations and ideals of virtuous character are properly classified as moral rather than religious action guides is an extremely complex and hotly debated question that goes considerably beyond the scope of this essay (See Outka and Reeder, ed., 1973; Gustafson, 1975). Roughly, I believe obligations are religious in character if they follow from a historically particularistic *way of life* (beliefs, attitudes, and practices) based on a concept of sacred authority with sufficiently broad interpretive powers both to explain anomalies in the existing understanding of reality (natural as well as social) and to cope with anxieties caused by suffering and death (cf. Geertz, 1966:1–46; Little and Twiss, 1973:60–77). Obligations are moral if they are "universalizable" (in the sense of applying to any similar person in similar circumstances and to the same agent in all relevantly similar situations),[5] and if they consider the fundamental interests of persons. On the basis of this distinction, dietary laws and meditative practices would be religious obligations, because they are closer to cultic worship offered the deity than universalizable prescriptions affecting human interests.

A significant number of obligations within any religious tradition combine religious and moral elements. Since there are several ingredients in the definitions of each obligation, a complex variety of patterns exist. Some obligations shade toward the religious side; others are more clearly moral. The evangelical counsels of perfection in Roman Catholicism are closer to the religious side, because they are legitimated almost exclusively by the distinctive way of life commanded by the sacred authority, Jesus of Nazareth. The counsels of perfection have more to do with a disciple's relationship to God than to other persons, although they place heavy emphasis on service to others. The love commandment in Judaism and Christianity is closer to the moral side, at least in its usual modern presentation as a universalizable prescription explicitly directed toward the neighbor. But it would not be a religious commandment if it were not something more than a consistent rational principle, if it did not derive from the special relationship of Jews and Christians to God. As a consequence of this relationship, the love commandment asks more in the way of self-sacrifice from believers than its purely rational analogues.

The similarities between these two examples illustrate the difficulty of applying analytic distinctions between religious and moral obligations within a religious community, where something more than morality alone is involved. From the point of view of adherents, obligations are complexly intertwined with religious and moral considerations within a general framework that makes no sharp distinctions between the two types of judgment. Indeed, a number of key terms—like sin, repentance, and reconciliation—fuse moral and religious meanings. Still, it is generally possible analytically to distinguish the moral from the religious element. Even when this is done, however, it is clear that religious faith adds requirements to moral obligations that follow reasonably, if not by strict logical entailment, from the beliefs, attitudes, and practices fostered by the community. The greater degree of self-sacrifice required of Jews and Christians than reasonable principles of justice require is a case in point. This requirement makes sense, not as a strict logical conclusion, but in light of all the other beliefs and attitudes of the adherents in question.

The three foregoing ways in which religion positively influences morality deal exclusively with the justificatory side of this impact, that is, with the religious contribution to practical reasons for moral action. In addition, religion has profound causal affects on moral affections and dispositions. A distinctive "spirit" is often encouraged by the way of life to which the believer is committed which shows up in how he or she is moral. The symbols, myths, and stories of the tradition qualify the affections, dispositions, and intentions of the religious person's moral character (Gustafson, 1968, 1974, 1975). My concern in this chapter has not been to delineate these motivational influences, but, rather, to treat the question of justification raised by Kohlberg's central assumption regarding the autonomy of morality. Kohlberg appears to be correct that religion is neither necessary nor sufficient for the derivation of morality. But religion positively affects practical moral reasoning in ways missed by this logically sharp delineation of the two realms. These influences, even on matters of justification, can be appreciated without making sweeping claims for either the logical derivation of morality from religion or the necessity of being religious in order to be moral.

AFTERWORD

Fowler has responded to my invitation to criticize the discussion of his theory in this chapter with several important clarifications that deserve further analysis. His specific criticisms fall under three main objections.

First, Fowler believes I overly distinguish his faith stages from Kohlberg's moral stages, whereas he actually incorporates Kohlberg's stages as one of his "windows" or apertures on faith. Aside from the fact that this inclusion of Kohlberg's stages among these "windows" on faith is a very recent, unpublished change in Fowler's theory, which has been made available to me only after most of the foregoing was written on the basis of his writings between 1974 and 1976, a serious tension between morality and faith remains that is not handled adequately in this manner. Fowler himself, after all, sharply distinguishes faith from morality when he criticizes Kohlberg for not seeing that "every moral perspective, at whatever level of development, is grounded in a broader system of beliefs and loyalties" (Fowler, 1976:209). The stages of faith are said to go beyond Kohlberg's work precisely insofar as they involve

apprehension of ultimate conditions of existence or "some kind of
pattern or coherence in the welter of being, value and power that
impinges upon the self from beyond the self" (Fowler, 1976:
175n3). Fowler apparently views morality as causally and logically dependent on this wider view of reality. At least he asserts
that "every principle of moral action serves some (ultimate) center or
centers of value" (Fowler, 1976:209). Fowler cannot sustain these
claims while maintaining, against my interpretation of him, that
morality enters into apprehension of the ultimate. Either morality
really is one of the windows on faith, in which case it is not dependent on the outcome to which it contributes, or it is, as the foregoing quotes suggest, a consequence of faith. Given Fowler's own emphasis on the inclusiveness and pervasive influence of faith, I take it
he means what he says about the dependence of morality on faith.
He may now wish to choose the other horn of this dilemma by
underscoring how morality enters into faith. But I do not see,
without further clarification from Fowler, how he can argue both
sides of this position, unless he wants to see a continuous dialectical
relationship between morality and faith. If the latter is the case, he
needs to soften his bold claims against Kohlberg regarding the
dependence of morality on religion.

Secondly, Fowler denies my suggestion that he relativizes ethical
judgments by making them dependent on nondemonstrable or nonrational faith commitments. Insofar as Kohlberg's moral stages are
viewed as windows on faith, their substantive ethical content guards
against the possibility that nonrational faith commitments (at the
highest stages) may be used to justify morally outrageous judgments. This response seems to involve Fowler in another dilemma.
If he builds moral development into his faith stages, he rules out
most non-Western forms of postconventional religiosity (for failing
to demonstrate the requisite moral principles). Kohlberg's claims
about the universality of moral stages is hard enough to believe; it is
even less plausible that all forms of postconventional faith within
the world religions incorporate either Western ethical standards of
utilitarianism (Kohlberg's stage 5) or universal respect for persons

(stage 6). But this is what Fowler apparently must believe, if he is going to build moral criteria into his postconventional faith stages. If, on the other hand, Fowler does not build moral criteria into his stages, the centrality accorded faith in nondemonstrable ultimate center or centers of value may lead to the justification of morally odious behavior, even at advanced stages. This problem becomes increasingly more acute, the more formal the descriptions of the stages become in accordance with structuralist methodological guidelines. There is, I believe, a hint of this undercurrent of ethical relativism in Fowler's statement that Kohlberg's commitment to "autonomy, rationality and universality as justification for Stage Six morality are... expressions of faith" (Fowler, 1976:209). If so, other faith commitments are equally justifiable, unless one builds into postconventional faith substantive ethical criteria that tend to rule out seemingly postconventional faith elsewhere. The avoidance of ethical relativism in a theory that closely ties morality to faith is scientifically costly. The universal applicability of the stage theory is sacrificed.

Once again, Fowler may be thinking of a more dialectical relationship between faith and morality than he has heretofore formulated. If so, he may be in danger of undermining the plausibility of Kohlberg's claims regarding the universality of moral development. Kohlberg insists that morality is based on logic and role taking alone. Clearly, a broadening of these necessary and sufficient conditions will begin to erode the plausibility of his claims about the universality of this particular sequence of development. If Fowler pushes the conditions of moral development in the direction of dialectical interaction between Kohlberg's two conditions on the one hand and his own exceedingly broad, nondemonstrable faith commitments on the other hand, he would appear to be undermining the foundations of the ethical theory that he has recently built into his model.

Finally, Fowler denies that he wants to defend the necessary moral superiority of that which is taken to be ultimate. There are, he says, distinct levels within developmental stages which permit the sort of conflict between faith and morality that I brought forward with the example of the Purta clan. From this perspective, utilitarianism may be a person's moral standard without being part of a faith commitment. Aside from the difficulties this distinction creates for the earlier charge that I overly distinguish morality from faith in Fowler's work, how are we to understand Fowler's position on the linkage of morality to an ultimate "center or centers of value"? Are these faith values nonmoral? What, indeed, does the word "ultimate" mean, if not that these values are morally superior in some sense? If the "ultimate" is only superior in power, is this sufficient to integrate the "total self," where ultimacy would seem to refer to a hierarchy of subjective values? I would think psychic integrity would demand some morally evaluative sense of ultimacy. Perhaps Fowler is looking for a notion of faith values that are only *sometimes* morally superior. If so, the self is sometimes *not* integrated around these faith values, but, rather, around moral principles that also preserve the self's sense of integrity. Do moral principles turn into faith values when this happens? Clearly, we need further clarification from Fowler on precisely how faith differs from morality as well as on the interaction between the two. And this brings us back to the main line of my argument about preserving the distinctiveness of both religion and morality, while being alive to the precise ways in which they are related.

NOTES

1. Fowler telescopes several types of claims regarding the dependence of morality on religion in the following passage: "There is, I believe, always a faith framework or matrix encompassing and supporting the motive to be moral and the exercise of moral logic" (Fowler, 1976:209). Clearly, Fowler believes religion always influences moral motivation, although whether other motives are also always involved is not at all clear. Fowler is more ambiguous about what "supporting . . . the exercise of moral logic" means. I could refer either to the causal or logical dependence of morality on religion. Fowler apparently does not feel a need to distinguish between these two very different claims, because he wants to assert both, together with the above motivational point as well as the metaphysical

dependency discussed below. The ambiguity of expression obscures for the reader what he or she is being asked to buy.

2. In recent years, several religious ethicists have developed Roderick Firth's suggestions that the ideal observer theory in ethics might clarify why God's commandments are considered right or good. See Roderick Firth, "Ethical Absolutism and the Ideal Observer," *Philosophy and Phenomenological Research*, 12 (1952): 317–45; Arthur Dyck, "Referent-Models of Loving: A Philosophical and Theological Analysis of Love in Ethical Theory and Moral Practice." *The Harvard Theological Review*, Vol. 61 (1968): 525–45; Charles H. Reynolds, "The Significance of Firth's Ideal Observer Theory for the Logic of Ethics" (unpublished Ph.D. dissertation, Harvard, 1968).

3. In saying that the ideal observer criteria must be known independently to be "good ones for moral decision making," I am presupposing that the theory is not a correct reportive definition of what everyone means by the use of terms like "ought," "right," and "good" in moral contexts. A number of examples can be imagined in which these criteria are not implied, and Kohlberg's research indicates that only subjects at stage 5 accept this type of moral reasoning. The ideal observer theory is what Frankena calls a "normative definition," that is, it is a proposal about how we *should* use moral terms (Frankena, 1970).

4. The arguments for this claim go back at least as far as Socrates's question in Plato's *Euthyphro:* "Is what is holy holy because the gods approve it, or do they approve it because it is holy?"

Modern apologists for faith have abandoned traditional natural law theory partly in order to buttress lagging religious enthusiasm in a secular age by wailing that morality lacks all foundation in the absence of faith. Fowler's verbal acceptance of Kohlberg's developmental work on morality notwithstanding, he clearly argues in the apologist's vein when he writes that "world maintenance— the holding together of a shared vision of reality in human communities— requires interpersonal faith and faithfulness. It also requires, I maintain, a common awareness of relatedness to the Transcendent. 'World maintenance' involves a tri-polar or covenantal relationship between persons, and between them and shared visions of excellence of being. In a real sense the answer to Ebeling's question, 'What happens if God is removed?" is that the world of interpersonal faithfulness collapses. Solipsism sets in—both *epistemological* solipsism, in which each person construes the world and the ultimate conditions of existence after his/her own fashion; and *moral* solipsism, in which each person acts solely out of an ethics of maximizing one's own survival, security and significance" (Fowler, 1974:7). It should be noted that an apologist of this persuasion cannot turn around, without self-contradiction, and use Kohlberg's theory of moral development beyond the hedonist stage described or defend the existence of God on moral grounds.

5. The scope of "morality" depends, to a large degree, on how the universalizability criterion is defined. I have not defined it so as to preclude particularistic moralities, because I believe such in-group moralities are conceptually possible. If I had insisted that a "moral" prescription apply to all mankind, this third type of influence would be virtually defined out of existence.

REFERENCES

Austin, J. L. *How to Do Things with Words.* Oxford: Oxford University Press (Clarendon), 1962.

Brunner, Emil. *The Divine Imperative.* London: Lutterworth Press, 1947.

Downie, R. S. and Telfer, Elizabeth. *Respect for Persons.* New York: Schocken Books, 1970.

Duska, Ronald and Whelan, Mariellen. *Moral Development: A Guide to Piaget and Kohlberg.* New York: Paulist Press, 1975.

Eysenck, H. J. *Handbook of Abnormal Psychology: An Experimental Approach.* New York: Basic Books, 1961.

Fowler, James W. "Faith Liberation and Human Development: Three Lectures." *The Foundation.* Atlanta, Georgia: Gammon Theological Seminary, 1974.

_____. "Stages in Faith: The Structural-Developmental Approach," in Thomas C. Hennessy, ed., *Values and Moral Development.* New York: Paulist Press, 1976.

_____. "Faith and the Structuring of Meaning." Paper presented at the Convention of the American Psychological Association. San Francisco, California, August 26, 1977.

Frankena, William K. "The Concept of Morality," reprinted in G. Wallace and A.D.M. Walker, eds., *The Definition of Morality.* London: Methuen, 1970.

_____. "Is Morality Logically Dependent on Religion," in Gene Outka and John Reeder, eds., *Religion and Morality.* New York: Doubleday (Anchor), 1973.

Furer-Haimendorf, Christoph von. *Morals and Merit: A Study of Values and Social Controls in South Asian Societies.* London: Weidenfeld and Nicolson, 1967.

Geertz, Clifford. "Religion as a Cultural System," in Michael Banton, ed., *Anthroplogical Approaches to the Study of Religion.* London: Tavistock, 1966.

Gewirth, Alan. *Reason and Morality.* Chicago and London: University of Chicago Press, 1978.

Hare, R.M. *The Language of Morals.* Oxford: Clarendon Press, 1952.

_____. "Religion and Morals," in Basil Mitchell, ed., *Faith and Logic.* London: George Allen & Unwin, 1957.

_____. *Freedom and Reason.* London and New York: Oxford University Press, 1963.

Kohlberg, Lawrence. "From Is to Ought: How to Commit the Naturalistic Fallacy and Get Away with It in the Study of Moral Development," in T. Mischel, ed., *Cognitive Development and Epistemology.* New York: Academic Press, 1971.

_____. "The Claim to Moral Adequacy of a Highest Stage of Moral Judgment." *The Journal of Philosophy,* Vol. LXX (1973), 630–46.

Little, David and Twiss, Sumner B., Jr. "Basic Terms in the Study of Religious Ethics," in G. Outka and J. Reeder, ed., *Religion and Morality.* Garden City, N.Y.: Doubleday, 1973.

Moore, G. E. *Principia Ethica.* Cambridge: Cambridge University Press, 1903.

Nielsen, Kai. *Ethics Without God.* Buffalo, N.Y.: Pemberton Books, 1973.

Outka, Gene and Reeder, John P., Jr., eds. *Religion and Morality.* Garden City, N.Y.: Doubleday (Anchor), 1973.

Rawls, John. *A Theory of Justice.* Cambridge, Mass: Harvard University Press, 1971.

Ross, Sir David. *The Right and the Good.* London and New York: Oxford University Press (Clarendon), 1930.

Wallwork, Ernest. *Durkheim: Morality and Milieu.* Cambridge, Mass.: Harvard University Press, 1972.

————. "Ethical Issues in Research Involving Human Subjects" and "In Defense of Substantive Rights," in Eugene Kennedy, ed., *Human Rights and Psychological Research.* New York: Thomas Crowell, 1975.

————. "Attitudes in Medical Ethics," in William Rogers and David Barnard, eds., *Nourishing the Humanistic in Medicine: A Dialogue with the Social Sciences.* Pittsburgh: University of Pittsburgh Press, 1979.

———— "Baldwin's Theory of Religious Development," in John Broughton and D. J. Freeman-Moir, eds., *The Foundations of Cognitive-Developmental Psychology.* New York: Johnson-Ablex Press, 1980.

Warnock, G. J., *The Object of Morality.* London: Methuen and Company, 1971.

Chapter 10

Jewish Education and Moral Development

BARRY CHAZAN

INTRODUCTION

One of the important dynamics of Judaism throughout the ages has been its interaction and juxtaposition with prominent philosophies, motifs, and practices of general society. Jewish education, too, has often related to and been influenced by movements, theories, and practices of general education. Our concern in this chapter is to examine the relationship between Jewish education and Lawrence Kohlberg's theory of moral development and moral education. Specifically, we shall focus on two questions: Is there any relationship between Kohlberg's cognitive-developmental theory of moral development and education and the theory and practice of Jewish education? To the extent that there is a relationship between the two theories, are they compatible or contradictory?

The discussion of this topic is predicated on an understanding of the theory and practice of the Kohlberg view, and of the Jewish educational perspective. We shall assume the former and hence shall not undertake a detailed analysis of it. However, the concepts and world of Jewish education are likely to be less known; hence, we shall devote some time to the elucidation of aspects of that world in order to pursue our comparative analysis.

It must immediately be noted that "Jewish education" is neither a homogeneous nor monolithic term. Rather, it has numerous con-

298

notations which reflect alternative historical periods, ideological perspectives, and geographical locales. Thus, Jewish education of the Talmudic period is not the same as Jewish education in the contemporary State of Israel; modern Reform and Orthodox Jewish education are dissimilar phenomena; and Jewish education in Mexico City looks different from Jewish education in London. It would be impossible to relate the Kohlberg position to all of these meanings of "Jewish education" (historical, geographical, and ideological). Therefore, we shall focus on two senses of the term: the classical rabbinic notion of Jewish education, rooted in the Talmudic period (100 B.C.E. to 500 C.E); and contemporary non-Orthodox American Jewish education.

Rabbinic Jewish education (which I shall interchangeably denote as classical Jewish education) refers to a theory and practice of Jewish education which is elaborated and described in the Mishnah and the Talmud and which was to become a central paradigm of and influence on Jewish educational systems throughout the centuries. Contemporary non-Orthodox American Jewish education refers to Jewish education which developed and is widespread in twentieth century American society and which reflects the impact of the Enlightenment, Emancipation, and modernity on Judaism and its educational systems.

I have chosen to focus on these two senses of the term since each is representative of a fairly normative, mainstream genre of Jewish education which influenced or is reflective of significant eras or groups of people. Thus, the notion of Jewish education rooted in the Rabbinic period spread throughout many lands and generations, and while not exclusive, is probably characteristic of what has come to be denoted as "the traditional approach to Jewish education."[1] Contemporary non-Orthodox American Jewish education[2] reflects a type of education and a condition representative of the majority of Jews living today outside of the State of Israel (Jewish education in Israel is a unique subject not dealt with in this context[3]) who are no longer Orthodox but continue to have Jewish ties.

Our pattern of analysis will be as follows: 1) a discussion of aspects of the classical Jewish view on the moral sphere; 2) an

analysis of key dimensions of classical Jewish education, particularly
as they relate to the moral sphere; 3) a comparison of the classical
Jewish approach and the Kohlberg approach to moral education;
4) an analysis of key dimensions of contemporary non-Orthodox
American Jewish education; 5) a comparison of the latter and the
Kohlberg approach.

THE MORAL SPHERE AND JUDAISM

Classical Judaism and Jewish education were not elucidated in
terms of tightly developed logical systems; instead, they were presented and expounded in specific value concepts, legislation, and
practice.[4] Moreover, as we have already noted, there were several
emphases and nuances in classical Judaism and Jewish education.
Thus, there is no neatly presented philosophy of Judaism and Jewish
education in the classical period (such philosophic endeavors were
undertaken in later periods as Judaism became more influenced by
system-building philosophic approaches), and the elucidation of
Jewish views on morality and moral education is dependent on the
analysis of specific laws, rabbinic discussions, homiletic literature,
and actual practices and behavior. There has emerged, however, a
corpus of analyses of classical Judaism and Jewish education which
makes possible a systematic discussion of the moral sphere and
moral education. In our discussion, we shall particularly follow
interpretations presented by three distinguished students of the
subject: Kadushin, Guttman, and Heschel.[5]

The first characteristic of the classical Jewish view of the moral
sphere is that the modern distinction between religion and morality
(implicit in much of the theory and practice of contemporary moral
education, including Kohlberg) is nonexistent and inconceivable.
Instead, religion and morality are regarded as an organic unity:

The conclusion is inescapable that, if Rabbinic Judaism is a criterion, religion
and morality have a common positive character . . . because all the concepts are
dynamically related to each other as elements of a single organismic complex.[6]

The living reality in Judaism has always been that religion is unthinkable without
ethics, and ethics are intrinsically intertwined with religion.[7]

To have asked of traditional Judaism how it conceived of the relation of religion to morality would have been to have asked an incomprehensible question. "Religion" and "morality" did not exist for Judaism as separate categories distinct from one another: rather Judaism understands faith—the way a man stood in relation to God—to be fundamentally ethical.[8]

The terms religion and morality are united and integrated in the classical view by the fact of God; he is the source and object of both spheres, and *all* of human life is the endeavor to emulate his ways and be like him. The uniqueness of the Jewish ethic, then, was not so much in its emphasis on the moral way, but on the unification of the moral with the godly. A.J. Heschel has argued that the uniqueness of Sinai was not the moral imperative, but "the idea that justice is an obligation to God."[9] Similarly, he and others contend that the prophets were not simply moralizers and the prophetic message was not solely justice, but rather the unity and inevitable oneness of morality and godliness.[10] Thus, whether rabbinic Judaism believed in some notion of a natural moral law or not is somewhat irrelevant, for its larger purpose was to postulate an entirely new language system which denied the religion/morality dichotomy.

This point has several sophistications and complications. It does not simplistically mean that God equals good, and has no contact with evil. Indeed, the commitment to God's omnipotence forced some of the rabbis to explain that God was also the creator of evil ("I form the light, and create darkness, I make peace and create evil, I the Lord do these things"—Isa. 45:7). The fact is that there is evil in the world, and according to one (central) rabbinic tradition, it is somehow related to God and his handiwork.[11]

Moreover, the interrelationship of morality and religion in classical Judaism did not mean the absorption of the latter by the former. Judaism did not imply the abdication of the ritual, the divine, and the religious to the moral; rather, it meant some sort of unique and innovative interrelation between them.

Religion and morality in classical Judaism are, then, interrelated and are rooted in the godly way. Hence, the goal of Judaism is to enable man to emulate and imitate the godly way.[12] The resource, expression, and indication of how this is to be done is contained in the written law (Torah) and elaborated in the oral law (the Talmud). Study of and adherence to these texts will help one approach the good life. The classical text was regarded as a living compendium of moral and religious truth, not in a narrow, fundamental sense, but as a document to be elaborated, expounded, and applied. Moreover, the very act of study of these texts was regarded as a moral (religious) act. Thus, while the text and its study had an instrumental dimension, namely, that they could lead to moral-religious practice, they also had intrinsic value as moral truths and practices.[13]

Thus, there is a compendium and source of moral truth in the classical Jewish position which has a definitive—if interpretable—dimension. At the same time, the classical literature also emphasizes the notion of intentionality in godly and human action. According to this notion, God's behavior is not blind or capricious, but rather the outcome of consciousness, intention, will. Since man is created in God's image and his ideal is to emulate the godly way, man too has the possibility of acting out of intention (*Kavanah*) and motivation.[14] Moreover, the nature of God implies the possibility and even necessity of man's choice of good or bad, saintliness or sin. This principle meant that the notion of intentionality of actions was regarded as a relevant factor in the Jewish conception of the moral-religious sphere.

There is much discussion in Jewish tradition as to the doctrine of free will, i.e., whether man has the power to choose between good and evil. There is strong support in the tradition for the existence of free will as a fact and a desideratum in the moral-religious sphere, as exemplified by two famous rabbinic quotations: "Everything is foreseen but freedom of choice is given" (Avot, 3:15); "Everything is in the hand of Heaven, except the fear of Heaven" (Berachot, 33b), or in another version, "Everything is in the hands of Heaven except the fear of God" (Niddah, 16b). Thus the role of man's intentions and choice in the moral-religious sphere was at least an issue and probably an assumption in the classical perspective.

This notion of the role of man's will in the ethical sphere should not, of course, be understood in modern, individualistic, autonomous terms.[15] Jewish ethics are not a question of one man's lonely confrontation with life and fate, detached from values and social contexts. In the classical Jewish view the godly way is rooted in a collective tradition and context.[16] It is presented in the Torah (which specifically refers to the Pentateuch, but which more generally refers to the concept of study of the holy texts) and explicated in subsequent religious literature (especially the Talmud). Thus, as noted, man has an indispensable resource for coming to know how to be godly, i.e., the classical texts.

Another crucial dimension of the collective, nonindividualistic nature of the Jewish ethic is the concept of *Am Yisrael*—the Jewish people. Judaism had an inherently collective, peoplehood dimension from the outset. It is the sins or good deeds of Israel, *the people,* which influence their relationship with God. Prayers for repentance and atonement are in the plural in the Jewish liturgy. The life of the people in history is the setting in which the moral way manifests itself or is impeded.

Finally, the Jewish ethic is a practical rather than contemplative[17] art: "A Jew is asked to take a leap of action rather than of thought."[18] Jewish ethics are formulated in specific laws, practices, parables, and tales which are all aimed at daily practice and behavior. While motivations, intentions, and understanding are important, classical Judaism is very much concerned with specific moral actions and behaviors and it presents moral principles and practices which spell out that moral lifestyle. It would be inaccurate to describe this ethic as noncognitive or emotivist; indeed, the key means for realization of the good life is study. (In a famous discussion, the rabbis argued about what was more important, study or action, and they concluded that study was more important since it leads to action.[19]) However, this is not an intellectual ethic whose aim is the contemplation of God.[20] The crucial arena is action, and study is important *because* of its central impact on right action.

CHARACTER EDUCATION AND CLASSICAL JEWISH EDUCATION

Classical Jewish education in the moral sphere flows very neatly from these principles. First, classical Jewish education was primarily character education in the sense of education for the good (holy) life, i.e., for the life of Torah and Jewish citizenship.[21] Hence, classical Jewish education was not intellectual education per se, education for Jewish culture per se, or training for Jewish socialization. Rather, it was concerned with the development of a lifestyle, mentality, and behavior system in individuals which reflected the life of Torah.

This approach to character education was, however, not of the modern view. It was not essentially about moral deliberation about God, not about clarification of one's own moral feelings and beliefs, and not about the verbal inculcation of moral laws. Rather the concern was for doing the good, internalizing it, and understanding it as part of one's being. At the same time, this was not a depersonalized educational tradition; the child and his motivations were regarded as important, and the pedagogy of the Jewish school reflected this individual concern.

Thus, for example, pedagogic methods emphasized student declamation and explication, rather than lectures by teachers. Rabbis were instructed to individualize instruction in terms of differences in student ability. Instruction was conducted in small units, and teachers had a one-to-one relationship with students, hence enabling an intimate sense of their achievements and problems. Many schools were constructed on a nongraded classroom model, in which students progressed at different levels and paces, according to their abilities.[22] However, this individualization was aimed at helping the child to see, accept, and perform the good life, rather than to "realize" or "express" himself.

This overriding aim was closely connected with the contents and pedagogy of Jewish education, which were Torah. As we have already noted, the ethical and godly way were regarded as rooted and reflected in tradition and the classical texts.[23] Hence, the careful study of these texts and of Jewish tradition comprised an indispensable content and method for Jewish character education. The study of Torah, once again, is not intellectual contemplation, but rather the tasting of practical wisdom and lifestyle from a "living fountain."

Text study has several uses in the process of character education in the classical view.[24] First, it presents specific contents, judgments, and principles concerning what is good and what is bad. These principles are presented in a variety of ways: story, history, law, literature. However, it is clear that the purpose of the text is not to be a cookbook or list of "do's" and "don'ts," but rather the presentation of a total moral outlook and world view. Second, the texts and the method of teaching them are utilized to develop the individual's powers of moral judgment. The assumption is that morality is also a matter of moral judgment and the precise, critical study of the classical texts (especially the Talmud) is of great value in that process. Third, the study of classical texts can also stimulate one's motivation or desire to be moral. The contact with creative, exciting, and often passionate moral texts can inspire, excite, and encourage one to follow the moral way. Finally, as we have repeatedly emphasized, Jewish tradition sees the study of texts as a moral act in itself. Thus the very act of studying the text contributes to a child's moral development by enabling (or forcing the child) actually to perform a moral deed. What is important in this context is that while classical Jewish moral education was text centered, this did not imply an exclusively doctrinal or rule-focused moral education. The text was utilized for several purposes, in addition to being the definitive statement of good.

A second central source of learning and method of classical Jewish education was the deed. The Jewish student both studied Torah and did Jewish deeds (*mitzvot*). Originally, the home taught deeds; eventually the school, too, encompassed these activities. The method used to teach prayer, the recitation of blessings, and the performance of acts of loving kindness was practical; one actually prayed, recited blessings, and performed acts of loving kindness. The Jewish school, then, functioned as a total educative community, using both the text and the deed to mold Jewish character.

There was no systematic psychological theory underlying classical Jewish education,[25] and educational practice was probably guided by prevalent pedagogic and psychological norms and precepts. However, rabbinic psychology would at least seem to include the following elements. The person is regarded as being born morally neutral, with a good inclination (*Yezer HaTov*) and an evil inclination (*Yezer HaRa*),[26] with the will and the ability to use both and enable one to overrule the other. Indeed, the psychological tension between these two forces was regarded as present throughout the life of an individual. Thus a person sins, but can repent and return; a person can improve his ways and defeat *Yezer HaRa*. Indeed, it probably was assumed that people would sin and for that reason the concept of *T'shuva* (repentance) and *Yom Kippur* (the Day of Atonement) were central. Finally, the rabbis recognized that people's choices and behaviors were influenced by their environment, and that a person was a social creature. In short, the psychological assumption is of a human being operating in a social context and undergoing a constant back-and-forth movement between the godly way, distraction, and return. (There is a notion of a truly pious person who attains a consistent level of moral and religious excellence; however, this person is unique.)

Finally, the teacher as model is an important dimension of classical Jewish character education.[27] Since Jewish morality is primarily focused on doing, and since Jewish tradition constitutes a compendium of such deeds, the teacher as catalyst and conveyer of tradition must exemplify the godly way. Hence, the teacher was to be a pious, behaving Jew whose actions and character were no less important than his knowledge. Moreover, the school structure went out of its way to emphasize the piety of the teacher, especially the headmaster, and to bring the child into direct contact with him. The teacher was to behave properly, exemplifying a moral lifestyle through behavior, thoughts, judgment, and feelings.

KOHLBERG AND CLASSICAL JEWISH CHARACTER EDUCATION

Some very clear comparisons emerge between Kohlberg and the classical Jewish perspective on morality and moral education. First, while both Kohlberg and classical Jewish education are concerned with moral education, they are, in fact, concerned with two different phenomena. The classical Jewish view is of the type that Kohlberg's system apparently comes to reject.[28] Kohlberg's moral education is about moral development in terms of patterns of thinking; classical Jewish moral education is about the study and acceptance of a very specific and definitive lifestyle and behavioral style. Now it is true that Kohlberg, too, is concerned with moral action, arguing that moral thinking leads to moral doing. Similarly, Jewish tradition is concerned with the motives and thinking underlying the deeds done. Nonetheless, they begin from opposite sides of the pole. Jewish moral education is about a normative, substantive Jewish life practice and style; Kohlberg's moral education is about modes of thinking and confrontation with problems. The difference is between a principled-behavioral framework as compared with a cognitive-developmental approach.

Second, classical Judaism and Jewish education differ with Kohlberg vis-à-vis the autonomy of the moral sphere. Whereas Kohlberg sees morality (and moral education) as an independent domain, Judaism sees it as one with religion. Kohlberg's morality and moral education can, and probably should, operate independent of prior religious assumptions; Jewish moral education functions inextricably bound to its religious assumptions.

Kohlberg does briefly (and sympathetically) discuss the relationship of moral development and faith, arguing that moral education indeed may operate in terms of the larger faith context.[29] In that sense, he does not contend that morality and religion are necessarily contradictory. However, he argues that moral development precedes faith development, and that faith is grounded in moral reasoning. There may be a stage 7, a faith stage which is characterized by the "contemplative experience of a nondualistic variety" and "an escape from despair by identifying with the cosmic or infinite perspective." However, this stage is an appendage, and not integral to moral development in the Kohlberg scheme, and if it is at all real (which is not clear from Kohlberg's discussion of stage 7 where he calls it a metaphor),[30] it is not "higher" or more developed in the sense that stage 6 is higher than stage 5.

Thus, while both the classical Jewish view and Kohlberg deal with the relationship between religion and morality, for the former the relationship is indispensable and one; for the latter it is possible, although not necessary.

Third, classical Jewish moral education is much more collectivist and tradition-informed than Kohlberg's system. In the classical Jewish view, tradition is the valid compendium of the truth about the godly way. Hence, its study via the great texts is an end rather than simply a pedagogic means. For Kohlberg, moral traditions and literature are suggestions, references, and resources for the ultimate goal of stimulating independent moral thinking. What matters for Kohlberg are the principles, rather than the tradition in which they are encased. For Judaism, the principles and the tradition are one; hence, the performance and study of the latter is both a means and end at the same time. In the Jewish perspective, the educator has a legitimate tradition expressed in social norms and behavior which must be a part of the practice of moral education. For Kohlberg, the tradition is much less central and ultimate, and essentially is an instrumental tool.

Moreover, classical Jewish education gives greater emphasis to the combined educational effects of an integrated social setting than Kohlberg. In the classical Jewish world, the school joined with the home, communal institutions, holidays, prayer, the neighborhood, and social networks to engage in moral-religious education. The community as a whole, as moral (religious) community, is a central concept of classical Jewish educational theory. Kohlberg does emphasize the importance of the communal setting;[31] however, his moral community is much less inclusive and all-encompassing than the classical Jewish view. This difference may be partially explained by the very basic structural and substantive differences between the notion of community in classical and modern times (and specifically between "Jewish community" then and "community" today); however, it is also probably attributable to the inherently more social and collective orientations of the classical Jewish view as opposed to Kohlberg.

Fourth, Kohlberg and classical Jewish moral education differ concerning the contents of moral education. For Kohlberg, the contents of moral education are case studies, situations, examples which are used instrumentally to enable debate so as to advance students to a more sophisticated level of moral thinking.[32] It is true that Kohlberg's case studies are not simply a discussion of methodology in the sense of values-clarification techniques; and they often have a historical or functional legitimacy of their own. However, they do not comprise, as they do in the classical Jewish view, a compendium of a priori legitimate principles or behavior. The stories about Abraham, Joseph, Jeremiah, may contain possibilities of moral reflection and discussion;[33] however, that would not be the main reason for their inclusion in the classical Jewish curriculum. Such stories are part of the curriculum because they are Torah, and Torah is truth.

Fifth, classical Jewish education does not contain the sophisticated hierarchical notion of moral development which appears in Kohlberg's theory. As noted, if there is any psychological theory of Jewish moral development in the classical view, it is more likely related to the good inclination-bad inclination tension. Moreover, while the Jewish view, as we have already noted, was not noncognitivist; its notion of cognition is different from Kohlberg's. The classical Jewish view is probably closer to a social psychological conception which places emphasis on the complex interrelationship between cognitions, attitudes, behaviors, social settings, norms, and backsliding, than to a linear cognitive-developmental model.

Up to this point, we have discussed differences between the two stances. There are several themes and motifs which have surfaced in our discussion of the two systems which may be regarded as common to both. First, both systems are sensitive to the individuation of moral education. That is, both assume that moral education is about some sort of development in the individual child; hence, both argue that teaching must be so constructed so as to speak to and affect the individual personally.[34] Second, both Kohlberg and Jewish education are sensitive to the school as a social setting of great educational potential. Both systems imply the utilization and integration of all dimensions of the school, curricular and extracurricular, for the enterprise of moral education. Teacher-student interaction, student activities, school environment are not irrelevant factors in the moral development process. Third, both systems reject a narrow behavioral notion of moral education as exclusively concerned with the inculcation of moral laws. Both systems believe that moral laws are not the exclusive content of moral education (for Kohlberg, moral thinking is of the essence; for Jewish education, moral life). And both systems assume that motivation and intention are not irrelevant factors in the moral sphere (for Kohlberg, they are indispensable; for classical Jewish education, they are desirable). Fourth, both systems are rooted in ultimate universal principles which they regard as true and which they posit as the objects of moral education (for Kohlberg the principle is justice; for Jewish education it is God).

Fifth, both systems assume a link between study and deed, i.e., that the intellectual and action spheres are not completely separate. For Kohlberg the link is apparently tight, i.e., true knowledge leads to good action. The classical Jewish view, while committed to study, is more sensitive to human foibles and weakness which combat the desirable influence of study.

The existence of these similarities has led some people to argue that Kohlberg and Jewish education are complementary.[35] In arguing this case, Linda Rosenzweig claims the following: Kohlberg is concerned with justice; justice is very central to classical (and modern) Judaism; hence, Kohlberg's system of moral education for justice is relevant for Jewish education. The problem with this approach is its reductionism, whereby two common terms are extracted from their natural, complex settings in order to prove similarity. Such a methodological approach neglects the fact that both Kohlberg's work and Jewish education are multidimensional educational models in which ultimate being is defined by the complex as a whole, rather than by one constituent element. Hence, to extract justice from each system and then equate the systems or argue that they are similar is a misleading procedure. Justice is, admittedly, an important part of the Jewish moral view. However, it is not the only dimension, and it is understandable only in terms of its interaction with other indispensable Jewish value concepts. Indeed, our analysis of the classical Jewish educational perspective, and its comparison with Kohlberg would seem to indicate that the two are more dissimilar than similar. The Kohlberg approach is either generally inconsistent with the classical Jewish educational view or it deals with different issues and assumptions. In terms of contents and goals, the two systems are contradictory; in terms of psychology and pedagogy they are operating on different wave lengths. Thus, the attempt to Judaize Kohlberg or to Kohlbergize classical Jewish education is ultimately an artificial attempt to amalgamate two disparate approaches.

MODERN AMERICAN JEWISH EDUCATION

Modern American (non-Orthodox) Jewish education is significantly different from its classical forebears. It has been shaped by the general confrontation of tradition with modernity and by the specific context of the open, democratic society. The result has been the emergence of some radically new patterns and functions of Jewish education.

Among the important distinguishing factors between classical as opposed to modern American Jewish education are: the diminution of Torah, tradition, *Halacha* (Jewish law) as central concepts; the heterogeneity and diversity of modern Jewish lifestyles as compared with classical forms; the impact of secularism on the life of the modern Jewish child and adult; the metamorphosis of the role and status of the Jewish teacher; the supplementary nature of Judaism and Jewish education to the American Jew's lifestyle; the diminished role of the classical text in Jewish lifestyle.[36]

Some of these changes directly relate to the changed theological and ideological perspective of contemporary Judaism. However, the most important changes, at least in terms of Jewish education, are more related to the new sociological situation of the modern Jew than to the theological sphere. (For that reason, whereas our discussion of classical Jewish education dealt with philosophic concepts, our discussion of contemporary Jewish education makes a dramatic shift to the sociological domain. The phiolsophy of contemporary Jewish education has increasingly been superseded by the sociology of contemporary Jewish life.) The major issues of Jewish life today relate to the nature and perpetuation of the individual and group life of modern Jews. Classical Jewish education took place within the context of a supportative, reinforcing Jewish society, but Jewish life in America occurs in an open, democratic, pluralistic secular society. In the classical Jewish society, the school did not have to be primarily or exclusively concerned with group socialization, since the family, the marketplace, the neighborhood, and the culture served these functions. Thus, the school was able to focus on the development of conscious normative religious lifestyle in children, in addition to more basic socialization functions. Today, the family, the community, the marketplace, and the peer group do not serve as agents for making the young Jew aware of his or her Jewishness. Indeed, they usually work in just the opposite direction. Thus the classical structural division of functions between Jewish society and school has been radically altered. The result is a new structural and functional basis for contemporary Jewish education.

Structurally, the predominant model of American Jewish education is the part-time supplementary school (79 percent of all Jewish children of school age who receive Jewish education do so in supplementary schools). Such education encompasses up to six hours a week (either once a week on Sunday morning or Sunday plus one or two weekday afternoons after public school). The education occurs in synagogues or Jewish community–sponsored schools. In such schools, students deal exclusively with Jewish studies. A minority of the children who receive Jewish education (21 percent) study in Jewish day schools, private schools which teach Jewish and general subjects. Moreover, not all American Jewish children receive Jewish education. According to a recent estimate, one–third of all American Jewish children of school age are likely never to set foot in a Jewish classroom. Finally, the majority of those who do receive any sort of Jewish education do so only until age thirteen; only 20 percent of American Jewish children of school age receive Jewish education on the high school level.[37]

Functionally, the shift is from (a) the classical presentation, analysis, and transmission of a carefully delineated lifestyle and value system to young Jews whose primary reference group was Jewish, to (b) the contemporary emphasis on the stimulation of links and alignment with the Jewish people for young Jews whose primary reference group is secular and American. Jewish education has had to become increasingly devoted to the development of a basic awareness of and receptivity to the Jewish subgroup membership of young American Jews. Moreover, Jewish education also has seen its role as preventing assimilation and intermarriage—and hence guaranteeing the perpetuation of the Jewish group—rather than education which attempts to transmit and develop a substantively Jewish character or moral-religious lifestyle. Categorically, then, the movement in modern Jewish education is from the domain of character education to education for group or ethnic affiliation.

This is, I believe, the emerging focus of much of contemporary Jewish education, and many of the subjects, topics, and programs of Jewish schools are utilized to serve this function. It is not, however, the only focus. Thus, many programs in contemporary Jewish education continue the concern for teaching Jewish religious-moral values and worldview. Two directions have emerged in programs which are concerned with this second function. One direction has been to return to the classical texts to discover the great moral-religious values in them, and intelligently and creatively to teach them, via the texts, to the modern child.[38] The tone of this approach is moral inquiry, rather than moral exhortation. It assumes that the classical texts are valid and relevant for today's world and moral dilemmas, and it attempts both to uncover the classical values and to exemplify their relevance for today.

The second approach concerns itself with the translation and explication of Jewish moral-religious values for today's life and child.[39] In this approach, the classical text is considered neither basic nor accessible to the child. Instead, the child learns about the Jewish moral way via contemporary textbooks on Jewish morality (e.g., *The Still Small Voice; Love, Sex, and Marriage: A Jewish View; Our Religion and our Neighbors; Jewish Values and Social Crisis*) or by dramatizations of the lives and behaviors of certain exemplary personalities (e.g., Moses, Rabbi Akiba, Abraham, Golda Meir). This approach assumes that classical Jewish values are still valid, but that they must be presented in a vivid, updated, and concise context and style. Both systems make no major claims vis-à-vis the centrality of the teacher as a moral personality and force, mostly out of an awareness of the problematic state of the profession today. The role of the teacher—out of necessity, not choice—becomes limited to creatively explicating the Jewish moral tradition.

A common thread runs through these approaches to moral education in the Jewish school. They both conceive of their task in the moral sphere as the presentation and explication of a specific, substantive moral system which is legitimate and relevant for the modern age.

The modern Jewish practice of moral education differs from the classical perspective in many areas: the role of the teacher in moral education; the emphasis on deeds; the study of the text as a moral act; and the source and force of moral principles. However, the modern approach does continue the classical commitment to the validity and value of such a moral system for the life of the individual and society.

The contemporary Jewish educational world, then, is defined by two parameters. The first is the new social setting of the modern Jew, a free member of an open, secular society. This means that much of the focus of Jewish education has had to shift to the concern for creating a sense of Jewish group affiliations, thereby contributing to Jewish survivalism. As I have indicated, this parameter has increasingly become the predominant one. The second parameter has been the concern to present, explicate, and defend in the modern context the contents and meaning of the classical Jewish religious-moral outlook.

KOHLBERG AND MODERN JEWISH EDUCATION

This brief description of the parameters of the contemporary Jewish educational world implies either contradiction or irrelevance between Kohlberg and the Jewish approach. We saw that the dynamics between Kohlberg and the classical Jewish perspective were generally those of contradictory positions on similar questions. The difference between Kohlberg and the modern Jewish educational world lies in contradictory perspectives, in concern for totally different objectives.

Kohlberg focuses on moral education; contemporary Jewish education increasingly is concerned with group affiliation, the first parameter discussed above. These different orientations mean that the two educational systems deal with a host of theoretical and practical questions which are radically dissimilar. Kohlberg centers on such questions as the role of moral principles in moral thinking; the role of society in determining moral action; educational strategies for enabling the student to reflect on moral issues. However, Jewish education, as education for group identification, focuses on such questions as educational techniques which will appeal to the child and stimulate positive Jewish feelings; behaviors and beliefs which are crucial to alignment with the Jewish group; subjects and contents which lend themselves to the development of a sense of group loyalty (i.e., the Holocaust, Israel). Thus, in terms of the first parameter of Jewish education today, Kohlberg is totally irrelevant.

In terms of the second parameter, i.e., Jewish education's concern for teaching a specific, substantive value system, there is the same sort of contradiction as we saw between Kohlberg and the classical Jewish perspective. The Jewish system of moral education presents and argues for a specific religious-moral lifestyle and system. Kohlberg at least purports not to be about the teaching of specific (or even general) substantive values or behaviors, but rather about the development of moral thinking. It is true that the modern as opposed to the classical Jewish educational perspective focuses more on verbal rather than behavioral elements; however, this is to a

great extent more a matter of educational realities than of principles. It simply is difficult to effect the classical principled-
behavioral moral education today; hence, there is more emphasis on
talking. It is clear, however, that whereas Kohlberg's moral deliberation is about the development of moral reasoning skills, moral
deliberation in the contemporary Jewish educational context is
about the defense and justification of a specific moral world view.
Thus, even when Kohlberg and modern Jewish education are on the
same wavelength and deal with the same concerns, they present two
contradictory approaches to moral education.

There are two other areas of contrast between Kohlberg and
modern Jewish education. Kohlberg's theory of moral development
reflects a carefully developed psychological structure which is based
on intensive longtitudinal and latitudinal research. Similarly, the
educational practice which emerges from it reflects a tightly organized pedagogy which is based on and develops carefully delineated patterns of moral thinking. Contemporary Jewish education is not based on any such carefully delineated psychological
theory. It is difficult to delineate any one dominant psychological
theory in Jewish education; instead, one witnesses a haphazard
amalgam of behavioristic, Gestalt, Freudian, and developmental
psychological assumptions. Similarly, no logical, planned approach
coordinates educational practice or curriculum development in contemporary Jewish education. The quilt or patchwork approach predominates; programs, texts, and curricula are developed on the basis
of "workability," chronology, personal experience, or "hit and
miss." Thus, whereas the Kohlberg model has a defensible educational psychology and potential theory of educational practice and
curriculum, modern Jewish education is a much more pragmatic
enterprise, lacking a unifying theory.[40]

As in the case of classical Jewish education, there also have been
attempts to argue for the similarity of Kohlberg and modern Jewish
education. These attempts, however, reflect the same methodological flaw we noted in the classical-Kohlberg comparison. In both
instances, comparisons mistakenly have extracted one phenomenon
(usually the term "justice"), and from it have deduced similarity.

The reasons for the dissimilarity between Kohlberg and the modern Jewish educational perspective are not exactly the same as between Kohlberg and the classical Jewish educational perspective; however, in both cases our contention is that the differences are greater than the similarities.

One area in which there has been some attempt to relate Kohlberg to contemporary Jewish education, with perhaps some limited success, is the sphere of practice. Jewish education is constantly on the lookout for techniques, practices, and materials of general education which might be used to increase student interest, motivation, and learning. Thus, contemporary Jewish schools have, at different times, adopted green boards, overhead projectors, language laboratories, open classrooms, values clarification. The Kohlberg discussion technique occasionally has been considered an interesting procedure for involving students in matters of Jewish concern. Sometimes, standard Kohlberg dilemmas are used; sometimes specifically Jewish adaptations are constructed. The relationship here is solely on the level of practice and didactics, with little reference to or concern for the theory. The question in such instances is, "Does it work?" in the sense of "Does it involve and interest students?" rather than "Is it right?" Indeed, it could be argued that the Kohlberg technique is being used in the Jewish school in this instance for the non-Kohlberg concern of having children be positive toward and involved in their Jewishness. Indeed, the use of Kohlberg in Jewish schools may be a vivid example of the fact that the same educational practices often may be used in totally different and even contradictory educational settings.

SUMMARY: IS KOHLBERG CONSISTENT WITH JEWISH EDUCATION?

Is there a relationship between Kohlberg and Jewish education? Are Kohlberg and Jewish education compatible or contradictory? I have argued that there is little relationship between Kohlberg and modern Jewish education, and there is an essentially contradictory relationship between Kohlberg and classical Jewish education. In both cases my arguments have been logical. That is, in terms of parameters, assumptions, and functions, these two Jewish educational systems seem either to be concerned with different sorts of issues from Kohlberg or to contradict Kohlberg. *Could* there be an accommodation between Kohlberg and Jewish education? I doubt it—unless Jewish education changes drastically in the coming years—despite certain potentially significant points of agreement, e.g., the importance of motivation, the school as community, and the centrality of the individual. The Kohlberg model is ultimately too Platonic, too individualistic, and too traditionless to be applicable to the Jewish educational world, past, present, or future.

NOTES

I would like to thank Dr. Michael Rosenak and Dr. Elliott Dorff for their helpful comments on this paper.

1. This phrase, as the expression "classical Jewish education," is somewhat problematic, if it implies a monolithic, unanimously-agreed-upon conception of Jewish education. The fact is that there were different approaches within the Rabbinic period, and certainly in subsequent periods of Jewish history. Nevertheless, it can be argued that there were certain mainstream assumptions which did emerge in the Rabbinic period, and which, if not unanimously accepted, were at least the starting point from which agreement or dissent began. See: Louis Ginzberg. *Students, Scholars, and Saints* (Philadelphia: Jewish Publication Society, 1928), pp. 64–65; David Goodblatt. *Rabbinic Instruction in Sasanian Babylonia* (Leiden: E. I. Brill, 1975); Yishayahu Gafni, "The Babylonian Yeshiva: Internal Structure and Spiritual and Social Functions among the Jewish Community in the Period of the *Amoraim*" (Hebrew). Unpublished Ph.D dissertation, Hebrew University of Jerusalem, 1979.

2. For discussions of major dimensions of contemporary American Jewish education, see: Walter Ackerman, "Jewish Education—for What?" *American Jewish Yearbook*, volume 70 (New York and Philadelphia: American Jewish committee and Jewish Publication Society, 1969), pp. 3–36; Zvi Adar. *Jewish Education in Israel and in the United States* (Jerusalem: Melton Press, 1977).

3. For discussions of Jewish education in Israel, see: Z. Adar, op. cit.; Aaron Kleinberger. *Society, Schools and Progress in Israel* (London: Pergamon Press, 1969); J. Schoneveld. *The Bible in Israeli Education* (Amsterdam: Van Garcum, Assen, 1976).

4. Julius Guttman. *Philosophies of Judaism* (New York: Schocken, 1964), pp. 43–44; Max Kadushin. *The Rabbinic Mind* (New York: Bloch Publishing Company, 1952), p. 6.

5. Some examples of this literature are contained in: Julius Guttman. *Philosophies of Judaism,* op. cit.; Max Kadushin. *The Rabbinic Mind, op. cit.;* A.J. Heschel. *God in Search of Man* (New York: Meridian Books, 1959); Haim Dimitrovsky (editor). *Exploring the Talmud. Volume I: Education* (New York: Ktav, 1976); Adin Steinsaltz. *The Essential Talmud* (New York: Basic Books, 1976). Of course, the best way for us to elucidate the issues in which we are interested would be via detailed references to and analyses of the primary sources in Hebrew and Aramaic. However, in order to facilitate the flow and argument of this chapter, and because of the existence of a reputable corpus of secondary sources, we shall generally refer to the latter in our discussion.

6. Max Kadushin. *The Rabbinic Mind,* op. cit., p. x.

7. Zvi Yaron. "Religion and Morality in Israel and in the Diaspora" in *Modern Jewish Ethics,* Marvin Fox, editor (Columbus: Ohio State University Press, 1975), p. 232.

8. Joseph Reiner. "The Moral Component of Religious Education: Theories of Character Development and their Relationship to Jewish Education." Brandeis University, Unpublished Master's Thesis, 1970, p. 1.

9. A.J. Heschel. *God in Search of Man,* op. cit., p. 288; also: Aaron Lichtenstein, "Does Jewish Tradition Recognize an Ethic Independent of Halakah?" in *Modern Jewish Ethics,* Marvin Fox, editor (Columbus: Ohio State University Press, 1975), pp. 62–88.

10. Y. Kaufmann. *The Religion of Israel* (Chicago: University of Chicago Press, 1960), pp. 343–446.

11. Both Heschel and Lichtenstein agree that it probably did believe in some notion of natural law; A.J. Heschel. *God in Search of Man, op. cit.;* Aaron Lichtenstein, "Does Jewish Tradition Recognize an Ethic Independent of Halakah?", op. cit.

12. Solomon Schecter. *Aspects of Rabbinic Theology* (New York: Macmillan Company, 1908), p. 270.

13. Aaron Kirschenbaum, "Students and Teachers: A Rabbinic Model", *Conservative Judaism,* XXVI (1972), pp. 20–32; Bernard Mandelbaum, "Two Principles of Character Education in the Aggadah", *Judaism,* XXI (1967), pp. 84–92.

14. Solomon Schecter. *Aspects of Rabbinic Theology,* op. cit., p. 271.

15. See the following comments on the difference between classical Jewish and contemporary notions of autonomy: David Hartman. *Maimonides: Torah and the Philosophic Quest* (Philadelphia: Jewish Publication Society 1976), pp. 236–237; footnote 2.

16. See the following discussions of the role of tradition in Judaism: Natan Rotenstreich. *Tradition and Reality* (New York: Random House, 1972), pp. 7–20; Gershom Scholem, "Tradition and Commentary as Religious Categories in Judaism", *Judaism,* XV, (Winter, 1966), pp. 23–39.

17. Max Kadushin. *The Rabbinic Mind,* op. cit., pp. 45–47; Emil G. Hirsch,

320   BARRY CHAZAN

"Ethics", *The Jewish Encyclopedia*, (New York, 1901), Volume 5, pp. 245–258.

18. A.J. Heschel. *God in Search of Man*, op. cit., p. 283.

19. "Rabbi Tarfon and the Elders were once reclining in the upper story of Nitza's house in Lydda, when the question was raised before them: Is study greater or practice? Rabbi Tarfon answered, saying: Practice is greater. Rabbi Akiba answered, saying: Study is greater for it leads to practice. Then they all answered and said: Study is greater for it leads to action." Sifre Deuteronomy, Kiddushin 40B.

20. Maimonides is sometimes mentioned as an exception to this noncontemplative tradition. See Hartman's analysis of and argument with this view. David Hartman. *Maimonides: Torah and the Philosophic Quest*, op. cit.

21. David Gordis, "Towards a Rabbinic Philosophy of Education". The Samuel Friedland Lectures, Jewish Theological Seminary, 1974, pp. 11–28; N. Drazin. *History of Jewish Education from 515 BCE to 220 C.E.* (Baltimore: Johns Hopkins Press, 1940), p.12; Nathan Morris. *The Jewish School* (London: Eyre and Spottiswoode, 1937), p. 100; Alvin Roth. *Rabbinical Foundations of Jewish Education as Reflected in Talmudic Literature, 10 C.E. - 499 C.E.* Northwestern University, Unpublished Doctoral Dissertation, 1957; J. Maller, "The Role of Education in Jewish History" in *The Jews*, Louis Finkelstein, editor. (New York: Harper and Row, 1949, p. 1235.

22. J. Maller, op. cit., pp. 1235–1237; L. Ginzberg "The Jewish Primary School" in *Students, Scholars and Saints*, op. cit., p. 1–34.

23. Natan Rotenstreich, *Tradition and Reality*, op. cit., pp. 1–14.

24. These comments draw upon insights presented by my colleague Professor Elliot Dorff in a paper and discussion presented at a faculty seminar in Jerusalem. I am grateful to him for his comments: Elliott Dorff, " 'Because Study Leads to Action': The Use of Text Study to Teach Morality" (Jerusalem, January, 1977).

25. Nathan Morris. *The Jewish School* (London: Eyre and Spottiswoode, 1937), p. 99.

26. Solomon Schecter. *Aspects of Rabbinic Theology*, op. cit., Chapters 14–17.

27. Max Arzt, "The Teacher in Talmud and Midrash" in *Mordecai M. Kaplan Jubilee Volume*, Moshe Davis, editor (New York: Jewish Theological Seminary, 1953), pp. 1–13; David Gordis, "Towards a Rabbinic Philosophy of Education", op. cit.; Aaron Kirshenbaum, "Students and Teachers: A Rabbinic Model", op. cit.

28. L. Kohlberg and E. Turiel, "Moral Development and Moral Education", in: *Psychology and Educational Practice* (Glenview, Ill.: Scott, Foresman, 1971), pp. 411–417.

29. Lawrence Kohlberg, "Education, Moral Development, and Faith", *Journal of Moral Education* IV (1974), pp. 5–16; see also James Fowler's work (in this book and others) in relating Kohlberg to the religious sphere.

30. Ibid., p. 18.

31. Lawrence Kohlberg, "Education for Justice", in *Moral Education: Five Lectures*, Theodore and Nancy Sizer, editors. (Cambridge, Mass.: Harvard University Press, 1970), pp. 82–83; see also: Elsa Wasserman, "Implementing

Kohlberg's "Just Community Concept' in an Alternative High School", *Social Education* (April, 1976, pp. 203–207).

32. Moshe Blatt, Ann Colby, Betsy Speicher. *Hypothetical Dilemmas for Use in Moral Discussions* (Cambridge, Mass.: Moral Education and Research Foundation, 1974); see also the film-tape program "Teacher Training in Values Education: A Workshop". (Guidance Associates, 1976) (4 color filmstrips, 4 cassettes, 36 duplicating masters, teacher's guide).

33. The Melton Research Center of the Jewish Theological Seminary of America has developed an approach to Biblical analysis and instruction which particularly focuses on ethical issues of the Biblical text and personalities (although it does not reflect a Kohlberg approach). See, for example: Nahum Sarna. *Understanding Genesis* (New York: McGraw-Hill, 1966); L. Gardner. *Genesis: The Teacher's Guide* (New York: Melton Research Center, 1966); L. Newman. *Genesis: The Student's Guide* (New York: Melton Research Center, 1969).

34. For a modern Jewish expression of this position, see: Martin Buber, "The Education of Character" in *Between Man and Man* (London: The Fontana Library, 1947).

35. See, for example: Linda Rosenzweig, "Towards Universal Justice: Some Implications of L. Kohlberg's Research for Jewish Education", *Religious Education*, LXXIII (November—December, 1977), pp. 605–615.

36. See the following discussions of these metamorphoses in the American Jewish community: Marshall Sklare. *America's Jews* (New York: Random House, 1971); pp. 155–179; Walter Ackerman, "Jewish Education—For What?" op. cit.; David Sidorsky (editor). *The Future of the American Jewish Community* (New York: Basic Books, 1973), pp. 3–21; 46–64; 65–154.

37. See the following for a summary of some of these facts: Harold Himmelfarb, "Jewish Education for Naught: Educating the Culturally Deprived Jewish Child," *Analysis,* LI (September, 1975), pp. 1–11.

38. The Melton materials (see footnote 33) reflect this approach. For a discussion of the dialectic of study and moral action in several contemporary Jewish educational programs, see: Barry Chazan, "Study and Action in Contemporary Jewish Education", a paper presented to the faculty seminar of the Centre for Jewish Education in the Diaspora, Hebrew University of Jerusalem (1979).

39. This approach is best exemplified by the curriculum of the Reform movement: *An Interim Outline of the Curriculum for the Jewish Religious School* (New York: Commission on Jewish Education of the Union of American Hebrew Congregations and the Central Conference of American Rabbis, 1977).

40. For discussions of the lack of theory and philosophy in contemporary Jewish education, see: Seymour Fox, "Towards a General Theory of Jewish Education in *The Future of the American Jewish Community,* David Sidorsky, editor, op. cit., pp. 261–264; Michael Rosenak, "The Tasks of Jewish Religious Educational Philosophy", *Religious Education* LXXIII (1978), pp. 513–528; Barry Chazan, "The Nature of Contemporary Philosophy of Jewish Education", *Philosophy of Education, 1972* (Edwardsville: Philosophy of Education Society, 1972), pp. 175–187.

REFERENCES

Ackerman, Walter. "Jewish Education—For What?" *American Jewish Yearbook 1969*. New York and Philadelphia: American Jewish Committee and Jewish Publication Society, 1969.

Adar, Zvi. *Jewish Education in Israel and in the United States*. Jerusalem: Melton Press, 1977.

Arzt, Max. "The Teacher in Talmud and Midrash" in *Mordecai M. Kaplan Jubilee Volume*. Moshe Davis, editor. New York: Jewish Theological Seminary, 1953.

Blatt, Moshe, Colby, Ann, Speicher, Betsy. *Hypothetical Dilemmas for Use in Moral Discussions*. Cambridge, Massachusetts: Moral Education and Research Foundation, 1974.

Blatt, M. and Kohlberg, L. "The Effects of Classroom Moral Discussion upon Children's Level of Moral Judgment", *Journal of Moral Education*, IV (February, 1975).

Baron, Salo. *A Social and Religious History of the Jews* Vol. II. New York: Columbia University Press, 1952.

Buber, M. "The Education of Character" in *Between Man and Man*. London: The Fontana Library, 1947.

Chazan, Barry. "The Nature of Contemporary Philosophy of Jewish Education", *Philosophy of Education, 1972*. Edwardsville: Philosophy of Education Society, 1972.

Dimitrovsky, H.Z. (editor). *Exploring The Talmud, Volume I: Education*. New York: Ktav, 1976.

Donin, Hayim. "An Inquiry into the Value Presuppositions Underlying Jewish Education in Metropolitan Detroit". Unpublished Ph.D. dissertation, Wayne State University, 1976.

Dorff, Elliot. "Because Study Leads to Action: The Use of Text Study to Teach Morality". Jerusalem (1979). Stencil.

Dorph, Sheldon. "A Model for Jewish Education in the United States: Guidelines for the Restructuring of Conservative Congregational Education". Unpublished Ed.D. dissertation. Teachers College, Columbia University, 1976.

Drazin, N. *History of Jewish Education from 515 B.C.E. to 220 C.E.* Baltimore: Johns Hopkins Press, 1940.

"Ethics" *The Jewish Encyclopedia* Vol. V (New York: Jewish Encyclopedia, 1901).

Fox, Marvin (editor). *Modern Jewish Ethics*. Columbus, Ohio: Ohio State University Press, 1975.

Fox, Seymour. "Towards a General Theory of Jewish Education" in *The Future of the American Jewish Community*. David Sidorsky, editor. New York: Basic Books, 1973.

Gafni, Yishayahu. "The Babylonian Yeshiva: Internal Structure and Spiritual and Social Functions among the Jewish Community in the Period of the *Amoraim*" (Hebrew). Unpublished Ph.D. dissertation, Hebrew University of Jerusalem, 1977.

Gardner, L. *Genesis: The Teacher's Guide*. New York: Melton Research Center, 1966.

Ginzberg, L. *Students, Scholars, and Saints.* Philadelphia: Jewish Publication Society, 1928.

Glosser, Joanne Katz. "Moral Development and Jewish Education: In Search of Synthesis". Unpublished M.A. dissertation, Hebrew Union College, 1977.

Goldin, Judah. "Several Sidelights of a Torah Education in Tannaite and Early Amoraic Times", *Ex Orbe Religionum,* I (1972).

Goodblatt, David. *Rabbinic Instruction in Sasanian Babylonia.* Leiden: E.I. Brill, 1975.

Gordis, David. "Towards a Rabbinic Philosophy of Education" in *Exploring the Talmud, Volume I: Education.* H.Z. Dimitrovsky, editor. New York: Ktav, 1976.

Guttman, Julius. *Philosophies of Judaism.* New York: Schocken, 1964.

Hartman, David. *Maimonides: Torah and Philosophic Quest.* Philadelphia: Jewish Publication Society, 1976.

Heschel, A.J. *God in Search of Man.* New York: Meridian, 1959.

Himmelfarb, Harold. "Jewish Education for Naught: Educating the Culturally Deprived Jewish Child", *Analysis,* LI (September, 1975).

An Interim Outline of the Curriculum for the Jewish Religious School. New York: Commission on Jewish Education of the Union of American Hebrew Congregations and the Central Conference of American Rabbis, 1977.

Kadushin, Max. *The Rabbinic Mind.* New York: Bloch Publishing Company, 1952.

Kaufman, Y. *The Religion of Israel.* Chicago: University of Chicago, 1960.

Kirschenbaum, Aaron. "Students and Teachers: A Rabbinic Model", *Conservative Judaism,* XXVI (1972).

Kleinberger, A. *Society, Schools and Progress in Israel.* London: Pergamon Press, 1969.

Kohlberg, L. "Cognitive-Developmental Theory and the Practice of Collective Moral Education" in *Group Care: The Educational Path of Youth Aliya.* M. Wolins and M. Gottesmann, editors. New York: Gordon and Breach, 1971.

Kohlberg, L. "Education, Moral Development, and Faith", *Journal of Moral Education,* IV (1974).

Kohlberg, L. "Education for Justice: A Modern Statement of the Platonic View" in *Moral Education.* N. and T. Sizer, editors. Cambridge: Harvard University Press, 1970.

Kohlberg, L. "From Is to Ought: How to Commit the Naturalistic Fallacy and Get Away with It in the Study of Moral Development" in *Cognitive Development and Epistemology.* T. Mischel, editor. New York: Academic Press, 1971.

Kohlberg, L. "Indoctrination Versus Relativity in Value Education" in *ZYGON,* Spring (1972).

Kohlberg, L. "Moral and Religious Education and the Public Schools: A Developmental View" in *Religion and Public Education.* T. Sizer, editor. Boston: Houghton-Mifflin, 1967.

Kohlberg, L. "Stages of Moral Development as a Basis for Moral Education" in *Moral Education: Interdisciplinary Approaches.* C.M. Beck, B.S. Crittenden and E.V. Sullivan, editors. Toronto: University of Toronto Press, 1971.

Kohlberg, L. and Turiel, E. "Moral Development and Moral Education", *Psychology and Educational Practice*. Gerald Lesser, editor. Glenview, Illinois: Scott, Foresman and Co., 1971.

Kurzweil, Z.E. "Fundamental Principles of Jewish Education", *Judaism*, XVI (1967).

Leipziger, Henry. "Education Among the Jews", *Educational Monographs*, III (1890).

Lichtenstein Aaron. "Does Jewish Tradition Recognize an Ethic Independent of Halakah?" in *Modern Jewish Ethics*. Marvin Fox, editor. Columbus, Ohio: Ohio State University Press, 1975.

Lipnick, Bernard. *An Experiment that Works in Teenage Religious Education*. New York: Bloch Publishing Co., 1976.

Maller, Julius. "The Role of Education in Jewish History" in *The Jews*. Louis Finkelstein, editor. New York: Harper and Row, 1949.

Mandelbaum, B. "Two Principles of Character Education", *Judaism*, XXI (1967).

Morris, N. *The Jewish School*. London: Eyre and Spottiswoode, 1937.

Neusner, Jacob. *First Century Judaism in Crisis*. Nashville: Abingdon, 1975.

Newman, L. *Genesis: The Student's Guide*. New York: Melton Research Center, 1969.

Rabinovitch, Nahum. "Halakah and Other Systems of Ethics: Attitudes and Inter-Actions" in *Modern Jewish Ethics*. Marvin Fox, editor. Columbus, Ohio: Ohio State University Press, 1975.

Reiner, Joseph. "The Moral Component of Religious Education: Theories of Character Development and their Relation to Jewish Education". Unpublished M.A. thesis, Brandeis University, 1970.

Rosenak, Michael. "Education for Jewish Identification: Theoretical Guidelines", *Forum* 28–29 (Winter, 1978).

Rosenak, M. "The Tasks of Jewish Religious Educational Philosophy", *Religious Education*, LXXIII (1978).

Rosenzweig, Linda. "Towards Universal Justice: Some Implications of L. Kohlberg's Research for Jewish Education", *Religious Education*, LXXII (November–December, 1977).

Rotenstreich, Natan. *Tradition and Reality*. New York: Random House, 1972.

Roth, Alvin. "Rabbinical Foundations of Jewish Education as Reflected in Talmudic Literature 10 C.E. - 479 C.E. Unpublished Ph.D. dissertation, Northwestern University, 1957.

Safrai, Samuel. "Elementary Education: Its Religious and Social Significance in the Talmudic Period", *Cahiers D'histoire mondiale*, XI (1968).

Sarna, N. *Understanding Genesis*. New York: McGraw-Hill, 1966.

Schecter, Solomon. *Aspects of Rabbinic Theology*. New York: Macmillan, 1909.

Scholem, Gershom. "Tradition and Commentary as Religious Categories in Judaism", *Judaism*, XV (Winter, 1966).

Schoneveld, J. *The Bible in Israeli Education*. Amsterdam: Van Gorcum, Assen, 1976.

Sidorsky, David. "The Autonomy of Moral Objectivity in *Modern Jewish Ethics*. Marvin Fox, editor. Columbus, Ohio: Ohio State University Press, 1975.

Sklare, M. *America's Jews*. New York: Random House, 1971.

Steinsaltz, Adin. *The Essential Talmud*. New York: Basic Books, 1976.

Wasserman, Elsa. "Implementing Kohlberg's 'Just Community Concept' in an Alternative High School", *Social Education* (April, 1976).

Yaron, Zvi. "Religion and Morality in Israel and in the Diaspora" in *Modern Jewish Ethics*. Marvin Fox, editor. Columbus, Ohio: Ohio State University Press, 1975.

Chapter 11

Christian Religious Education and Moral Development

JAMES MICHAEL LEE

INTRODUCTION

More than any other social scientist, Lawrence Kohlberg has dominated the field of moral reasoning and moral development since 1960. From the 1960s to the present, Christian religious educationists have been paying increasing attention to Kohlberg's work, probably for two reasons. First, virtually every Christian denomination strongly affirms that morality occupies a major position in its theory and practice. Consequently, moral judgment and moral development are emphasized in the religious education activities which the various Christian denominations sponsor or otherwise support.[1] Second, in an age of natural science and social science, many Christian religious educationists like to feel that they have scientific findings on their side—even if they know little about the nature and workings of natural science or social science.

Those whom religious educationists would wittingly or unwittingly destroy, they first trivialize. There is a certain sense in which Christian religious educationists who write or speak enthusiastically or semienthusiastically about Kohlberg have indeed trivialized his work. Seldom have Christian religious educationists done more than rattle off Kohlberg's six stages of moral reasoning, followed by some low-level remarks about how Kohlberg's data "prove" that a person grows step-by-step in consciousness and in conscience.[2] Rarely do Christian religious educationists offer extended treatments of the deeper issues raised by Kohlberg's data and his conclusions.[3] Indeed, when Christian religious educationists do treat Kohlberg with anything resembling requisite seriousness, they not infrequently spend considerable time drawing attention to the so-called "dangers" which Kohlbergianism poses for Christianity and Christian religious education. It is the purpose of this essay to examine the relevance and significance which some of Kohlberg's fundamental contentions have for Christian religious education.[4]

THE BASIS OF MORAL JUDGMENT

For Lawrence Kohlberg, the basis of moral judgment is human development. Kohlberg conceptualizes development as the fundamental, molar, structural, processive form of the human organism, rather than as any particular isolated change in an individual's cognitive, affective, or lifestyle behavior. Development thus involves: (1) change in the general shape, pattern, or organization of response; (2) the emergence of a new, qualitatively different structure of response; (3) an irreversible, nonextinguishable character.[5] In my language, development is structural content, as contrasted to substantive content.[6]

Drawing on both John Dewey and his own research findings, Kohlberg defines development as the consequence of the ongoing interaction between the growing organism and the environment. The human being, then, is an *interactive emergent.* Cognitive activity, or mind, is not a *res* or substance; rather it is a function. Cognition is the way in which the human being cognitively organizes and deploys himself.[7] Kohlberg calls his theory "cognitive-developmental" because he maintains that normal human development has a basic cognitive-structural component which tends to organize but not control the developmental process. Cognitive development, therefore, is a necessary but not a sufficient condition for overall human development.[8]

At the center of Kohlberg's cognitive-developmental theory of moral development is the tenet that each person is basically good. Therefore, each person has a fundamental orientation toward increasingly higher levels of moral development.[9] Attainment of successively higher stages of moral development is hastened or thwarted by the quality, variety, and intensity of one's encounters with one's environment.[10] Experience brings with it either an upward reorganization or a congealing of a person's cognitive stance toward right and wrong. Kohlberg, then, is a developmentalist rather than a maturationalist.[11]

In Kohlberg's view, the basis or fundamental course of moral judgment lies in the process of human development itself. His research suggests that moral judgment, like overall moral development, is the process of personal self-constructed and self-regulated advance as one interacts with the environment. Thus it is the natural developmental process and not primarily any extrinsicist system such as theologizing or Christian rules of conduct, which entails in each stage the progressive organization of moral structure for resolving moral problems.[12]

From what I have written in the last few paragraphs, Kohlberg's fundamental position clearly runs counter to the basic tenets advanced by the advocates of the theological approach to religious education.[13] Defenders of the theological approach argue that growth in personal morality as well as in other phases of Christian living comes from an extrinsicist source, typically identified as the mysterious and unfathomable action of the Holy Spirit. Hence, to truly understand and chart development, one must look to theology because only theology can discern, however dimly, the workings of the Holy Spirit. To understand development, therefore, the Christian religious educator should be a theologian.

Supporters of the theological approach to Christian religious education assert that empirical research data such as those gathered by Kohlberg are irrelevant because they cannot measure or otherwise get at the mysterious and unfathomable way in which God works.[14] In other words, advocates of the theological approach to religious education attempt to sidestep or evade Kohlberg's data by spookifying reality.

The net effect of the position advanced by the adherents of the theological approach to Christian religious education is to make God an extrinsicist variable in the process of moral development. Indeed, Françoise Darcy-Bérubé, a staunch supporter of the theological approach to Christian religious education, uses this very word *variable* to describe God's action with respect to humans.[15] It is here, as in many other places as well, that fundamental contradictions inherent in the theological approach manifest themselves. I am referring in this instance to the fundamental tenet in both classical and modern Christian theology that God is not a variable, but rather is the ground of all being and the existential context of all man's actions.

Instead of begging the profound question raised by Kohlberg in his research-based conclusions that moral development is rooted in human development, Christian religious educationists could profit immensely by forthrightly confronting his data and his theory.

To accept Kohlberg's findings is not to de-godize God. Rather, Kohlberg's findings suggest how God works in this world. Kohlberg's research data clearly imply that if God does exist, then he works in and through the process of human development, rather than by some extrinsicist "zap" of grace.[16] To assert the existence of God is to assert that God is in all reality by his presence, power, and existence. Thus God is not outside human development, but works in all its operations. God erupts in human living rather than irrupting into it. God *in se* is utterly transcendent, yet God in the world is radically immanent.[17]

THE AUTONOMY OF MORAL DEVELOPMENT FROM RELIGION

For Kohlberg, an adequate explanation and prediction of moral judgment and moral development can be found in the social-scientific study of human development. Thus any philosophizing (or theologizing) about the way in which a human being becomes increasingly moral must be based in part upon social-scientific evidence.[18] From the Christian perspective, human development can be the basis of moral judgment and moral development *only if* this is the way in which God works with respect to persons. To assert otherwise is to take the position that moral judgment and moral development are independent of God's action.

What do Kohlberg's research findings say about the relationship between morality and religion? The Harvard educationist and psychologist unequivocally states that the evidence from his empirical studies strongly suggests that moral development takes place independently of religion. He emphasizes that "no differences in moral development due to religious belief have yet been found" in his investigations.[19] Regardless of their religious affiliation, children "go through the same sequence of moral stages" identified in Kohlberg's research. In other words, a child's religion does not significantly affect the progress of his or her moral development.[20] This finding appears to hold true cross-culturally. In the United States, children make remarkably little use of religion in responding to moral dilemmas, irrespective of the denomination of these children.[21] Kohlberg's studies also found the same stages of moral development to exist in Israeli and Formosan Chinese children, as well as in middle- and working-class children, and in socially popular and socially isolated children—regardless of the various religious denominations of these children.[22] In his empirical investigation of the efforts by members of different religious groups to support their moral judgments, Kohlberg discovered that regardless of their religious affiliation, these individuals relied upon those types of moral judgment charted and described in his research.[23] Kohlberg's findings are consistent with those of other empirical research studies which conclude that membership in a particular religious denomination appears to have no pivotal relationship with ethical conduct, humanitarianism, altruism, or nondelinquency.[24]

What response can Christian religious educationists make to Kohlberg's research data and conclusions? Predictably, those holding to the theological approach to Christian religious education would offer one set of responses, while those espousing the social-science approach would offer a contrasting set.

It should be noted that supporters of the theological approach to religious education typically ignore Kohlberg's findings and conclusions concerning the autonomy of morality from religion. However, from what these individuals have written on other, related matters, it is possible to construct what they would answer if they were to open their eyes and honestly face his data and conclusions.[25] The axis of their answer would be that Kohlberg's research deals only with the outer surface of religion, and so it is incapable of locating the essential, mysterious, and unfathomable religious wellsprings and mainsprings of morality. Thus Alfred McBride writes that Kohlberg's social-scientific research is confined solely to observable, rational phenomena. Consequently, Kohlberg's research does not address itself to what McBride terms "the mysterious realm of human faith."[26] Françoise Darcy-Bérubé claims that no social-scientific theory can adequately explain religious lifestyle, because this constitutes an interior act of God's free giving and man's free responding—an interior act which she claims is essentially mysterious and unknowable by the human mind.[27] Some individuals like Berard Marthaler,[28] John Westerhoff,[29] and Alice Gallin[30] posit a substantial difference between faith and religion. In their view, faith is the inner, mysterious, lived, graced relationship which a person has with God, while religion is the set of outward practices related to an individual's contact with the divinity.[31]

The response to Kohlberg such as that delineated in the previous paragraph is manifestly unsatisfactory on at least four counts. First, it gratuitously asserts that faith and other kinds of God's workings in the human heart are mysterious and unfathomable. What is gratuitously asserted can just as gratuitously be denied.

Second, it adopts an ostrich-like approach to the empirical evidence. Advocates of the theological approach to religious education cannot legitimately brand empirical research evidence as irrelevant simply because they do not like it or agree with it. It is sheer spookification to retreat into the mists of mystery whenever empirical research evidence is brought against one's position. It is also intellectually dishonest. In this respect, I note a conspicuous tendency on the part of Christian religious educationists to trumpet forth every shred of empirical evidence supporting one or another of their theologically inspired tenets, while simultaneously remanding to the world of mystery all evidence which disagrees or even questions their assumptions.

Third, it posits a radical duality in man, a duality which they by and large claim to reject. Virtually all Christian educationists strongly support the notion *homo integer*. If this notion is true, then the workings of God in the human soul are not restricted to the human soul but are operative in the whole person. Consequently such divine workings are manifested in one or another way in the ongoing personality, and therefore are amenable to empirical investigation.

Fourth, it reifies faith. It must be remembered that faith is a construct. Faith is a logical being and not a real being. Faith is a label given to a certain set of behaviors perceived to have similarity to one another. The purpose of a construct is functional, namely to help us analyze particular behaviors more clearly and more carefully. Faith, therefore, does not exist in the soul or anywhere else. What exists is that set of behaviors which certain human beings classify as "faith." Because man is in all likelihood *homo integer,* these behaviors have simultaneously an inner and outer face, and consequently are amenable to empirical research. Thus when John Westerhoff writes that "religion . . . is faith's expression,"[32] he not only posits a basic dualism (inner faith and outer religion) but reifies faith. If faith is not a lived human reality, then it does not exist. But all lived human realities are manifested in one way or another, directly or indirectly. Faith is not something "in there." Faith is a function. Faith is a way in which people organize their lives. A person is a man of faith or he is not; one cannot say a person is an inner man of faith but an outer man of faithlessness.

How would advocates of the social-science approach to Christian religious education respond to Kohlberg? They would approach Kohlberg's data with a mixture of respect and skepticism—respect because all data (as does all reality) demand respect owing to their existential character; skepticism because conclusions derived from data require frequent scrutiny to ascertain with confidence that they accurately reflect the data from which they are drawn. The social scientists would examine the research design, the methodology, the data, and the conclusions derived from these data to determine the degree to which these elements harmonize. If, after this process, the research design is found to be sound, the methodology well executed, the data valid and reliable, and the conclusions warranted, then the social scientists would accept the evidence, especially if it is corroborated by other studies. As a proponent of the social-science approach to religious instruction, I maintain that the validity of Kohlberg's conclusions concerning the autonomy of morality and religion can be seriously questioned on two fundamental grounds, namely his research methodology and his developmental theory.

In terms of his research methodology, Kohlberg's data are invalid because they do not measure what he claims they measure. In his investigations, Kohlberg operationally defines religion as religious affiliation. Thus his data do not show that morality is autonomous from *religion,* but rather from *religious affiliation.* Social scientists investigating religious behavior typically draw a sharp distinction between religiosity and religious affiliation.[33] It is surprising and disappointing that a social scientist as sophisticated and methodologically rigorous as Kohlberg did not acquaint himself more assiduously with the corpus of empirical data and theorizing on the social-scientific study of religion before interpreting his own data concerning the relationship between moral development and religiosity.

The second reason why I maintain the invalidity of Kohlberg's claim that moral development is independent of religion is a theoretical one. In order for Kohlberg's claim to be true, he first has to deny the developmental character of religion. Such a denial would necessitate jettisoning either the entire developmental theory and thus Kohlbergianism itself, or discarding the contention that religion is a human (and therefore developmental) phenomenon capable of being empirically investigated and hence invalidating his research before it even began. Kohlberg is thus caught on the horns of a cruel dilemma. The first horn is as follows. The Kohlbergian thesis states that activities engaged in by the self are developmental. But religion is an activity engaged in by the self. Therefore religion is developmental, and hence in Kohlberg's organismic theory of development, cannot be autonomous from morality. The second horn is as follows. In order to psychologically study the relationship between religion and morality, religion has to be amenable to empirical investigation. Kohlberg's research methodology and conclusions indicate that he believes he did study that set of behaviors which he operationally identifies as religion. Hence religion must be a set of human behaviors, rather than a set of behaviors peculiar to the empirically unresearchable *mysterium tremendum*. Therefore to deny that any set of human behaviors is autonomous from every other set is to deny Kohlberg's entire theory of organismic human development.

Underlying the point I made in the last paragraph is the fundamental distinction between structural autonomy and operative autonomy. The structure of religious development, if one subscribes to Kohlberg, is independent or autonomous from the structure of moral judgment. But the major issue is: How do these parallel human structures actually operate in the person's moment-to-moment, day-to-day life? As an advocate of the organismic, holistic, interactionist school of psychology and philosophy, Kohlberg maintains that psychological structures do indeed interact and affect one another. The interaction among ongoing structures affects each one of them in such a way as to advance the development of the person qua person while still preserving the integrity of the different structures themselves. This point takes on added significance for Lawrence Kohlberg, who maintains that psychological structures are functions (as contrasted to *res* or static entities) which dynamically interact with each other in such a processive manner as to cause each person to be properly regarded as an interactive emergent. Hence on theoretical grounds Kohlberg is inconsistent when he claims total (structural *and* functional) autonomy of moral development from religious development. The fundamental issue of the influence which ongoing human psychological structures have on each other is crucial in adequately addressing one of the principal problems confronting any religious educationist, theologian, moral philosopher, or psychologist of moral development—the issue of how the *cognitive* structure and content (structural content and substantive content, in my language) of moral judgment actually do influence other human psychological structures in such a way that the person *conducts* himself morally. How does knowledge lead to virtue? To my mind, Kohlberg has not yet satisfactorily resolved the all-important issue of how moral judgment actually affects either religious conduct or what for him would be nonreligious or areligious conduct. He is, of course, acutely aware of the problem of locating just how the parallel structures of faith-knowing, moral-reasoning, and global cognitive activity affect each other.[34] To be sure, I find no indication in Kohlberg's writings of Geulincxianism. In fact, Kohlberg's key doctrine of the person as interactive emergent constitutes a fundamental rejection of the Geulincxian position.[35]

Parenthetically, I should note at this juncture that there seems to be a certain spirit and flavor of Occasionalism in the theological approach to Christian religious education. Occasionalism, it will be recalled, was a post-Cartesian seventeenth- and early eighteenth–century philosophy. One branch of Occasionalism viewed human activity, especially mental and spiritual activity, as being directly and immediately caused by God. People—particularly in their mental and spiritual functions—were regarded as instruments of here-and-now occasions of God's action. Thus a certain strain of Occasionalism attempted to solve the problem of mental and spiritual causality strictly on the basis of here-and-now divine intervention. Being more intellectually sophisticated than most modern-day advocates of the theological approach, Occasionalists such as Nicolas Malebranche did not propose a series of continuous individual "zaps" from an on-high God as the proximate cause of each person's mental and spiritual action. Rather, these Occasionalists viewed God's proximate efficient causality of each person's mental and spiritual actions as a more global, ongoing, seamless kind. The "zap" theory held implicitly and dearly by the modern-day proponents of the theological approach to religious education seems to have much in common with aspects of the theory of causality advanced by the pre-Occasionalist Mutakallimic philosophers of the early Middle-Age Arabic world. The Mutakallims viewed the regular sequence of events as simply the willed occasions for God's efficient causality. For example, a person does not move a pen because of his or her own efficient, here-and-now causality. Rather, it is God's *hic et nunc* direct intervention which creates four separate but related accidents to simultaneously occur: the person's will-act to move the pen; the power to move the pen; the movement of the hand; the movement of the pen. The advocates of the theological approach typically claim that it is not the religion teacher or the teacher's pedagogy or the structured learning environment which teaches religious and/or faith outcomes to the learner. Instead, it is God who is said to directly, proximately, efficiently, and above all mysteriously cause these "gifts" to be learned. Each learning outcome, therefore, is a miracle, that is, a here-and-now result of the direct proximate intervention of God who brings to pass that which the regular laws of nature are unable to effect. Thus a major weakness in the metaphysics of the theological approach to religious education lies in its inadequate explanation of how learning is caused.

The fatal methodological and theoretical flaw in Kohlberg's research on the relationship between moral development and religion highlights once again the extremely important perspective which Kohlbergianism offers Christian religious education. Kohlberg states that all human behavior is developmental. Since religion is quintessentially a human behavior (God has no religion), then religion is developmental. Since social science can with validity empirically investigate human development, it also can with validity investigate religion in all its dimensionalities, including that of faith. Kohlberg also states that all human development is of a piece. Thus if religion does exist, it is intimately bound up with other areas of human development, including morality. Consequently, research on how an individual develops morally will shed important light on how that individual develops religiously.

MORAL DEVELOPMENT AS A LEARNING PROCESS

Lawrence Kohlberg maintains that moral judgment and indeed overall moral development are learned in a manner inextricably tied to the way in which an individual acquires other learnings. Like most social scientists, Kohlberg contends that a person's moral standards and moral activity are not "stamped in" by any external force, group, or institution. From the perspective of cognitive-developmental psychology, moral judgment and overall moral development are the outcome of a set of transformations of earlier learned attitudes and conceptions. These transformations take place within the ongoing development of the person as interactive emergent, that is, through the dynamic interaction between the growing person and his or her environment.[36]

One of the chief ways in which a child learns morality is through the process of identification. Identification is a construct, a hypothesis formulated to explain how internalized principles are in fact learned in the absence of specific, didactic-type instruction in these principles.[37] For Kohlberg, a person's motivation to identify with this individual person or that societal ideal is intrinsic. The motivation to identify flows from the individual's inbuilt need to develop and thus to fulfill himself or herself. The way in which the child learns to progressively identify is organically related to the child's successive developmental stages. The attainment of each new stage of development *eo ipso* brings with it a need totally or partially to discard previous models and to identify with new models. This need leads to the person's affective attachment to and social dependency on the new or revised model.

Like most other social scientists, Kohlberg contends that the development of conscience is intimately related to the identification process. His research has led him to conclude that conscience occurs developmentally, and later than psychoanalysts claim. His investigation found that four-year-olds tended to judge an act good or bad on the basis of how and when it was externally reinforced rather than on the basis of any moral judgment or standard of behavior derived from conscience. In the period from five to seven years of age, children in the Kohlberg study tended to judge an act in terms of the moral label which adults attached to it, rather than in terms of immediate external reinforcement of conscience. For children of this age group, reinforcement still played a significant role in the sense that they viewed punishment as a sign that a particular act was bad. Thus the Kohlberg study concluded that the development of conscience or internalized moral judgments is intimately and organically related to overall cognitive development and social experience.[38]

For Kohlberg, one of the principal ways in which the developmental process of identification takes place is through role-taking. In his view, "social cognition always involves role-taking, i.e. awareness that the other is in some way like the self, and that the other knows or is responsive to the self in a system of complementary expectations."[39] The concept of role-taking fits in nicely with overall developmental theory, since it suggests that a person progressively grows through the ongoing interaction between his or her developing self and the changing environment. As I observe elsewhere,[40] role-taking is an exercise in empathy.[41] It is primarily on this account that role-taking is so pivotal in the identification process. After all, identification necessitates that the person empathize with the model to be able to experience the model as closely as possible as the model experiences himself or herself. Indeed, empathy accelerates the model's own power as an identificand, since the model experiences the reinforcing consequences of the identifier's empathy. These reinforcing consequences tend to motivate the model to intensify those behaviors with which the identifier is empathizing.[42] From Kohlberg's cognitive-developmental vantage point, role-taking is necessary for moral development since the latter involves an identification or at the very least some kind of progressive personal involvement with a person or a culture outside the self. For Kohlberg, the fundamental import of the word *moral* is the structuring of one's personal internal and external behavior on the basis of role-taking, that is, by treating the other as the other treats and perceives himself or herself. "Do unto others as you would have others do unto you." Thus the most universal and fundamental of all moral principles, namely justice, can result only when a person role-takes.

Kohlberg is very clear in his view that moral judgment, like the other dimensions of molar moral development, requires appropriate environmental contours and stimuli. Hence moral judgment and all of moral development can be significantly enhanced by providing certain structured sets of experiences with which the individual can fruitfully interact. In all likelihood the individual does not learn progressively higher moral behaviors simply by being exposed to any environment. Exposure suggests passivity. Rather, the individual should actively encounter the structured environment, since advancement in one's level of moral development flows from the interaction between the individual's structuring tendencies and the structural features of the environment. Kohlberg maintains that preparing a structured environment which is dissonant to the learner's present level of development is a particularly fruitful pedagogical procedure for enhancing the probability that an individual will advance in moral judgment. The internal conflict which the individual experiences while interacting with a dissonant environment whose moral texture is higher than the individual's own will tend to lead to a higher level of internal reorganization and thus to increased moral development, or at least to accelerated moral judgment at first.[43]

There is a corpus of empirical research which lends support to Kohlberg's views on moral development as a process which is learned. These data come from a wide variety of studies, including those conducted by scholars whose overall theoretical orientation is at variance with that of Kohlberg.

An experimental study conducted by David Bearison and Leora Isaacs found that children ranging in age from 6 years 6 months to 7 years 6 months typically base their moral judgments on the objective consequences of another's act rather than on the other's intentions because they do not infer the moral intentionality of another's act. However, when the teacher (in this case, the experimenter) gave the children selected cognitive prompts, the children did indeed infer the moral intentionality of another's act. [44] The Bearison and Isaacs study suggests that children can be taught to increase the level of their moral judgment. Michael Riccards's review of the pertinent research literature concludes that eight distinct stages of religious development quite possibly exist, and that these stages are intimately and organically related to other aspects of personal development. [45]

Kohlberg's research data and theory on moral judgment/development as a process which is learned through normal human activity goes completely counter to the opinions expressed by the advocates of the theological approach to Christian religious education. Kohlberg's data puts the advocates of the theological approach in a bind. If they deny Kohlberg's findings, they are forced to admit that moral development is completely independent from religious development. On the other hand, if they admit the validity of Kohlberg's findings, they are compelled to abandon the theological approach to religious education.

It seems to me that the only logical and honest course of action open to the advocates of the theological approach in the face of Kohlbergianism is to discard the theological approach. After all, it is virtually impossible for any religionist to claim that God does not operate in all areas of life. God patently cannot be present in religion but absent in moral development. Indeed, religion typically claims to be the source, spirit, raison d'être, and ultimate sanction for moral behavior. Hence the only other course of action is to honestly face the facts, and concede that Kohlberg's data, like the data from the research conducted by other social scientists, indisputably show that moral development—and therefore, one can conclude, religion, including faith—is acquired in a manner at one with other kinds of learning.

Like the data of many other social scientists, Kohlberg's data suggest that a young child develops morally through identification. Conscience, moral judgment, and to a certain degree moral affectivity seem to be learned early in life by identification. This is a natural process which seems to take place in all children. It appears not to be a "zap" from an outside or extrinsic Holy Spirit. Indeed, the whole thrust of the research by Kohlberg and others on identification, role-taking, and conscience development strongly suggests that moral development is learned in a natural, human way. It is indicative of the low state of most current Christian religious education theory that Berard Marthaler, a prominent advocate of the theological approach to religious education, holds that: (1) religion and faith are mysterious gifts from God which cannot be taught because these gifts come to man in a hidden and ineffable manner; (2) socialization—and therefore, to a large extent, identification—is the way in which a person learns and lives religion and faith.[46] To simultaneously hold both of these tenets is, of course, to hold a contradiction.[47]

Kohlberg's research shows that from a developmental standpoint, a person's stage of moral-judgment thinking typically lags slightly behind his or her general or overall stage of cognitive development.[48] This kind of Kohlbergian data raises a serious problem for many advocates of the theological approach to religious education, notably those holding the blow or afflation "theory." If the Holy Spirit does indeed mysteriously teach each and every person *individually* from on high, then each person should develop morally and religiously at significantly different rates. Indeed, the Holy Spirit blows *where it wills* (John 3:8), say the afflationists—which is quite different from asserting that children *typically* grow in moral thinking at a slower rate than they do in overall cognition. The issue I am making salient is this: whereas the afflationists present a theologically based hypothesis on how people learn, Kohlberg offers hard empirical data on how in fact they do learn. Kohlberg's data, like the data offered by other social scientists, not only negate the afflationists' hypothesis, but also offer important information for drawing adequate inferences about how the Holy Spirit actually does work. The Holy Spirit seems to work in and together with the laws of that nature which God has made, keeps in being, and pervades. It is social science, not primarily theology, which explains and predicts human developmental behavior—behavior which includes those specific functions and actions which comprise the wider constructs called learning, teaching, religion, and faith. Here, then, is one of the fundamental challenges which Kohlbergianism presents to Christian religious education. It is a challenge which the centuries-old theological approach to religious education is utterly unable to resolve satisfactorily.

When confronted with data such as those offered by Lawrence Kohlberg, advocates of the theological approach to religious education attempt to manufacture categories or invent realities which they believe will bolster their position. Françoise Darcy-Bérubé, for example, speaks of faith as God's free gift.[49] Alice Gallin claims that faith is a gift from God which cannot be taught—thus, she states, faith-learning cannot be the purpose of any church-related educational institution.[50] Yet these two women are begging the question, and begging it frightfully. The whole world, after all, is God's free gift. The issue is thus not the gift or the freeness of the gift. The issue is how and under what mode the free gift is given. Kohlberg's data suggest how and under what mode the free gift is given. His findings indicate that the free gift is given in a developmental manner, a manner by which children and youth and adults naturally grow. The gift is not given as an extrinsicist "zap," but rather as a processive flow of human development. The dimensionalities of personality development are amenable to social-scientific investigation in direct or at least indirect fashion. Hence there are social-scientific laws governing moral development, religious development, faith development, vocational development, social development, and so on. There are also social-scientific laws governing the way in which each of these dimensions of development occur.[51]

Many Christian religious educationists do not seem to have learned much from the history of the past four hundred years concerning the relationship of religion and science. Yet it seems evident that the one thing we should have learned from the Galileo fiasco, and from other fiascoes which Christian church leaders subsequently had with great men of science such as Darwin and Freud, is that it is a grievous error to conceptualize faith as something radically apart from the laws governing humankind and the universe. If Christians are to grow in their understanding of faith, they must conceptualize it in such a manner as not to exempt it from rational or scientific elements in either its genesis or its growth. The notion of faith posited by Darcy-Bérubé, Gallin, and other advocates of the theological approach to religious education is an enfeebling, debilitating, and indeed, at bottom, an anti-human one. By detaching faith and other religious encounters with God from the developmental human fabric, these people transmogrify faith into a spooky, otherworldly, and basically unreal affair—an affair which has little appeal to modern man who wishes his faith to be real in and for him.

Kohlberg's view of moral development as a learned process which takes place within the overall context of the person as interactive emergent has great import for the Christian conception of theology and of God. In his fine essay relating developmental psychology to Christian theology, Howard Grimes observes that the work of Kohlberg, Jean Piaget, James Fowler, and other developmentalists seriously challenges such long-held theological notions of God as static absolute, and faith as a once-then gift of God. Kohlbergianism offers a vision of God as quite possibly a dynamic *becoming* rather than an immutable *being*. Kohlbergianism offers a vision of faith as embedded in each person's ongoing, developmental self.[52] Theology is a science which attempts to make statements about the nature and workings of God by drawing intelligent inferences from the data which God has revealed about himself in the bible, in the church, and in the universe. Kohlberg and other developmental psychologists provide theologians with empirically established facts and provisional social-scientific theories about how God does indeed operate in the world. Christian theologians would do well to investigate the research of Kohlberg and other social scientists more intensely, so that the speculations of these theologians would be rooted in reality rather than in wishful thinking or in fantasy.

DEVELOPMENT AS THE AIM OF EDUCATION

Kohlberg views the process of development as itself being the aim or end of *all* education.[53] Development is the psychological, and indeed the existential axis around which a person's life revolves.

As such, the basic way individuals improve themselves both in terms of their own selves and in terms of their relationship to *every* reality outside themselves is through concerted efforts to enhance their own ongoing developmental quality. Kohlberg's fundamental position is that any adequate theory of the aim of education must be based on adequate psychological facts and explanations of development. Conversely, no satisfactory theory of education can be erected primarily on forces, hypotheses, or institutions outside of or extrinsic to the developing person. This does not mean that the aim of education is devoid of extrinsic philosophies or ideologies. Rather, Kohlberg maintains that the way in which extrinsically derived aims are incorporated into educational activity in its processes or goals must be done in a manner consistent with and indeed based upon the learner's developmental self. Learners critically test the educational value of what they have learned by the criterion of how it has objectively furthered their own developmental processes.

Kohlberg writes that the "method of 'empirical' or 'experimental' philosophy is especially central for an educational philosophy prescribing educational aims. Philosophical principles cannot be stated as ends of education until they can be stated psychologically. This means translating them into statements about a more adequate stage of development. Otherwise the rationally accepted principles of the philosopher will only be arbitrary concepts and doctrines. . . ."[54]

From what I have written thus far in this section, it is readily apparent that Kohlberg's view of development as the aim of *all* education poses a serious challenge to many of the advocates of the theological approach to Christian religious education.

Whereas Kohlberg views development as the aim of *all* education, many Christian religious educationists holding the theological approach view the aim of religious education as residing primarily in some reality outside the person and his or her developmental becoming. John Westerhoff, for example, regards Christian religious education as taking its aims (as well as its pedagogical procedures) from something outside human development, namely from theology.[55] Like most other leaders in the Catholic Catechetical Establishment, Alfred McBride[56] and Berard Marthaler[57] also claim that the goals of Christian religious education emanate from outside the person's developmental processes, namely from the *General Catechetical Directory* and from other official statements of the Roman Catholic Church. Françoise Darcy-Bérubé, one of the theological approach's most uncompromising hardliners, holds that it is theology, and not human development, which underlies all the goals and pedagogical procedures of Christian religious education.[58] Some other advocates of the theological approach attempt to weasel out of this challenge which Kohlbergianism poses to their extrinsicist conception of the aims of Christian religious education. These individuals contend that while Kohlberg's statements might hold true for so-called "secular" education, they are not true for Christian religious education.

It seems to me that what Kohlberg is affirming is an extension of the familiar Scholastic principle that all learning occurs according to the mode of the learner. A child learns the Ten Commandments according to his or her own developmental activity, and not according to the logical structure or eternal import of the Ten Commandments themselves. When young people are confirmed, they receive the sacrament according to where they are and where they are going developmentally; hence each person receives and actualizes this sacrament differently. When adults give themselves in matrimony or in Orders, they learn their new lifeway according to their own developmental processing. Thus the goals of education lie in the way in which individuals develop as they interact with their environment. To accept Kohlbergianism is not to remove God or God's will as the goal of education. Rather, it is to appreciate that God and his will are not extrinsic or "out there" but instead are immanently enfleshed in the outgoing, human, developmental process itself. An illustration of how almost totally blind so many Christians are to this central fact of Christian existence can be seen by Edward Erpelding's dismissal of a collection of psychological essays on value development as a book "wherein God and the spiritual nature of man are not addressed," and therefore a book of little value to the Christian religious educator.[59]

Another related serious challenge which Kohlbergianism presents to the theological approach to religious education is the Harvard social scientist's assertion that the aim of *all* education should be based on psychological data about how a person grows and learns. In other words, the goals of Christian religious education must be based on and flow out of what *is*.[60] This does not preclude the incorporation into religious education activity of principles derived from Christian theology or any other set of principles prized by one Christian group or another. Rather, Kohlbergianism implies that theological principles be subsumed into the goals of Christian religious education according to the developmental realities of the processing person. To do otherwise is not only foolhardy; it is arbitrary and antihuman. One cannot take seriously, for example, Françoise Darcy-Bérubé's statement that God's living revelation causes everything to become unpredictable.[61] To make this claim, as Darcy-Bérubé does, one has to surrender not just the goals of Christian religious education, but also the workings of the whole world to arbitrariness. But Kohlberg's research has shown that there is a basic developmental predictability in people. This is a psychological fact, and neither Darcy-Bérubé's theology, nor the theology of anyone else who takes a theological position different from hers, can alter this fact. If the history of much of Christian religious education is one of building pedagogical structures of unreality, then this unfortunate history is largely traceable to Christian religious educators who based their programs and procedures on what they thought their theology told them ought to be the way people learn, rather than on what social science indicated about how people actually do learn and develop.

Christian religious educators seem to believe that the worth and faith–richness of their educational goals are directly related to the loftiness of the theological rhetoric in which these goals are expressed. But Kohlbergianism suggests that theological principles cannot be stated *as ends of education* until they are stated social-scientifically. This is simply because education is primarily a social-scientific activity, an activity whose goal is to consciously, deliberatively, and systematically foster the learner's development. Education in one or more of its concrete forms will, of course, have theological, religious, social, linguistic, and historical import and content—but the base, the process, and the goal of educational activity are first and foremost social-scientific. Therefore, its goals must be conceptualized and stated social-scientifically if it is to be effective.

CONCLUSION

In terms of this essay, it should be noted that Lawrence Kohlberg does not claim that his empirical research findings and theories on moral judgment and moral development are directly applicable to religious education. As I have observed previously, Kohlberg contends that moral development and religious development are separate realms. He interprets his research findings as suggesting "that there is no relation between religious experience and moral character," and therefore "religion is not a necessary or highly important condition for the development of moral judgment or conduct." While religious education in formal settings may possibly be capable of playing a role in enhancing an individual's moral development, nonetheless religious education in formal settings "has no specifically important or unique role to play in [fostering] moral development as opposed to the role of the public school and the family in this area. . . . " Hence Kohlberg argues for a complete separation of moral and religious education, a separation which he states is required if moral education is to be constitutionally part of American public school education. He notes that this view is supported by the United States Supreme Court in its post-World War II decisions on religion in the public school.[62]

In light of Kohlberg's claims about religious education and moral development, is my essay in this book irrelevant or even anti-Kohlbergian? I think not, for several reasons. First, Kohlberg's conclusion that religious development is basically separate from moral development flows from a major methodological error in his research design. This error is of such a magnitude as to invalidate his conclusions in this regard. I elaborated on this point in the body of this essay. Second, Kohlberg's posited *radical* separation between structure and content with respect to moral and religious development appears to be at sharp variance with his overarching theoretical principle of the whole person developing as a whole. My demurrer here is not to deny the difference between structural content and formal content, but to challenge Kohlberg's contention on how these relate to one another in the area of moral development vis-à-vis religious development. Third, Kohlberg does admit the possibility that religious education in formal settings (such as church schools) may indeed be capable of playing a role in fostering moral development. Fourth, Kohlberg does not rule out, and perhaps even concedes, that religious education in informal settings does indeed play an important role in enhancing moral development. The purpose of my essay in this volume is to explore religious education in its global aspect, without respect to the setting in which it is enacted.[63] Fifth, some Christian religious educationists, particularly among the Protestants and among those Catholics not in the Catholic Catechetical Establishment, have written essays, given speeches, and conducted seminars on the relationship of Kohlbergianism to Christian religious education.

If one major point emerges from the present essay, it is this: Kohlberg's research and theory go basically counter to the fundamental principles, assumptions, and starting points of the theological approach to Christian religious education. Conversely, Kohlberg's work supports the social-science approach to religious education. Thus I ask, even plead, that Christian religious educationists and educators confront the essential Kohlberg, and desist in their continuing efforts to use his research simply as frivolous adornments to one or another fanciful a priori notion. I am asking the advocates of the theological approach to Christian religious education to face up to Kohlberg honestly, and see if his basic research findings and central theoretical tenets square with their views of how development and education do indeed occur.

This essay is quite sympathetic to Kohlbergianism. However, it should not be interpreted as representing anything like my complete advocacy of Kohlbergianism and the concomitant rejection of "humanistic" psychology, behavioristically-oriented psychology, or psychoanalytically-inspired psychology. The overall social-science approach to Christian religious education which I advocate in my writings, teaching, and speeches is such that it can accommodate any school or theory of social science. I have not yet elaborated my own particular psychological preference within the social-science approach, despite my obvious sympathy for certain aspects of Dewey's philosophy of education and of developmental psychology, a sympathy which has characterized my professional writings since the publication of my first book.[64]

One final note. Throughout this essay I have shown that the advocates of the theological approach to Christian religious education have an innate tendency to invoke an *ab extrinsico* Holy Spirit as the explanation of religious development or "faith-life." My position is that the Holy Spirit does not have to be brought into the picture from the outside, since he is already immanently in and with and through all reality in all its being and becoming. It seems to me quite possible that the advocates of the theological approach who drag the Holy Spirit into the picture by the heels really do not trust him to effectively do his work from the withinness of the world which he has made and pervades in his immanence.

NOTES

1. I am using the term "religious education" in this essay to include religious instruction, religious guidance, and the administration of religious education activities.

2. See, for example, Alfred McBride, *Creative Teaching in Christian Education* (Boston: Allyn and Bacon, 1978), pp. 61–67.

3. Some Christian scholars from outside the ranks of Christian religious education (ranks where real scholars are seldom found or appreciated) do offer a somewhat protracted in-depth treatment of Kohlberg's theory. See, for example, Walter E. Conn, "Postconventional Morality: An Exposition and Critique of Lawrence Kohlberg's Analysis of Moral Development in the Adolescent and Adult," in *Lumen Vitae,* XXX (June, 1975), pp. 213–230.

4. For two adequate overviews of the surface of Kohlbergianism and its relation to Christianity, see James Youniss, "Kohlberg's Theory: A Commentary," in *Living Light,* X (Fall, 1973), pp. 352–358; see also Ronald Duska and Mariellen

Whelan, *Moral Development* (New York: Paulist, 1975). Both of these works are introductions to Kohlberg's thought, and so presumably are not intended as in-depth treatments.

5. L. Kohlberg and R. Kramer, "Continuities and Discontinuities in Childhood and Adult Moral Development," in *Human Development,* XII (Second Quarter, 1969), pp. 98–99.

6. On this point, see James Michel Lee, "Process Content in Religious Instruction", in Iris V. Cully and Kendig Brubaker Cully, editors, *Process and Relationship: Issues in Theology, Philosophy, and Religious Education* (Birmingham, Al.: Religious Education Press, 1978), pp. 23–24.

7. John Dewey, *Democracy and Education* (New York: Macmillan, 1916), pp. 153–158. ". . . mind is not a name for something complete by itself; it is a name for a course of action in so far as that is intelligently directed . . . " (p. 155).

8. Lawrence Kohlberg and Carol Gilligan, "The Adolescent as a Philosopher: The Discovery of the Self in a Postconventional World," in *Daedalus,* C (Fall, 1971), p. 1071.

9. Lawrence Kohlberg, "The Claim to Moral Adequacy of a Highest Stage of Moral Judgment," in *Journal of Philosophy,* LXX (October 25, 1973), pp. 630–646.

10. This view is similar to that of John Dewey, *Experience and Education* (New York: Macmillan, 1938), pp. 23–52.

11. I suspect that Gloria Durka and possibly some other Christian religious educationists do not understand the difference between maturation and development. For example, Durka characterizes Kohlberg as a theorist who has "extended Erikson's interpretation of the identity crisis" by "rounding out" Erikson's theory (pp. 24–25). Erikson, of course, is a maturationalist, while Kohlberg is a developmentalist. Although acknowledging the general compatability of his theory with that of Erikson, Kohlberg is nonetheless careful to emphasize that Erikson's formulations represent a variant of maturational stage theory. I also find Durka's adherence to the neo-Freudian theorizing of Erikson rather odd. Durka is an ardent feminist, and feminists typically abhor Freudianism in all its forms. Gloria Durka, "Identity—The Major Task of Adolescence," in G. Temp Sparkman, editor, *Knowing and Helping Youth* (Nashville, Tenn.: Broadman, 1977), pp. 13–30; see also Lawrence Kohlberg, "Continuities in Childhood and Adult Moral Development Revisited," in Lawrence Kohlberg, "Collected Papers on Moral Development and Moral Education," unpublished document, 1973, pp. 46–48 (of essay); Lawrence Kohlberg, "The Implications of Moral Stages for Adult Education," in *Religious Education,* LXXII (March-April, 1977), p. 187.

12. Lawrence Kohlberg, "Stages of Moral Developments as a Basis for Moral Education," in C.M. Beck, B.S. Crittenden, and E.V. Sullivan, editors, *Moral Education: Interdisciplinary Approaches* (Toronto: University of Toronto Press, 1971), pp. 48–49.

13. The theological approach to religious education claims that religious education derives both its fundamental theory and its practice from theology. This approach is the traditional and dominant one used in Christian religious education. The validity as well as the fruitfulness of the theological approach has been

seriously challenged in James Michael Lee, *The Shape of Religious Instruction* (Birmingham, Al.: Religious Education Press, 1971). Lee argues that religious instruction, like all of religious education, is a mode of social science and thus must draw its basic theory and practice from social science rather than from theology.

14. Françoise Darcy-Bérubé, "The Challenge Ahead of Us," in Padraic O'Hare, editor, *Foundations of Religious Education* (New York: Paulist, 1978), pp. 115-120.

15. *Ibid.,* p. 116.

16. For a brief discussion of the "zap" theory of grace, so dearly prized by advocates of the theological approach to Christian religious education, see James Michael Lee, "Toward a New Era: A Blueprint for Positive Action," in James Michael Lee, editor, *The Religious Education We Need* (Birmingham, Al.: Religious Education Press, 1977), pp. 130-131.

17. For a careful treatment of the issue of immanence versus transcendence in Christian religious education, see Ian P. Knox, *Above or Within?: The Supernatural in Religious Education* (Birmingham, Al.: Religious Education Press, 1976).

18. In Kohlberg's view, psychological findings and the fruits of philosophical speculations are consistent with each other when philosophical speculation is based upon an adequate understanding of how reality does in fact work. Philosophy approaches reality from a different vantage point; hence in a *complete* explanation of reality, philosophical and psychological explanations of reality are fundamentally consistent and complementary to each other.

19. Lawrence Kohlberg, "Moral and Religious Education and the Public Schools: A Developmental View," in Theodore Sizer, editor, *Religion and Public Education* (Boston: Houghton Mifflin, 1967), p. 180.

20. Lawrence Kohlberg, "Stage and Sequence: The Cognitive-Developmental Approach to Socialization", in David A. Goslin, editor, *Handbook of Socialization Theory and Research* (Chicago: Rand McNally, 1969), p.427.

21. Lawrence Kohlberg, "Moral and Religious Education and the Public Schools: A Developmental View," p. 179.

22. Lawrence Kohlberg, "Development of Moral Character and Moral Ideology", in Martin L. Hoffman and Lois Wladis Hoffman, editors, *Review of Child Development Research,* volume I. (New York: Russell Sage Foundation, 1964), p. 406; Lawrence Kohlberg, "Cognitive-Developmental Theory and the Practice of Collective Moral Education", in Martin Wolins and Meir Gottesmann, editors, *Group Care: An Israeli Approach. The Educational Path of Youth Aliyah* (New York: Gordon and Breach, 1971), pp. 342-371.

23. Lawrence Kohlberg, "Moral and Religious Education and the Public Schools: A Developmental View," p. 180.

24. For a review of some of the pertinent pre-1965 studies, see James Michael Lee and Nathaniel J. Pallone, *Guidance and Counseling in Schools: Foundations and Processes* (New York: McGraw-Hill, 1966), p. 442.

25. I am assuming logical consistency on the part of the advocates of the theological approach to religious education. Such an assumption, however, frequently fails to be operative, primarily because no advocate of the theological

approach has ever developed an overarching macrotheory explaining (1) the inter-relationship of his or her theoretical hypotheses with one another and (2) how and in what manner pedagogical practices can be explained by and predicted from theology. Because no overall macrotheory for the theological approach has been developed, the writings of the advocates of this approach frequently are internally inconsistent and indeed often contradictory. Thus, for example, Berard Marthaler at one point denies that religion and faith can be studied social-scientifically, yet at another point endorses Fowler's attempt to social-scientifically chart the development of faith. Berard L. Marthaler, "Review," in *National Catholic Reporter,* VIII (November 19, 1971), p.8; Berard L. Marthaler, "Socialization as a Model for Catechetics," in Padraic O'Hare, editor, *Foundations of Religious Education,* pp. 84–87.

26. Alfred A. McBride, *Creative Teaching in Christian Education,* pp. 63–64.

27. Françoise Darcy-Bérubé, "The Challenge Ahead of Us," pp. 115–120.

28. Berard L. Marthaler, "Socialization as a Model of Catechetics," p. 75.

29. John H. Westerhoff III, *Will Our Children Have Faith?* (New York: Seabury, 1976), pp. 21–23.

30. Alice Gallin, "A Response," in John H. Westerhoff, editor, *The Church's Ministry in Higher Education* (New York: United Ministries in Higher Education, 1978), p. 208.

31. Darcy-Bérubé seems confused on this point. Within a few short pages she first identifies the lived, mysterious relationship which a person has with God as "faith, hope, and charity"; later she goes on to identify the relationship just simply as "faith." She also makes a substantial differentiation between faith and religion, without bothering to adduce any evidence for her posited distinction. Françoise Darcy-Bérubé, "The Challenge Ahead of Us," pp. 115–120.

32. John H. Westerhoff III, *Will Our Children Have Faith?* p. 21.

33. See, for example, Charles Y. Glock, "On the Study of Religious Commitment," in *Religious Education,* research supplement, LVII (July-August, 1962), pp. s-98 to s-110; Gordon W. Allport and J. Michael Ross, "Personal Religious Orientation and Prejudice," in *Journal of Personality and Social Psychology,* V (April, 1967), pp. 432–443.

34. Lawrence Kohlberg, "Education, Moral Development and Faith," in *Journal of Moral Education,* IV (October, 1974), pp. 5–16; Lawrence Kohlberg, "Stage and Sequence: The Cognitive-Developmental Approach to Socialization," pp. 347–353; Lawrence Kohlberg, "From Is to Ought: How to Commit the Naturalistic Fallacy and Get Away with It in the Study of Moral Development," in Theodore Mischel, editor, *Cognitive Development and Epistemology* (New York: Academic Press, 1971), pp. 151–235.

35. Arnold Geulincx was, of course, an important seventeenth-century philosopher interested in, among other things, the relation of mind to body and of one mental process to another. For Geulincx, the correspondence between bodily operations and mental functions can be illustrated by analogy with two clocks which kept the same time, not because one causatively interacted with or affected the other, but because both were set in motion by one and the same maker.

36. Lawrence Kohlberg, "The Development of Children's Orientations To-ward a Moral Order: I. Sequence in the Development of Moral Thought," in *Vita Humana*, VI (First Quarter, 1963), p. 11.

37. Rightly or wrongly, many theorists conceptualize identification as a general modeling process, whereas they conceive of imitation as copying specific actions. See Albert Bandura, "Social-Learning Theory of Identificatory Processes," in David A. Goslin, editor, *Handbook of Socialization Theory and Research*, p. 219.

38. Lawrence Kohlberg, "The Development of Children's Orientations To-ward a Moral Order: I. Sequence in the Development of Moral Thought," pp. 11–33.

39. Lawrence Kohlberg, "Stage and Sequence: The Cognitive-Developmental Approach to Socialization," p. 349.

40. James Michael Lee and Nathaniel J. Pallone, *Guidance and Counseling in Schools: Foundations and Processes*, p. 329.

41. Role-taking is, of course, different from role-playing.

42. See Albert Bandura, "Imitation," in David L. Sills, editor, *International Encyclopedia of the Social Sciences*, volume 7 (New York: Macmillan, 1968), p. 97.

43. Lawrence Kohlberg, "Stages of Moral Development as a Basis for Moral Education", pp. 49–52. In *The Content of Religious Instruction*, I place Kohlberg's match-one pedagogical procedure in a wider context of instructionally productive conflict and dissonance. See James Michael Lee, *The Content of Religious Instruction*, in preparation.

44. David J. Bearison and Leora Isaacs, "Production Deficiency in Children's Moral Judgments," in *Developmental Psychology*, XI (November, 1975), pp. 732–737.

45. Michael P. Riccards, "The Structure of Religious Development: Empirical Evidence for a Stage Theory," in *Lumen Vitae*, XXXIII (March, 1978), pp. 97–123.

46. Berard L. Marthaler, "Socialization as a Model for Catechetics," pp. 64–92. Marthaler's prominence stems primarily from the fact that he heads the religious education program at The Catholic University of America, an episcopally controlled institution of higher learning. This position tends to automatically catapult its occupant into a leading role in the academic wing of the Catholic Catechetical Establishment. To date, Marthaler has made no major or original contributions to "catechetical" or religious education theory and practice. John Westerhoff states that the theory and process of "catechesis" are "understood best by a socialization model." John Westerhoff, "A Discipline in Crisis," in *Religious Education*, LIV (January-February, 1979), p. 14. In another place, Westerhoff describes "catechesis" as the deliberate and intentional process by which a religious educator can assist others to learn and grow in faith. John Westerhoff III, editor, *Who are We?: The Quest for a Religious Education* (Birmingham, Al.: Religious Education Press, 1978), pp. 269–271.

47. In his chapters John Westerhoff, for whom I have warm personal affection, also seems to hold this contradiction. (See, for example, Gwen Kennedy

354   JAMES MICHAEL LEE

Neville and John H. Westerhoff III, *Learning Through Liturgy* (New York: Seabury, 1978), pp. 89–181. I regard Westerhoff as one of the most imaginative and zealous of all Christian religious educationists.

48. Lawrence Kohlberg and Carol Gilligan, "The Adolescent as a Philosopher: The Discovery of the Self in a Postconventional World," pp. 1071–1075.

49. Françoise Darcy-Bérubé, "The Challenge Ahead of Us," pp. 116–119.

50. Alice Gallin, "A Response," in John H. Westerhoff, editor, *The Church's Ministry in Higher Education*, p. 208.

51. The Catholic religious educationist Martin Lang also holds this position. Lang contends that faith-development participates in the same basic human dynamics which govern all human development, and that faith is communicated according to the laws of communication. Martin A. Lang, "Faith as a Learned Life-style," in Gloria Durka and Joanmarie Smith, editors, *Emerging Issues in Religious Education* (New York: Paulist, 1976), pp. 69–75.

52. Howard Grimes, "A Process/Developmental View of the Divine/Human Relationship," in Iris V. Cully and Kendig Brubaker Cully, editors, *Process and Relationship: Issues in Theology, Philosophy, and Religious Education*, pp. 82–90.

53. Lawrence Kohlberg and Rochelle Mayer, "Development as the Aim of Education," in *Harvard Educational Review*, XLII (November, 1972), pp. 449–496.

54. *Ibid.*, p. 485.

55. It should be noted that Westerhoff claims that Christian religious education is a subdiscipline of the main discipline "religion and education," while "catechesis" is a form of pastoral ministry. In my view, Westerhoff's dichotomy is a false one because it is not based upon adequate principles of distinguishability. An activity can be a discipline or subdiscipline and at the same time be used in a pastoral, ministerial manner. For example, religious psychology and religious counseling are branches of the discipline of psychology. However, when used in spiritual direction, retreats, and so on, these subdisciplines are employed in a pastoral ministry context for pastoral purposes. Few areas of life are pastoral in themselves. This is a fortiori true for scientific disciplines and fields. What makes one or another area of life or of science a form of pastoral ministry is the use to which it is put, and not its nature. John H. Westerhoff, "A Discipline in Crisis", pp. 10–11. I think Westerhoff also errs in his claim that Christian religious education is a discipline. Elsewhere I have shown, conclusively, I believe, that religious instruction, and therefore a fortiori religious education, is a field. On this point see James Michael Lee, *The Shape of Religious Instruction*, pp. 94–100.

56. Alfred McBride, *Creative Teaching in Christian Education*, pp. 188–189. McBride contradicts himself, since he consciously takes his educational aims from one science (theology) and his pedagogical procedures from a basically different science (social science). Such an *en marche* dichotomy between aim and procedure, ends and means, product and process is, of course, as fallacious logically as it is impossible existentially.

57. Berard L. Marthaler, *Catechetics in Context* (Huntington, Ind.: Our Sunday Visitor, 1971).

58. Françoise Darcy-Bérubé, "The Challenge Ahead of Us," pp. 117–118.

59. I should note that this book was published by a character research group. Edward E. Erpelding, "Review," in *Living Light,* XV (Winter, 1978), p. 567.

60. Lawrence Kohlberg, "From Is to Ought: How to Commit the Naturalistic Fallacy and Get Away with It in the Study of Moral Development," pp. 151–235; also Lawrence Kohlberg, "Stages of Moral Development as a Basis for Moral Education," pp. 66–70.

61. Françoise Darcy-Bérubé, "The Challenge Ahead of Us," p. 153.

62. Lawrence Kohlberg, "Moral and Religious Education and the Public Schools: A Developmental View," pp. 164–165, 179–181. Quotations from p. 181.

63. From a scientific, pedagogical standpoint, Kohlberg would do well to eschew the phrase "formal religious education" in favor of "religious education in formal settings." This verbal distinction is no mere literary nicety or example of logic-chopping. Rather, it is a crucial one in conceptualizing and applying the teaching act. For a further discussion of this point, see James Michael Lee, *The Flow of Religious Instruction* (Birmingham, Al.: Religious Education Press, 1973), pp. 5–9.

64. A Catholic reviewer of this 1963 book pointed what he probably thought was a finger of scorn at me when he accused me of being a "Catholic Deweyizer."

Part VI

BASIC ISSUES IN MORAL EDUCATION

Chapter 12

Kohlberg in the Classroom: Moral Education Models

LINDA ROSENZWEIG

INTRODUCTION

Teachers have always been moral educators whether or not they are conscious of this role. Their comments in the classroom, their manner of speaking, their behavior, and their treatment of other people convey important "moral messages" to students. Indeed, these factors comprise a significant portion of what Philip Jackson has described as the "hidden" curriculum, the structural organization of the school. Many teachers have traditionally stressed ethical considerations explicitly in the context of their courses. In this sense, moral education certainly is not a new phenomenon. Nor is it new in terms of American educational tradition, which reflects a strong belief that schools have a duty to teach children a set of approved traits so that they will know right from wrong and behave accordingly. Despite the fact that from the 1930s until recently, public school educators basically ignored this aspect of education, moral education is and has been a part of the school experience of every student.

Lawrence Kohlberg traces the history of the cognitive developmental approach to moral education back to classical Greece, to Socrates's belief in a universal rational or cognitive conception of justice which develops through levels as people experience doubt,

359

questioning, and social dialogue with regard to moral issues. Kohlberg's longitudinal and cross-cultural research findings, described elsewhere in this volume, offer contemporary support for this Socratic hypothesis concerning the development of the idea of justice and for the application of the Socratic method to the process of moral education. The Kohlberg theory suggests that rather than attempt to indoctrinate or socialize students, moral education should seek to stimulate the natural process of development toward more mature moral reasoning. Hence the role of the educator ought to be that of a supportive but questioning guide—a Socratic teacher—who encourages the articulation and examination of students' own reasoning about ethical issues and facilitates exposure to higher stages of reasoning. Kohlberg believes the latter is a necessary component in the process of cognitive moral development.

The first documented effort to implement this type of moral education in a classroom setting was that of Moshe Blatt, who conducted a series of discussions of moral dilemmas with junior high school students in Chicago and in Boston about ten years ago. After one semester, Blatt found measurable moral stage change in one-fourth to one-half of his students, a change not found among students in control groups.[1] In an attempt to replicate Blatt's findings, Edwin Fenton and Lawrence Kohlberg undertook a cooperative project designed to train high school social studies teachers in the Boston and Pittsburgh areas to lead developmental moral discussions of hypothetical dilemmas in their classes. As in the Blatt study, students in control groups demonstrated no measurable moral stage change after nine months. Little change occurred in half of the experimental classes, but in the remaining experimental classes, Blatt's findings were replicated. Between one-quarter and one-half of these students exhibited significant upward movement in moral reasoning.[2]

The teaching methodology employed by Blatt in engaging his students in Socratic moral discussions was extended and systematized in the course of the Fenton-Kohlberg work with social studies teachers. The teachers were trained to conduct moral discussions utilizing a five-step process: 1) introducing and clarifying the nature of the dilemma and the facts and circumstances involved; 2) asking students to take a tentative position on the appropriate action for the main protagonist in the dilemma; 3) dividing the class into small groups to discuss the reasoning behind their positions; 4) testing and questioning student reasoning in a full class discussion; and 5) encouraging students to reevaluate their own positions and their reasoning individually.

For several years, educational intervention to foster cognitive moral development followed this model. Classroom discussion of hypothetical moral dilemmas patterned on those used by Kohlberg in his research served as the major vehicle for moral education. However, the middle and late 1970s witnessed the emergence of different intervention models designed to achieve the objectives of developmental moral education as conceptualized by Kohlberg. The scope and variety of these interventions in public schools, colleges, universities, and even in prisons, define a continuum ranging from the occasional use of hypothetical moral dilemmas or dilemmas growing out of course content to stimulate classroom discussions to comprehensive efforts linking the formal curricular materials with the hidden curriculum and offering students opportunities to analyze real-life dilemmas in a democratic framework as well as to examine moral questions in an academic context.

No single summary can possibly do justice (at any stage of the Kohlberg scale!) to the many efforts in cognitive developmental moral education currently underway in this country and elsewhere, in Canada and Great Britain, for example. The literature on moral education includes detailed descriptions of many current programs as well as several excellent general surveys of the state of the art.[3] This chapter discusses several representative programs generally and presents a more detailed case study of one program at the secondary school level, the Carnegie-Mellon Civic Education Project. Due to its comprehensive nature, this program incorporates many of the aspects of other interventions, including efforts to design new formal curricular materials, to link the formal and hidden curricula through a participatory governmental experience, and to instruct teachers in the theory and practice of developmental moral education. For this reason, the program offers a useful in-depth perspective on the Kohlbergian approach to moral education. The final section of this chapter analyzes some of the strengths and weaknesses that are apparent in the developmental moral education movement at present and offers some general conclusions.

INTERVENTION MODELS

Since Blatt's pilot project, programs in cognitive developmental moral education have involved virtually every subject area and every age level from the elementary school through college. The Fenton-Kohlberg effort to integrate discussions of moral dilemmas with the teaching of social studies represents a major step in the evolution of developmental moral education from an area of theory and research to an area of practical classroom application. That project provided the first clear and concrete illustration of the idea that moral education need not be a completely separate area of the curriculum or something that takes place only under the rubric of an ethics or civics course. Since the original Fenton-Kohlberg work, the conception of moral education as an integral part of substantive academic studies has been extended and applied in different directions by educators representing a variety of disciplines and backgrounds.

For example, Kohlberg's theory of cognitive moral development has been united with the perspectives of guidance and counseling to construct several curricula for deliberate psychological and moral education. Ralph Mosher, Norman Sprinthall, and Paul Sullivan have produced and tested courses which successfully integrate opportunities for analyzing moral dilemmas, opportunities for learning counseling skills, role-taking abilities, basic knowledge of moral psychology and philosophy, and opportunities for peer-counseling and cross-age tutoring. The results of their interventions indicate that such experiences facilitate the development of social perspective-taking abilities, and thus enhance the cognitive moral development of the students who serve as counselors and teachers.[4]

Other experiments with cross-age tutoring lend support to the findings that experiences of this type have a positive developmental effect.[5]

By extending the deliberate psychological education model to address the developmental needs of women, V. Lois Erickson also has achieved positive results in the area of cognitive moral development. Erickson found measurable stage change, based on pre- and post-moral judgment interviews, among twenty-three sophomore women in a Minneapolis high school following their participation in an experimental course consisting of both field experiences and seminar discussions designed to examine social issues related to the women's movement.[6] In another project which addresses the particular needs of a special subgroup of students, Robert Selman and his colleagues are constructing and evaluating developmental curricula for children with learning problems and interpersonal adjustment problems. Building on research findings regarding the interrelatedness of cognitive and social development, their work, which is currently in progress, focuses on three general areas: logical skills; perspective taking and interpersonal and communication skills; and fairness and social reciprocity skills.[7]

In contrast to moral education interventions designed to implement one course or to reach a specific group of students, the Ethical Quest in a Democratic Society Project in Tacoma, Washington, offers an example of a program which aims to stimulate the moral development of students at all grade levels in the school system through integrating an explicit focus on ethical considerations with the existing humanities program. During the initial phase of this project, 1975–76, twenty-three teachers from nine schools were introduced to the theory and practice of moral education and were asked to participate in curriculum development workshops. These teachers analyzed their own current curricular materials, identified the moral issues present, and created supplementary materials and appropriate teaching strategies to stimulate the moral development of their students. Twenty-two additional teachers joined the group in 1977. At present, forty-five teachers are using revised versions of the project materials in English, social studies, and health classes at the elementary, junior high, and senior high school level, and the project evaluation is continuing.[8]

Like those involved in the Tacoma Ethical Quest Project, many other educators are working to achieve the objectives of developmental moral education by emphasizing the moral issues which are an integral part of the subject matter they teach. Most literary works, most historical events, and most scientific problems as well as many aspects of vocational education encompass a moral dimension. Current efforts to integrate a focus on moral issues with literature, history, science, and vocational courses have substantially expanded the parameters of moral education.

For example, students in Brookline, Massachusetts, frequently participate in simulations and role-playing experiences as they analyze complex moral issues embedded in the rich context of American history.[9] Similarly, students in Scarsdale and Mamaroneck, New York, examine moral questions in the context of a new interdisciplinary English, social studies, and science curriculum.[10] The "Bio-Medical" Curriculum created by curriculum developers at the University of California integrates chemistry, biology, and public health concerns with ethical questions. Elsewhere in California, the Newport-Mesa Schools in Newport Beach offer a program in developmental vocational education which is designed to provide adolescents with meaningful, real-life work experiences and to help them reflect on the moral and social issues involved in the world of work.[11] A similar program in Minneapolis, Minnesota, Project ACT, offers additional support for the idea that community-based learning experiences, or experiences beyond the classroom, can have a positive effect on moral development.[12]

Developmental moral education addresses the needs of late adolescent college students as well as those of precollege students, as indicated by the results of an undergraduate experiment conducted at Harvard and replicated at the University of Washington. Focusing on the state of inner conflict, doubt, questioning, and the tendency toward relativism which are characteristic of many college freshmen and sophomores, Dwight Boyd designed an introductory ethics course with the general objective of facilitating the transition from conventional moral reasoning to principled moral reasoning. Students were exposed to readings in moral philosophy and to intensive discussion of both hypothetical and real-life moral dilemmas. Based on their responses to pre- and post-moral judgment interviews, the students enrolled in the experimental version of the course moved approximately one-fifth of a stage toward principled moral judgment, while those who took the revised version of the course moved approximately one-third of a stage.[13]

The Sierra Project, currently underway at the University of California at Irvine, exemplifies a more comprehensive college-level developmental intervention. This project involves a residential living experience as well as academic experiences designed to facilitate the transition to college life, stimulate psychological development, examine different life and career choices, and apply education through community services. A four-year longitudinal study to measure the effect of the program on cognitive moral development is in progress.[14]

Comprehensive developmental moral education in elementary and secondary schools in the form of participatory democratic community government experiences illustrate the far end of the continuum that begins with early efforts to replicate Moshe Blatt's experimental moral discussion classes. Adopting the Platonic view that education for justice, i.e., developmental moral education, must start with a just society, Lawrence Kohlberg and his colleagues have developed the concept of the "Just Community School," a school which attempts to establish congruence between the hidden curriculum, the way the school is organized and governed, and the formal curriculum, the content of the academic courses. In two alternative schools in Massachusetts, the Cluster School located in Cambridge High and Latin School and the School-within-a-School located in Brookline High School, students, faculty, and consultants, among them Professor Kohlberg himself, have established two models of the "Just Community School." The organization and operation of these schools are described in detail in the literature, and their programs have become the prototypical examples of

Kohlbergian educational interventions.[15] (See Kohlberg's discussion of such programs in chapter 16 of this volume.)

Differences between the student bodies and the settings of Cambridge High and Latin School and Brookline High School, as well as differences in the composition of the student populations of these alternative schools, account for functional differences between the two models. But the important common element is an ongoing effort to build and maintain a participatory democracy where school governance matters are handled in a community meeting and each member of the community, teachers and students alike, has one vote. Both schools have coped with countless problems as they attempt to give students real responsibilities relating to school governance and to build congruence between the hidden and formal curricula. And if the preliminary evidence is accurate, both schools appear to be providing viable experiences in developmental moral education.[16]

At least two attempts to establish "Just Communities" at the elementary school level also appear to have achieved a measure of success in enhancing the moral atmosphere of the school. In cooperation with elementary teachers in central New York, Project Change at the State University of New York at Cortland has been working to scale down the "Just Community" to make it developmentally suitable for younger children. Employing Glasser's concept of the class meeting, Project Change teachers have provided children with a participatory democratic experience which offers them a real share in classroom decision making.[17] A similar effort in the Falk Laboratory School at the University of Pittsburgh supports the idea that Kohlbergian education for justice can take place in the elementary school.[18]

THE CIVIC EDUCATION PROJECT

The Carnegie-Mellon Civic Education Project incorporates many of the elements of other Kohlbergian moral education programs in an attempt to develop an integrated and comprehensive approach to citizenship education for high school students. The project offers a three-year, three-part experience for tenth, eleventh, and twelfth grade students who work together for a three-period block of time during the school day in Civic Education units organized within the wider school. The students enroll in specially designed social studies and English courses. These include an integrated writing program and a community activities period which involves participation in a Civic Education community government and in a variety of community-building experiences and projects. The students take the remainder of their courses with the rest of the student body in the wider school. Currently, Civic Education units are functioning in four Pittsburgh-area high schools and in two schools in Bakersfield, California. Dissemination of the project model to additional school systems in other areas is in progress.

In an effort to expand on the traditional conception of civic education, the Carnegie-Mellon project focuses on five sets of goals: the development of knowledge; the development of basic participatory skills; the development of basic intellectual skills; personal development, including the development of self-knowledge, self-esteem, and personal identity; and the development of the ability to understand democratic values, in other words, cognitive moral development. These goals link the three components of the Civic Education project and serve as the criteria for the selection and design of educational experiences which aim to help students develop the skills and abilities necessary for responsible participation as citizens in a democratic society.

The project rationale defines such skills and abilities in a far more detailed and comprehensive fashion than do traditional statements regarding the fostering of vague traits such as "an appreciation of the democratic way of life." It specifically addresses the development of knowledge of American society and government, both past and present; the development of knowledge of contemporary social problems; the development of knowledge of literary works representing the various genres; the development of communication and data-gathering skills; the development of critical thinking skills; the development of knowledge about one's own ideas and beliefs; and the development of a sense of respect for one's own abilities. In addition, the rationale argues that civic education should include developmental moral education designed to help students develop the ability to understand the post-conventional principles of justice and fundamental human rights on which American society was founded.[19]

Civic Education students encounter experiences designed to foster progress toward the development of more mature moral reasoning through both formal, planned discussions of moral issues and informal, spontaneous discussions of ethical questions in the context of their academic classes. For example, the introductory social studies course, which emphasizes concepts drawn primarily from sociology and political science, investigates the various ways in which individuals are organized into groups, examines the different forms and functions of government, analyzes the concepts of power and leadership, and finally considers issues of justice through a study of the Constitution and the Bill of Rights. As a culminating activity, students try to write a constitution for their own Civic Education community. The course materials stress moral issues in context—should elected representatives vote as their constituents prefer or as their own consciences dictate—and also include supplementary moral dilemmas for class discussion.

The introductory English course parallels the social studies course, presenting literature which focuses primarily on the themes of the individual in the family, the individual in the wider community, and organization in the community. Discussion of the moral issues which form an integral part of the literary works as well as discussions of dilemmas presenting analogous conflicts occur throughout the course.

Through their participation in the third-period component of the project, students have opportunities to relate the content of their academic courses to their own needs and experiences and to discuss moral issues arising from their membership in a democratic Civic Education community. The focal point of the community activities period is an institution known as the community meeting. The entire Civic Education unit meets at regular intervals in a town meeting format based on Kohlberg's "Just Community" model to deal with matters of school governance. Under the terms of an agreement negotiated with school administrators and the school board, Civic Education students are required to obey the rules of the school and of the wider society, but they are permitted to design alternative sanctions for members of their community who violate those rules.

This agreement means, for instance, if the wider school has a rule prohibiting smoking except in designated areas, the Civic Education community cannot permit its members to smoke in Civic Education classrooms. The community is authorized, however, to determine an appropriate sanction for one of its members who violates the school rule. Students may appeal decisions of the community meeting through designated procedures which differ in each individual Civic Education community. In addition to community meetings and meetings of smaller advisory groups to consider discipline problems and other governance matters, third-period activities include planning and implementing projects designed to develop feelings of belonging and group identity, such as fund drives, community service projects, parties, room decorating contests, etc. Many of the issues which arise in the course of these community-building activities, as well as during formal community meetings, trigger discussions involving moral reasoning.

Second-year students in the Civic Education Project study American history and American literature and continue to participate in community governance and projects. Their history and English courses, built around a general theme of the quest for justice in America, include an ongoing, integral emphasis on issues of justice in the context of the American past and of American literature. Parallel social studies and English courses projected for the first semester of the third year will emphasize selected contemporary problems and their ethical aspects in a global perspective. Plans for the second semester of the third year call for a community-based learning experience which will offer students an opportunity to work outside the classroom in agencies and institutions which deal locally with various practical aspects of the problems to be studied during the first semester.

A two-year developmental writing program which spans the social studies and English components comprises an additional part of
the Civic Education Project's effort to equip students with the broad
spectrum of citizenship skills defined in the rationale. The writing
program combines a systematic approach to the teaching of writing
with a view of writing as a learning process derived from the work of
A. D. Van Nostrand. Exercises designed to teach writing through a
series of sequential steps are included with the English curricular
materials, while writing assignments designed to reinforce this
learning are included with the social studies materials.

In-service training in the form of weekly, after-school staff development seminars preceding the opening of the Civic Education
units introduced participating teachers to the rationale and goals of
the project, to model curricular materials, and to practical matters
such as procedures for organizing community meetings. All of the
teachers involved in the project attended these seminars. In addition, eight teachers from participating schools were released from
the classroom for a semester or part of a semester to work at
Carnegie-Mellon on curriculum development. Because the projected
dissemination of Civic Education involves implementation in
schools located in diverse geographic areas with students of varying
backgrounds, interests, and abilities, the curricular materials prepared at Carnegie-Mellon have been and will continue to be adapted
by individual teachers to meet the needs of their own students.

The Civic Education Project represents an ambitious effort to
introduce fundamental changes into high schools through a comprehensive program which integrates Kohlberg's model of moral
education with a variety of other educational aims. Preliminary
evaluation data from standardized tests administered to every student in the project and moral judgment interviews administered to
a sample of participating students offer some evidence of progress
toward the five sets of goals.[20] But it is too soon to draw
conclusions—particularly with regard to cognitive moral development, which is a long, slow process.

The longitudinal quantitative project evaluation is supplemented
by quantitative research conducted by two participant-observers

during the initial year of project implementation.[21] Their copious field notes based on observations and experiences in two of the original participating schools illustrate the complexity of an undertaking which proposes to introduce structural and normative innovations into secondary schools. In addition to the characteristic problems involved in piloting experimental curricular materials in schools, the Civic Education Project has confronted special difficulties stemming from the effort to socialize teachers simultaneously to major changes in significant areas: the internalization of a new body of knowledge regarding educational theory and research; the pursuit of five sets of goals through both the formal and hidden curricula; the adoption of innovative instructional techniques, including Socratic questioning to elicit moral reasoning, and new roles as members of a democratic school community; the sharing of power with students; and the need for flexibility in altering classroom routines to cope with unexpected, community-related intrusions into teaching time.

The ethnographic data collected by the participant-observers document the varying degrees of conflict and stress experienced by teachers in the course of their efforts to implement the components of the Civic Education Project in their own schools. The data also provide evidence of the impact of the project on the attitudes and behaviors of students. While some students have regarded particular aspects of their social studies and English courses as especially noteworthy, for both positive and negative reasons, most students have regarded the sharing of power through the community governance structure as the most significant feature of their experiences in Civic Education.[22] The significance of participation in community government apparently derives from a combination of both positive and negative experiences. Students respond very positively to the opportunity to become "more equal" with their teachers. But responsibility accompanies power, and frustration often accompanies responsibility. Civic Education students learn these lessons repeatedly as they attempt to devise efficient and fair procedures for the transaction of community business and the preservation of order and cooperation in the community—and to solve the "real-life" moral dilemmas that inevitably accompany these tasks. If this impact is reflected in the final evaluation data from the Civic Education Project and the other school democracy interventions, the significance of Kohlberg's concept of "evaluation for justice" will be demonstrated graphically.

A CRITICAL APPRAISAL

The resurgence of concern over values and moral education, including the current interest in developmental moral education, does not represent a revolutionary movement; actually, it could be characterized as a form of conservatism or a "back to basics" trend. But the phenomenon which Jack Fraenkel has characterized as the "Kohlberg Bandwagon" testifies to the appeal of the cognitive developmental approach for educators at virtually every level. A variety of factors have been cited to account for the "bandwagon" phenomenon: the events of the troubled decade of the 1960s; Watergate; high crime rates; and a decline in traditional family life and sexual morality. Lawrence Kohlberg attributes the "bandwagon" phenomenon, at least in part, to a rediscovery by liberals of the principles of justice which underlie American society and a concomitant realization that those principles ought to enter into education.[23] Whatever the explanation, the influence of developmental moral education is growing, and educators need to be cognizant of the implications of this growing influence.

What are the ramifications of the developmental moral education movement? Current intervention efforts reflect four basic models: occasional classroom discussions of moral dilemmas; introduction of special courses designed to focus on moral issues through academic and experiential components; extensive infusion of ethical considerations and supplementary materials dealing with moral issues into existing formal curricular materials; and establishment of participatory democratic governance structures designed to work toward curricular congruence. Some efforts incorporate aspects of all four, while others remain narrower in scope. The general thrust of the evidence thus far is positive; it appears that educational intervention can affect the process of cognitive moral development in students. But both theoretical and practical aspects of developmental moral education reflect problems and weaknesses which will require the continued attention and concerted efforts of researchers and practitioners.

Critiques of Kohlberg's theory and research have raised important questions reflecting both philosophical and empirical considerations. While a full discussion of these critiques belongs elsewhere, it is appropriate at this point to indicate the general nature of at least some of the issues that have been raised. Kohlberg's claims regarding the universality and invariance of his six stages of moral reasoning and the existence of stage 6 have been challenged by scholars who argue that the empirical evidence does not document these claims conclusively.[24] In connection with the latter claim, Kohlberg himself has expressed some reservations concerning the evidence for the existence of a sixth stage which exhibits the characteristics he originally attributed to it.[25] Several critiques question the evidence for the relationship between moral judgment and action and the reliability of the moral judgment interview as a research instrument.[26] Other areas of critical examination emphasize possible conflict between the element of elitism inherent in a hierarchical structural system of moral reasoning and the idea of democracy; the ahistorical nature of the liberal-ideal conception of the moral person which is implicit in Kohlberg's notion of moral maturity;[27] the possible ethnocentric bias reflected in the research model;[28] the omission of any consideration of the role of the affective domain in the process of moral judgment;[29] and the failure to include female subjects in the longitudinal sample on which most of Kohlberg's claims have been based.[30]

Critiques which raise important empirical and philosophical issues for theoreticians to consider underline the fact that much additional research is needed to determine the validity of Kohlberg's hypotheses regarding moral development. Such critiques also encourage the type of dialogue and openness which is essential for a realistic assessment of the strengths and weaknesses of classroom applications of the cognitive developmental approach to moral education. And certainly an examination of the problems and difficulties involved in developmental moral education offers a healthy balance to the "bandwagon" effect noted previously.

Such an examination must consider the fact that any attempt to implement developmental moral education asks a great deal of the classroom teacher. Most, if not all, of the pilot intervention programs reflect the efforts of highly trained and experienced researchers, university professors, and graduate students in developmental psychology, philosophy, and education. Such people have a thorough knowledge of Kohlberg's research and have read widely and in depth in related fields. Furthermore, they usually have been able to devote a concentrated amount of time and attention to moral education projects. In contrast, the typical classroom teacher has little or no knowledge about developmental psychology and has to cope with a multiplicity of duties and concerns, of which moral education is only one small part. While many teachers may be interested in the implications of developmental moral education, comparatively few have the time or the opportunity to acquire the necessary background to implement Kohlberg's approach in any really meaningful way in their own classrooms.

This situation clearly indicates that the developmental moral education movement must continue to devote careful attention and effort to the areas of teacher training and in-service education. Certainly adequate preparation is essential if teachers are to be comfortable with the new roles and new methods demanded by this approach. Such preparation is also of critical importance as a safeguard against possible teacher misuse of the theoretical framework on which developmental moral education is based. For example, a superficial understanding of stage theory and the nature of stages of moral reasoning could result in a teacher's misapplication of Kohlbergian stage labels as a measure of the human worth of individual students or as a standard for establishing positive and negative expectancies for students in the same way that some teachers have used IQ scores.[31] Without adequate comprehensive teacher preparation, developmental moral education will most likely prove ineffective, and may also prove detrimental through the creation of unnecessary stress and pressures for both teachers and students.

The possibility that attempts to infuse curricular materials with a cognitive moral developmental perspective may result in over-simplification or distortion of subject matter also reflects the importance of providing educators with a solid theoretical and practical foundation for implementing developmental moral education. Focusing on the moral dimension in the context of a literature course or a history course, for example, can enhance course content, but such a focus must preserve the integrity of the discipline. Hence designing moral dilemmas for use in such courses can be an intricate task which requires scrupulous attention to the constraints imposed by the data or the literary object, if the objectives of both academic instruction and cognitive moral development are to be appropriately addressed.

An additional problem faced by teachers who want to use moral dilemmas in their courses is the fact that students quickly become bored with "moral dilemma day" unless both the format for presenting moral issues and the method of discussion or analysis are varied. Providing this necessary variety poses a formidable task for teachers who already are burdened by too many such tasks and a challenge even for experienced curriculum developers who are thoroughly familiar with cognitive moral developmental theory.

Undoubtedly, the most challenging task of all is the establishment and maintenance of democratic schools which provide congruence between the hidden and formal curricula and thus work toward the "Just Community" which Kohlberg believes serves as an important stimulus to the development of mature moral reasoning. Both environmental and human limitations offer formidable obstacles to the successful implementation of the participatory democracy model in schools. The structure of the hidden curriculum and the general conception that the main purpose of the school is the transmission of knowledge by subject matter specialists work directly against the "Just Community" approach, which distributes responsibility for school governance to all members of the community and views the purpose of the school in much broader developmental terms.

The size of many contemporary high schools and the reluctance of both administrators and teachers to share power with students also limit the possibility of effective student participation. In addition, although the rhetoric of school democracy may support student input in substantive areas such as curriculum planning or faculty hiring, few students have the background to contribute constructively in these areas, and few teachers are willing to trust them to do so. These factors, combined with the parameters established by the concept of democracy that is held by the majority of the members of the wider community outside the school, impose severe constraints on school democracy projects.

The limits of human development also impose constraints which may be even more critical in terms of the creation of a "Just Community" in the classroom. If Kohlberg's theory is accurate, understanding and implementing democracy may be beyond the ability of many students. The theory suggests that individuals define concepts like democracy in stage-related terms and that they cannot understand definitions which involve reasoning more than one stage above their own.[32] This means that a student who thinks at stage 2 will not understand a stage 5 conception of democracy which encompasses the ideas of liberty and justice for all, individual freedom commensurate with equal freedom for all others, majority rule, protection of minority rights, etc. Because the research evidence indicates that most high school students reason at stages 2 and 3, with some stage 4 thought present among older students, it appears that very few students at the secondary level are capable of implementing a stage 5 democracy. In addition, as Ralph Mosher has pointed out, Kohlberg's findings indicate that most teachers probably reason at stage 3 and 4. Hence their interpretations of democracy may also emphasize stage 3 interpersonal concordance concerns or stage 4 societal maintenance concerns rather than stage 5 human rights and welfare concerns. As a result, many teachers may be ambivalent about Kohlberg's notion of a "Just Community," and some will never be comfortable with it.[33]

Despite both the environmental and human constraints on the implementation of school democracies, the "Just Community" model appears to have the potential to significantly enhance cognitive moral development. Building and maintaining a viable community exposes students to many opportunities for moral growth. Coping with situations involving conflicts between community welfare and the welfare of individuals—sanctioning a rule breaker who also happens to be one's best friend, for example—can facilitate the transition from stage 3 to stage 4 thought. Such experiences also stimulate students' role-taking abilities and help them to acquire the broad social perspectives which are necessary for the development of principled moral reasoning. Hence the experience of creating a "Just Community" may prove to be the means by which "Just Community members" also are created.

Certainly much educational research regarding the effects of developmental moral education will be necessary before the validity of Kohlberg's approach can be demonstrated conclusively. The many philosophical, empirical, and practical questions which remain unanswered testify to the still hypothetical nature of the Kohlbergian moral universe. But there can be no doubt that the moral dimension of human experience, in all its aspects, is an appropriate area of examination and study. Insofar as Kohlbergian developmental moral education models focus on and illuminate that area, their contributions to the education of students at all levels must be considered positive.

NOTES

1. Moshe M. Blatt and Lawrence Kohlberg, "The Effects of Classroom Moral Discussion Upon Children's Level of Moral Judgment," *Journal of Moral Education*, 4, 2 (February, 1975), 129–161. Blatt's data have been reevaluated according to the revised version of Kohlberg's scoring system for moral judgment interviews. Although his conclusions regarding stage change have been revised downward, the evidence still supports the claim that measurable cognitive moral development occurred.

2. Anne Colby, Lawrence Kohlberg, Edwin Fenton, Betsy Speicher-Dubin, and Marcus Lieberman, "Secondary School Moral Discussion Programmes Led by Social Studies Teachers," *Journal of Moral Education*, 6, 2 (January, 1977), 90–111.

3. The following accounts describe moral education programs in the United States: Elsa R. Wasserman, "Implementing Kohlberg's 'Just Community Concept' in an Alternative High School," *Social Education*, 40, 4 (April, 1976), 203–207. Also in Peter Scharf, ed., *Readings in Moral Education*. Minneapolis: Winston Press, Inc., 1978, pp. 164–173. Ralph L. Mosher, "A Democratic High School: Damn It, Your Feet are Always in the Water," in Norman A. Sprinthall and Ralph L. Mosher, eds., *Value Development . . . As the Aim of Education*. Schnectady, New York: Character Research Press, 1978, pp. 69–113.

For accounts of moral education programs elsewhere, see Edmund V. Sullivan and Clive Beck, "Moral Education in a Canadian Setting," in David Purpel and Kevin Ryan, eds., *Moral Education . . . It Comes with the Territory*. Berkeley, California: McCutcheon Publishing Company, 1976, pp. 221–234 and Peter McPhail et al., *Moral Education in the Secondary School*. London: Longman Group Ltd., 1972.

Moral education in a prison setting is discussed in Lawrence Kohlberg, Peter Scharf, and Joseph Hickey, "The Justice Structure of the Prison: A Theory and an Intervention," *The Prison Journal*, 51 (Autumn-Winter, 1972), 3–14.

For general surveys see Ralph L. Mosher, "Theory and Practice: A New E.R.A.?", *Theory Into Practice*, 16, 2 (April, 1977), 81–88, and James Rest, "Developmental Psychology as a Guide to Value Education: A Review of 'Kohlbergian' Programs," *Review of Educational Research* (Spring, 1974), pp. 241–259. A comprehensive bibliography of materials related to moral education appears in the *Moral Education Forum*, February, 1977.

4. Ralph L. Mosher and Norman A. Sprinthall, "Psychological Education in Secondary Schools: A Program to Promote Individual and Human Development," *American Psychologist*, 5 (October, 1970), 911–924; Ralph L. Mosher and Norman A. Sprinthall, "Deliberate Psychological Education," *The Counseling Psychologist*, 2 (1972), 3–82; Ralph L. Mosher and Paul Sullivan, "A Curriculum in Moral Education for Adolescents," *Journal of Moral Education*, 5, 2 (1976), 159–172, also in Scharf, ed., op. cit., pp. 82–97.

5. Philip V. Cognetta and Norman A. Sprinthall, "Students as Teachers: Role Taking as a Means of Promoting Psychological and Ethical Development During Adolescence," in Sprinthall and Mosher, eds., op. cit., pp. 53–68; Robert D. Enright, "Promoting Interpersonal Growth in Elementary Schools," in Sprinthall and Mosher, eds., op. cit., pp. 27–40.

6. V. Lois Erickson, "Deliberate Psychological Education for Women, from Iphigenia to Antigone," *Counselor Education and Supervision* (Winter, 1975), and "The Development of Women: An Issue of Justice," in Scharf, ed., op. cit., pp. 110–123.

7. Robert L. Selman and Dan Jaquette, "To Understand and to Help: Implications of Developmental Research for the Education of Children with Interpersonal Problems," in Scharf, ed., op. cit., pp. 124–136.

8. Paul J. Sullivan and Mary F. Dockstader, "Values Education and American Schools: Worlds in Collision?" in Sprinthall and Mosher, eds., op. cit., pp. 135–156.

9. Thomas J. Ladenburg, "Cognitive Development and the Teaching of Social Studies," in Scharf, ed., op. cit., pp. 98–109.

10. The Scarsdale-Mamaroneck project, entitled "Ethical Issues in Decision-Making," is supported under Title IV-C funds by the New York State Education Department. This project includes a teacher training component as well as a curriculum component.

11. Peter Scharf, *Moral Education*. Davis, California: Responsible Action, 1978, p. 130; pp. 158–163.

12. Diane Hedin and Byron Schneider, "Action Learning in Minneapolis: A Case Study," in Ralph Tyler, ed., *From Youth to Constructive Adult Life: The Role of the Public School*. Berkeley, California: McCutcheon Publishing Company, 1978, pp. 149–167.

See also Dan Conrad and Diane Hedin, "Citizenship Education Through Participation," in *Education for Responsible Citizenship*, The Report of the National Task Force on Citizenship Education. New York: McGraw-Hill Book Company, 1977, pp. 135–155.

13. Dwight R. Boyd, "Education Toward Principled Moral Judgment: An Analysis of an Experimental Course in Undergraduate Moral Education Applying Lawrence Kohlberg's Theory of Moral Development," unpublished dissertation, Harvard University, 1976; Dwight R. Boyd, "The Problems of Sophomoritis: An Educational Proposal," *Journal of Moral Education*, 6, 1 (May, 1977), 36–42.

14. John Whiteley, "A Developmental Intervention in Higher Education," Paper presented at the Eighth Annual Piagetian Theory and the Helping Professions Conference, Los Angeles, California, February 3–4, 1978. A shorter version appears in the *Moral Education Forum*, 3, 4 (September, 1978), 1–13.

15. Wasserman, op. cit.; Mosher, "A Democratic High School."

16. Mosher, "A Democratic High School," p. 101.

17. Thomas Lickona, "Creating the Just Community with Children," in Scharf, ed., op. cit., pp. 174–185, also in *Theory Into Practice*, 16, 2 (April, 1977), 97–104.

18. Cheryl Kubelick, "An Instructional Design for Values Education," unpublished dissertation, University of Pittsburgh, 1977.

19. Edwin N. Fenton, "A Rationale for a Civic Education Project," unpublished paper, Carnegie-Mellon University.

20. The evaluating instruments for the Civic Education Project include: Educational Testing Service Sequential Tests of Educational Progress and Cooperative Social Studies Test for Senior High School American History, for the social studies components; Houghton-Mifflin Tests of Academic Progress in Composition, Reading, and Literature, for the English components; Coopersmith Self-Esteem Inventory and Rotter's Sentence Blank Completion Form, for personal development; Piagetian Cognitive Tasks, for cognitive development; and the Kohlberg Moral Judgment Interview, for cognitive moral development.

21. G. Dale Greenawald, "Civic Education and the Implementation of Structural and Normative Changes in Secondary Schools: A Case Study Analysis," unpublished dissertation, Carnegie-Mellon University, 1978; Bette L. Hutzler, dissertation in progress.

22. Greenawald, op. cit.

23. "Foreword," Scharf, ed., op. cit., pp. 11–12.

24. Jack R. Fraenkel, "The Kohlberg Bandwagon: Some Reservations," *Social*

Education, 40, 4 (April, 1976), 216–222. The Fraenkel critique also appears in Scharf, ed., op. cit., pp. 250–263 and in Purpel and Ryan, eds., op. cit., pp. 291–307. Elizabeth L. Simpson, "Moral Development Research: A Case Study of Scientific Cultural Bias," *Human Development,* 17 (1974), 81–106. John Gibbs, "Kohlberg's Stages of Moral Judgment: A Constructive Critique," *Harvard Educational Review,* 47, 1 (February, 1977), 43–61.

25. "The Contributions of Democratizing Schooling to the Education of Citizens," Plenary Session Address, First Annual Civic Education Conference, Los Angeles, California, August 26–September 1, 1978.

26. William Kurtines and Esther B. Greif, "The Development of Moral Thought: Review and Evaluation of Kohlberg's Approach," *Psychological Bulletin,* 81 (August, 1974), 453–470. Roger Brown and Richard J. Herrnstein, "Moral Reasoning and Conduct," in *Psychology,* Boston: Little, Brown and Company, 1975, pp. 287–340. For a reply to the Kurtines and Greif critique, see John Broughton, "The Cognitive Developmental Approach to Morality: A Reply to Kurtines and Greif," *Journal of Moral Education,* 7, 2 (January, 1978), 81–96.

27. Edmund V. Sullivan, *Kohlberg's Structuralism, A Critical Appraisal.* Toronto, The Ontario Institute for Studies in Education, 1977.

28. Elizabeth L. Simpson, op. cit.

29. See, for example, John Flowers, "A Behavioral Psychologist's View of Developmental Moral Education," in Scharf, ed., op. cit., pp. 264–271 and Richard S. Peters, "The Place of Kohlberg's Theory in Moral Education," *Journal of Moral Education,* 7, 3 (May, 1978), 147–157.

30. Carol Gilligan, "In a Different Voice: Women's Conceptions of Self and of Morality," *Harvard Educational Review,* 47, 4 (November, 1977), 418–517.

31. Daniel J. Bolt and Edmund V. Sullivan, "Kohlberg's Cognitive-Developmental Theory in Educational Settings: Some Possible Abuses," *Journal of Moral Education,* 6, 3 (May, 1977), 198–205.

32. These findings are reported in James R. Rest, "The Hierarchical Nature of Moral Judgment: A Study of Patterns of Comprehension and Preference of Moral Stages," *Journal of Personality,* 41 (March, 1973), 86–109. See also James R. Rest, Elliot Turiel, and Lawrence Kohlberg, "Level of Moral Development as a Determinant of Preference and Comprehension of Moral Judgments Made by Others," *Journal of Personality,* 37 (1969), 225–252.

33. For a more extensive discussion of the implications of students' and teachers' stages of moral reasoning for school democracy, see Mosher, "A Democratic High School," pp. 103–106. Edmund V. Sullivan also addresses this issue in *Moral Learning: Some Findings, Issues and Questions.* New York: Paulist Press, 1975, p. 103.

Chapter 13

A Look at the Kohlberg Curriculum Framework for Moral Education

JAMES B. MACDONALD

INTRODUCTION

It seems only "just" that the attempt to critique and/or analyze any position or set of ideas be self-reflective, as well as other-reflective.[1] By this I mean that my value position and assumptions should be clear, since no analysis or critique could possibly be neutral.

I long ago came to the conclusion that curricula were political statements shot full of moral and ethical decisions. Further, a curriculum, in plan and action, has the intention to reproduce the social order of things as they presently exist, or to create new possibilities by helping to discover and foster the capabilities of the learners. Curricula, in other words, by intention at least, either are controlling or liberating. Since I am committed to the liberation side, I shall look at Kohlberg's work critically from that perspective.

A second conviction I hold is that curriculum is much more than a plan for learning with appropriate materials and methods. Curriculum is the environment we construct, within which the so-called learning is observed. As such, it has implicit, latent, or hidden action components, as well as explicit, substantive "subject matter." The environment involves the leadership and managerial

381

realms (with our rules and policies); the curriculum planning area (resources and materials); the instructional arena (methods, interpersonal relationships, etc.); *and* the qualities, characteristics, past experiences, capacities, and possibilities of all the people involved.

A third general value that I hold is a commitment to participatory social democracy as the best answer to the humanistic question, "How shall we live together?" This I couple with a fourth value grounded in the individual's search for meaning found in such questions as, "Who am I?" and "What does life mean?" Thus, I find a spiritual or transcendental concern necessary. Any curriculum worth developing should (by my values) reflect a real concern for helping find answers to these kinds of questions.

BASIC CURRICULUM QUESTIONS OR CRITERIA

Herbert Kliebard[2] proposed four basic traditional questions that have to be answered in order to create a curriculum. Other persons have done similar analyses, but Kliebard's will serve the purpose of seeing whether Kohlberg's approach *is* a genuine curriculum in the traditional sense. The questions listed here are:

1. Why should we teach this rather than that?
2. What rules should govern the teaching of what is selected?
3. Who should have access to what knowledge?
4. How should various parts be interrelated?

An appropriate question now becomes, "In terms of answering these four traditional curriculum questions, does Kohlberg have a curriculum?" The answer is definitely yes! Throughout Kohlberg's writings and materials produced by collaborators, these questions are addressed clearly and directly.

The question of what goals are of most worth is answered by the assertions that moral virtue is the goal of the curriculum; that virtue is one (not a bag of discreet behaviors); and that *virtue* is best reflected in the concern for justice and human welfare. Thus, the long-range goal of the Kohlberg curriculum is to bring a person's moral reasoning to the highest possible level of principle in the following categories of principles: prudence (and self-realization); welfare of others; respect for authority, society, or persons; justice.

As Kohlberg says, "All these 'principles' or reasons are present in one form or another from Stage 1 onwards, except that prudence and authority have dropped out as reasons by Stage 6. From Stage 1, these reasons have two characteristics. First, they are ultimate terms, they refer to states of affairs which seem right or good in themselves and are in that sense 'principles.' Second, they refer to states of affairs that are involved in all moral situations and are potentially relevant to all people."[3] Thus, what knowledge (reasons) is of most worth is clearly indicated.

Goals are not stated as behaviors (i.e., in behavioral terms) in the sense that the substantive content of any moral principle embodied in a reason is relative to context, intentionality, personal experience, and culture. This still leaves the question of the connection of moral reasons to actual behavior. (In Kohlberg's framework conduct would be more apt a word than behavior.)

The question of methodology is reasonably clear. There is a broad approach which relies on the heterogenity of groups (varying stages and backgrounds) to provide a richness of experience within which a conflict strategy operates. Dialogue and discussion, or in broad generality even the simple increasing of intercommunication about value issues is stimulating for moral development.

A central element of the Kohlberg methodological procedures is recognition of "role-taking" opportunities (i.e., recognition of others and putting oneself in the place of various people involved in a moral conflict).[4] It isn't clear whether the methodology suggests setting up the "acting out" of conflict situations or (as it seems) simply the recognition of broad experiences in the person's social life from which moral value discussions eventuate. This, it should be remembered, takes place in the context of a "just community."

There is a distinct conflict strategy within a group discussion setting. First, identify the stage(s) (1–6) of moral reasoning that the group represents. Then present a moral conflict story or situation for discussion. Next, accept, help develop, reinforce, etc., a moral level of reasoning *one* stage *above* the majority of the group in the discussion. (It should be clear that Kohlberg is speaking about the *form* of the argument or reasoning, not the content or substance, per se.) The moral cognitive dissonance in the story will, of course, be related to the substantive "categories of principles" mentioned above.

The question of differentiation is dealt with in terms of the stages of development. As a developmental approach, each youngster should be accepted at his or her own stage and be encouraged to move into the next higher level. This in effect means that "acceptable" action and response is individualized in terms of the general supporting theory.

The problem of relationship is also dealt with. Not only is it premised that moral and ethically conflictual situations may arise in any aspect of the total curriculum, but also the very idea of the importance of the *hidden* curriculum in Kohlberg's work is a fundamental recognition of the relational realities of curriculum.

Kohlberg recognizes that moral development is related to all aspects of the self, society, and other curricular substance. Thus, he posits the hidden curriculum—i.e., "The fact that teachers and schools are engaged in moral education without explicitly and philosophically discussing or formulating goals and methods." Thus, the hidden curriculum is a set of "learnings" or goals of socialization constantly in operation through the action contexts and their implicit intentions and meanings for the development of the learner.

To make the hidden curriculum explicit, and to create an environmental context consonant with moral development, Kohlberg offers the idea of the "Just Community." By this, he suggests that schools should have a shared governance of a participatory social democratic flavor where the social arrangements, the answer to "How shall we live together?" reflect a *just society*. That is, they should reflect a living arrangement which is consonant with higher-level moral reasoning, capped by overriding concern for the principles of welfare, equality, and justice.

The explicit part of the curriculum, that is, where moral education gets located in traditional terms, seems to be in the social studies area. This, however, appears more as a convenience than logic, since Kohlberg makes it clear in many places that he is speaking about human cognitive development in relation to moral concerns, and thus, any place in the curriculum where moral concerns are relevant (almost any place, in other words) could involve persons in explicit moral education.

The conflict situations that are utilized might better be labeled interdisciplinary studies with many implications for philosophical, psychological, anthropological, and social awareness and understanding involved integrally in the resolution of moral conflicts. These are apparent in, among other places, "Just Community" building projects underway in various places.

Furthermore, several people from a variety of areas have been working on the development of instructional materials and strategies appropriate to their concerns, based upon Kohlberg's broad statement about stages of moral development. Thus, the methodological status of the framework is in a dynamic development phase at the present.

However, as far as the explicit curriculum is concerned, Kohlberg adheres to Dewey's conviction that "the aim of education is growth and development both intellectual and moral." Because moral development leads to the virtue of justice and justice is a social concept involving active thought about and concern for society, then social studies would appear to be a logical home for the moral development curriculum.

Kohlberg[5] praises "new social studies" for embodying Deweyan postulates of 1) active thought and reasoning, 2) distinguishing between the form and substance of thinking, 3) the interdisciplinary nature of content, 4) the use of relevant concrete social problems, 5) recognition of the need for value clarification; and 6) emphasis on controversial issues. He, however, suggests that his moral education curriculum embodies two further Deweyan postulates that are critical. These are 1) the awareness of cognitive and moral stages; and 2) recognition of ethical principles defining the aims of social education, specifically the principles of social justice.

There is a question of time that is left askew in Kohlberg's curriculum methodology. Are we to assume that over the years the same procedure will be used over and over again? What would appear in his experimental situations as exciting and stimulating new discussions could become rather jaded over a period of months and years. There is a general lack of variety in the materials.

This suggests that Kohlberg should back away from Piaget a bit and go back to Dewey in the development of the possibilities in the immediate social lives of the school community. In other words, teachers would better interact with students in the immediacy of their social lives to find meaningful moral situations if they are to keep the interest at a high motivational level.

Further, is it really necessary to move mechanically through stages in groups? If teachers were aware of the framework, understood it, used it as a guide in their work, would it not make sense to help teachers relate to *individual* and *group* problems as they arise? Would it be more effective this way?

What about the methodology itself? What level is the moral level of the relationship (let's say on authority concerns) suggested in the teacher-pupil relationships in the method? It really seems to me to be "authoritarian" and level 3 or 4. If this is so, then how can we expect to move people beyond what they are if we do not embody the highest moral principles in our own behavior? Would a "Just Community" allow persons to choose not to have "moral education" experiences?

Examination of Kohlberg's curriculum perspective reveals a sophisticated understanding of curriculum in both contemporary and traditional terms. Kohlberg has clear answers to the basic questions and (as we shall see) strong *reasons* for the answers. He further is well aware of the impact of hidden, latent, or implicit aspects of the environment upon the possibilities for learning. Thus, we may say that Kohlberg's work satisfies professional curriculum criteria.

JUSTIFYING THE CURRICULUM

Having decided a bona fide curriculum exists for moral education, it is now critical that we seek the justification for it. Here, again, Kohlberg's work is far ahead of many "curriculum" experts' proposals. He has reasons for practically everything he includes in his proposals. We shall look at these reasons and ask questions and make comments.

Kohlberg's major sources and methods for justification are to be found (according to him) in the work of Plato, Immanuel Kant, John Dewey, Jean Piaget, empirical studies by Kohlberg and colleagues, and deductive logic. All of these sources or methods are brought to bear on the construction of the curriculum.

Fundamental to the whole structure is the developmental point of view.[6] This is really vintage Dewey with, of course, close agreement with Piaget on the developmental and action orientations.

It is at this point that I begin to have some difficulties with the material. As an approach to morality, it reflects a secular humanism. There is no recognition of "other" than human. In fact, Kohlberg on more than one occasion makes the point that morality is not synonymous or necessarily related to religion, ergo we may talk meaningfully and fully about morality without entering the realm of religious discourse.

I'm not sure this follows logically, but I am sure that I disagree with the assertion. Although it might not make any practical difference in the actual curriculum, I would feel better about it if the rationale recognized the realm of religious mysticism and/or intention and revelation as a source of virtue for human beings. I very much doubt that the concept of justice as a cornerstone of virtue and morality is knowable or possible without intuitive experiential "reinforcement" (from God?). This may suggest that a stage 7 with a transcendental orientation is a possible development of the theory.

Kohlberg discusses this briefly in "Notes toward a Seventh Stage."[7] Essentially, he recognizes that the questions "Why be moral?" and "Why be just?" are still left, in fact, even more insistent at the stage 6 level of rational principle. For this he feels we must move from a humanistic universal awareness to a cosmic perspective. However, it is apparent that this recognition has not affected the conceptualization of the moral development framework up to this point.

Paul Tillich[8] presents just such a cosmic theological perspective not found in Dewey or Kohlberg. The religious source of moral demands is love (as agape), in unity with the imperative of justice to recognize each person, guided by the wisdom of the past, and acted on courageously on the basis of these principles. Combined with the religious concern for the ultimate found in the moral imperative, and a religious element found in moral motivation, Tillich says that morality is religiousness in its very essence: "The unconditioned character of the moral imperative, love as the ultimate source of the moral commands, and grace as the power of moral motivation are the concepts through which the question of the relation of religion and morality is fundamentally answered."[9]

This is related to the cognitive psychology that pervades the whole framework. There is a limit, for manageability's sake, on the possible meaning of morality. Although Kohlberg does well in refuting the emotive theory and the bag of virtues position, he also buys a rational limitation for morality when he defines it completely as cognitive growth in moral reasoning. In other words he brings morality into the curriculum but he also may be losing important aspects of it in the process.

It is a very difficult problem since perceiving morality from Kohlberg's position has major educational advantages—it is identifiable, it has known dimensions, it is observable, it is manipulatable, and it can be assessed. Having managed this, he also, as was said, takes morality out of the morass of emotions unamenable to logic or empirical study. All to the good! In the back of our minds, however, we may well wonder what price in exclusion we have had to pay for the positive gain.

There is some possible evidence in the more recent right-brain/left-brain work[10] that might raise questions of the left-brain approach to morality reflected in Kohlberg's work. The right brain apparently operates on a much more holistic, intuitive basis, but is still intellectual and not *just* emotional. Questions such as how moral understanding develops in holistic and intuitive terms need to be asked. It is possible, for example, that movement from stage to stage is done on an intuitive holistic basis, only observable in the reasoning patterns (i.e., the left-brain translations) of the individual.

Michael Polanyi's[11] suggestion of hierarchy based on a holistic approach would posit that at each level of organization the new organizational level is more than a sum of previous parts, although dependent upon the parts.

This very need to take a more holistic look at moral development is discussed by Simpson.[12] She suggests a cognitive-affective-conative developmental theory is necessary. Selecting Maslow's work with a hierarchy of needs, she parallels Kohlberg's and Maslow's theories. She concludes:

> . . . In contrast to Piaget and Kohlberg—I believe that morality is fundamentally irrational—that is, that differences in even such obviously cognitive phenomena as moral reasoning and judgment derive from essential personalogical structures. Moral reasoning and behavior are a function of the *person,* and not simply his capacity to think logically or to learn concepts and norms.
>
> . . . I see personality development as a whole—and not cognitive development alone—as the basis of morality.[13]

Thus, Kohlberg's stages may not reflect the organizing principle that makes movement to higher levels of moral reasoning possible. Somehow, Kohlberg's discovery by practical trial and error that one presents moral arguments one stage above the level of the person's present reasoning for best results does not satisfy any basic need for understanding what is actually involved.

Also, research reported by Leslie Hart[14] concerning the recent discoveries about the function of the brain may suggest that Kohlberg's conception of moral reasoning is too narrow. Apparently, the brain performs in a holistic manner, processing a great deal of complex multidimensional data and casting out probabilities. This is a far cry from the generally forced, linear, one-item-at-a-time, "computer" model we operate with in an attempt to develop rationality in our reasoning process. Formal logic may work and it may be the highest "testable" stage for Piaget; but it may also be fundamentally brain-antagonistic in the sense of being a highly specialized and forced performance. Thus, moral reasoning defined as evidence of formal logic may also be a highly restricted and forced performance, and not reflective of total human moral capacity.[15]

In summation, one cannot argue the efficacy of this approach to moral education for purposes of constructing a curriculum. On the other hand, it appears to me that the philosophical, physiological, and psychological justification for defining the development of goodness, virtue, etc., in terms of rational cognitive reasoning is still very problematic.

There also may be some question as to whether Dewey and Piaget are really compatible bedfellows. There may be an epistemological problem since Dewey, to my knowledge, did not talk about genetic epistemology and the emergent biological structuring of experience in the manner (or at all?) of Piaget.

Kohlberg accepts a structuralist position in his insistence on the form of the rational moral discourse and his reported empirical data on the sequence of emergence of his stages. This combined with his "discovery" of universal moral categories of principles brings him much closer to a "realist's" position than his oft-stated identification with Dewey's pragmatism.

This appears also in the axiological implications of the theory. For example, are we to believe, as Dewey would have us, that value is created in terms of our actions in the world reflected upon in terms of their consequences? Or are there built-in (biologically structured) moral categories that will emerge in form (but vary in cultural substance) wherever human beings are? If so, our moral values are determined by more than the consequences of our action (although that might then be said to create the specific substance). Kohlberg seems to leave us with some puzzlement in relation to his axiological premises.

In terms of philosophical justification for the curriculum, there are questions that can be raised about the metaphysical, epistemological, and axiological positions and possible inconsistencies. At this point, it would be extremely difficult and not worth the effort to project possible changes in curriculum from differing assumptions (other than the traditional programs).

I would agree with Kohlberg (and Plato) that virtue is one (not a bag of characteristics like honesty, etc.). However, it is worth asking if virtue translates into justice in its highest and most general form. Kohlberg assumes this to be true. This is, in fact, the cornerstone of his theory and its educational implications. He presents both logical and empirical evidence of its validity.

Essentially, as you view the six stages and move up the ladder of moral reasoning, justice is the "end point" (defined as operating on principle out of respect for persons and their equality) and it is the only principle higher than the social contract with respect to the welfare of the community. Thus, the rule of law (democratically developed) can only be subject to one higher level—that of whether the spirit of the law (i.e., justice) is achieved. It is the final moral criterion and highest stage of moral reasoning. According to reported studies, empirical data validate the existence of moral choice and reason based on the principle of justice (as well as prudence, welfare of others, and respect for authority, self, and persons).

At some point in his work Kohlberg mentions that as far as he can discern, the only other candidate that philosophers have seriously proposed in place of justice as the highest virtue is compassion. He talks a little bit about love in this context, but gives it short shrift. "It (love) is primarily another stage 3 virtue label, not a guide to action."[16]

This may very well reflect intellectual, cultural, and biographical historical differences. Our ideas and theories are certainly influenced by our biographies. It is clear that justice is the cornerstone of Judaism, and Moses led the Israelites out of Egypt to "the promised land"—the kingdom of heaven on earth, the just society.

Jesus was another matter, and the message of love was the highest virtue. Without love, can there be justice? How else will we know what is just? The kingdom of heaven lies within and beyond rather than *in* the society and its structures, per se.

This represents a different orientation, the Christian tradition. Perhaps love is stage 7 if only in an implicit and intuitive manner; but in any case, it is not accounted for adequately by Kohlberg's theory.

William Kay[17] seems to agree in general with much of Kohlberg's orientation, although he only mentions his work briefly. However, he develops at length the idea that both rationality and altruism or a "rational-altruism" are necessary for a moral orientation in the personality, so that one responds to people with love and to problems with reasons. This seems to be a broader end point and a more satisfying understanding than Kohlberg's.

Joseph Fletcher[18] posits that love is always good and is the only norm. Thus, in place of Kohlberg's concept of justice, a moral development schema developed out of Fletcher's philosophical and theological position would substitute love as the highest and only intrinsic "good." Or, virtue is one and this is love. Fletcher probably would categorize Kohlberg's moral education as a legalistic approach, at least in terms of principles or categories of form, whereas Fletcher proposed a situational approach with love as the basic guide for interpreting what moral behavior is right in any given situation. We must do, in other words, the loving thing.

Fletcher also disputes Kohlberg's allegation that love is a stage 3 virtue by saying that love "is a 'formal' principle, expressing what types of real actions Christians are to call good (exactly the same as is true of justice)."[19] It is not a virtue at all; it is the "one and only regulative principle of Christian ethics."[20]

Love and justice are the same for Fletcher; love is justice and justice is love. As Paul Tillich says of love, "(it) is the ground, the power, and the aim of justice," and "love without justice is a body without a backbone." Justice, then, is Christian loving using its head, calculating its duties, obligations, opportunities, resources. Justice is love coping with situations where equality and the problems of distributive welfare come into play. Thus, justice is love distributed and nothing else. For Tillich, "love becomes the ultimate moral principle, including justice and transcending it at the same time."[21]

Carol Gilligan[22] presents a compelling argument attributing a male orientation to the Kohlberg theory. In general, she claims that justice and principled rationality (acting on) are male-assigned cultural virtues. Further, women in our culture may exhibit higher moral reasoning in other ways than this.

It is especially interesting to see her definition of female moral development along the major theme of compassion and love (caring and responsibility for others), plus her tying of morality to concrete contexts related to hurting others (nonviolence) as the highest moral category principle. One is reminded of Fletcher's situation ethics. In any case, Kohlberg's commitment to justice as the definition of virtue can be questioned legitimately.

I suggest that justice is a much more rationally manageable concept and one which has become so noticeably lacking in our contemporary arrangements of living together. This does not substitute, however, for an awareness that as a set of premises, commitment to justice as the highest virtue has not been satisfactorily justified.

What I would hate to think is that love as a phenomenon of human existence would be interpreted *after* the creation of Kohlberg's theory in terms of that theory. Whenever a reflection on a criticism is made in terms of the theory itself, you know the theoretician is in trouble. When Kohlberg says love is just a stage 3 virtue with no action implication, he is coming close to propounding a closed system which is characterized by reducing criticism to meaninglessness by using the system to refute it rather than dealing with it on a broader philosophical basis. Surely, love as a human quality, so clearly described by many persons, deserves more consideration in our concern for virtue.

When we arrive at consideration of the sociocultural justification for Kohlberg's moral education curriculum, we encounter the intellectual *piece de resistance.* It reflects some of the niftiest intellectual footwork in all of curriculum. In one fell swoop Kohlberg eliminates the dual problems of cultural relativism (ethical) and concrete absolutism. Thus, the so-called liberals who abhor specific moral dictates and the so-called conservatives who despise wishy-washy relativism both can be somewhat satisfied. It is not fair to call Kohlberg's position a compromise, but it has that effect.

Essentially, Kohlberg argues that his cross-cultural empirical studies reveal that there are universal (cross-cultural) categories of principle (justice, etc.), and that there are universal stages of development in these categories. On the other hand, his data tell him that although the form (in Piaget's terms) is universal, the substance is relative. That is, for example, the principle of justice may be expressed in a culturally relevant and specific form, whereas the substance per se will not be universal to all cultures.

These data allow him to refute the "bag of virtues" approach (along with other arguments) and also allow him to engage in a rationally constructed program of moral education rather than an implicit socialization process in schools. This is so because if the forms are universal but substance relative and if a person naturally prefers a higher level of rational explanation (an assumption Kohlberg offers), then moving people to higher levels of moral reasoning is not coercive. It is, in fact, facilitating their natural development and autonomy.

Further, Kohlberg clearly states that an effective moral educator "is something of a revolutionary rather than an instiller of virtues."[23] He says he stressed the revolutionary nature of moral education in that statement because it was comforting to think that it wasn't only America that killed its moral educators (e.g., Martin Luther King). He thinks that it is the men who are too *good* rather than those who preach hate and power that are assassinated.

I am not totally sure whether Kohlberg has escaped the relativism-absolutism problem, for I need much greater assurance through further anthropological or cross-cultural research, but I am willing to go along with it for now in the hope that he has. In general, his theoretical framework as a justification for the moral education curriculum is very appealing and intellectually satisfying.

Further, I do see Kohlberg's approach as basically liberating and not controlling. Although he rejects the A. S. Neill type "freedom" position and the Durheim-Russian "socialization" efforts, his approach is not part liberating and part controlling in a compromised sense. That it is fundamentally liberating may be illustrated in two ways.

To begin with, the virtue of justice as respect for persons and equality is a liberating principle. Thus, to reach the highest level of moral reasoning is to enter a perspective which is both liberating to the person and liberating to others through a person's acts. Further, the refusal to commit social definitions (honesty, etc.) to instructional formats, and the willingness to accept wide, substantive variations of the various forms of reasoning is a noncoercive and liberating procedure. In sum, it would appear that Kohlberg is correct when he refers to moral educators (from his theory) as revolutionaries, although there is grave reason to doubt that he is aware of the complex and long-range implications of this awareness.

This leads to an aspect of discourse that I have not found in Kohlberg's writing (perhaps it is somewhere). Although Kohlberg is aware of the *general* function of moral education in a society and talks about this in a number of places, he does not appear to connect the hidden curriculum with specific social structures. He does not seem to ask "in whose interest" is the traditional pattern of moral education.

In this, he is much like Phillip Jackson,[24] whom he quotes in a number of places, in that he appears to play a descriptively neutral role when he looks at the hidden curriculum. For instance, Jackson says crowds, power, praise are the critical descriptions of elementary classroom life but makes no effort to connect that school description with any broader social perspective. Similarly, Kohlberg seems to not consider the structural meaning of his moral educational curriculum in broader terms.

This can readily be seen by a paucity of report or comment on the nature and implication of social class differences in moral reasoning. According to Kay[25] the summary of a goodly number of research studies shows that higher social status is associated with greater moral maturity; and, equally, lower social status is associated with greater moral immaturity.

Kay[26] further discusses at length the idea of moral embourgeoisement; that is "the fact that our educational system should be engaged in introducing the best of our middle-class values to the whole community." He goes on to say, ". . . it is simply a recognition that the abundance of money, time, culture, concern and enlightened, educative experiences, both in the home and the school, ought to be equitably distributed."[27]

Whether or not one agrees with Kay he has at least recognized the problem. It is doubtful that Kohlberg has examined his moral development framework (or Piaget for that matter) in terms of its social class implication and potential role in educating the "lower classes."

Thus, Kohlberg is open to the radical social-structuralist critique that all developmentalists are open to when they focus primarily on individual development and do not integrate their approaches into a broader conceptualization of society. In this sense, it is possible that "moral education," sounding liberal, can be "used" by the power structure to ameliorate "problems" and maintain the present oppressive system. In any case, Kohlberg has not seen fit to present his thinking in any depth about the relationship of his program to the broader societal structures.

I think this is unfortunate, as much as I like and agree with this approach. It is very useful to be able to predict the kind of difficulties that will arise when connections to broader social structures are made.

It would, for example, not be fair to say that Kohlberg's moral education is anticapitalistic, yet it would be quite fair to say that exercising the highest moral reasoning in terms of justice will most assuredly bring us face to face with many positive aspects of social democracy (socialism). Under the circumstances, someone sometime may well label Kohlberg's moral education as communist inspired. Just being intelligent and rational won't solve that problem.

We should also be reminded that regardless of economic structures, there is no special reason growing out of self-interest why those in the power structure of societies or bureaucracies would be interested in a whole citizenry of persons exercising stage 6 moral reasoning. On the contrary, one reasonable hypothesis would be that the power structure would prefer people to operate on stage 3–4 conventional level in accepting the status quo, with the power structure justifying the status quo on a stage 5 contract basis. In neither case would stage 6 thinking be especially appreciated. It would, in fact, impose a terrible burden of dissent and trouble, undoubtedly resulting in a redistribution of power and resources. Consequently, it seems to me that the success of a Kohlberg curriculum may well necessitate political allies and alliances within and without the profession. The history of the progressive education movement would support this contention and suggest that moral education curricula need special political thinking.

COMPARED TO ALTERNATIVES

A short commentary appears to be in order on the Kohlberg moral education curriculum compared to the major alternatives available. The alternatives appear to me to be the teaching of specific virtues (bag of virtues) in an absolute sense; the indoctrination approach through hidden, implicit, or latent aspects of the environment; and the Simon-Raths value clarification procedures. In my judgment, the Kohlberg curriculum is far and away the sounder and better approach.

Considering a position in terms of its concrete alternatives is an important aspect of critique. Dealing with abstract intellectual problems is one viable and critical way of proceeding. In the long run, however, we must still ask what the *alternative* is, and this becomes part of the judgmental process in decision making.

I would accept Kohlberg's refutation of the bag-of-virtues approach when he says, as a psychologist, that we must object to the bag of virtues because there is no such thing. Virtues and vices, he goes on, are labels by which people award praise and blame to others, but these are not the ways people make moral decisions. Virtues, in other words, are not reality descriptions and, therefore, have little, if any, educational value.

An indoctrination approach, I think, should be rejected on three grounds: (1) it is not democratic, therefore it does not represent a model for a just society; (2) it is not rational and explicit, therefore it is not open to criticism and improvement; and (3) it is intended to control the individual in the service of the society. Any one of these reasons is enough for me in terms of my value perspective.

The real rival would appear to be the values-clarification approach. As Kohlberg says, "our approach differs from the values clarification approach, then, not in giving right answers but in operating under the assumption that some answers, or rather some reasons, are more adequate than others."[28]

This is, I believe, a real distinction between Kohlberg and Simon-Raths. There is an operational relativism in the Simon-Raths approach which tends to "hide" the ethical agenda of the clarifier. It implies some sort of Rogerian nondirective neutrality which is not really possible. The Kohlberg curriculum adds to the general concern for rational reflection about values found in value clarification, a commitment to universals and hierarchies of valued moral reasoning which are open and which give guidance and direction to activity in the moral education curriculum. In this sense Kohlberg represents a better alternative.

What is still left is the question of whether any moral education curriculum is justified at all (or at least any we know about). Kohlberg says yes because there will be a "moral" education going on no matter what we do in schools, as part of the hidden curriculum.

Even so, granting this point, it still doesn't answer the question of whether any of the alternatives are worthwhile. Relatively speaking, Kohlberg's may be best, but is it "good"?

This calls for a lengthy and involved answer which needs to be made. My own opinion at this point is yes and no. Yes, in relation to its accessibility to intellectual appraisal and its inner completeness and integrity; no, in relation to its limitations to formal reasoning in methods of development, methods of operation, and end points. In science this might not make a difference, but in matters of morality, this could effect a major disaster.

SUMMARY OF OPINIONS

In summary, the Kohlberg curriculum for moral education receives high marks. It is a complete curriculum in the sense of dealing with the relevant curriculum concerns; it is intellectually sound and pleasing in the sense that the justification given for curriculum decisions is well thought through. It is, of course, possible to disagree with a number of assumptions and premises along the way. Finally, the Kohlberg curriculum represents the best of the curriculum alternatives that are available.

The final comment here would be a word of caution. The moral education theory can easily become a closed system—constructive criticism of it can be thwarted by forcing an interpretation of critics' behavior "within" the theory. Further, the theory is an intellectual joy, but Kohlberg has not explored its political ramifications, nor has he explained to what extent it is socially and emotionally satisfying. I don't think we can afford to make the rational animal mistake over again. Thus, it remains to be seen how well the moral education curriculum in a "Just Community" can be put into practice. Let's hope it has great success. It probably will depend upon how *lovingly* the curriculum is employed.

NOTES

1. Special appreciation is extended to my colleagues, David Purpel and Charity James, who carefully critiqued earlier drafts of this chapter and helped considerably in the final outcome.

2. Herbert Kliebard, "Curriculum Theory: Give Me a 'For Instance,'" *Curriculum Inquiry,* Vol. 6, No. 4, 1977, pp. 257–268.

3. Lawrence Kohlberg, "Stages of Moral Development As a Basis for Moral Education," in C. M. Beck, B. S. Crittenden, and E. V. Sullivan (eds.) *Moral Education: Interdisciplinary Approaches,* Toronto: University of Toronto Press, 1971, p. 59.

4. Lawrence Kohlberg, "Moral Stages and Moralization", Chapter 2, in *Moral Development and Behavior,* Thomas Lickona, (ed.), Holt, Rinehart, Winston, 1976, pp. 31–53.

5. Lawrence Kohlberg, "Moral Development and the New Social Studies," in *Collected Papers on Moral Development and Moral Education.* Edited by L. Kohlberg, Harvard University, 1973.

6. Lawrence Kohlberg, "Development As the Aim of Education," *Harvard Educational Review,* 42 (4), November 1972.

7. Lawrence Kohlberg, "Continuities and Discontinuities in Childhood and Adult Moral Development Revisited," *Collected Papers on Moral Development and Moral Education.* Edited by L. Kohlberg, Harvard University, 1973.

8. Paul Tillich, *Morality and Beyond,* Harper Torchbooks, 1963.

9. Ibid., p. 64.

10. Robert Ornstein, *Psychology of Consciousness,* Penguin Books, 1972.

11. Michael Polanyi, *The Tacit Dimension,* Anchor Paperback, 1972.

12. Elizabeth Leonie Simpson, "A Holistic Approach To Moral Development and Behavior," *Moral Development and Behavior,* Chapter 9, edited by Thomas Lickona, Holt, Rinehart and Winston Co., 1976.

13. Ibid., pp. 168, 169.

14. Leslie Hart, "The New Brain Concept of Learning," *Phi Delta Kappan,* Feb., 1978, pp. 393–396.

15. Note: Kohlberg does discuss intellectual development as a *necessary* but not *sufficient* condition for moral reasoning. Thus, they are not seen as synonymous. The point here, however, is that both are correlated cognitive abilities.

16. Kohlberg, "Stages of Moral Development As a Basis for Moral Education."

17. William Kay, *Moral Education,* Unwin Books, 1975.

18. Joseph Fletcher, *Situation Ethics,* Westminster Press, 1966.

19. Ibid., p. 60.

20. Ibid., p. 61.

21. Tillich, p. 39.

22. Carol Gilligan, "In a Different Voice," *Harvard Educational Review* Vol. 47, No. 4, November 1977.

23. Lawrence Kohlberg, "Education for Justice," in *Moral Education,* edited by N. Sizer and T. Sizer, Cambridge: Harvard University Press, 1970, p. 65.

24. Phillip Jackson, *Life in the Classroom,* Holt, Rinehart, and Winston Co., 1968.

25. Kay.

26. Ibid., p. 154.

27. Ibid.

28. Lawrence Kohlberg, "Implications of Moral Stages for Problems in Sex Education," in *Collected Papers on Moral Development and Moral Education.* Edited by L. Kohlberg, Harvard University, 1973, p. 19.

Chapter 14

Moral Education: The Formalist Tradition and the Deweyan Alternative

ISRAELA ETTENBERG ARON

INTRODUCTION

The philosophical problems[1] raised by Lawrence Kohlberg's theory of moral development are of more than academic interest to educators, because Kohlberg and his colleagues have actively promoted the adoption of the theory as a basis for moral education programs in schools: "The educational conclusion we derive from the existence of universal stages of moral development . . . is that it is a valid and legitimate aim of education to stimulate the upward development of all children, to stage 6 if possible" (Kohlberg and Turiel 1971, p.440). Moral stimulation, Kohlberg claims, is different from indoctrination because it does not inculcate specific beliefs, but rather teaches the student a form of reasoning which develops naturally in the best moral thinkers: "The developmental approach to moral education is based not on social authority but upon the natural authority of the more advanced stage for the developing child" (ibid., p. 443).

Kohlberg's critics, however, disagree (see Alston 1971; Aron 1977; Bressler 1976; and Peters 1971). They argue that Kohlberg has failed to demonstrate that stage 6 ought to be the highest level of morality. To quote William Alston:

401

It is notorious that moral philosophers agree no more about what is distinctive of the moral than about anything else; and a large number of distinct accounts of what makes a judgment, a reason, an attitude, a rule, or a principle moral have been put forward. Kohlberg chooses one of these, but fails to do anything by way of showing that this is more than a choice of what seems most congenial or interesting to him. That is quite acceptable if it is just a matter of carving out a subject for empirical research. But if he wants to use the developmental approximations to the purely moral in his sense as a basis for pronouncements as to how people ought to reason in their action-guiding deliberations, that is another matter. If these pronouncements are to carry any weight, he will have to show that this sense of "moral" which is functioning as his standard has itself some recommendation other than congeniality to his predilections. [1971, pp.276–77]

Kohlberg's response to his critics has been to insist that his definition of morality is not simply one congenial to his predilections, but is grounded in a firm philosophical tradition, that of formalist moral philosophy.

A formalistic normative theory says, "Stage 6 is what it means to judge morally. If you want to play the morals game, if you want to make decisions which anyone could agree upon in resolving social conflicts, stage 6 is it."

In this connection, Alston's comment that "it is notorious that moral philosophers agree no more about what is distinctive of the moral than about anything else" is somewhat misleading. While there are an infinite variety of definitions of the moral, there is a fairly high degree of agreement among formalists as to the formal properties of moral judgment. Philosophers who offer alternative definitions of morality do so because they ignore formal features of morality, and define it instead in terms of the particular content of the normative theory they advocate. To my knowledge, those who object to a formalist definition of morality have no positive alternative to offer except (a) morality is what is in accord with my own system, or (b) morality is relative. Regardless of psychology, then, our conception of morality has a strong philosophical base. Anyone who tries to criticize it must provide a stronger positive alternative. [Kohlberg 1971, pp. 217–18]

In this article I wish to take up Kohlberg's challenge. In the first part I explore the contributions of the formalist tradition in moral philosophy, and discuss at length the problems which arise when the formalist approach is used as the entire basis for a theory of moral education. In the second part of the article an alternative ethical theory, that of John Dewey, is presented. Dewey's philosophical assumptions, I argue, provide a more adequate framework for values education.[2]

FORMALIST MORAL PHILOSOPHY

The term "formalist" has been used to describe the methods and assumptions underlying the works of contemporary moral philosophers such as R. M. Hare, William Frankena, R. S. Peters, and John Rawls. The philosophers thus classified do not by any means comprise a monolithic bloc; the differences between them are varied, serious, and complex. Nonetheless, they are united in their belief that morality may be described in purely formal terms, irrespective of its content. A judgment or action, according to the formalists, is moral if and only if it has certain formal characteristics—that is, if it conforms to certain criteria which are held, by the formalists, to define morality. Frankena gives the following description of this position:

The formalist maintains that there is something which may be called the moral point of view. This point of view can be described in purely formal terms— readiness to think and make practical decisions by reference to principles which one is willing to take as supreme, even in the light of the best available knowledge. A judgement, however it is worded, is moral only if it is made from this point of view, only if it is supported by reasons involving principles chosen in this spirit, whatever the content of these reasons may be. [Frankena 1963, p.8]

According to the formalist philosophers, what makes a judgment moral is that it rests on or derives from a principle or a set of principles which meet certain formal conditions or criteria.[3] These criteria are delineated and classfied in different ways by different philosophers. The condition that generally receives priority is universality; a moral principle satisfying this criterion would be applicable to all persons, irrespective of race, social class, sex, etc. This criterion thus assures that moral principles will be impartial and will not become the instruments of a dictator, a ruling elite, or a "master race." Philosophers who follow R.M. Hare consider universality to be the only formal condition by which the validity of a

moral principle should be tested. Others have proposed other requirements, such as that the only valid principles are those which
can be taken as supreme and overriding, or those which take into
account the welfare of society as a whole. John Rawls, for example,
proposes five formal criteria: generality, universality, ordering, finality, and publicity (Rawls 1971, pp. 130–36).

In an article of this scope and purpose it is obviously impossible
to do justice to the range and intricacy of the issues that arise within
the formalist camp itself. One issue, however, bears mentioning
because it is relevant to Dewey's philosophy and will be discussed
later on. This school is divided on the question of whether morality
should be considered primarily an individualistic or a social institution. Some formalist philosophers claim that a moral principle is
only valid if it is likely to be shared by others who adopt the "moral
point of view"; others argue that this condition is too stringent, that
it restricts the autonomy of the moral agent.

Variations, refinements, and disagreements notwithstanding, the
main thrust of the formalist tradition is straightforward, and its
attraction for those interested in values education is clear. The
emphasis on formal requirements for the validity of moral judgments neatly sidesteps the issue of indoctrination. Educators who
accept the formalist framework allegedly concentrate their efforts on
developing their students' ability to reason analytically, an ability
which, they claim, transcends particular contents. Kohlberg, for
example, states repeatedly that he is concerned with the form, not
the content, of moral reasoning. He seeks to remove his theory from
the arena of controversy in which most ethical discourse takes place.
He is not, he claims, attempting to inculcate particular values or
dispositions, but rather to strengthen the students' reasoning
capabilities.

LIMITATIONS OF THE FORMALIST APPROACH TO
MORAL EDUCATION

The importance of this tradition in moral philosophy is beyond
question. The issues raised by these philosophers have added a new

dimension to the study of ethical theory. These successes do not, however, insure equally felicitous results in the field of moral education, since moral philosophy and moral education differ in significant ways, as the theoretical differs from the practical. It is my contention that the assumptions and methodology of the formalist school, useful as they may be to the moral philosopher, impose certain limitations on the moral educator. In order to demonstrate these limitations, three corollaries of the formalist approach are discussed, together with their implications for educational practice.

The Separation of Metaethics and Normative Ethics

Contemporary philosophers commonly distinguish two subject areas which they term "normative ethics" and "metaethics." "Normative ethics" refers to the discussion of substantive moral issues, abstract or concrete, factual or hypothetical, common or esoteric. "Metaethics," on the other hand, is the discussion of ethical discussion itself; the analysis of ethical terms and the discussion of the functions of principles, rules, maxims, intuitions, and concrete judgments lie within the province of metaethics.

Philosophers have not always made so much of the distinction between the two levels of discourse. Although they were no doubt aware of the difference prior to the twentieth century, they slipped easily from one mode to the other. In Plato's dialogues, for example, the opening metaethical statements are examined in the light of substantive problems and are modified continually in the course of this examination. Even Kant, who wrote separate volumes on metaethics and normative ethics, considered them to be of equal importance. Although his most popular work today is his metaethical work, *Groundwork of the Metaphysic of Morals,* Kant himself considered this work to be a prelude to his normative ethical work, *Metaphysic of Morals.*[4]

The formalist philosophers, however, have occupied themselves almost exclusively with metaethics, since they hold that morality can be defined in terms of form alone, without entering into a discussion of its content. The concrete cases which appear in their writings are for purposes of illustration only and are usually limiting cases of one sort or another. They rarely deal with substantive ethical issues.

For most students of moral philosophy the absence of normative ethical discourse in the writings of these philosophers does not present a serious problem. They have had their share of firsthand experience with ethical problems and conflicts and thus have a store of concrete instances with which to illustrate and test out metaethical generalizations and abstractions. They have, in addition, a familiarity with the works of moral philosophers, playwrights, novelists, and social commentators who deal more extensively with normative issues; thus they have an additional fund of practical examples on which to draw. They can very quickly evaluate a metaethical abstraction with a series of appropriate test cases. For the student of moral philosophy, the abstract language of metaethics functions as a kind of shorthand, easily decoded and fleshed out.

In moral education, on the other hand, the situation is quite different. Students for whom programs of moral education are intended are relatively young and inexperienced; even those in college have had only a limited range of ethical choices to make. They are less likely to be familiar with a variety of moral problems and conflicts which adults face in their daily lives. These students need more than analytical reasoning skills; they need actual or vicarious experiences which will give substance and life to the abstractions of metaethics.

Kohlberg has not ignored this problem, and has tried to integrate normative ethical issues into his educational method in a way consistent with the formalist viewpoint. His solution involves the discussion of hypothetical moral dilemmas carefully structured to highlight conflicts between moral principles.[5] The problem with these dilemmas, however, is that they are so abstracted and oversimplified that they bear only a faint resemblance to actual human experience. For example, the Kohlberg dilemma most often quoted involves a conflict between the law against stealing and the principle of saving a human life:

In Europe, a woman was near death from cancer. One drug might save her, a form of radium that a druggist in the same town had recently discovered. The druggist was charging $2,000, ten times what the drug cost him to make. The sick woman's husband, Heinz, went to everyone he knew to borrow the money, but he could only get together about half of what it cost. He told the druggist that his wife was dying and asked him to sell it cheaper or let him pay later. But the druggist said, "No." The husband got desperate and broke into the man's store to steal the drug for his wife. Should the husband have done that? Why? [Kohlberg 1969, p.379]

This dilemma is simply too pat to be believed. In a comparable real-life situation, the contingencies would be less certain and much more ambiguous. The drug, for example, would have only a certain probability of saving the patient; its use, moreover, might well result in harmful side effects. Thus a decision would have to be made as to whether the cost and the risk involved were justified. Heinz might be able to get a loan (albeit at an exorbitant interest rate) or apply for public assistance. The druggist, in actuality, might not appear to be simply selfish. He would be more likely to have a complicated rationalization for charging such a high price. The high price might, moreover, be justified in the light of expenses and debts the druggist has incurred. Finally, the drug itself might be in short supply, and Heinz's wife might be only one of a number of individuals whose life would depend on its use.[6]

Without these complicating factors the Heinz dilemma is reduced to "a shallow melodrama . . . played by three stock characters, whose broad gestures signal the audience for whom to applaud, hiss, or weep" (Bressler 1976, p.6). How much can students learn by dealing with an abstract and artificially limiting case? From a discussion of cases like this, will they learn enough to deal with the infinitely more complex problems which arise in everyday life?

Kohlberg has tried to straddle the gap between metaethics and normative ethics by utilizing abstract and artificial limiting cases; he has stayed as close as possible to metaethics while still employing the case method. In doing so, however, he may be failing to equip his students with a method for dealing with the complexities of actual situations.

The "Autonomy of Moral Discourse"

A second corollary of the assumption that moral judgments are governed by a set of formal conditions is the notion that the domain of morality is unique, set apart from other domains. This concept is alluded to in Frankena's description of "the moral point of view" quoted above; formalist philosophers commonly formulate this notion as a claim for the "autonomy of moral discourse." The primary argument in support of this claim is that moral judgments, which contain prescriptive statements, are not entirely reducible to judgments in other realms, which are only descriptive. Thus, the "autonomy of moral discourse" implies a separation of the prescriptive from the descriptive, of facts from values, of the ideal from the real.

The issue of the autonomy of moral discourse has a long and controversial history. Fortunately, it is not necessary to enter into the controversy to point to the problem that arises when this notion is applied to moral education. The primary purpose of moral education is to increase the students' ability to make intelligent, thoughtful, and responsible choices in actual situations; and, in actuality, values are not so neatly separated from facts. Moral discussion which confines itself to questions of principle and avoids questions of fact is likely to become pedantic and sterile. Its ability to be illuminating to those who are grappling with genuine ethical problems is thus severely limited.

The shortcoming of this approach to moral education may be seen if we turn again to the Kohlberg dilemma quoted above. The Heinz dilemma is carefully structured to elicit a series of stock responses concerning principles, rules, obligations, and rights. As formulated by Kohlberg, the dilemma can be resolved in one of two ways: Heinz can steal the drug, or he can sit by while his wife dies. But a comparable dilemma occurring in real life would be open to a range of additional solutions. Heinz might organize a protest against the druggist; he might seek public assistance; he might, in addition, attempt to publicize the case and lobby for stricter governmental regulation of pharmaceuticals, for more research on cancer, or for local credit associations. The issues embedded in such a situation would go far beyond those of the moral principles involved; they would include questions pertaining to socialized medicine, the responsibility of doctors and druggists, and the policies of banks in granting loans.

If Kohlberg were to present to his students a case rich in plausible detail and which provided a context for the discussion of these issues, he would be going far beyond the confines of "morality" as defined by the formalists. He would, in fact, be undercutting the autonomy of moral discourse. But he would also be encouraging his students to think creatively, to explore new possibilities, to see human relationships as more than a zero-sum game. He would, in short, be educating responsible, ethical decision makers, as opposed to formalist moral philosophers.

Divorced from science, politics, art, law, and economics, morality becomes insular and rarefied. The separation of prescription and description into strictly defined and mutually exclusive categories reduces normative ethical discussion to an abstract recitation of principles.

The Equation of Justification and Decision Making

A final problem with the formalist approach lies in the preoccupation with justification of moral decisions as opposed to the process of decision making itself. For the moral philosopher concerned primarily with metaethics, the formalist emphasis on justification is highly appropriate; for the moral educator, on the other hand, the absence of any discussion of the process of decision making is problematic. If a program of moral education does not teach students about the process of making moral choices, is it not failing in a crucial respect? Is it sufficient to provide students with knowledge of principles and skills in analytical reasoning without assisting them in the task of bringing their knowledge and skills to bear on the actual process of decision making?

Kohlberg's view of the matter seems to be that decision making is equivalent to justification. According to Kohlberg, one ought to go about resolving a moral dilemma in the same way that one evaluates a proposed solution, namely, by enumerating the principles involved and deciding which principle should take precedence over the others. Kohlberg allows that emotional factors may motivate particular suggestions but holds that these factors are irrelevant to a determination of the correct solution.

I wish to argue that the process of decision making is, in actuality, quite different from after-the-fact justification. To paraphrase Dewey, ethical problems arising out of genuine situations do not present themselves neatly labeled and defined; they are a good deal more complex and confusing. When a problem is first recognized, it is likely to be characterized in different ways by different people. Each person's perceptions may be clouded in a different manner; emotional factors account for this difference, as do factual determinations.

Were justification equivalent to decision making, Kohlberg's dictum that the solution to a dilemma is not as important as the reasons which lie behind it would be acceptable. But in fact this notion is appropriate to academic discussion only. In real life, the reasons for our decisions are certainly important, but so are the decisions themselves. Because Kohlberg assumes that decision making is the same as justification, his methodology fails us when it comes to making actual choices which will have actual repercussions.

THE NEED FOR ALTERNATIVE APPROACHES

The difficulty of deriving appropriate directives for moral education from formalist moral philosophy is yet another instance of the problem of "the practical" discussed by Joseph Schwab (1970, 1971). In brief, the problem is that education is a practical field which can profit from the insights and data of a variety of disciplines: philosophy, psychology, sociology, economics, etc. Because of the way in which inquiry in these disciplines is structured, however, the knowledge of any one discipline and of any particular theory within that discipline is both partial and academic. Thus, the educator is faced with a paradox: inquiry in the social sciences and the humanities (at its present level of development, if not by its very nature) can proceed only through the delimitation and simplification of subject areas; but this process of limitation and simplification reduces the usefulness of these theories in the educational enterprise.

Schwab proposes that educators utilize a variety of competing theories to inform their practice. Since "truth" and "fact" are—given the present state of the social sciences—contextual, educators must be able to work with a number of diverse, even conflicting, truths, to borrow knowledge from a variety of contexts. This task is arduous and complex and is fraught with pitfalls, but, if Schwab's analysis is correct, it is unavoidable.

Thus, those interested in moral education must turn to moral philosophies outside the formalist tradition. They must try to complement the formalist approach with insights and directives from competing ethical theories. If the foregoing critique of the formalist approach is valid, the alternatives will have to be particularly strong in three respects: they will have to lend themselves to dealing with normative ethics, they will not separate morality from other domains, and they will deal with the process of ethical decision making itself rather than with the justification of past decisions. One likely candidate, which deserves more attention from moral educators than it has received, is the moral philosophy of John Dewey, to which we now turn.

DEWEY'S ETHICAL THEORY

Dewey's ethical theory, once much discussed in philosophical and educational circles, has, over the past forty years, receded from public view. It seems particularly appropriate to reintroduce it at this point, since it has a great deal to contribute to values education, being strongest in precisely those areas in which the formalist tradition is weakest.

Dewey's primary concern is with the process of ethical decision making. One of the core concepts in his philosophy is that of "an experience," the interaction of the living creature with its environment. His claim is that the same basic pattern characterizes all human experience, including that of survival, artistic creation, aesthetic appreciation, scientific inquiry, and day-to-day decision making (Dewey 1958, pp. 35–57). In each instance, different aspects of the basic pattern are emphasized; in aesthetic appreciation, for example, the emphasis is on the emotional quality of the experience, whereas in scientific inquiry the emphasis is on the symbolic manipulations and intellectual maneuvers in which the inquirer engages. In day-to-day decision making the emphasis is on the outcome, the decision. The class of experiences occasioned by practical problems or conflicts and governed by the need to reach a definite conclusion or decision is termed by Dewey "practical deliberation."

Dewey defines practical deliberation as "a dramatic rehearsal (in imagination) of various competing lines of action" (Dewey 1930, p. 179). Human beings, in his view, normally act according to habits, acquired predispositions which they follow without reflection. In problematic situations, however, prior habits fail the individual in some way. Perhaps they no longer satisfy his or her desires; perhaps two habits conflict and a choice must be made between them. The result is a temporary suspension of action, during which there is an opportunity for reflection. "There is but one issue involved in all reflection upon conduct: the rectifying of present troubles, the harmonizing of present incompatibilities by projecting a course of action which gathers into itself the meaning of them all" (Dewey 1930, p. 196). It is important to emphasize Dewey's contention that deliberation can only arise out of concrete and actual dilemmas and conflicts. Only if the problem is felt can deliberation come to a satisfactory conclusion.

Deliberation begins with the formulation of the issue, the conversion of the preliminary sense of indeterminacy into a stated problem. This first step is crucial, since the statement of the problem determines the form of proposed solutions. The initial formulation need not remain fixed, however; at a later stage the deliberator may decide that the situation is best defined in a different way.

Once the problem is formulated, the task of the deliberator is to actively entertain as many solutions as possible. He or she must consider a broad range of possible actions and must imagine the results of each. The competing lines of action cannot, according to Dewey, be evaluated by an a priori or abstract standard (such as an

ultimate principle), but must be assessed in terms of their consequences. These consequences must be construed broadly; not only
direct and immediate results, but also indirect and long-term ones,
must be taken into account. There is not one consequence of an act
but a plurality of consequences. Moreover, the consequences of an
act include the effects it will have on the character of the deliberator
as well as its effects on the physical and social environment.

The forecasting of consequences is a delicate operation, requiring
knowledge of one's physical surroundings, the society, human nature in general, and one's own character in particular. It often
involves a search for new knowledge. The more acute the deliberator's assessment of human nature and dispositions, the more
accurate will be his or her projection of consequences. A memory of
the outcomes of comparable actions and decisions is an important
aid in deliberation; yet the deliberator must bear in mind the possibility that conditions have changed. Principles and ideals, too, are
useful tools for deliberation, for they represent the results, in summary form, of age-old deliberations. Precisely because of their long
history, however, certain principles or rules may be outdated, not
suitable for current situations. Thus the deliberator must be aware
of the need to modify and readapt traditional principles and rules.

The forecasting of consequences is continually endangered by the
biases of both habit and desire. "We see what we want to see, we
obscure what is unfavorable to a cherished, probably unavowed,
wish. We dwell upon favoring circumstances till they have become
weighted with reinforcing considerations. We don't give opposing
consequences half a chance to develop in thought" (Dewey 1930,
p. 228). The deliberator must be constantly on guard against the
biases which may distort his or her perception of consequences.

Once the consequences of as many different courses of action as
possible have been projected, how is the final decision reached? At
this point, Dewey's account differs most sharply from those of most
philosophers, for Dewey claims that one cannot know the correctness of a decision intellectually. Instead, he says, one feels the
desirability of a consequence, one experiences the appropriateness of
a particular choice. Just as one's feelings of confusion or conflict give

rise to the deliberation, so one's feelings of unity, harmony, and resolution are an indication that is has terminated successfully. This is not to say that the doubt arises from subjective factors alone; Dewey states explicitly that genuine problems arise from indeterminacies that are objective characteristics of situations. Yet the deliberator can only sense an indeterminacy through direct and immediate perception; he or she does not know there is a problem in the sense that one knows a fact. Likewise, though the solution of a problem is an objective occurrence, the feelings attendant upon it are the best indicators of its appropriateness. Once the deliberator knows the reasons for and against different courses of action, he or she can feel that a particular one is most appropriate. "Complacency and annoyance follow hard on the heels of any object presented in image as they do upon its sensuous experience. Some objects when thought of are congruent to our existing state of activity. They fit in, they are welcome. They agree, or are agreeable, not as a matter of calculation, but as a matter of experienced fact" (Dewey 1930, p. 188). The fact that one can experience the correctness of a choice explains why Dewey refers to deliberation as a "dramatic rehearsal."

The feeling of harmony and unity which comes at the close of a successful deliberation is qualitatively different from the feeling of a momentary or chance pleasure. "Enjoyments that issue from conduct directed by insight into relations have a meaning and validity due to the way in which they are experienced. Such enjoyments are not repented of; they generate no aftertaste of bitterness. Even in the midst of direct enjoyment, there is a sense of validity, of authorization, which intensifies the enjoyment. There is a solicitude for perpetuation of the object having value, which is radically different from the mere anxiety to perpetuate the feeling of enjoyment" (Dewey 1930, p. 267). Thus, experienced deliberators come to have a sense of confidence in their ability to perceive directly and immediately that a particular consequence is desirable. Likewise, with experience, deliberators may learn to be more accurate in their estimation of consequences; they also learn what their particular biases are and in what ways these biases are likely to prejudice their deliberations. Of course, even the best of deliberations may fail to foresee a particular consequence, and a course of action decided upon may prove, in the end, to have been mistaken. This possibility is unavoidable. Yet in most cases a careful attention to consequences, the anticipatory generation of alternatives, and a diligent avoidance of prejudices will result in judgments and actions that will not be regretted later.

TWO COROLLARIES OF DEWEY'S POSITION

Two corollaries of Dewey's conception of practical deliberation are worth spelling out in detail, since they point up the differences between him and the formalist philosophers. First, in his discussion of practical deliberation, no separation is made between moral and nonmoral decisions, since deliberation itself is simply a form of inquiry with a special emphasis. Dewey takes strong exception to the notion that morality is an autonomous domain with its own criteria for the adequacy of judgments. "Morals has to do with all activity into which alternative possibilities enter. For wherever they enter a difference between better or worse arises. . . . Potentially every and any act is within the scope of morals, being a candidate for possible judgment with respect to its better-or-worse quality" (Dewey 1930, pp.257–58).

The second corollary of Dewey's position is that metaethical discussion alone is of limited value, and that normative ethical discussion should focus on concrete problems or conflicts. "A theory of valuation *as* theory can only set forth the conditions which a method of formation of desires and interests must observe in concrete situations. . . . It does not purport to solve the problems of valuation in and of itself; it does not claim to state conditions that inquiry must satisfy if these problems are resolved, and to serve in this way as a leading principle in the conduct of such inquiries" (Dewey 1966, pp. 57–58). The task of the moral philosopher in the Deweyan tradition, then, is to consider actual cases in the context in which they arise and to draw from these deliberations certain generalizations and methodological rules regarding the process of deliberation itself. "An actual theory can be completed only when inquiries into things sustaining the relation of ends-means have been systematically conducted and their results brought to bear upon the formation of desires and ends. For the theory of valuation is itself an intellectual or methodological means and as such can be developed and perfected only in and by use" (Dewey 1966, pp. 53–54).

THE DEWEYAN APPROACH TO MORAL EDUCATION

The task of translating Dewey's theory into a series of programs for moral education is a formidable one. Some curricular suggestions have been made in a number of specialized contexts (Aron 1975; Cohen 1974), but the bulk of the task remains to be done. Nevertheless, it would be useful to sketch briefly the outlines of a Deweyan approach, if only to see the ways in which this approach would differ from currently fashionable alternatives.

This approach to moral education would be premised on Dewey's contention that educational efforts must be grounded in the experiences of the students. Thus, in order to teach students to deliberate, one would give them a great deal of practice in deliberation. Student deliberations might concern actual situations or they might be based on fictional or hypothetical case materials. A case study involving an ethical decision would be presented to the class, and the task of the students would be to deliberate and to arrive at a defensible decision for one or more of the actors in the situation. Within this context, the teacher might emphasize the principles and ideologies which lie behind various choices, and which will often conflict with one another. But in each case the process of deliberation would be exemplified in full, from the formulation of the problem to the final choice of a solution.

The cases to be used in the teaching of deliberation might be taken from a variety of sources, fictional as well as nonfictional. Not all materials, however, would be equally appropriate. There are a number of requirements which would have to be met in order for a case to qualify as the subject matter of deliberation.[7] First the case would have to be emotionally compelling: the students would have to feel that there was a genuine problem worthy of their attention; that there was a need for a definite decision; and that they had a stake in the decision. Although the deliberations would generally pertain to a matter removed from the students' immediate concerns, the students would have to feel some of the emotional force of the problem, enough, at least, to motivate them to attend carefully to the various alternatives, and to search diligently for the best solution. The success of the teacher in focusing the attention of the students and in harnessing their energies in service of a particular problem would depend, in part, upon the teacher's knowledge of the students.

A second requirement for the teaching of deliberation would be that enough details of the case be available so that the students could project the consequences of a variety of alternatives. The case, in other words, would have to be a reasonable facsimile of an actual situation; it might be fictional, but it could not be sketchy or stereotyped. The students would have to be able to obtain considerable information concerning the characters, their historical circumstances, social conditions, etc.[8] This is not to say that all this information would be presented to the students at the outset; rather, it would be made available to them as the need arose. The ease or difficulty with which such information might be retrieved is a variable which could be controlled by the teacher. In some situations, and with certain students, the information might be placed, at the outset, in a data bank, upon which the students might draw directly. In other situations, students might be required to do research in order to obtain the information.

A third requirement for the teaching of deliberation concerns the degree of definition given to the problem at the outset. It has been noted that the formulation of the problem is, in itself, part of the process of deliberation. Dewey's assumption is that actual problems are perceived only vaguely at first. The definition of the problem is a first step in deliberation, a step which may be retraced at a later point, when a different formulation of the problem is found to be more appropriate. Thus, the materials presented to the students should not be overdefined. The first question, "What is the problem?" should not be a giveaway. Again, the optimal degree of definition would vary according to the ability of the students and their experience in deliberation. In the early stages problems which are more defined might be more appropriate, while in the later states problems which are less defined would be preferable.

Within the general area of problematic ethical and political situations, any case study which met the above requirements would potentially be appropriate for use in the teaching of deliberation. The preparation of case materials is, however, difficult and time consuming, and materials for deliberation might well be adapted from a variety of sources: the Oliver-Shaver (1966) Public Issues Curriculum, for example, contains cases suitable for this purpose, as does the Hart and Sacks (1958) Law Curriculum. Novels such as Robert Penn Warren's *All the King's Men* and Tom Wicker's *Facing the Lions* provide excellent source materials, as do films such as Maximilian Schell's *The Pedestrian* and Bertrand Tavernier's *The Clockmaker*. In addition, legal controversies with broad moral and political implications, such as the DeFunis case, the Karen Ann Quinlan case, and various cases involving busing to achieve racial integration, would be easy to use; some of these would have the added advantage of allowing the students to take action in accordance with their decisions.

The choice of materials for deliberation and the manner in which deliberation is taught would vary according to particular characteristics of the students, with the most obvious factors being age and intellectual ability. For younger students, who have had less personal experience in decision making, and less need of a methodology for decision making, the teaching of deliberation might well be more schematic and less rigorous. It would seem inappropriate, in a high school setting, to devote a whole course to deliberation. Instead, instances of deliberation could be taken up in connection with social studies and history (using, for example, the Oliver-Shaver materials) or in a general humanities course (using fictional or dramatic cases). In college settings, on the other hand, the students' need for a method of decision making increases, as does their ability to utilize it, and an entire course devoted to deliberation would be appropriate.

The intellectual ability of the students would determine the complexity of the cases to be considered. The more capable the student of digesting and ordering quantities of information, and of reasoning from principles to concrete circumstances, the more complex would be the cases that could be considered. When the students' powers of analysis could not be taken for granted, the cases utilized would have to be a good deal simpler, involving fewer options, fewer competing principles, and more predictable consequences. With practice, the students would improve in their ability to generate alternatives, weigh principles, and predict consequences, and would be ready to deliberate on more complex issues.

The extent to which students were dependent or independent, cooperative or competitive, is another variable which would also influence the way in which deliberation would be taught. In situations in which students were generally highly competitive, the teacher would do well to emphasize the corporate nature of deliberation, and to encourage group deliberations. The aim of cooperation, however, must be balanced against the aim of developing independent judgment. In situations in which students were more docile and tended to accept uncritically the opinions of others, the teacher would do well to encourage the students to exercise and evaluate their own judgments.

Finally, there are a host of student characteristics, such as social class, religion, ethnicity, location, and sex, which the teacher or curriculum writer should take into account in selecting case materials for deliberation. Here, too, two principles must be kept in a delicate balance: the need for the students to find the materials relevant and compelling, and the desirability of stretching the students' field of experience. Case materials could be chosen to answer both needs; students could be given practice in deliberating as both men and women, tenants and landlords, parents and children, voters and politicians, etc. Giving students the opportunity to imagine themselves in situations which are foreign to them would have the added advantage of putting to the test some of the ideologies and principles which they take for granted, and, consequently, of making them less dogmatic in their thinking.

The greatest temptation for the teacher of deliberation would be to break up the process of deliberation into a number of smaller components and fashion out of them a series of mechanical exercises. The process of inquiry outlined by Dewey in *How We Think* has been treated in this fashion innumerable times, with uniformly disappointing results. This reductionist and disjointed strategy destroys the organic unity of the process of deliberation and makes deliberation abstract and academic.

LIMITATIONS OF THE DEWEYAN APPROACH

The emphasis in this paper on the strengths of Dewey's philosophical position should not be taken as an indication that this approach has no shortcomings. In fact, Dewey's ethical theory seems to have a serious limitation in that it endorses a highly individualistic morality. If one accepts Dewey's contentions that moral discussion should focus on decision making in concrete cases rather than on abstract rule making and justification, and that, ultimately, moral choice, though informed by rational considerations, is best made by a reliance on direct emotional perception, then morality becomes an individualistic endeavor. In a concrete deliberation no one but the deliberator is in a position to ascertain how he or she will feel about alternative outcomes. It seems likely, then, that occasions will arise in which two deliberators in similar circumstances will choose different courses of action. A more formidable problem is raised by cases in which the actions of a group of people are in question. Group deliberation is not guaranteed to yield consensus; on the contrary, Dewey's emphasis on the emotional factor in moral choice all but guarantees that different deliberators will arrive at different decisions.

Thus, Dewey's ethical theory strips morality of its prescriptive power. A recognition of this has led some critics to charge that

Dewey's ethical theory is relativistic. But Dewey's position is not that of a relativist, who claims that all questions of value are mere matters of opinion and are not worthy of serious discussion and consideration.[9] On the contrary, he holds that inquiry into ethical issues is of utmost importance. Although he assigns a crucial role to the emotions in the process of deliberation, he never claims, as do the emotivists, that there is no place for rationality in the process of valuation. Dewey would, however, agree with the emotivists that a primary function of ethical discourse is that of persuasion. While the ethical deliberation of one individual does not bind others to the same decision, there is always the possibility of influencing others through discussion and debate.

Dewey's denial of the prescriptive power of moral judgments seems to be the most troublesome aspect of his ethical theory. But what, in actuality, is the prescriptive power commonly attributed to moral judgments? Consider the following hypothetical case: a friend of mine plans to do something that I consider to be immoral; what means are at my disposal for persuading him or her? Following Dewey's methodology I conduct a deliberation with my friend. Together we project the consequences of the proposed action and examine these consequences in the light of various principles and ideals. Suppose, however, that at the end of the discussion my friend and I are still in disagreement. Is there anything to be gained by my saying, at this point: "But it is *immoral* to do what you are planning, as you will be directly violating certain moral principles!" Will this final appeal really strengthen my case? Should it, moreover, represent an added imperative?

If my assertion that the act in question is immoral does change my friend's mind, it is likely that the change will have been caused by emotional rather than strictly rational factors. In the first place, my claim might serve as an indication to my friend of the degree to which the proposed action disturbs me. In the second place, my claim might serve as an appeal to my friend's vanity or fears; it would be tantamount to saying, "What would so-and-so think of you if they knew you did that?" But beyond the merely rhetorical force of my claim that the act is immoral, what could it add to the rational process of deliberation which already has been undertaken? Does the use of a moral imperative in this case have any additional bearing on the rational decision-making process? I think not.

Moral judgments can have a prescriptive power only within a unified moral community. When the preservation of a unified and harmonious community is of value to its members, individual members will have a strong reason for taking account of each other's opinions and acting accordingly; this system of mutual accommodation and compromise might come to be embodied in a set of shared principles. In the absence of a unified community, however, the moral principles adhered to by one individual have as much force for others as the laws of a foreign country. Such moral principles might arouse a certain curiosity and interest, but they will not be perceived as imperatives for action.[10]

The problem in our own age, of course, is that there are few unified moral communities. A group of young men may be unified in their adherence to principles related to conscientious objection; but how many of their fathers and mothers will accept these principles above others? Furthermore, this very group of conscientious objectors may well be divided with respect to other moral issues. How many of us have friends with whom we are in substantial agreement on a wide range of moral issues?

Dewey's moral theory is highly appropriate to contemporary individuals precisely because it recognizes the complex nature of our society and does not hold onto an image of a past era when life was a good deal simpler. Dewey's theory is individualistic because our society, ultimately, is individualistic. A moral commitment proclaimed by one group carries less weight when a second group is proclaiming, just as vociferously, an opposing moral imperative.

Dewey himself was extremely disturbed by the atomization of contemporary society, and devoted an entire volume to this subject. Whether or not we agree with the diagnosis put forth in *The Public and Its Problems* (1927) and whatever our reactions to the solutions he proposes in that work, we cannot deny that our society is, at present, highly polarized and fragmented. There are those who hope to ameliorate this condition by establishing moral imperatives. My own opinion (and Dewey's, I believe) is that moral judgments can only function as imperatives when they are shared by all or most of the members of a true community of interests.

In the absence of such a community, however, individuals are not entirely at sea. Those who employ Dewey's method of practical deliberation will be led to consider the effects of their actions on others and on the society at large. While this will not lead to a total consensus, it should increase cooperation between individuals, and may, in fact, represent a first step in the formation of a moral community.

THE NEED FOR AN ECLECTIC APPROACH TO MORAL EDUCATION

In a previous article (1977), I argued that moral education cannot be limited to the adoption of a particular curriculum or technique, since each approach has both advantages and disadvantages. In this article, I have tried to extend this argument to include the philosophical theories which underlie particular approaches to moral education. I have tried to show that the formalist philosophical tradition is limited in a number of ways, and that those concerned with values education would do well to consider the philosophical position of Dewey in this respect. It seems likely that other philosophical positions, from the Platonic and Aristotelian to the existentialist, would serve to enrich our conception of moral education even further and would complement both the formalist and the Deweyan approaches in ways we cannot yet specify but may well imagine. A thorough examination of some of these ethical theories, with an eye to their implications for moral education, would be most welcome.

It is not my intention to advocate the rejection of the formalist approach in toto or the dismissal of Kohlberg's techniques and materials. Rather, I have argued for a more critical and open approach; at this stage, values educators would do best to pick and choose from among valuable approaches and to develop their own curricular materials and strategies to supplement them. This mode of operation is often dismissed out of hand as a "mindless eclecticism." It is certainly eclectic, but it need not be mindless. In his writings on "the practical," Schwab has outlined some of the arts and techniques by which several theoretical perspectives can be brought to bear on a practical problem. The "arts of eclectic," as he terms them, involve, for the scholar, an analytical approach to subject matters and a detailed knowledge of the philosophical underpinnings of particular theories. For the teacher and curriculum writer, an eclectic approach requires flexibility, a tolerance for complexity, a willingness to experiment, and a willingness to acknowledge the number of failures which inevitably will occur.

This may sound like an impossible requirement of both teachers and scholars in education. Certainly a task which requires constant criticism of accepted knowledge and practices and continual research into new areas is a difficult and demanding one. But it is the only reasonable and viable course of action in a field in which the issues are complex and the answers not readily forthcoming. The history of American education is replete with instances of short-lived innovations. Unless moral education is viewed in a more critical and judicious light, unless its complexity is honored, it will be doomed to failure along with the innumerable fads and fancies which come and go with depressing regularity.

NOTES

1. Some of the material contained in this chapter appeared in the author's article, "Moral Philosophy and Moral Education II. The Formalist Tradition and the Deweyan Alternative." *School Review* 85 (1977): 513–534.

2. Throughout this paper the terms "ethics," "values," and "morals" are used interchangeably, contrary to contemporary philosophical conventions. A majority of contemporary philosophers, in adherence to the formalist tradition, use the term "morality" for an even more restricted sphere concerned with obligations, rights, and duties. One of the contentions of this paper, however, is that the formalist position is not the only one available to moral educators; hence, the term "ethics" and "morals" will be construed broadly, in accordance with the Deweyan tradition.

3. It should be noted that the words "rests on" and "derives from" are highly ambiguous. The nature of the relationship between principles and particular judgments is an issue which divides the formalists (see Boyd 1976, pp. 37–44).

4. For a discussion of this point see Kemp (1968, p. 73).

5. This is not Kohlberg's only approach, but it has been, thus far, the dominant method employed by his colleagues and students. Kohlberg has lately begun to see the limitations of this approach and has proposed the notion of "the school as a just community" (Wasserman 1976). However, the discussion of moral dilemmas remains the most popular means of implementing Kohlberg's approach and is the only method for which curricular materials are currently available.

6. I am indebted to Martin Bressler (1976, p. 6) for several of these observations.

7. Much of the following discussion is based on Schwab's treatment of deliberation in *College Curriculum and Student Protest* (1969, pp. 148–173).

8. Information on the consequences of various alternatives, on the other hand, deliberately should be kept incomplete.

9. There are, of course, many forms of ethical relativism. The most serious charge of relativism, and that with which I am concerned here, is described by John Ladd (1963) as "destructive ethical relativism."

10. For a cogent discussion of this point, see Aiken (1963, pp. 95–105).

REFERENCES

Aiken, H.D. "The Concept of Moral Objectivity." In *Morality and the Language of Conduct,* edited by H.N. Castaneda and G. Nakhnikian. Detroit: Wayne State University Press, 1963.

Alston, William. "Comments on Kohlberg's 'From Is to Ought.'" In *Cognitive Development and Epistemology,* edited by T. Mischel. New York: Academic Press, 1971.

Aron, Israela. "Curricular Proposals for the Ethical and Political Education of Adolescents: Overcoming Dogmatism and Relativism and Teaching Deweyan Deliberation." Ph.D. dissertation, University of Chicago, 1975.

Aron, Israela. "Moral Philosophy and Moral Education: A Critique of Kohlberg's Theory." *School Review* 85 (1977): 197–217.

Boyd, Dwight. "Education towards Principled Moral Judgment: An Analysis of an Experimental Course in Undergraduate Moral Education Applying Lawrence Kohlberg's Theory of Moral Development." Ph.D. dissertation, Harvard University, 1976.

Bressler, Martin. "Kohlberg and the Resolution of Moral Conflict." *New York University Education Quarterly* 7 (1976): 2–8.

Cohen, Burton. "Criteria for Developing Proposals for the Teaching of Deliberation." Ph.D. dissertation, University of Chicago, 1974.

Dewey, John. *The Public and Its Problems.* Chicago: Swallow Press, 1927.

Dewey, John. *Human Nature and Conduct.* New York: Modern Library, 1930 (originally published 1922).

Dewey, John. *Art as Experience.* New York: Capricorn Books, 1958 (originally published 1934).

Dewey, John. *Theory of Valuation.* International Encyclopedia of Unified Science, vol. 2, no. 4. Chicago: University of Chicago Press, 1966 (originally published 1939).

Frankena, William. "Recent Conceptions of Morality." In *Morality and the Language of Conduct,* edited by H.N. Castaneda and George Nakhnikian. Detroit: Wayne State University Press, 1963.

Hart, Henry, and Sacks, Albert. "The Legal Process: Basic Problems in the Making and Application of Law." Mimeographed. Cambridge, Mass.: Harvard University, 1958.

Kemp, John. *The Philosophy of Kant.* Oxford: Oxford University Press, 1968.

Kohlberg, Lawrence. "Stage and Sequence: The Cognitive Developmental Approach to Socialization." in *Handbook of Socialization Theory and Research,* edited by D.A. Goslin. New York: Rand McNally & Co., 1969.

Kohlberg, L. "From Is to Ought: How to Commit the Naturalistic Fallacy and Get Away with It in the Study of Moral Development." In *Cognitive Development and Epistemology,* edited by T. Mischel. New York: Academic Press, 1971.

Ladd, John. "The Issue of Relativism." *Monist* 47 (1963): 585–609.

Oliver, Donald P., and Shaver, James P. *Teaching Public Issues in the High School.* Boston: Houghton Mifflin Co., 1966.

Peters, R.S. "Moral Development: A Plea for Pluralism." In *Cognitive Development and Epistemology,* edited by T. Mischel. New York: Academic Press, 1971.

Rawls, John. *A Theory of Justice.* Cambridge, Mass.: Harvard University Press, 1971.

Rest, James. "Developmental Psychology as a Guide to Values Education: A Review of Kohlbergian Programs." *Review of Educational Research* 44 (1974): 241–59.

Schwab, Joseph J. *College Curriculum and Student Protest.* Chicago: University of Chicago Press, 1969.

Schwab, Joseph J. *The Practical: A Language for Curriculum.* Washington, D.C.: National Education Association, 1970.

Schwab, Joseph J. "The Practical: Arts of Eclectic." *School Review* 79 (1971): 493–542.

Wasserman, Elsa. "Implementing Kohlberg's 'Just Community Concept' in an Alternative High School." *Social Education* 40 (1976): 203–207.

Part VII

POSTSCRIPT: UPDATING KOHLBERG'S POSITIONS AND RESPONSE TO THE ISSUES

Chapter 15

Kohlbergian Forms and Deweyan Acts: A Response

BILL PUKA

INTRODUCTION

There are complex relationships among the philosophical, psychological, and educational aspects of Kohlbergian theory. Many have applauded Kohlberg's attempt to march into moral development on all these fronts at once. Yet it is often objected that in following the lead of a formalistic and rule-oriented metaethic, the projected Kohlbergian advance has been deflected off course. For example, in this book Aron, Munsey, and Rosen criticize the leadership of formalism, and campaign for a Deweyan, pragmatic alternative. We should like to discuss the pros and cons of their sophisticated critiques.[1]

Several comments can be made about their accounts, taken together. First, their attention to the subtleties of real-life moral decisions and their call for most precise decision procedures and skills is a welcome complement to the Kohlbergian approach. The focus of Kohlbergians has been on cognitive structure more than on skill, on justification more than decision making. This focus seems most appropriate for assessing and stimulating natural development, in the Piagetian sense, and for avoiding indoctrinative education. An ideally complete approach to moral psychology and education will concentrate more intently on decision-making skills, as well as on ego strength and moral conduct. It is a mistake, we believe, to see such concerns as incompatible or even out of spirit with Kohlberg. Such a misconception is likely to arise where the role of formalism in Kohlberg's theory is grossly exaggerated, as it has been in the critiques of Aron, Munsey, and Rosen.

It is predictable that Deweyan critics would exaggerate the influence of formalism in Kohlberg, given their specialized conception of the nature of moral theory. Each of their metaethical critiques begins with the assertion that a necessary or primary role of normative ethical theory is to render singular justified moral judgments. Rosen sees normative theory as a "device" enabling people to arrive at such judgments. This position does not distinguish the role of a decision procedure which generates judgments from the role of a justification procedure which determines which judgments or decision procedures are valid. As these critics themselves point out, the primary aim of moral theory in the formalist tradition is explanation and justification, not decision making. The principles of such theories are meant to embody the underlying rationale of our most indubitable moral judgments. The metaethical criteria which these principles fulfill are meant to help justify or explicate their form.

When comparing formalistic rule-theory with the pragmatic, act-theory alternative, these critics use concrete and detailed decision making as the primary if not sole criterion of adequacy. They argue that formal rules cannot render accurate (justified) decisions because they are not amply sensitive to the situational contingencies of real-life dilemmas; more detailed methods of practical deliberation are needed. As might be expected and will be discussed, the pragmatic, act-theory approach is much better at decision making than it is at justification or explanation. It seems to approach justification as a facet of decision making. A fair comparison of formalism with pragmatism would consider their relative adequacy in each of these areas, with regard to these two different approaches to justification, unless it could be shown that the decision-making variety is of overriding importance. This is unlikely. Normally we approach theory building in any area of philosophy with most of our data, our particular beliefs, in hand. We seek a fundamental explanation of these beliefs to increase our understanding of their logic, to expose their underlying laws. This is especially true of theorizing on the meta-level. We seek a justification of these beliefs, also, to help ensure against arbitrariness or prejudice as well as to resolve certain usually narrow areas of controversy or uncertainty. If we were concerned almost exclusively with this last issue or with particularizing our moral beliefs to fit the novelties of particular situations, it would hardly seem sensible to construct a philosophical theory, especially at the meta-level. Some more rough and ready devices, a few rules of thumb, a recipe, a set of procedures would be more appropriate. If these were questioned, there might be some need to go deeper into the logic of morality.

To make their case, Aron, Munsey, and Rosen must show a) that a justification procedure must be a decision procedure or b) that it is impossible for formal rules to be constructed which could capture all the distinctively moral elements of concrete moral decisions or c) that a formalist theory cannot utilize a decision procedure containing significantly nonformalist elements. None of these points has been shown. While Aron and Munsey overlook Kohlberg's ideal role-taking decision procedure in their attack on formal rules, Rosen criticizes Kohlberg's reliance on intuitive judgments in that procedure. In the first case decision-making capabilities are not those which are evaluated. In the second, the nonformal capabilities of formalist decision making are actually admitted. This leaves open the possibility that act-theory can be encompassed by formalistic rule-theory rather than functioning as its replacement.

FORMALISM AND EDUCATION: ARON

Israela Ettenberg Aron's emphasis on the concrete, practical, and skillful is particularly appropriate in the context of public or precollege education. Educational institutions are explicitly designed to fulfill certain social functions which require efficient training in practical competencies. When Aron opposes her position to that of Kohlberg, however, three overarching problems arise. First, she fails to demonstrate a logically necessary or natural relation between formalist ethics and even her own overly formalized vision of Kohlbergian education. Thus she leaves open the question of whether the alleged limitations of one need trouble the other, or whether the virtues of her own approach cannot be claimed for the Kohlbergian cause. Second, Aron offers a greatly distorted picture of what actually goes on, or should go on, in Kohlbergian interventions. She fails to maintain a sharp enough distinction between using moral dilemmas as a research tool for assessing levels of reasoning and discussing moral dilemmas in the classroom to stimulate cognitive development. Third, Aron fails to demonstrate that Deweyan ethics provide an adequate basis for moral education at all, much less one which is superior to formalist alternatives. She suggests no way to get past the grave difficulties in Dewey's account, although she seems aware of many of these difficulties.

Aron opens her discussion, paradoxically, with an overly general characterization of formalism. She notes that this view describes morality in purely formal terms, irrespective of content, according to such criteria as universality, finality, and ordering. It conceives of morality as a distinct realm, independent from facts, for example. Serious confusions arise from the lack of clarity of this definition. First, and most important, no distinction is made between defining the moral realm of judgments as opposed to determining the relative adequacy of such judgments. A formalist may define the moral realm using content considerations such as "pertaining to basic needs and minimum freedom" and yet insist on formal criteria for evaluating judgments on these contents. Indeed it would be difficult to call a nonuniversalizable practice such as lying wrong or immoral if by being so it fell outside the moral-immoral dimension. A justificatory formalist of this sort could not be said to ignore content nor to support a strict separation of fact and value, as Aron is too hasty to claim. Formalists themselves are misleading on this point in not explicating the close relationship between the adequacy and distinctiveness of moral reasoning. Consider Kohlberg's claim, "Stage 6 is what it means to judge morally. If you want to play the moral game, if you want to make decisions which anyone could agree upon in resolving social conflicts, stage 6 is it." Here he seems to be defining morality in terms of universalizability. Actually, however, he is defining what it means to play the moral game well, to make decisions which are ideally justified from the moral point of view. When we recognize that making adequate moral judgments involves distinguishing (to some degree) between relative and egoistic interest and obligations, conventional values and reflective or principled ones, we are tempted to call this process "true" or distinctive morality. In general, this temptation should be resisted to avoid confusing formal definition with formal justification.

Aron is also unclear when she says formalism has to do with the separation of form and content, "form regardless of content." She does not mention that the adequacy of formal criteria is to a large extent determined by how accurately the criteria match our particular moral beliefs, distinguishing those acts we term right from those we term wrong. Aron also fails to consider how form typically reflects particular contents. The universality criterion reflects our beliefs in the equality of persons or the implications of shared needs. It also reflects a belief that duties should be voluntarily accepted, that moral rules should be self-legislated. The same may be said for other formal criteria: moral principles or values must be ranked or ordered because we need to resolve practical conflicts of interest in reliable ways. They must be public so that people will not have to live in fear of being held liable for injustices they unknowingly commit. Formal criteria reflect very concrete needs, particular beliefs and values. The picture Aron paints of abstracted forms on one side and practical content on the other is simply simplistic.

Aron's view of formalism in education brings with it the same problem. For example, when formalists such as Kohlberg claim to develop "reasoning ability at a general level" rather than the "inculcation of particular beliefs," this does not imply that they or the logic of formalism spurn content. It merely means that they approach the content of judgments with a certain logic of organization, emphasizing the rationale involved in moral judgment in relation to the judgment this rationale supports. Such an approach does not avoid indoctrination via abstraction but by resisting the kind of mindless authoritarianism characteristic of traditional "do or don't" or virtue training. Students provide the particular beliefs; Kohlbergians urge them to reflect on them. For Kohlberg, an emphasis on reasoning and rationales is also recommended by the structural criteria of Piagetian theory and research, which appear to demonstrate the formal, logical, and holistic character of moral cognition along with its developmental, problem-solving characteristics. This is another way in which fact and real-world practice inform the formalist. In view of these considerations it becomes difficult to accept Aron's assumption that formalist ethics and education merely reflect formalist predilections.

Aron begins her criticism of formalism by noting that formalists emphasize metaethics, though she excludes Kant, the foremost formalist, from this characterization. Notably, she does not define formalism on the normative ethical level except to say that it "confines itself to questions of principle." Aron does not relate normative to metaethical formalism; does one imply the other? Given the casual way in which all three critics define rules, moving from deciding to justifying, from "Do not steal" to "Maximize the good" with ease, it is unclear how a general-rule orientation could distinguish normative formalism. The decision procedures sketched by Aron and elaborated by Rosen can certainly be represented as sets of general rules. If these procedures or their facsimile must be gone through to arrive at justified moral judgments, then it is not clear why such procedures, represented as rules or principles, do not constitute a formalist theory at the normative level. A distinction between types of rules seems called for.

In any event, Aron somehow relates the philosophical concern for metaethics with depriving young students of ample experience with concrete decision making. "These students need more analytical reasoning skills, they need actual or vicarious experiences which will give substance and life to the abstractions of metaethics." It is hard to believe that Aron would fault the pedagogical abilities of formalist philosophers simply because they choose to do technical work in metaethics. Yet the apparent alternative is to assume that Aron is faulting educators for instructing children in formalist theory. I do not know anyone who would try such a thing, especially at the metaethical level or with young children. At the very basis of Kohlberg's approach is the belief that it is futile even to present children with moral philosophy at the metaethical or normative level. Such theory is too abstruse and cognitively complex to be understood by children and may also contain certain ideological biases. Kohlbergians merely elicit or offer the raw data on which children might reflect, reason, and build theories, if they wish.

Lurking behind Aron's criticism of metaethical emphasis seems to be the assumption that metaethical inquiry is unenlightening for a person faced with practical decision making and real-life dilemmas. This is untrue. Metaethical reflection, especially at a nontechnical level, can help us distinguish our needs or demands from our obligations and rights. It can help us separate our rationalizations from reasons and give us a basis for ranking values and ideals. Such rankings can affect choice of occupation, friends, lifestyles, and so forth. Having a greater understanding of values and rationales can greatly affect our degree of commitment to moral character-development and behavior. Virulent moral skepticism and irresponsibility often follow the rejection of social conventions. Why? The answer may well be that when the skeptics, the irresponsible, were children, they never reflected deeply on why people are equal or valuable.

Aron claims that because Kohlberg is aware of this alleged problem of metaethical emphasis in education, he has adopted the dilemma-discussion technique. She then quotes Kohlberg's Heinz dilemma,[2] without its supporting probe questions, and proceeds to criticize this dilemma as follows: "It is simply too pat to be believed. In a comparable real-life situation, the contingencies would be less certain and much more ambiguous . . . the Heinz dilemma is . . . a shallow melodrama . . . whose broad gestures signal the audience to applaud, hiss, or weep." Aron believes that students cannot learn a great deal from such an "abstract and artificially limiting case" and will certainly not learn enough to deal with the "infinitely more complex problems which arise in everyday life."

Of primary interest to the Kohlbergian is Aron's admission that discussing particular cases is compatible with the formalist approach. Thus, just as Aron offers no compelling reason for why formalists need typically emphasize metaethics or for why metaethical emphasis need typically translate directly into educational curricula, she cannot use the formality of formalism to exclude content-ridden moral debate. (Her arguments seem based on a guilt by abuse or association rationale.) Aron's criticism of the Heinz dilemma, however, is meant to demonstrate the *logical* limitations of formalism. Here Aron finally claims, though falsely, that to detail the Heinz dilemma and its discussion would violate the formalist separation of fact and value, the formal autonomy of the moral domain. We have previously noted that a justificatory formalist such as Kohlberg (as opposed to the formalist who defines the scope of morality formally) need not invoke such a distinction on formal grounds. Moreover we should hardly assume that being a formalist makes one a total ignoramus. Even people who rely on formal criteria to justify moral decisions or to focus on the distinctively moral elements of a dilemma recognize that a moral decision cannot be made without weighing facts and values or calculating probabilities. Could someone try to maximize the social good without knowing in particular what people thought was good or how good could be produced, increased, or distributed? Could a modern formalist dealing with conflicts, deceits, and unfair treatment among family members not consider in detail the psychological harms which different courses of action might cause to different members, the rationalization people use to justify lies, the ideology of parental authority?

There is nothing about the Heinz dilemma per se, nor certainly about its typical use in the classroom, which limits discussion to formal principles or criteria. In fact, Kohlbergian education has no particular commitment to the use of hypothetical dilemmas in education and has for the past three quarters of its existence been utilizing real-life dilemmas. Despite a footnote in which Aron concedes that post-Heinz dilemma techniques have been "proposed," Aron gives the clear impression that Kohlbergian education consists of discussing conflicts between moral principles in hypothetical dilemmas in which speculations on factual contingencies are cut short. In the first place, the conflicts embodied in the Heinz dilemma are claims, interests, or values, not (formal) principles. Second, the Heinz dilemma was designed for research purposes, to assess moral reasoning on conflict-resolution. It is accompanied with probe questions designed to elicit reasoning which covers the conflicts among values, interests, rights, duties, and fairness. It is true that research interviewers may ask respondents not to alter the dilemma factually when this alteration will eliminate the conflict involved or get around the use of moral concepts. This is not meant to cut off deliberation but to be sure that needed data is obtained. In moral discussions students should never be prevented from filling in dilemmas in as many ways as they see fit, so long as they do not discuss merely factual issues only.

Before Kohlberg became directly involved in moral education, a few of his graduate students devised and experimented with the hypothetical dilemma, moral discussion technique. This trend has had educational impact, as Aron points out. Yet from the inception of Kohlberg's personal entry into developmental education, an entry which occurred in a prison rather than a school, the emphasis has been on creating a moral (just) community which discusses the moral, practical, and emotional aspects of the daily lives of members in community meetings, discussion groups, and peer-counseling groups. Members discuss all sorts of decisions down to the last detail, from how their discipline system should be set up and should work or how chores and privileges should be shared, to whether a member should keep calling a former spouse who has done her or him wrong in the past and is likely to do so in the future. Their discussions do not stop at (nor even proceed to) "Do not treat me as a means only but always as an end in myself." Rather, they involve considerations such as "You keep trying to bring drugs in this unit, man, and they're going to close our thing right down. What have you been thinking of?" If this is formalism, it at least does not sound "sterile and pedantic" or "rarefied and insular," as Aron predicts. We have heard the most detailed, relevant, lively, soul-searching, heart-warming, and developmentally stimulating discussions take place in these "just communities" around issues of who should be responsible in what way to whom in their daily interactions.

It is ironic that Aron ends her critique of Kohlberg's formalism by claiming that he equates justification with decision making, requiring students to resolve dilemmas utilizing moral principles. It is Aron who makes this confusion and the accompanying erroneous claim. She does not even discuss the Kohlbergian decision procedure of ideal role-taking which, by the way, does not invoke principles. Of course, Kohlberg never educates students even in this procedure, but allows them to generate whatever reasoning or decision strategies they find to be most adequate after discussion and reflection. This may indeed be a fault in Kohlberg's approach since it certainly would be useful to students to learn various decision strategies for weighing facts, probabilities, and values. Exposing students to such strategies and to the range of alternative strategies would hardly constitute moral indoctrination. It is in this area that Aron-like criticisms make sense and Aron-like alternatives may prove to be useful additions to Kohlbergian education.

The Deweyan alternative, which Aron suggests, shares the following assumptions with Kohlberg. 1) Moral reflection arises spontaneously from coping with problems and is directed toward a resolution of them. 2) Efficient deliberation involves defining problems clearly, considering alternative solutions, consulting rules to help weigh alternative contingencies. 3) An adequate solution to these problems should yield a unification of meaning and a feeling of satisfaction or reflective equilibrium.

According to Aron, the Deweyan approach differs in being more attentive to emotional and empathetic considerations, relying more fully on feeling for determining valid solutions, recognizing the continuity of moral and nonmoral considerations, and recognizing the need for an emphasis on normative rather than metaethical consideration in deciding cases. Where these differences represent a matter of degree, it is difficult to know why we should prefer Dewey to Kohlberg or why we could not bridge the gap between these approaches by merely altering emphases. Can formal criteria be violated in degrees? Moral and nonmoral considerations should be neither totally distinguished nor identified. But how much and in precisely what ways should they be related? The same question might be asked of the emotional-empathetic involvement of the sober reflection-and-role-taking continuum. Aron provides no guidelines here.

Without greater clarification and justification, we can hardly accept Dewey's conception of valid conflict resolution. What is this "unifying" of meanings and feeling of satisfaction or validity that Dewey speaks of through Aron? How can we distinguish it from (the delights of) prejudice or vice? Such a test of validity seems too arbitrary, unreliable, irregular, and untestable to outdo formal criteria or principles. As noted earlier, the Deweyan approach is weak in the area of justification. In admitting these difficulties Aron raises the dangers of individualism or relativism caused by consulting our feelings on a decision's validity. She notes how difficult it is to reach consensus on a decision among members of a group using this criterion and, therefore, how Dewey's ethical theory strips morality of its prescriptive force. Aron tries to mitigate this problem by noting that the prescriptive force of moral judgments is often rhetorical or persuasive. This is especially so where the judgments are voiced to bring consensus after a Deweyan process of rational deliberation has failed.

"But it is *immoral* to do what you are planning, as you will be violating certain moral principles!" Will this final appeal really strengthen my case? . . . If my assertion . . . does change my friend's mind, it is likely that the change will have been caused by emotional rather than strictly rational factors.

Aron is claiming, in effect, that the Deweyan methodology is superior because inclusive of formalism. It is a rational deliberation process which can consult rules and principles but which is more rigorous in its procedures, more attuned to factual detail, and more willing to avail itself of the emotional aspects of sound judgment. However, given what I have previously said regarding formalism and decision making, we can pose a formalist methodology based on criteria and principles, yet able to consult rigorous procedures for decision making, factual details, and emotional considerations. Would there be any reason to prefer this latter methodology to its

Deweyan alternative? Yes. Even procedures of rational deliberations can go awry when used in particular cases; especially where they are tailored to the particular facts and feelings involved in a situation. General principles represent a more reliable, trans-situational measure of moral reasoning and belief. Furthermore, by resting on the greater authority of rational principles, we might become less vulnerable to the influence of prejudice, unanalyzed sentiments, and, indeed, to the rhetorical force of principles and persuasion techniques. At least this would seem to be the case if formal principles reflect an attitude of rational detachment, as Aron suggests. In an educational context where much more feeling and prejudice attend moral deliberation and debate, and where there are serious dangers of indoctrination, cajolery, and intimidation, this case for preferring a formalist methodology is especially powerful. Imagine training children to feel or identify these feelings of unity and validity Aron speaks of, incoming to (or justifying?) a moral decision. What does one do with disagreements? What does one do with the few students whose moral feelings may differ markedly from those of the class? How does one guard against emotional shaping due to teachers' reinforcements of their own possibly prejudicial and difficult-to-evaluate predilections?

The Deweyan approach would have initial appeal in any area of education which required careful thinking. It seems, after all, simply a step-by-step procedure for careful decision making regarding any sort of issue. Ironically, however, it is not attuned to the particular concerns and dangers of *moral* education. One must watch out for its last step; it's a big one. As noted previously, however, there is no reason to uphold Kohlberg at Dewey's expense. An attempt to synthesize these approaches in a mutually supportive way should be undertaken.

RULE THEORY AND COGNITIVE DEVELOPMENT: MUNSEY

Brenda Munsey considers the relationship between Kohlberg's formalist assumptions and his stage theory of cognitive-moral development. She agrees with Kohlberg that a moral philosophical basis is needed for defining development change, for claiming that a later developing stage is a better stage. However, she argues that a Deweyan ethic should replace a formalistic one in Kohlberg's system. This substitution, she claims, would save Kohlberg's theory from arbitrary assumptions and unscientific consequences. Let us consider her interesting arguments in detail.

Munsey seems to attack formalism at the level of normative ethical theory. She identifies formalism with rule-theory and the view that rules are necessary for justifying singular moral judgments. Act-theorists, by contrast, believe that such judgments can be justified simply by reference to particular facts involved in the situational contexts. In a critical context, this characterization of formalism is problematic. It makes it seem that formalists are rule-fixated and rule-burdened, whereas act-theorists are free to tailor their justifications to the particular realities of any situation or judgment. Because rules are general in form, they appear to be less flexible in this regard. Yet formalists need not care about the rule-quality of their positions apart from the underlying rationales or forms of judgment these rules embody. Such underlying rationales could be represented in motley ways via particularized descriptions of this or that element of moral form: the equality of persons, the implications of free will, the need for consensus on moral rules, and the like. Finding general rules which can capture and unify such descriptions in a smooth, economical, and fundamental way is a theoretical advance on such descriptions. Consider the like case of "discovering" a general law in science. Rules such as "Do not steal" do not capture formalist criteria well. General principles such as "Always act so as to maximally express and respect individual autonomy" do so much better. This is one reason why the Deweyan should be much more careful to distinguish particular rules which may be useful in applying general principles to cases, from general principles of justification. As noted previously, until a more discriminating conception of rules and principles is offered, the crucial influence this concept plays for these critics in distinguishing their views from formalism is a bit worrisome.

Perhaps we will be helped here by the distinction Munsey offers

between constitutive and summary rules. Act theories view moral
rules as summary statements or "empirical generalizations purportedly identifying general categories of facts which have *tended* to be
relevant in making justified moral decisions." They can always
admit of exceptions and can become outdated, as they often do,
because they do not "define (a priori) moral justification." Act
theories retain the logical independence of moral rules and the
identification of morally relevant particular facts. According to the
rule-theorist, by contrast, "the morally relevant facts cannot even be
identified without moral rules, since it is the rules which make
them relevant." Rule theorists claim that there are valid constitutive rules. Act theorists can now be distinguished by claiming
that all valid moral rules are summary rules which can admit of
a posteriori exceptions.

This way of distinguishing the two types of theory is perhaps
more problematic than the first. For one thing it seems to involve an
even more subtle confusion between formalist definition and formalist justification than we saw in Aron's account. Though Munsey
concentrates on justification, she speaks here of what facts are
morally relevant to justifying a judgment. Moral relevance and sufficient moral warrant are two quite different things, as previously
noted. Kohlberg does not use universalization to determine whether
this or that claim may be *considered* from the moral point of view,
but whether it will meet the criteria of moral adequacy. To use an
overly-Kantian example, one can consider whether to tell a lie so as
to save onself from embarrassment. Certainly it can be a claim
advanced in Kohlberg's ideal role-taking procedure. The question
is, however, can this policy be justified, does it meet criteria of
adequacy sufficiently? The answer will probably be no, depending
on certain circumstances.

The characterization of formal criteria as a priori and exception-
less is also misleading. The issue of validity is left unclear. Is the
claim that there are valid constitutive principles of justification a
description of our current level of philosophical attainment or a
logical, "in principle" remark? I think most formalists at the normative ethical level agree that we have not yet formulated totally

adequate principles of justice, right, obligation, or whatever. Furthermore, there is still significant dissatisfaction among formalists over their metaethical criteria, as Aron points out. If Munsey is making the logical claim that constitutive rules are logically impossible, then formalists or anyone else might indeed object. We might ask to see the impossibility theorem or even a plausibility argument which should accompany this strong and seemingly a priori claim.

To say that constitutive rules are a priori could mean that they are purely dependent on logical considerations and therefore beyond experience or that they are generated by logical procedures and therefore not based on experience. For a modern, inductive formalist, and especially for Kohlberg, neither of these options holds true. Let us take the second one first. We have already considered two ways in which content figures into the formulation of formal principles. The first way is by reflecting certain beliefs, needs, values, and ideals: universalization reflects our need to resolve conflicts in a consensual way, our belief in the equality of individuals, and the like. The second way is by matching or explaining our most sound moral judgments. A universal rule or the criterion of universality which it embodies is valid if it can differentiate the right from the wrong, the good from the bad accurately. In this way a formal rule may have the same inductive history and justification as a summary rule. It is a serious mistake to believe that this is not so, even if on certain formalist conceptions they were derived and justified in more analytical ways.

Why do act theorists formulate or consult summary rules? Why do they find summary rules useful in the way Aron and Munsey state? It is because they add plausibility to a piecemeal justification. They are more simple, unified, and elegant theoretically, and are often more useful in moral deliberation and discussion because of these features. They also may have an intuitive or rational appeal of their own. Consider: "All actions should be directed at maximizing the greatest good for the greatest number over time." This principle does seem to capture what many of us consider an adequate morality to be most about. The rule-theorist goes one step beyond empirical generalization in generalizing and elevating a rule to the level of a standard for justification. The reason behind this additional step is similar to that which motivated the last one—namely, increased theoretical adequacy, practical utility, and plausibility. Formalists put forward their principles as a standard in precisely the way that act theorists may put forward their procedures of deliberation. The former feel that their principles are correct; the latter feel that their procedures are correct.

Does advancing a rule as a standard for justification make it a priori, unfalsifiable, incapable of exceptions? Ask this of the Deweyan regarding his or her procedure. The answer is: at one level, no; at another level, maybe. When you use your standard to justify judgments you do not at the same time question its competence. It is being used to eliminate such questions. Here it *defines* adequate justification. However, you may at any time reflect on the competence of its performance using content considerations. It should have been formulated to reflect such considerations to begin with, so we have good reason to trust it. It is also likely to have had a history of success in matching our judgments, so it is not likely to go wrong. Only the best summary rule would ever be considered for a standard-bearer position. Yet if its use causes us to justify judgments or acts we consider on other bases of sound judgment to be significantly counterintuitive, its adequacy becomes questionable.

Note that as I have pictured justification, formalists have all the situational apparatus of the nonformalist at their command, but merely give greater credibility to certain rules. Counterexamples can be recognized by the formalist, as they have been in the philosophical literature, on the basis of nonformalized considerations. This is symmetrical with the Deweyans' relation to summary rules. Seen logically, a formalist's rule may be a logical standard. Seen historically, it is an hypothesis. When it fails to handle counterexamples, it becomes discredited.

Munsey claims that on an act-theory, "it is always possible to recognize *novel situational* factors as relevant to a justified resolution; factors which might not be covered by a present structure of summary moral rules (no matter how 'generally' adequate it might be)." (Note again the phrase, "*relevant* to a justified resolution.") The formalist would not have to claim that his or her current formulation of rules is necessarily the correct one. Thus exceptions to it might arise. Yet the formalist could ask why it is assumed that novel situational exceptions could not in principle be handled by some more adequate rule formulated in the future. (The formalist's hope here may seem more plausible when we recognize that a rule theory can have a variety of rules to handle different functions at different levels of generality or specificity.) How, after all, will the nonformalist be able to distinguish a novel situational factor which biases the moral decision by its influence, as opposed to one which aids it? A rule could provide the rationale which would allow us to make the necessary discrimination. A procedure for how to deliberate carefully or debate vehemently might only steel our judgment against being easily swayed by arbitrary factors. It probably would not provide us with the mechanism by which this discrimination between a biasing and legitimizing factor should be made. If this mechanism or rationale can be found and if it stands the test of time as a more reliable basis for justification than alternatives, why should it not be accorded superior status? If the Deweyan procedure for justification were not only always reliable but if it also comprised a fundamental explanation of why it were so reliable, as rules can do, it should become the standard of justification.

How does this relate to Kohlberg's psychological stage theory of moral development? Munsey advances several critical points against the formalistic and a priori nature of Kohlberg's metaethics. The first is that formalist criteria are not adequate for defining the direction of development because they are not neutral (or objective?). They do not say why a later developing stage is a better or more developed stage, but only say that it is more in accord with formalism. Formalist criteria must be replaced by truly objective criteria of moral philosophical adequacy which do not favor formalists over nonformalists. Second, because formalist criteria are not objective or neutral, they cannot be assumed to define the deep structure of moral cognition or development (accommodation). The ability to reflectively evaluate the adequacy of one's own stage relative to a superior stage as well as the tendency to "reconstruct" one's stage in the direction of superior stages, can be explained by a nonformalist metaethic. Third, in performing the functions of a formalist metaethic, the pragmatic alternative can avoid stipulating an arbitrary highest stage and end-point to development which bears the scientific embarrassment of unfalsifiability.

Let us take these claims in turn. The choice of a formalist metaethic seems most controversial to the nonformalist. In our judgment formalism is the most widely respected view, the received view in the field of metaethics. Even if this judgment is incorrect, there is an overriding reason for preferring it. The formal criteria of metaethics are well matched to the structural assumptions of Piagetian psychology. They are prima facie isomorphic with the logical operations (formal operations) of Piaget which have received so much empirical support. In formulating a theory of cognitive moral development within the Piagetian tradition, one must set out on the most promising path. The findings of Kohlbergian research seem to support the path taken.

The characterization given by Munsey of how Kohlbergians relate metaethical criteria to cognitive structure and development is both implausible and inaccurate. Though there is no explicit Kohlbergian theory of cognitive structure and accommodation beyond that which can be provided by Piagetians, it is certainly not assumed that metaethical criteria are implicit in the psychological processes of reasoning or reconstruction except in the sense that they are isomorphic logically with structural criteria such as reversibility, integration, and differentiation. Munsey offers an overly intellectualistic and reflective picture of the processes of disequilibration and accommodation. Kohlbergians do not and need not claim individuals typically reconstruct their cognitive systems according to an implicitly metaethical preference for a more formalistically adequate stage. What seems most likely is that people become frustrated by their inability to resolve problems using their spontaneous form of reasoning. They accommodate to a higher stage (whether or not they encounter or prefer that stage beforehand) because it resolved those problems more competently.

Munsey's account totally ignores the structural criteria, on the psychological side, which support the greater adequacy of later developing stages. These criteria also help account for developmental change, and support the philosophical criteria of adequacy themselves. It has been found, for example, that the attainment of higher moral stages is dependent upon the development of higher logical stages in the Piagetian sense. This gives some support to the notion that later developing moral stages are more logical, more adequate at problem solving. It appears also that later developing stages are more integrated and differentiated in their organization of moral concepts and that, most important, a later stage is inclusive of an earlier one. Someone reasoning at a later stage can solve all the problems solved by reasoning at an earlier stage, and more besides. Inclusiveness is perhaps the most likely indicator of superior adequacy. If, as Kohlberg has argued, structural criteria of adequacy are isomorphic with formal criteria in ethics, then each set of criteria supports the other in terms of the problem-solving competence of developing processes. Moreover, through the use of criteria such as integration, differentiation, and inclusiveness (which are isomorphic to prescriptivity and universality), we may define the relative adequacy of any two or three stages locally without referring to psychological or philosophical forms of the highest stage. It is noteworthy that when Kohlberg presented his argument to philosophers for the moral adequacy of stage 6, he relied directly on the structural criteria of differentiation and integration to make his case.[3]

Munsey claims several times that pragmatic metaethic can function at least as well as its formalist alternative in explaining the developmental sequence. However, she offers precious little detail regarding how this story might go. Certainly she does not offer enough of an account to allow an ample comparison of their relative merits. From our discussion of Aron, we have reason to suspect the reliability of the pragmatic procedure for justification. Moreover, we have no reason at all to think that a Deweyan alternative would offer the same valuable opportunity to relate the structural form of cognition to the moral form of ethics in a mutually supportive way.

On Munsey's reflective reconstruction of moral development, the developing person disequilibrates and later accommodates by recognizing counterexamples to her or his current system of reasoning. Because the stage 6 system of reasoning embodies those rules which define or constitute adequate justification, however, this becomes impossible at stage 6. As a result, stage 6, unlike all the other stages, is unfalsifiable. That is, stage 6 structures lack the capacity to disequilibrate on the basis of moral experience. For the Deweyan, this situation is anathema. Encountering novel grounds for justification which can represent exceptions to summary rules is always possible.

Were these criticisms valid, the Kohlbergian would be hard pressed to explain the differences in structural capacity between stages 1–5, and 6. It appears that the ultimate end-point of psychological sophistication has been defined in advance, a priori, by the choice of philosophical criteria. If this is not unscientific enough, the unfalsifiability of an empirical phenomenon, stage 6, is.

Previously, I offered an inductive account of formalism which was designed to highlight its a posteriori characteristics. On this account formal rules could be challenged by counterintuitive cases. It would be possible, on these same grounds, for stage 6 reasoning to encounter cases which it cannot solve in a reflectively satisfying (equilibrating) way. This does not mean that such a situation would arise, of course. It does mean, however, that the rules or criteria of stage 6 need not define the logic of adequate moral justification at all levels for a person who might reach that stage. Kohlberg's claim—that the fulfillment of psychological criteria by developing processes supports philosophical criteria—demonstrates an inductive stance toward these criteria. Perhaps the a posteriori falsifiability of stage 6 rules is best expressed in the following passage.

The isomorphic assumption is a two way street. While moral philosophical criteria of adequacy of moral judgment *help* define a standard of psychological adequacy or advance, the study of psychological advance *feeds back* and *clarifies* these criteria . . . a later stage is "objectively" preferable or more adequate by certain moral criteria. This philosophical claim, however, would for us be thrown into question if the facts of moral advance were inconsistent with its psychological implications.[4] (My emphases.)

If people became more logically sophisticated, more able to dif- ferentiate and integrate physical and moral concepts, more able to imaginatively assume and coordinate subjective and social perspec- tives, more competent across the board at problem solving, and yet less able to make morally adequate judgments according to certain formal criteria of moral adequacy, goodby criteria. As this appears to us from the outside, as researchers looking at development, so can it appear to developing or developed persons looking out through their cognitive structures.

DILEMMAS, MORAL BARGAINING, AND IDEAL ROLE-TAKING: ROSEN

Because Bernard Rosen's account has less critical relevance to Kohlbergian theory than those of Aron or Munsey, we will be more cursory and selective in our analysis. Rosen's approach to moral dilemmas is to schematize them in the form of a deductive argu- ment, to break down each unit of meaning in the premises and reflect on our beliefs about it, and when we have come to some degree of surety about what to believe, to accept the conclusion which must follow. He describes each step in this process carefully both in the contexts of individual deliberation and of group discus- sion. Rosen then contrasts this method with the approach of rule theory to dilemmas, especially as it relates to Kohlberg's role-taking procedure. He criticizes the rule approach for being much less rich, accurate, and satisfying than this step-by-step, moral bargaining procedure. Kohlberg's ideal role-taking procedure is faulted for rely- ing on intuitions at a most crucial point in deliberation.

One problem with Rosen's analysis is that he uses an extremely general rule of justification to represent the rule theory approach.

If action A should maximize my good (good for the greatest number), then A is obligatory.
If action A should not maximize my good (good for the greatest number), then A is not obligatory.
Therefore A is obligatory or not.[5]

Note that this formalistic formulation of the dilemma gets nowhere near its problem. This is because the problem is an "epistemological" one, one of not knowing which action would maximize the good. Though Kohlbergians would agree that this is a serious problem which must be decided before acting, there is no reason to think that general principles of moral justification should have anything to say about it. What we need is a fact-finding procedure. The dilemma posed by Rosen is a factual dilemma within a moral choice. There is no dispute over the distinctive morality of the situation, no conflict over what is good or whether we should maximize the good. Kohlbergian dilemmas and decision procedures are designed to focus on these moral aspects of the dilemma. Yet it is just for this reason that they can accommodate and indeed must seek and welcome fact-finding techniques and procedures for calculating probabilities.

A principle of the generality Rosen cites would be informative were we wondering whether a proposed solution was arbitrary or had a justifiable rationale, or if we needed to hear morality's position on the most adequate rationale for guiding our deliberations. Such a principle might tell us in a general way how individual rights should be treated relative to social welfare, but it would need greater specificity to tell us even how to deal with specific rights, or how to rank values. Consider how patently ridiculous it is to think, prima facie, that such general principles of justification could be meant to resolve concrete dilemmas. Could a utilitarian principle resolve a dispute between its rationale and a more Kantian one? Could it resolve a dilemma over what sorts of things are good, or the logistics of attaining them? Of course not. More specific and perhaps quite different rules and/or procedures are called for.

There is no reason at all why Rosen's bargaining procedure could not be used as a part of Kohlbergian or formalist decision making. Indeed it is hard to know how a sound judgment could be made without thinking carefully about every fact and value aspect of a dilemma and trying to resolve it in as close to a deductive way as is possible. What could be more in line with the spirit of formalism than to deal with our decisions in a logical form which has become the standard of reasoning? Yet why should we not go beyond the particularistic step of this procedure and consult summary rules? If some of these rules have proven more reliable than other bases for justification, why should we not accord them superior or supreme authority? It is important to notice that we cannot go directly to rules without passing a Rosen-like procedure, even if we are formalists. We need to interpret the dilemma to be sure that all relevant facts and values are considered as well as the possible courses of action available (including those which would skirt the problem felicitously). Note that these steps of formalist process are not embodied in the formal principles or criteria normally cited. Yet "rule-theory" is much more than such principles. A sophisticated rule-theory which justifies and decides cases will involve several levels and types of rules as well as rules or procedures for ranking rules.

We should note that Kohlberg describes his ideal role-taking without reference to moral rules or criteria. We are to imagine ourselves in the position of each party to the dilemma and consider all the claims that could be made from each position. Then we are to imagine that we do not know which position we are to occupy once the decision is made. We ask ourselves which claim we would uphold, given that we might have to live with its effects on any of the people involved. Finally, we are to act in accordance with these claims.[6] Kohlberg notes that these claims are reversible in the logical-structural sense. We know also that reversibility maps into universality on the moral domain. Could it be claimed then that Kohlberg's procedure builds formalistic criteria into the constraints on reasoning such that people who are ideal role-taking may just as well be utilizing rules? Let us consider ways in which this does not seem the case. First, the warrant for the structural criterion of reversibility is psychological. A more extensively reversible cognitive structure shows greater problem-solving competence within the logical-physical domain. If a reversible decision-making procedure yields judgments which match our core moral belief, support is gained for the validity of the corresponding universality criterion in ethics. Second, we should notice that a reversible decision procedure also has intrinsic appeal from the moral point of view. It matches our considered intuitions regarding impartiality in "bargaining," the equality of persons, the need in making moral decisions to see things from the other's point of view. This need not have been the case. It could not have been known a priori that a system of thought containing symmetrical relations between concepts of right over the domain of right-holders would appeal to our value commitments and beliefs about various qualities of moral thought. Neither can it be known a priori that reversible reasoning will generate decisions which match our considered judgments in particular cases.

The validity of the ideal role-taking procedure can also be evaluated relative to the actual decisions it renders in practice. Successful, imaginative role-taking at this high level requires a variety of accurate judgments and successfully exercised skills. We must decide who to include in our perspective-taking, we must coordinate perspectives adequately, and we must calculate the relative weight of claims and degrees of probability for a variety of outcomes. Such skill requirements may lead to less reliability than is found in an alternative decision procedure. We must remember that a rule-theory does not require a decision procedure which invokes or embodies its rules. It only requires that its decision procedure generate outcomes which can be justified by its principles. Taking the advice of a wise and sensitive friend could be a reliable decision procedure, as could Rosen's step-by-step method of moral bargaining.

When Kohlberg uses ideal role-taking to deal with the Heinz dilemma, he notes that the rational solution is to steal the drug (to save the wife's life). This solution "leads to the least loss (or most gain) to an individual who could be in any role," among the wife, husband, and druggist. Note that this is a rational solution expressed in a rational, minimax rule. Kohlberg then notes that this solution "corresponds to our intuition of the primacy of the woman's right to life over the druggist's right to property . . . " Rosen criticizes this reference to intuitions as a "totally mysterious step." He claims all prima facie rule-theories revert to this step to decide conflicts of rights. Act-theory, according to Rosen, need not take this step.

It is being automatically assumed here that the correspondence Kohlberg notes between his resolution of the Heinz dilemma and our intuitions on the proper weighting of rights is the basis for decision, or need be. Rosen also seems to assume that there is something more to the term "intuition" here than " as yet unanalyzed plausible belief." Neither of these assumptions is warranted. The ranking of rights to life over property can be based on the logical priority of life to property and the corresponding relation of rights to these conditions. It can also be based on the structural implications of the naturally developing value-hierarchy which Kohlbergian research has discovered. People becoming more competent at resolving problems in a variety of domains tend to differentiate and integrate values and rights such that the value of life and its right are judged increasingly prior to those of property over time.[7] If we wished we could formulate the logical priority of life over property in a rule and support it with these psychological findings. This rule could then be used in the ideal role-taking. The problem of specifying exceptions to this rule could be handled within the provisions of the rule itself or through additional rules, depending on how rule-oriented we wished to become.

POSTSCRIPT UPON POSTSCRIPT

It is extremely discomforting to be at odds with Deweyan positions, given the central role many of Dewey's notions have played in shaping the Kolbergian approach. Much of what has been said here in response to critics is more controversial than one would desire. Some criticisms have not been responded to. Others may have been poorly understood. It might be hoped that the Deweyan perspective will continue to inform Kohlbergian theory and practice in the future and that allies will be found within the ranks of our current opposition.

NOTES

1. Though I often found myself on the side of criticisms discussed here, I have tried to respond to them in the way a more orthodox Kohlbergian might. It is

important to consider how such an argument might go. The use of "we" rather than "I" in the text represents an attempt to speak for a school of thought, though I am not certain this school would endorse my defense.

2. This is the dilemma (presented in Chapter 2) that asks whether a man should steal an overpriced and stubbornly withheld drug which could save his wife's life.

3. These claims regarding structural criteria and their relation to formalism are discussed in L. Kohlberg, "The claim to moral adequacy of a highest stage of moral judgment," *Journal of Philosophy*, Vol. LXX, No. 18, Oct., 1973, pp. 633, 634.

4. Ibid., p. 633.

5. As Rosen has constructed this dilemma, the moral principle involved is being used to define the moral problem or the very scope of moral relevance. It is on such a formulation that the Deweyan launches claims regarding the a priori character of formalistic rules and criteria. I have tried to argue that this is not the way to view Kohlbergian formalism.

6. L. Kohlberg, "The claim to moral adequacy of a highest stage of moral judgment," *Journal of Philosophy*, pp. 643, 644. All cited passages on ideal role-taking are contained on these pages.

7. L. Kohlberg, "From is to ought: How to commit the naturalistic fallacy and get away with it," in *Cognitive Development and Epistemology*, T. Mischel (ed.), Academic Press, Inc.: New York, 1971, p. 174.

Chapter 16

Educating for a Just Society: An Updated and Revised Statement

LAWRENCE KOHLBERG

INTRODUCTION

The first lecture I gave on education for a just society was given in 1968, shortly after the death of Martin Luther King (Kohlberg, 1970). In it I advocated the Platonic vision of moral education that commenced with the execution of Socrates and ended with the assassination of Martin Luther King. Socrates and King attempted to stimulate a higher level of morality, a level of principles of justice, by questioning and confrontation. I called their level of morality a sixth and highest stage of moral development, a stage of universal principles of justice, equity, and respect for human personality.

I claimed our research on moral development, both cross-cultural and in experimental programs of moral discussion in American schools, supported that Platonic vision of education for justice. I claimed the research supported the following elements of the Platonic view.

First, virtue is ultimately one, not many, and it is always the same ideal form regardless of climate or culture.
Second, the name of this ideal form is justice.
Third, not only is the good one, but virtue is knowledge of the good. He who knows the good chooses the good.

455

Fourth, the kind of knowledge of the good which is virtue is philosophical knowledge or intuition of the ideal form of the good, not correct opinion or acceptance of conventional beliefs.

Fifth, the good can then be taught, but its teachers must in a certain sense be philosopher-kings.

Sixth, the reason the good can be taught is because we know it dimly all along or at a low level and its teaching is more a calling out than an instruction.

Seventh, the reason we think the good cannot be taught is because the same good is known differently at different levels, and direct instruction cannot take place across levels.

Eighth, then the teaching of virtue is the asking of questions and the pointing of the way, not the giving of answers. Moral education is the leading of men upward, not the putting into the mind of knowledge what was not there before.

The 1960s were no more safe for stage 6 examplars than was Socrates's Athens. But the quest for justice and a concern for what I called the sixth stage of universal principles moved in the land.

In 1976, the bicentennial led me to a reassessment of education for justice in light of the contemporary scene (Kohlberg and Fenton, 1976). I gave a bicentennial lecture entitled "The Quest for Justice in American History and Education"—among other places, at Kent State. Even indirect reference to the martyrs of the sixties and the Platonic vision which moved them met with embarrassed silence in a student body which did not want to be reminded of the conflicts of the past.

My 1976 lecture on education for justice reasserted not the Platonic vision I had called stage 6 but the vision of Jefferson and the founding fathers I called stage 5. Stage 5 is the morality of the social contract and the rights of man which generated the Declaration of Independence and the Constitution. Our longitudinal research solidly confirmed that this was a natural stage of development found in Israel and Turkey as well as in the United States. While a natural stage, only a small minority of adults, even of college graduates, reached the fifth stage. In 1976, I said stage 5 was, as ever, in some danger because it was in the possession of only a minority.

Watergate supported this claim. President Nixon's willingness to violate the civil rights of his fellow citizens, I pointed out, was not sheer expediency but was at least partly moral ignorance or lack of civic and moral education. I pointed out that Mr. Nixon's public utterances displayed no clear usage or comprehension of fifth-stage thought. In this he was little different from the American majority which every year votes down the Bill of Rights presented unlabeled in the Gallup poll. Watergate supported the founding fathers' wisdom in constructing a system of checks and balances to support human rights. It also showed, I thought, the founders' wisdom in proposing that public education should focus on education for citizenship.

In this vision public education *was* civic education and the graduate of the public school would be a free citizen. A free citizen was someone who could sign our social contract, the Declaration of Independence and the Constitution, with informed consent to its stage 5 premises.

In 1976 Watergate provided the scenario to reassert the stage 5 vision of the founding fathers. In addition further research by my colleagues and myself also dictated a retrenchment from stage 6 Platonic idealism to stage 5 rational liberalism. Empirical research between 1968 and 1976 did not confirm my theoretical statements about a sixth and highest stage (Kohlberg, 1979). My longitudinal subjects, still adolescents in 1968, had come to adulthood by 1976, but none had reached the sixth stage. Perhaps all the sixth stage persons of the 1960s had been wiped out, perhaps they had regressed, or maybe it was all my imagination in the first place.

More accurately, the ideas of justice I called stage 6 are now the subject of slow, scholarly, philosophic dispute, revolving largely around John Rawls's (1973) stage 6 restatement of the liberal social contract. This restatement generates universal principles of social justice which include not only our familiar stage 5 civil libertarian assumptions of procedural justice and equal opportunity, but the more radical and substantive stage 6 principle of justice as equity in the distribution of income and respect.

My 1976 call to the schools to make the world safe for stage 5 democracy reflected not only rhetoric but a developing practice of civic and moral education supported by the Danforth Foundation

(Fenton, 1974). This practice linked together the new social studies curricula with developmental moral discussion. Ted Fenton at Carnegie-Mellon University and the Pittsburgh schools tied high school curriculum in civics and history to developmental moral discussion. Ralph Mosher at Boston University and the Brookline schools tied high school curriculum in psychology and social relations to developmental moral discussion. Chuck Quigley and Todd Clark in Los Angeles related new social studies law curriculum to developmental moral discussion.

This linkage between the new social studies curriculum and moral discussion around the goal of an understanding of the stage 5 premises of our society was a natural one in terms of educational theory. The new social studies had taken the Socratic inquiry method as the basis for reasoning about matters of social fact in relation to value issues in problematic cases. Our developmental moral discussion extends the Socratic method to systematic moral dialogues about values. The new social studies of the 1960s had assumed high school students could reason about social facts at Piaget's stage of formal reasoning and that they could reason about moral values and justice at my fifth stage of social contract. Developmental psychology suggested that stimulation to these cognitive levels, rather than assuming them, was a more reasonable goal of secondary civic education. But these differences between the new social studies of the sixties and our cognitive developmental curriculum of the 1970s represented minor differences in instructional means, not differences in educational ends. Both postulated as ends an understanding of the liberal principles of constitutional democracy in the context of reasoned discussion about controversial social and moral problems.

This new education for stage 5 which I advocated in 1976 looked attractive in comparison with available alternatives. Aside from neglect of civic education, the principal alternative was the old fashioned indoctrinative civic education for stage 4, teaching respect for law and order, authority, nation, and the free enterprise system on the value side, and straight facts on the cognitive side.

In summary, my 1976 lecture on education for justice stressed a retrenchment from my 1968 Platonic stage 6 to a stage 5 goal and conception of justice. The present paper reports a further retrenchment to stage 4 goals as the ends of civic education. It discusses my civic educational efforts for the last four years at Cambridge high school's alternative Cluster School. Our Cluster approach is not merely Socratic and developmental, it is indoctrinative. Its goal is not attainment of the fifth stage but a solid attainment of the fourth stage commitment to being a good member of a community or a good citizen. Its philosophy of civic education is in a certain sense, then, conventional or fourth stage. Only its educational approach is unconventional and new. The approach is the governance of a small school community by participatory or direct democracy. Rules are made and enforced through a community meeting, one-person-one-vote whether faculty or student. Later in this paper, I will report on one such meeting. First I need to indicate briefly why I have been led to advocate such a form of civic education from the point of view of contemporary social needs, research, and theory.

CIVIC EDUCATION AND PARTICIPATORY DEMOCRACY

The central rationale for representative constitutional democracy is still the founding fathers' rationale that democratic governance best protects justice or individual human rights. There is a second and somewhat different rationale for participatory or direct democracy, the rationale of community as something more than justice. Direct democracy promotes participation in society and a resulting sense of community. Athenian direct democracy was not as good as American representative democracy at protecting justice, Socrates's right to life, and free speech. Athenian direct democracy, however, was very good at creating that sense of participation and community which keeps a society alive and free of the death called privatism. Today the major problem in developing youth is privatism; its major educational solution is participation.

In August of 1978 a national conference on civic education was held in Santa Monica by the Danforth Foundation. A central theme was civic education through action or experiential learning, rather than curriculum improvement in the sense I discussed as education for stage 5. As reflected at that conference, the focus of experiential learning (in new civic education projects) is participation, either participation in the governance of the school through school democracy or participation in the outside community through service projects or projects working on community problems. Why the new emphasis on participation? Partly because that is where our developmental education theory has taken participants in the conference such as Fenton, Mosher, Dian Hedin, Fred Newmann, and myself. But what appeal would education for increasing participation have had in the sixties when half the country wanted students to stop participating and making trouble, to settle down in the classroom? On the other hand, today participation represents an educational response to the growing privatism of youth.

Each younger generation in America is diagnosed by its elders in academia in terms of its moral character, usually from a psychoanalytic perspective. In the 1950s David Riesman (1952) diagnosed the coming generation as "the lonely crowd," William Whyte as "the organization man." Their books bore those titles. In the 1960s Kenneth Keniston diagnosed the coming generation first as "the uncommitted" and then as the "young radicals." In the late seventies the diagnosis is given by Christopher Lasch (1978) as "the culture of narcissism," or more popularly as "the me generation." At the top of the best-seller list is Robert Ringer's (1977) *Looking Out for Number One*. These diagnoses and slogans are reminiscent of our second stage, of instrumental hedonism and exchange. Ringer's book starts with a preface explaining that you can trust the book's advice because he wrote the book to make money but not to give a fair dollar value. The best-selling ideological or theoretical fad is sociobiology featuring "the selfish gene." These signs and portents and diagnoses do not mean that today's youth are fixated at a second moral stage or a narcissistic level of ego development. This is no more true of them than of their "new conservative" elders who are doing the diagnoses. Rather the youth, like their elders, are responding to an overwhelming national mood of privatism.

"Privatism," the ideology of "look out for number one," is

exactly the attitude behind the new conservative elder's demand for more discipline in the schools and more "back to the basics." Behind the back to the basics movement is the basic of California's Proposition 13, money. In terms of outcomes of education, the recent Gallup poll indicates the most endorsed educational outcome is the ability to write a job application letter with correct grammar and spelling. In terms of education input, the most endorsed input is not spending money. Thus privatism underlies the back to the basics movement.

The new privatism unites the cynical or disillusioned liberal with the cynical or disillusioned conservative, "the new conservative." Until Mr. Nixon and Watergate, the conservative private property ethic was what Mr. Goldwater called the conscience of the conservative, a stage 4 moral commitment to maintaining American society or a stage 5 commitment to liberty and democracy threatened by Marxist socialism. The more recent new conservative ideology stresses not moral stage 4 but "look out for number one." It calls into question not only the stage 5 premises of the Declaration, but the stage 4 societal maintenance ideas which I took for granted as safe in 1976. Perhaps under Mr. Nixon's stage 4 rhetoric of law, order, and nation, we suspected a stage 2 "look out for number one." But at least the rhetoric was stage 4. Here is the rhetoric of the new conservatism which does not even pretend to stage 4: let me use as an example the words of Democratic candidate for governor, Edward I. King. I quote the *Boston Globe* (October, 21, 1978).

King yesterday denounced his Republican rival Hatch in a press conference reiterating his support of the death penalty, a 21 year drinking age, and an end to tax-funded abortions. He said these views were not extremist, they were moderate. "If you're a millionaire living off inherited wealth in Beverly like Mr. Hatch, you may think that those who care about capital punishment to deter murder are part of a hate group. But if you live in Winthrop like I do, you want capital punishment, and you don't do it out of hate, you do it out of fear. Up in Beverly, the crime rate is low. Maybe Hatch hasn't been mugged or doesn't know anyone who has."

King's Archie Bunker reasoning is not stage 4; it is stge 3. It asserts that what's right is right because it's what my group thinks is right or what's good for my group. Since King's group, the lower middle class, is more numerous than Hatch's group, the rich, King thinks not only that he'll get elected but that he's right. If he were fourth stage, he'd worry about what was best for the total community in Massachusetts. [1]

Whether King's reason is morally right or not, it seemed to be right by the criteria of "look out for number one." It got him elected governor. It appealed to the dissaffection of the voters, not only from our stage 5 civil-libertarian Constitutional premises, but from any stage 4 conception of government as rule by law, not by men, in the public interest. Here is this disaffection in the words of Laura, a senior graduating in the Cambridge High School. She comes from a stable, working class family and is part of our research sample.

> I don't know whether I'll go to college next year or take a year off to work. What I want out of life is to have a good job, I want to be happy at my job. I would like to be a stewardess and travel and learn about people and things. To a certain extent I want to travel to escape, the world depresses me and the government depresses me. I don't want to hear the truth about what my country is like. I know it is corrupt, they say it is a way of life and I'm still young enough to be a little frightened that I'll be like that. We say we have a democratic government but I don't think it treats people fair at all. In a way I think the government hates people, in a way I think it tries to bribe people. If we had a democratic government we wouldn't have ghettos and people on welfare and riots. But maybe that isn't fair, it's a big world out there and I don't expect it to run smoothly, I don't understand it but in a way I don't want to understand it.

Our research criterion indicated her moral reasoning was mostly stage 3, though a far more idealistic or "moral" stage 3 than that appealed to by King. She says: "I was brought up to be good but I chose on my own not to become selfish, to be considerate. It is okay to think of yourself but also you should give space to others and have your mind open to others and the world." She also shows some beginning fourth stage thinking about hypothetical moral dilemmas. She doesn't apply her beginning fourth stage capacities to her perception of government and the larger society; her disaffection, she says, is such that she doesn't really want to try to understand. She also does not approach government in terms of penalistic issues. Rather she approaches it as failing to meet her third stage moral expectations that it be a government of good people concerned about helping other people, and she is disappointed.

How can we fault her third stage privatism as a citizen when her privatism can be seen as a disillusioned response to the third stage privatism of political "leaders" like King?

In the sixties, we seemed to see youth groping toward principled fifth or even sixth stage reasoning, and recoiling from fourth stage political leadership while being misunderstood as immoral and lawless. Today the misunderstanding is a stage down. The youth groping toward some fourth stage conception of a political community are alienated at the personal and institutional or collective egoism of institutional leadership and are branded "the Narcissistic generation."

The purpose of our comments is not to seriously diagnose the times but to point to the current need for the American high school to take some active steps to help students like Laura to positive stage 4 conceptions and attitudes toward citizenship.

In a sense, then, our goals in high school civic education are old. Our approach, however, is very different from the old civics education prevalent in the 1950s. That approach was one of indoctrination of fourth stage values, with a conservative slant (Kohlberg, 1973). An example is the text, *Civics for Americans,* written by Clark, Edmonson, and Dondineau in 1954. They say:

Civics for Americans is a book designed to help young people develop the characteristics of good citizenship. Primarily these characteristics are devotion to the Constitutional government of the United States, respect for law and appreciation of the advantages of a free-enterprise economy, faith in God and man and in the tenets which distinguish our way of life. Willingness to assume the responsibilities of school citizenship is essential to developing these characteristics.

Clearly, too, our approach requires more than the integration of developmental moral discussion of dilemmas in history, civics, and human relations with new social studies analyses. Such analyses were described as the education for stage 5 in the curriculum projects of Fenton, Mosher, and myself (Kohlberg and Fenton, 1976). The additional educational experience required is the experience of civic participation, the focus of the Danforth conference on civic education.

The first form of participation discussed in the conference was participation in the outside community represented by the projects of Fred Newmann in Madison and Dian Hedin in Minneapolis. The second form of participation is real power and democratic participation in the governance of the high school itself.

The general educational rationale for both is still best given by Dewey's (1964) theory as this has been elaborated in the psychological theory of Piaget (1932). According to both, the fundamental aim of education is development, and development requires action or active experience. The aim of civic education is the development of a person with the structures of understanding and motivation to participate in society in the direction of making it a better or more just society. This aim requires experiences of active social participation as well as the learning of analytic understandings, of government, and the moral discussion of legal and political issues.

Newmann's paper provides the rationale for participation experience in terms of the basic psychological theory and research of Piaget (1932), David Hunt (1973), and myself. My own theory argues, following Dewey and G. H. Mead (1934), that if sociomoral development is the aim of social education, the central means of social education is the creation of opportunities and experiences for social role-taking and participation. In an earlier review of the research literature (Kohlberg, 1969), I conclude that both active power and decision-making responsibility and more passive belongingness in secondary groups correlate well with and stimulate social and moral development. Social development (or stage of social cognition, of moral judgment, of self-perception) is correlated with socioeconomic status, with participation in formal and informal voluntary organizations, with occupational status and responsibility. From this point of view, the primary "problem" of disadvantaged street youth is that they have no sense of power and participation in the wider organized society, in the secondary institutions of high school, of work, of government. Their world is the world of stage 2 instrumental exchange or of stage 3 informal loyalty or caring. The stage 4 world of organized society is not a world which they can either understand or identify with since they and their families have no roles of power and participation in that world. Newmann's paper reviews the research literature and comes to similar conclusions.

I have shown the educational need for experiences of political participation in terms of the stage psychologies of Dewey and Piaget. John Stuart Mill made the same claim for a different, perhaps more common-sense psychology:

Freedom has an invigorating effect upon the development of character. Character develops very differently when a human being feels himself under no other external constraint than the necessities of nature or of a society in which he has a share in imposing and the right to publicly dissent from and alter if he thinks them wrong. The effect of freedom on character development is only obtained, however, when the person is, or is looking forward to becoming a citizen as privileged as any other. What is still more important than this feeling is the practical discipline from the demands made upon the citizen to exercise some social function. It is not sufficiently considered how little there is in most people's ordinary life to give any largeness to their ideas or sentiments. Giving them something to do for the public supplies, in a measure, these differences. If circumstances allow the amount of public duty assigned to them to be considerable, it makes them an educated person. The practice of the assembly raised the intellectual standard of an average Athenian citizen beyond that of any other mass of people. An intellectual benefit of the same kind, though far less, is produced in Englishmen by their ability to be placed on juries and to serve parish offices. Still more salutary is the moral instruction afforded by participation in public functions. One is called upon while so engaged to weigh interests not one's own, to be guided in conflicting cases by another rule than one's private partialities, principles which have their reason for existence in the common good. Where the school of public spirit does not exist, scarcely any idea is entertained that private persons owe any duties to society except to obey the law and submit to the government. There is no unselfish sentiment of identification with the public, angry thought or feeling is absorbed in the individual and in the family. The man reasons thinking not of any collective interest, of any objects to be pursued jointly with others but only in competition with them.

So, one hundred years ago, did Mill state the necessity of participation for attaining what we call the fourth stage of civic attitudes, and point to it as the remedy for what we have called privatism.

Newmann's paper presents the Dewey-Mill psychology as part of the "participatory-idealist" philosophy of democracy. This classical ideal is embodied in the stage 5 educational and moral philosophies of human development and perfection running from Aristotle to Dewey. These philosophers assert that the educational aim of full individual human development can only be reached through an education for full participation in society or in a human community. Development to a fifth or sixth stage of human personality and experience, in this vision, cannot take place except in and through experiences of participation. Whether one's exemplars of human development are sixth stage exemplars like Socrates or Martin Luther King, or fifth stage exemplars like Aristotle and Dewey, their development will have been inextricably tied to participation in their political communities. Education by, and for, participation is not simply a concern of "citizen education." It is a concern for any educational philosophy which sees education as furthering human development.

Given the importance of actual experiences of participation in a political community for human and civic development, why does it devolve upon the high school to provide it? Why not leave it to spontaneous experience after high school? The answer is that unless a person leaves high school already at the fourth stage and with corresponding interests and motivations, he or she is unlikely to be in a position to have the capacities and motivation to enter positions of participation and public responsibility later. He or she will, as our graduating student says, avoid such situations, not seek them.

I cited both Newmann's and my own review of the research literature correlating participation experiences with attainment of higher stages of cognitive, moral, and ego development. The correlations are both cause and consequence. Experience of participation causes development. But higher stages of development are also causes or conditions of being in a position of participation (Candee, 1978). Opportunities for participation, then, are given to the mature in our society. Representative democracy, like our economic system, tends to give growth experience to those who don't really need it, to those already advanced.

The high school's expectation and help in entering participatory roles is required, then, especially for those students who would not seek them later. This, at least, is required of high schools or educators who take seriously the "developmental," "progressive," or "participatory idealist" philosophy of education and citizenship. It is almost universally accepted by educational sociologists that an informed definition of the school as an agent of social education rests on seeing the school as an intermediary between the family and the society. The bridging role of the school is conceived of in a system-maintaining perspective (or what Newmann calls an "elitist pluralist" perspective) by functional sociologists such as Durkheim (1906—early edition) and Parsons (1964). In this perspective, the school, like the government, is a bureaucratic or impersonally rule-governed organization stressing competitive merit or achievement. Through it, rather than directly through the family, children learn to respect general and impartial rules and to be concerned about collective goals. In the developmental or "participatory idealist" view of Dewey, the school was a necessary bridge between the family and the outside society in providing individuals with experiences of democratic community. Already in Dewey's day, the town-meeting forms of democratic community most amenable to creating experiences of participation were becoming rare. Today they are practically unknown for most adults and adolescents alike. The schools and universities need to help create roles of responsible participation as vehicles for social development because the civic and vocational roles which graduates enter are typically not roles of responsible participation. Furthermore, the school is needed to encourage rational and moral reflection and discussion of participation roles if participatory experience is to lead to growth. Otherwise such experiences may simply confirm the ignorance or alienation with which our graduating student (quoted above) approaches her civic role.

The most basic way in which the high school can promote experiences of civic participation is to govern itself through a process of participatory democracy. The learning and development required for democratic governing must come from doing or making a government, from being an active member of governance with the power to influence government to be more just. The only way school can help graduating students become persons who can make society a just community is to let them try experimentally to make the school themselves. The school can offer a chance for experience in making a just community immeasurably easier, safer, and less frustrating than the experience of adult participation in society. It can provide the adolescent with direct power and responsibility for governance in a society which is small and personal, like the family, but which is also complex, rule-governed, and democratic, and which is a stage 4 or 5 society like the society in which the student is to be a citizen.

I have made the Socratic argument for school democracy in terms of participatory experience for development to a fourth stage citizenship role orientation, as well as for developing some awareness of our fifth stage principles of constitutional democracy. The negative argument is perhaps even more compelling. This is the argument that bureaucratic-authoritarian high school governance actually teaches alienation and ignorance about a democratic society. In this argument, while the high school social studies curriculum teaches equal liberty, due process, and creates the high school "hidden curriculum," the governance and informal social relations of the school teaches something very different. Fred Newmann (1977) states this as follows:

Public education should teach students to function in a political-legal structure of representative democracy. This means there has to be a consistency between the principles of democracy being taught and the actual process of education, or the student will rightly come to distrust both the democratic principles taught and the process of education. Education must authenticate these central principles of democracy and apply them to the educational process. Equal liberty and consent of the governed are the two most fundamental principles behind representative democracy. These principles of equal liberty and consent can be embodied in the educational process by providing freedom of choice, intellectual openness, and active participation.

In the recent projects of Fenton, Mosher, and myself, school democracy is the central experience of participation necessary for moral and civic development. In the projects of Newmann and Hedin, internship and project experience in the community are the central experiences of participation for civic development. I question whether community internship and project experiences in themselves have the intimacy and duration, the democratic form, or the chance to combine action and reflection which school democracy can provide for stimulating civic development.

At the same time, participation in a democratic school is not enough to guarantee a development or transfer of fourth stage understandings and attitudes to the out-of-school society. Laura attacks a democratic school, i.e., the Cambridge Cluster School. She attributes much of her third stage moral concern to this experience of community in the Cambridge Cluster School:

I learned more or less on my own to be considerate, not to be selfish, though also from my mother and from the Cluster School. Cluster has signified that in this democratic school people should respect one another and care. That is what a community is, people caring for each other and watching out for each other and helping each other grow. In Cluster we all try to work together and when someone has a problem we try to approach it in a good way. Cluster is a democratic school in Latin High School, but it is different than Latin: I'm not saying Latin teachers aren't fair. It's just you come in, the teacher is in front, saying "Now you do this" and you just listen. In Cluster, you come in and the teacher says "How should we approach our lesson" and people try to work as one. So I have tried to be a good community member, to voice my opinions even when people don't agree with me. I think I'm respected and that makes me feel good about myself and I think I've helped the school.

Laura's moral and positive attitudes of participation in the democratic school, then, have not transferred to the larger civic world in the absence of a parallel process of participation in the broader community.

NOTE

1. Stages in thinking about capital punishment have been empirically studied (Kohlberg and Elfenbein, 1975). If King were fifth or sixth stage, he would respond to the John Rawls idea of universal justice. From the Rawls view, a law or punishment is just if it would be the result of a social contract made by people trying to choose impartially. They go behind a "veil of ignorance" as to their actual position in society, as rich or poor, as a possible victim of crime or a possible felon. As a possible victim of murder, and as a possible felon, you would want punishment to deter murder. But as a possible felon, you would not want capital punishment. If you did not know who you were to be, the additional gain to deterrence would not be acceptable if you had the chance of being a felon.

REFERENCES

Candee, D., Graham, R., & Kohlberg, L. Moral Development and Life Outcomes. Report to National Institute of Education. Grant # NIE-6-74-0096. 1978.

Clark, I., Edmonson, J., and Dondineau, A. *Civics for Americans*. New York: MacMillan, 1954.

Dewey, J. "Democracy and Education." In *Selected Writings* (Ed.) R. D. Archambault. New York: Random House, 1964.

Durkheim, E. *Moral Education*. New York: Free Press, 1961. (earlier edition, 1906)

Fenton, E., Colby, A., & Speicher-Dubin, B. "Developing Moral Dilemmas for Social Studies Classes." Cambridge, MA: Moral Education Resource Fund, 1974.

Hunt, D. "Education for Disciplinary Understanding," *Behavioral & Social Science Teacher, 1,* 1. (1973)

Kohlberg, L. "Stage and Sequence: The Cognitive-Developmental Approach to Socialization." In D. Goslin (Ed.) *Handbook of Socialization Theory*. New York: Rand McNally & Co., 1969.

Kohlberg, L. "Educating For Justice: A Modern Statement of the Platonic View." In T. Sizer (Ed.), *Moral Education*. Cambridge, MA: Harvard University Press, 1970.

Kohlberg, L. "Moral Education and the New Social Studies." *Social Education,* 1973, *37,* 5.

Kohlberg, L., & Elfenbein, D. "The Development of Moral Judgments Concerning Capital Punishment." *American Journal of Orthopsychiatry,* 1975, *45,* 4.

Kohlberg, L., & Fenton, E. "This Special Section in Perspective." From Special Section: "The Cognitive-Developmenal Approach to Moral Education." *Social Education,* 40, 4, p. 213–216. April, 1976.

Kohlberg, L. "Meaning and Measurement in Moral Development." *Heinz Werner Memorial Lecture,* Worcester, MA: Clark University Press, 1979.

Lasch, C. *The Culture of Narcissism*. New York: Norton Press, 1978.

Mead, G. H. *Mind, Self, and Society*. Chicago: University of Chicago Press, 1934.

Mill, John Stuart. *On Liberty,* (Ed.) A. Castell. New York: Crofts Classic Series, 1947.

Parsons, T. *Social Structure and Personality*. New York: The Free Press, 1964.

Piaget, J. *The Moral Judgment of the Child*. New York: The Free Press. 1965. (Originally published, 1932).

Rawls, J. *A Theory of Justice*. Cambridge, MA: Harvard University Press, 1973.

Ringer, R. *Looking Out for Number One*. New York: Fawcett Books., 1977.

Riesman, D. *The Lonely Crowd*. New Haven: Yale University Press. 1952.

Contributors in Order of Presentation

LAWRENCE KOHLBERG Harvard University
JAMES REST University of Minnesota
JAMES FOWLER Emory University
BRENDA MUNSEY University of Alabama in Birmingham
DWIGHT BOYD Ontario Institute for Studies in Education
JOHN WILSON Oxford University
BERNARD ROSEN Ohio State UNiversity
ERNEST WALLWORK Yale University
BARRY CHAZAN Hebrew University in Jerusalem
JAMES MICHAEL LEE University of Alabama in Birmingham
LINDA ROSENZWEIG Carnegie-Mellon University
JAMES B, MACDONALD University of North Carolina
ISRAELA ETTENBERG ARON Hebrew Union College
BILL PUKA Trinity College and Harvard University

Subject Index

Action, moral, motives for, 96–98

Christian religious education, 8, 9,
  326–349
  social-science approach to, 9, 329,
    331, 343–349
  theological approach to, 9, 328, 329,
    330–336, 340–349
  (*See also* Religion; Faith development)
Civic education, 85–89, 360–377,
  384–386, 456–469
  Carnegie-Mellon Civic Education Proj-
    ect, 361, 366–372
  Fenton-Kohlberg methodology, 360–
    362
  Kohlbergian models for, 85–86,
    360–377
  Kohlberg's approach, recent
    modifications in, 456–469
  participation experiences, uses in,
    86–89, 384, 385, 459–469
Cognitive developmental approach,
  37–51, 72–89, 362–366
  (*See also* Moral education: Kohlberg's
    approach to)
Cognitive developmentalism, 37–51,
  101–127, 161–179, 214–231,
  440–449
  characteristics of, 38, 166–175
  ethical basis of, 161–179, 440–449
  Kohlberg's theory, 37–51
  metatheoretical aspects of, 166–175,
    440–449

philosophical difficulties with
  methodology, 214–231
as psychological basis of Kohlberg's
  educational program, 37–51, 101–
  107
Cognitive processes, correlation with
  moral judgment, 38–51, 115–123
Cognitive structure, 38–51, 102, 103,
  107–119, 134, 135
  content, in relation to, 121, 122
  in developmental approach, 102, 103
  in moral judgment, its assessment,
    107–115
  (*See also* Cognitive developmentalism;
    Moral judgment; Moral stages)
Curriculum, moral educational, 359–
  377, 381–399
  (*See also* Moral education)

Defining Issues Test, Rest's, 109–119
Developmental sequence, 104, 105,
  113–115, 166–179
  in moral judgment, research on, 113–
  115
  its philosophical justification, 166–
  179
  (*See also* Moral development; Moral
    stages)

Education, (*See* Moral education)
Epistemology, 2, 3, 6, 7, 10, 137,
  166–179, 237–261

472

Name Index

476